Looking after the flock can be taxing enough.

So let us take care of the finance for you.

As a busy member of the clergy you have enough to do without having to worry about your tax affairs.

TMC is here to help. We were established to provide a tax management service to the clergy and are now one of the largest such specialist advisers in the UK. Our team offers telephone and virtual face to face appointments so that we can discuss your individual needs with:

General tax advice | Completion of tax returns
Tax credits | Payroll administration | Property accounts
Student advice | Annual Diocesan return

tax management for clergy

Call us on 01476 539000

Email: enquiries@clergytaxuk.com Visit: www.clergytaxuk.com

PO BOX 6621 Grantham Lincolnshire NG32 3SX

REFLECTIONS FOR DAILY PRAYER 2024/25

Reflections for Daily Prayer are the official daily Bible notes from the Church of England, designed to enhance your daily prayer through the year.

On Monday to Saturday each week, Reflections provides full lectionary details for Morning Prayer, an inspiring reflection on one of the Bible readings, and a Collect.

978 1 78140 457 7 • £17.99

REFLECTIONS FOR SUNDAYS YEAR C

Reflections for Sundays offers over 250 reflections on the Principal Readings for every Sunday and Holy Day in Year C.

For each Sunday it provides full lectionary details for the Principal Service as well as four reflections, covering both Old Testament readings, the Epistle and the Gospel.

978 1 78140 039 5 • £16.99

CHURCH HOUSE PUBLISHING

www.chpublishing.co.uk

Weave the latest news into your sermons

- On-the-pulse sermon ideas **linked to the lectionary readings**

- **Weekly inspiration** for leading worship with adults and all ages together

- Fresh **seasonal** and **themed** materials through the year

Now including

NEW Bread & Wine
Resources for Communion

Take a *free trial* at
rootsforchurches.com

The Roots ecumenical partnership

Discover the *Church Times* archive

Since the paper's launch in 1863, *Church Times* coverage has included two world wars, the coronations of four British monarchs, and protests against everything from Ritualism to climate change.

Explore over 150 years of history in the digital archive. Access is included with all Print + Digital and Digital subscriptions.

www.churchtimes.co.uk/archive

iChurch

Church websites from £9.99 per month

We design a WordPress site for your church with: secure domain and hosting, theme updates, security and plugin updates, training videos, quick customer support, membership of the iChurch community
£150 set up fee for a new website, £9.99 per month thereafter

As above, but with us uploading your updates quarterly and regular performance reviews
£150 set up fee for a new website, £14.99 per month thereafter

Emails

Unlimited domain-based emails for £4.99 per month
(eg minister@anytownurc.org.uk, secretary@anytownurc.org.uk treasurer@anytownurc.org.uk, lettings@anytownurc.org.uk)

www.ichurch.website
ichurch@urc.org.uk

The world's most famous hymn book
on your phone, tablet or computer

- Words for all 847 hymns and songs found in *Ancient and Modern* (2024)
- Find hymns by number, first line, author or composer
- Browse the collection by theme or lectionary reading
- Create and edit your own lists of hymns

Try the app free for 30 days.
Go to www.canterburypress.co.uk/apps

Did you hear the one about the church...

- with a Ukrainian ukelele Abba tribute band?
- where they take alpacas for a walk?
- which raised £11,000 by reading the Bible?
- with the largest ceiling of its kind in Europe?
- where hymns include Bob the Builder?
- which reaches further through community partnerships?
- which provided 4,000 books for a school?

There's so much in **Reform**

Call **020 7520 2721** or visit
www.reformsubs.co.uk

Thousands of Songs
ONE LICENSE

ONE LICENSE is a premier licensing source that covers all of your congregational reprint needs.

Featuring more than 160 Member Publishers and their divisions, ONE LICENSE gives you access to over 80,000 titles for congregational song. Included with your license is the music of GIA, OCP, The Taizé Community, Wild Goose and The Iona Community, The Royal School of Church Music, Oxford University Press, Kevin Mayhew, Stainer & Bell, and more!

Our comprehensive search allows you to browse by...

- Title
- Mass Setting
- Composer
- Psalm Number
- and much more!

Our reporting process is fast, easy, and intuitive. There is no online licensing resource that is as user friendly as ONE LICENSE.

| Annual License | Single-Use/Event License | Podcast/Streaming License | Practice-Track License |

ONE LICENSE
Inspiring congregational song

HYMNS Ancient & Modern
Bookselling | Publishing | Distribution | Grants | Events

onelicense.net | infoeurope@onelicense.net

jobs.churchtimes.co.uk

Advertise your vacancy with us

Your job advertisement will be seen by up to 40,000 readers in the print issue; another 50,000 online; 15,000 via App downloads and still more through email alerts, tweets and widgets.

Advertise for one week, two weeks or use our unique Until Filled facility: for one fee, your vacancy can run as many times as you like (terms and conditions apply).

To find out more about our brilliant recruitment package call us on 020 7776 1010 or email ads@churchtimes.co.uk

CHURCH TIMES

OUT OF THE SHADOWS
PREACHING THE WOMEN OF THE BIBLE

KATE BRUCE & LIZ SHERCLIFF

"Important, accessible and comprehensive... I commend it to you with urgency." Kate Bottley

"An important, accessible and comprehensive account of the too-long silenced voices of women of the bible."

THE REVD KATE BOTTLEY, PRIEST AND BROADCASTER

9780334060697 · PAPERBACK · £19.99
Available from www.scmpress.co.uk

 scm press  @SCM_Press

OVER 1,000 CHURCHES...

...Have purchased our bespoke Pew Cushions, Kneelers and Chair Cushions!

We have a comprehensive website, a 12-page brochure and Sample Packs available FREE of charge or obligation.

We are a family run business and have 27 years' experience of supplying high quality, affordable Church Pew Cushions, Kneelers/Hassocks and Altar Rail Kneelers.

THE CHURCH CUSHION Co.

Bringing *Comfort* to your Congregation

Call us today on:
FREEPHONE 0800 977 8006
or visit our website:
www.churchcushion.co.uk

CHURCH HOUSE BOOKSHOP

YOUR FIRST STOP FOR CHRISTIAN BOOKS, RESOURCES & CHURCH SUPPLIES

- We stock thousands of titles and cater for all traditions

- We can order almost any book available in the UK

- Visit us for reading and materials for all occasions — Diaries, Lectionaries, Years A/B/C resources and much more

- Visit us online at www.chbookshop.co.uk – and sign up for our e-bulletins to receive the latest offers and news

CHURCH HOUSE BOOKSHOP
31 Great Smith Street, London SW1P 3BN
Website: www.chbookshop.co.uk
E-mail: bookshop@chbookshop.co.uk
Tel: 01603 785918

A COURSE EXPLORING CHRISTIAN FAITH AND LIFE
Being With

SAMUEL WELLS AND SALLY HITCHINER

The *Being With* Course is an invitation to become a person who knows how to be with yourself, others, the world, and with God. Participants will discover the Christian faith in the context of friendship, their own stories, and the stories of others.

978 1 78622 439 2   Being With Leaders' Guide   **£12.99**
978 1 78622 442 2   Being With Participants' Companion   **£6.99**

www.being-with.org

CANTERBURY PRESS
www.canterburypress.co.uk

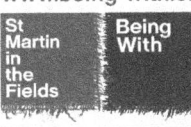

THE CANTERBURY PREACHER'S COMPANION APP

The new way to explore the Canterbury Preacher's Companion sermon collection

- Browse over 1500 sermons;
- Copy any sermon to edit, add new ideas, and easily rearrange text blocks;
- Access your saved notes and sermons from anywhere;
- Switch to read view to see a clean text version, ready for the lectern.

Try the app free for 30 days:

canterburypress.co.uk/preachers-companion

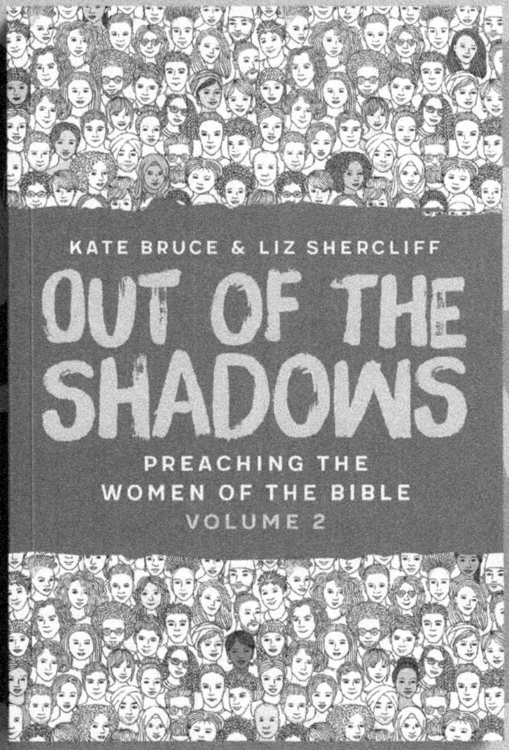

Saint Columba's House

t: 01483 766498
www.stcolumbashouse.org.uk
Maybury Hill, Woking, Surrey GU22 8AB

Situated in beautiful wooded gardens, our urban retreat house offers conference spaces, accommodation, quiet days and retreats.

- 9 flexible, well equipped meeting rooms
- Overnight accommodation for 31 guests
- On site Chapel and Oratory
- Home cooked food
- Easy access from London by rail and road

Contact us:

call: 01483 766498
email: admin@stcolumbashouse.org.uk
web: www.stcolumbashouse.org.uk

The Canterbury Preacher's Companion 2025

The Canterbury Preacher's Companion 2025

Sermons for Sundays, Holy Days, Festivals and Special Occasions Year C

Edited by Catherine Williams

© the Contributors, 2024

First published in 2024 by the Canterbury Press Norwich
Editorial office
3rd Floor, Invicta House
110 Golden Lane
London EC1Y 0TG, UK
www.canterburypress.co.uk

Canterbury Press is an imprint of Hymns Ancient & Modern Ltd
(a registered charity)

Hymns Ancient & Modern® is a registered trademark of
Hymns Ancient & Modern Ltd
13A Hellesdon Park Road, Norwich,
Norfolk NR6 5DR, UK

All rights reserved. No part of this publication may be reproduced,
stored in a retrieval system, or transmitted,
in any form or by any means, electronic, mechanical,
photocopying or otherwise, without the prior permission of
the publisher, Canterbury Press.

The Authors have asserted their right under the Copyright, Designs and
Patents Act 1988 to be identified as the Authors of this Work

Scripture quotations are from the New Revised
Standard Version of the Bible, Anglicized Edition,
copyright © 1989, 1995 by the Division of Christian Education of the
National Council of the Churches of Christ in the USA.
Used by permission. All rights reserved.

British Library Cataloguing in Publication data

A catalogue record for this book is available
from the British Library

ISBN 978-1-78622-555-9

Typeset by Regent Typesetting

Contents

Preface   xvii
Preaching in a Hurting World by Lucy Winkett   xix
Contributors   xxix

SUNDAYS AND MAJOR FESTIVALS

Unless otherwise stated, the readings and the verse numbers of the psalms are taken from *Common Worship: Services and Prayers for the Church of England* (Church House Publishing, 2000), with revisions, and are for Year C.

2024

1 Dec.	**First Sunday of Advent**	
	Principal Service: Luke 21.25–36	
	Straining Our Eyes for God's Kingdom	2
	Second Service: Joel 3.9–end Advent Hope	4
8 Dec.	**Second Sunday of Advent**	
	Principal Service: Luke 3.1–6	
	Potholes and Speed Bumps	7
	Second Service: Luke 1.1–25 The Last Prophet	9
15 Dec.	**Third Sunday of Advent**	
	Principal Service: Luke 3.7–18	
	Foreboding and Faith	12
	Second Service: Isa. 35 Fools on the Road	14
22 Dec.	**Fourth Sunday of Advent**	
	Principal Service: Luke 1.39–45 [46–55]	
	Leading Us to the Incarnation	16
	Second Service: Matt. 1.18–end Shame	19

25 Dec.	**Christmas Day**	
	Set I: Luke 2.1–14 Born in Us Today	22
	Set II: Luke 2.[1–7] 8–20 Good News Alert:	
	Do Not Be Afraid!	24
	Set III: John 1.1–14 The Squalid Stable	26
	Second Service: Phil 2.5–11 Making Choices	29
29 Dec.	**First Sunday of Christmas**	
	Principal Service: Col. 3.12–17; Luke 2.41–end	
	Growing Up with Jesus	31
	Second Service: Isa. 61 We Begin Again	33

2025

5 Jan.	**Second Sunday of Christmas**	
	Principal Service: John 1.[1–9] 10–18	
	Another Helping	35
	Second Service: 1 Sam. 1.20–end God Hears	38
12 Jan.	**Baptism of Christ** (First Sunday of Epiphany)	
	Principal Service: Luke 3.15–17, 21–22	
	'Well, So That is That'	40
	Second Service: Isa. 55.1–11; Rom. 6.1–11	
	Freedom in Christ	42
19 Jan.	**Second Sunday of Epiphany**	
	Principal Service: Isa. 62.1–5; John 2.1–11	
	God's Overwhelming Generosity	44
	Second Service: 1 Sam. 3.1–20 Here I Am	46
26 Jan.	**Third Sunday of Epiphany**	
	Principal Service: Luke 4.14–21	
	Personal, Political, Holy	49
	Second Service: 1 Cor. 7.17–24	
	Remain as You Were Called	51
2 Feb.	**Presentation of Christ in the Temple** (Candlemas)	
	Principal Service: Luke 2.22–40	
	Bucket List	53
	Second Service: Hag. 2.1–9	
	The Promised Presence	55

9 Feb.	Fourth Sunday before Lent (Proper 1)	
	Principal Service: Isa. 6.1–8; Luke 5.1–11 *Ego*	59
	Second Service: Hos. 1 *The Power of Naming*	61
16 Feb.	Third Sunday before Lent (Proper 2)	
	Principal Service: Luke 6.17–26	
	Blessings and Woes	63
	Second Service: Gal. 4.8–20	
	Turning Back – Moving Forward	66
23 Feb.	Second Sunday before Lent	
	Principal Service: Luke 8.22–25	
	The Power to Bring Calm to Chaos	68
	Second Service: Gen 1.1 – 2.3 *Beginning Now*	70
2 Mar.	Sunday next before Lent	
	Principal Service: Luke 9.28–36 [37–43a]	
	A Shining Face	73
	Second Service: John 12.27–36a	
	Storing Up in the Hump of Faith	75
5 Mar.	Ash Wednesday	
	Principal Service: John 8.1–11	
	Writing in the Dust	78
9 Mar.	First Sunday of Lent	
	Principal Service: Luke 4.1–13	
	The Weakness of Jesus	80
	Second Service: Luke 18.9–14	
	Lord, Have Mercy	83
16 Mar.	Second Sunday of Lent	
	Principal Service: Luke 13.31–end	
	Beware Foxes	85
	Second Service: Luke 14.27–33	
	Because He's Worth It	87
23 Mar.	Third Sunday of Lent	
	Principal Service: Isa. 55.1–9; Luke 13.1–9	
	Repentance and Salvation	90
	Second Service: Gen. 28.10–19a *God the*	
	Still-point in All Our Dreaming	91

30 Mar.	**Fourth Sunday of Lent** (Mothering Sunday) *Principal Service:* 2 Cor. 5.16–end	
	The Truth We Find	94
	Second Service: Isa. 40.27–41.13	
	Where is God?	96
30 Mar.	**Mothering Sunday** *Principal Service:* Ex 2.1–10; John 19.25b–27	
	Here is Your Mother	98
6 Apr.	**Fifth Sunday of Lent** (Passiontide) *Principal Service:* John 12.1–8	
	Out of Control?	100
	Second Service: 2 Chron. 35.1–6, 10–16	
	Lay Down Your Ark	102
13 Apr.	**Palm Sunday** *Principal Service:* Luke 19.28–40; Luke 23.1–49	
	Looking On from a Distance	105
	Second Service: Isa. 5.1–7	
	Speaking Truth to Power	107
14–16 Apr.	**First Three Days of Holy Week** Isa. 50.4–9a Carrying the Cross	110
17 Apr.	**Maundy Thursday** John 13.1–17, 31b–35 In the Upper Room: a reflective sermon	112
18 Apr.	**Good Friday** John 18.1–end of 19 The Stone Rejected	115
19–20 Apr.	**Easter Vigil** Ex. 14.10–end Free at Last!	118
20 Apr.	**Easter Day** *Principal Service:* John 20.1–18	
	While It Was Still Dark	120
	Second Service: 1 Cor. 15.1–11	
	I Am What I Am	123

27 Apr.	Second Sunday of Easter	
	Principal Service: John 20.19–end	
	I'll Leave You with This ...	125
	Second Service: Luke 24.13–35	
	Trauma and the Next Steps	128
4 May	Third Sunday of Easter	
	Principal Service: John 21.1–19	
	Resurrection Promise	130
	Second Service: Ps. 86; Isa. 38.9–20	
	What's Your Immediate 'Go-to'?	132
11 May	Fourth Sunday of Easter (Vocation Sunday)	
	Principal Service: John 10.22–30	
	Hear and Follow	134
	Second Service: Luke 24.36–49	
	God of Surprises	137
18 May	Fifth Sunday of Easter	
	Principal Service: Acts 11.1–18; John 13.31–35	
	What Does Love Look Like?	139
	Second Service: Dan. 6.[1–5] 6–23; Mark 15.46 — 16.8 Not that Kind of Messiah	141
25 May	Sixth Sunday of Easter	
	Principal Service: John 14.23–29	
	God the Home-maker	144
	Second Service: Zeph. 3.14–end	
	The Story and the Song	146
29 May	Ascension Day	
	Principal Service: Luke 24.44–end	
	Set Free to Serve	148
	Second Service: Rev. 5 Transforming Heaven	150
1 June	Seventh Sunday of Easter	
	(Sunday after Ascension Day)	
	Principal Service: Acts 16.16–34	
	The Business, Not Busy-ness, of Faith	153
	Second Service: Isa. 44.1–8	
	As Water on a Thirsty Land	155

8 June	**Day of Pentecost** (Whit Sunday) *Principal Service: Acts 2.1–21*	
	The Power of Wind and Flame	157
	Second Service: Ex. 33.7–20; 2 Cor. 3.4–end	
	Changed from Greyness into Glory	160
15 June	**Trinity Sunday** *Principal Service: John 16.12–15*	
	Love in Harmony	163
	Second Service: Ex. 3.1–15	
	On Holy Ground	165
22 June	**First Sunday after Trinity** (Proper 7) *Principal Service: Luke 8.26–39*	
	A Man on the Edge, and a Herd of Pigs	168
	Second Service: Gen 24.1–27	
	Never Go Back …	170
29 June	**Second Sunday after Trinity** (Proper 8) *Principal Service: Luke 9.51–end*	
	The Cost of Following Jesus	172
	Second Service: Mark 6.1–6	
	Not Just a Man	175
6 July	**Third Sunday after Trinity** (Proper 9) *Principal Service: Luke 10.1–11, 16–20*	
	Speaking Powerfully	177
	Second Service: Gen. 29.1–20	
	Food, Water and Love	179
13 July	**Fourth Sunday after Trinity** (Proper 10) *Principal Service: Luke 10.25–37*	
	Following the Family Way	181
	Second Service: Mark 7.1–23	
	But, it's Tradition!	184
20 July	**Fifth Sunday after Trinity** (Proper 11) *Principal Service: Luke 10.38–end*	
	An Invitation into Deeper Freedom	186
	Second Service: Gen. 41.1–16, 25–37	
	Living the Dream	188

27 July	Sixth Sunday after Trinity (Proper 12)	
	Principal Service: Luke 11.1–13 Just Ask	191
	Second Service: Gen. 42.1–25	
	Seeing Into the Life of Things	193
3 Aug.	Seventh Sunday after Trinity (Proper 13)	
	Principal Service: Luke 12.13–21	
	Abundant Living	195
	Second Service: Gen. 50.4–end	
	God Meant It for Good	198
10 Aug.	Eighth Sunday after Trinity (Proper 14)	
	Principal Service: Luke 12.32–40	
	Treasure Seekers?	200
	Second Service: Isa. 11.10 – end of 12	
	Homecoming	202
17 Aug.	Ninth Sunday after Trinity (Proper 15)	
	Principal Service: Luke 12.49–56	
	Lukewarm? As if!	205
	Second Service: Isa. 28.9–22	
	Which Bed Will You Choose?	207
24 Aug.	Tenth Sunday after Trinity (Proper 16)	
	Principal Service: Isa. 58.9b–end;	
	Luke 13.10–17 Be Expectant!	210
	Second Service: Isa. 30.8–21	
	Returning and Rest as Revolutionary	212
31 Aug.	Eleventh Sunday after Trinity (Proper 17)	
	Principal Service: Luke 14.1, 7–14	
	Tea Parties and Politics	214
	Second Service: John 3.22–36	
	The Best Man, Not the Groom	217
7 Sept.	Twelfth Sunday after Trinity (Proper 18)	
	Principal Service: Philemon 1–21	
	Giving the 'Useless' a Voice	219
	Second Service: John 5.30–end	
	You Search the Scriptures …	221

14 Sept.	**Thirteenth Sunday after Trinity** (Proper 19)	
	Principal Service: Luke 15.1–10	
	Lost and Found	224
	Second Service: John 6.51–69	
	Sustenance for Spiritual Life	226
21 Sept.	**Fourteenth Sunday after Trinity** (Proper 20)	
	Principal Service: Luke 16.1–13	
	God or Wealth?	228
	Second Service: John 7.14–36 Who is Jesus?	231
28 Sept.	**Fifteenth Sunday after Trinity** (Proper 21)	
	Principal Service: Luke 16.19–end	
	When the Tables are Turned	233
	Second Service: Ps. 134 Summoning Praise	235
5 Oct.	**Sixteenth Sunday after Trinity** (Proper 22)	
	Principal Service: Luke 17.5–10	
	Divine Dissatisfaction	237
	Second Service: John 9 Who Can You See?	240
12 Oct.	**Seventeenth Sunday after Trinity** (Proper 23)	
	Principal Service: Luke 17.11–19	
	Healing on the Way	242
	Second Service: Neh. 6.1–16	
	The Power of Walls	244
19 Oct.	**Eighteenth Sunday after Trinity** (Proper 24)	
	Principal Service: Luke 18.1–8	
	A Human Being Crammed Full of Heaven	247
	Second Service: Neh. 8.9–end	
	Home Rediscovered	249
26 Oct.	**Last Sunday after Trinity** (Proper 25)	
	Principal Service: Luke 18.9–14	
	Do Better, Be Better!	252
	Second Service: Eccl. 11 and 12 All is Vanity!	254
26 Oct.	**Bible Sunday**	
	Luke 4.16–24 Nobody's Poster Boy	256

2 Nov.	**Fourth Sunday before Advent**	
	Principal Service: Luke 19.1–10 Would the Real Zacchaeus Please Stand Up?	258
	Second Service: Lam. 3.22–33 Compassionate and Steadfast	260
9 Nov.	**Third Sunday before Advent**	
	Principal Service: Luke 20.27–38 Alive to God	263
	Second Service: Rom. 8.31–end 'I Am Convinced'	265
9 Nov.	**Remembrance Sunday**	
	Job 19.23–27a God is the God Who Always Sees	267
16 Nov.	**Second Sunday before Advent**	
	Principal Service: Luke 21.5–19 Looking for Security and Identity	270
	Second Service: Dan 6 Lion's Mouth	272
23 Nov.	**Christ the King** (Sunday next before Advent)	
	Principal Service: Luke 23.33–43 The King on a Cross	274
	Second Service: 1 Sam. 8.4–20 A King Over Us	277

SERMONS FOR SAINTS' DAYS AND SPECIAL OCCASIONS

2024

1 Dec.	**St Andrew the Apostle**	
	Matt. 4.18–22 Andrew: The Patron Saint of Community Activists	280
26 Dec.	**St Stephen, Deacon, First Martyr**	
	Acts 7.51–end Where is God to be Found?	282
27 Dec.	**St John, Apostle and Evangelist**	
	John 21.19b–end The Scandalous Maths of Grace	284

| 28 Dec. | The Holy Innocents
Matt. 2.13–18
Searching for Glimpses of Light | 287 |

2025

| 1 Jan. | Naming and Circumcision of Jesus
Num. 6.22–end   *A Face of Love* | 289 |
| 6 Jan. | Epiphany
Matt. 2.1–12   *Welcoming the New Things of God* | 292 |
| 18–25 Jan. | Week of Prayer for Christian Unity
Eph. 4.1–6; Col. 3.9–17   *One Body* | 294 |
| 25 Jan. | Conversion of St Paul
Acts 9.1–22   *The 'C' Word* | 296 |
| 19 Mar. | St Joseph of Nazareth
Matt. 1.18–end   *Guardians of Jesus* | 298 |
| 25 Mar. | Annunciation of Our Lord to the Blessed Virgin Mary
Luke 1.26–38   *Finding a Voice* | 301 |
| 28 Apr. | St George, Martyr
Rev. 12.7–12   *Battling in the Strength of Christ* | 303 |
| 29 Apr. | St Mark the Evangelist
Mark 13.5–13   *Calling Time* | 305 |
| 1 May | SS Philip and James, Apostles
John 14.1–14   *Enough* | 307 |
| 14 May | St Matthias the Apostle
Acts 1.15–end, John 15.9–17   *God's Friends* | 310 |
| 31 May | Visit of the Blessed Virgin Mary to Elizabeth
Luke 1.39–49 [50–56]   *Pregnancy and Prophecy – the Start of a Revolution* | 312 |

11 June	St Barnabas the Apostle *John 15.12–17 He Calls Us Friends*	315
19 June	Day of Thanksgiving for the Institution of the Holy Communion (Corpus Christi) *1 Cor. 11.23–26 Tokens of Love*	317
24 June	Birth of John the Baptist *Isa. 40.1–11; Luke 1.57–66, 80 Learning to Listen*	319
29 June	SS Peter and Paul, Apostles *Acts 12.1–11 Belt, Sandals, Cloak, Follow*	321
3 July	St Thomas the Apostle *John 20.24–29 Jesus of the Scars*	323
22 July	St Mary Magdalene *John 20.1–2, 11–18 All Desires Known*	326
25 July	St James the Apostle *Matt. 20.20–28 Not Sitting but Serving*	328
6 Aug.	Transfiguration of Our Lord *Luke 9.28–36 Mountain-top Experiences*	330
15 Aug.	The Blessed Virgin Mary *Luke 1.46–55 The Power and Potential of God*	333
24 Aug.	St Bartholomew the Apostle *Luke 22.24–30 Being Chosen*	335
14 Sept.	Holy Cross Day *Phil. 2.6–11 The Crucified God*	337
21 Sept.	St Matthew, Apostle and Evangelist *Matt. 9.9–13 Changing Perspective*	339
29 Sept.	St Michael and All Angels *John 1.47–end Fig Trees and Ladders*	341

18 Oct.	St Luke the Evangelist *Isa. 35.3–6; Luke 10.1–9* The Healing and Wholeness of God	344
28 Oct.	SS Simon and Jude, Apostles *John 15.17–end* So that You May Love	346
1 Nov.	All Saints' Day *Luke 6.20–31* A Chain of Blessedness	348
2 Nov.	Commemoration of the Faithful Departed (All Souls' Day) *Wisd. 3.1–9; John 6.37–40* In the Hand of God	351
	Harvest Festival *Deut. 26.1–11; John 6.25–35* God's Faithful Provision	353

ALL-AGE SERVICES

13 Apr.	Palm Sunday *Luke 19.28–40* When the Cheering Stops Will You Stay?	356
8 June	Pentecost *Acts 2.1–21* Empowered by the Holy Spirit	359
9 Nov.	Remembrance Sunday *Gen. 9.8–17* Stories to Remember	362
Notes		365

Preface

A new church year begins. Advent 2024 sees us embrace Year C in the church's lectionary. It's the Year of Luke. Luke was an apostle and evangelist, a doctor and a writer. Luke recorded the good news of Jesus in the Gospel which bears his name and in the adventures of the first Christians in the Acts of the Apostles. These books witness to God's kingdom being worked out in human history, first through Jesus and then through his body, the church. Luke focuses on the poor, the oppressed and the marginalized. God comes into ordinary lives bringing extraordinary promise and transformation. In Luke's hands, the good news of Jesus Christ is universal and the Holy Spirit is active, fiery and generative. You will encounter many of these features as you work with *The Canterbury Preacher's Companion*. Thank you for acquiring this book, either as a faithful devotee or a newcomer. Many of you have found this volume invaluable in the past. Do introduce others to this book and the associated App.

The well-honed format of the book remains the same. The first two-thirds offer two sermons for each Sunday of the church's year, working to the Principal and the Second Service provision in the lectionary. Several Sundays, such as Mothering Sunday and Remembrance Sunday, offer a third option. Christmas Day offers sermons for the four sets of readings, and there is material provided for Holy Week. The last third of the book has sermons for Saints' Days and a range of festivals often celebrated midweek. This edition also contains All-Age interactive material for Palm Sunday, Pentecost and Remembrance Sunday.

The word of God is to be preached in context, after prayerful preparation and with the inspiration of the Holy Spirit. Sermons, homilies and addresses are written for a particular community in a specified place, on a certain day. As such, each sermon is a 'one-off'. How strange then to produce a book of sermons as a resource! As I mention each year, these sermons are not to be copied verbatim and passed off as one's own. They are examples of good practice indicating how a particular preacher has responded to Scripture and developed ideas for their own context. Although they have been edited and reworked for publication, the majority of the sermons offered here have already been preached to real congregations in real-time. We offer them to you as a gift to spark your imagination and aid your preparation. They are a helping hand and a loving voice from the body of Christ to fellow preachers on the ground, preaching the gospel in season and out of season, week by week.

The contributors to this volume are a dedicated, gifted and hard-working group of preachers. They come from a variety of backgrounds, ordained and lay. Their voices are diverse in terms of background, gender, orientation, ethnicity and age, representing God's glorious rainbow people. It's always very inspiring to edit their work and I encourage you to read the sermons, not merely for sermon preparation but also for your spiritual well-being.

As this book goes to publication, we are in bleak and dangerous times. The climate chaos continues to alarm us with the speed of global warming and unprecedented weather events. Ukraine and Russia are at war, the escalating conflict and violence between Israel and Gaza harrowing. The cost-of-living crisis in the UK, with fuel, food and housing poverty, is a daily reality for many in our communities. These combined crises make the task of preaching the good news of Jesus urgent and complex.

The introductory article which follows is by Lucy Winkett, the Rector of St James's, Piccadilly, who is a gifted, creative and seasoned parish priest. In it, we are reminded that we preach from our baptismal promises. We turn to Christ, repent of our sins and renounce evil. We are challenged to preach truth with mercy in our current context. Drawing on the life and words of Quobna Ottobah Cugoano, an eighteenth-century parishioner at St James's who lived and worked in Pall Mall, Lucy demonstrates how to preach into the political, social and economic issues of the day, speaking with courage and hard-edged hope of the judgement, goodness and mercy of God. Lucy writes with intelligence, maturity and humility of the task of the preacher. I commend her words to you unreservedly.

So, as we enter into the Year of Luke, I pray that the God who calls you to preach will grace you afresh with passion to share the good news of Jesus in your words and daily living. May the Holy Spirit who dwells within you stir up the gift of preaching as she guides your imagination and empowers your creativity. So let's journey with Luke through Year C with courage, confidence and humility, preaching the lively oracles of God in word and deed.

Catherine Williams

Preaching in a Hurting World

Lucy Winkett

Every day I say morning prayer not far from the font where the poet and prophet William Blake was baptized in 1757. Itself a remarkable feature, the marble font, carved by the wood carver Grinling Gibbons, shows Adam and Eve in, to my eyes, a rather anarchic pose, certainly more bohemian than Puritan, more louche than virginal, draped around the trunk of the Tree of Life which holds the bowl in which that future excoriator of Christian hubris, and challenge to Christian preachers, William Blake was as a small baby exorcized, baptized and blessed.

At that same font, born in the same year as William Blake, came a 16-year-old young man in 1773 to be similarly baptized. Quobna Ottobah Cugoano was kidnapped as a child, as he says in his book, while he was playing with his friends in the West African village he grew up in. He was trafficked to Grenada in a slave ship, enslaved on a plantation, bought by an English man, taken to London and then freed. The first thing he did, on the advice of 'some good people', was to seek baptism, so that he not be 'carried away again'. He was a parishioner at St James's Piccadilly, living in Pall Mall, working in the household of Richard and Maria Cosway, and it was while living there and worshipping at the church that he wrote his fierce, seminal book *Thoughts and Sentiments on the Evil of Slavery*: the first book by an enslaved person of African descent to call for the total abolition of the transatlantic slave trade everywhere for ever.[1]

Unconventional preachers and the Spirit

Cugoano and Blake were both preachers, although not in the conventional sense. Neither would have been permitted in the church pulpit physically, but their writing, speaking, letter-writing and campaigning was an expression (sometimes in opposition to contemporary church teaching) of the fundamental call on Christians, rooted in their baptism promises, to 'renounce evil'.

Preachers promise to preach the gospel in and out of season, especially when things are difficult, compromised, contested or unclear. And in today's soundbite culture, where the strongest messages have to be instagrammable, it's a strange thing to do, to speak uninterrupted (usually ...) in a public setting where anyone can walk in, or walk out, and to do this week after week after week. Within contemporary British society, preaching a sermon is frankly quite weird. And 'preaching' has, in popular culture, pejorative tones, implying a judgemental attitude and a demeanour best described as 'holier than thou'.

And so, in the manner of Cugoano, Blake and many since, I suppose I don't want to lose the shock of the opportunity of being able to preach regularly. An overused word, it is truly a privilege that is not to be taken for granted.

Over the years that I have been preaching, from the small Methodist chapels of the Midlands to Anglican cathedrals, to gatherings on the street, at gravesides and any number of other settings, I've often wondered how I can stay close to the edge, stay close to the truth and keep looking for fresh perspectives. How can I remain attentive to the Spirit who blows where she wills, and not attempt to capture, domesticate or weaken (as if anyone really could ...) the clarifying, connecting, enlivening Spirit abroad in the world?

Divine mercy and the illusion of power

Preaching conventions don't really help this; in conventional sermons, one person speaks and while they speak others listen. Even in a sermon that has a measure of participation, or call and response, or element of discussion, it is still the case that one preacher has crafted what is often called 'the sermon slot' to be what it is. This gives power to the one who speaks. But the opposite reality is true too. For any preacher who is speaking from within a community such as a church congregation, the sermon is never created in isolation. It's a collective endeavour, as the meaning of Scripture is broken open for that community at that time. What's more, whenever one speaks and others listen, of course, the person speaking indeed holds power, but other sorts of power are being exercised too.

The power of the preacher is really an illusion. There are thoughts and feelings that the congregation experiences in the exchange that the preacher couldn't control if they wanted to, and will almost certainly never know. And a preacher throws themselves on the mercy of a congregation because (especially over time) there are things about the preacher that the congregation will learn that the preacher may never discover. A preacher is never able to be aware of all their biases, prejudices and hypocrisies. Despite our best efforts to find them all and name them all, these hypocrisies are resolutely hidden from us. They can often be seen by others and, of course, are seen by God. But the hypocrisies and prejudices are there for all to see. To be honest, whether or not I were a preacher, it is in part my growing awareness of this which takes me to church and, by and large, keeps me there. To follow Christ as a preacher of the word, to commit to my practice of religion, with others, has become my path precisely because I know my need of God's mercy. Because I live in the gap between the person I am and the person I want to be; because I recognize St Paul's 'flesh' and long for Christ's 'spirit'. Because there are times when I have sat in the valley of the dry bones of my life and begged them to remember how to dance. Divine mercy is the context for the exchange between preacher and congregation. Divine mercy sets the horizon and the boundaries within which the preacher and congregation are asked continually to forgive one another and, by so doing, build Christian community together.

The kerygmatic text

In contemporary culture, every day, congregations and preachers are bombarded by images, invitations to buy stuff, and persuasive copy of every kind created by every coms strategy of every institution, political party, church, business or charity. For preachers, context is everything. And so in the 2020s, preaching has to take into account this daily bombardment of words, information, images and stories.

Like the Gospels, sermons are, to use the theological word, kerygmatic. That is, they are not just text recounting facts or lists. They are telling stories, constructing arguments, and building a case that invites responses from the congregation. Sermons are written to persuade others of something.

To take the example of Quobna Ottobah Cugoano, his kerygmatic text takes the form of a sermon, yes, and a particular form at that. It's a jeremiad; in the manner of the prophet Jeremiah. A mixture of personal testimony and powerful rhetoric, all rooted in Scripture and Christian doctrine. Cugoano's courage is breathtaking. Because he was attending church services in a congregation that included parishioners who funded his abolitionist tract (168 of them listed in his text) and were clearly strongly supportive. But alongside them, he sat in the pews with people who were clearly benefiting from the transatlantic slave trade, and who received compensation on the abolition of the trade for the slaves that they had owned. To issue such a scriptural rebuke to them in his written sermon is astonishing, given his own experience of being enslaved. He preaches equality and freedom for all people everywhere for ever, based in the doctrine of creation found in Genesis and the story of Adam and Eve. He is unequivocal and clearly uncompromising, saying that if any person believes it is acceptable to own another person, they simply cannot be Christian. He takes on the racist theologies and ideologies that were espoused by Christian and church slave owners, who argued an inherent inequality based on skin colour from an interpretation of the story of Cain and Abel, known as the 'mark of Cain'. This inherent inequality argued on theological grounds provided Christians with the abominable justification for trading and owning slaves with darker skin. He challenges and re-interprets this theology head on and says clearly that the 'mark of Cain', as the brother who killed his brother inviting condemnation, does exist, but it is on the slave owners, not the slaves. Therefore, it is conditional on behaviour, not genetics. The key principle for Cugoano's preaching is that it is scriptural, personal, political and visionary. If ever preachers in local communities were needed with these characteristics, it is now. The task of the preacher is surely then not to be controversial for the sake of it, or be anxious about how creative or political or erudite or relevant they are. The task of the preacher is simply to return again and again to the source of all being – the presence of God – which is the most creative, generative and truthful presence in which all preachers live and move and have our being.

Turning to Christ

Like Cugoano, preachers preach as baptized people from the standpoint of someone immersed in that baptismal identity. And the promises taken at my baptism are the foundational promises of a preacher: I turn to Christ; I repent of my sins; I renounce evil. And over years of returning to the source of life, studying the Scripture, reading the newspaper and living the ministerial life: this is in itself a sort of continual baptism. Returning to the heart of things and making promises while there is a sort of continual process: spiritual drowning and death moving into new energy and life.

Over years of preaching, it's easy to become stale, uninterested or worn into a groove – oh yes, that parable, I know what I think about that one. Oh yes – of course, it's Ascension – I'm not sure I'm feeling it this year, but I'll dig out what I said before and see if I can adapt it. Ah yes, Mary Magdalene – well I've done my revisionist sermon on the fact that she wasn't actually a prostitute. Not sure what else there is to say …

In our quest for freshness, we can become too blown by the wind of current events, which are forever changing. Or, by contrast, we can become exhausted by the pace of current events to the extent that we retreat into a more risk-averse reliance on what's worked in the past, which is in reality more brittle than stable. This manifests itself in a reluctance in a preacher to try new approaches or let go of the script (or write a script), or find different interpreters or make a different path.

And there are always the voices that call preachers to account, reminding us that we take a risk every time we dare to approach the task. Quobna Ottobah Cugoano seems certainly to have had his fill of preachers who are given licence to speak in public by the church:

> Sometimes an old woman, selling matches, will preach a better, and a more orthodox sermon, than some of the clergy, who are only decked out with the 'external trappings of religion'. Much of the great wickedness of others lieth at their door, and these words of the Prophet are applicable to them: And first, saith the Lord, I will recompense their iniquity, and their sin double, because they have defiled my land, they have filled mine inheritance with the carcases of their detestable and abominable things. Such are the errors of men. Church, signifies an assembly of people; but a building of wood, brick or stone, where the people meet together, is generally called so; and should the people be frightened away by the many abominable dead carcases which they meet with, they should follow the multitudes to the fields, to the vallies, to the mountains, to the islands, to the rivers, and to the ships, and compel them to come in, that the house of the lord may be filled.[2]

Context matters

The novelist Iris Murdoch wrote back in 1970 that Christianity is 'not so much abandoned as unknown'. Even more true now than then. Of the people alive today, more generations have grown up without reference to Christian assumptions and teachings than have. The contemporary theologians John Baptist Metz and Rowan Williams talk of 'cultural amnesia' and 'cultural bereavement'.

Preachers in today's society and church are preaching to congregations who are themselves aware of and facing huge existential challenges of climate change, the forced migration of people, the inevitability of more pandemics and the instability of international relations in the context of weakening multinational organizations such as the UN. The necessary calls for justice following the Me Too and Black Lives Matter movements, a greater appreciation of the divergent identities of human beings concerning gender, neurology and disability, to name just three current issues, also cause deep and existential reflection on the nature of humanity, our interdependence with the earth and the increasing knowledge we have of the variety of people God has made.

And layered onto these global and existential challenges will be the local, the contingent, the community-focused, day-to-day realities that a preacher speaks into, with, please God, the energy and freshness of the good news.

Hard-edged hope

As I've reflected on the sermon of Quobna Ottobah Cugoano, his jeremiad, it seems to me that the theology from this former enslaved person speaks directly into the huge themes we face today.

Preaching in this context demands a combination of challenge to contemporary injustice with an insistence on the goodness and mercy of God. This sort of preaching reveals a hard-edged hope that addresses his hearers as perpetrators rather than victims. And in that combination is a manifesto for twenty-first-century preaching: to confront contemporary injustices honestly while relying utterly on the goodness and mercy of God. And vitally, understanding that these sermons are preached in a society where none of these themes can find ready or easy understanding or acceptance. In a world full of echo chambers and reinforcing beliefs, the ability to preach about difficult subjects in a merciful way is more necessary now than ever where Christianity is not so much abandoned as unknown.

Cugoano's language is of the eighteenth century (his sentences can be very long!) but his theological clarity is necessary for the twenty-first. And this brings me to my final reflection for today's preachers.

Strength, courage, judgement and mercy

Cugoano was challenging the great evil of his day: the transatlantic slave trade. He was doing this from within his own experience of that trade. And in the context of a church that owned and trafficked slaves. But his sort of preaching gives me, perhaps gives us, a blueprint for preaching into today's huge challenges. He insisted on vengeance and judgement being a necessary consequence for unrepentant slave traders. But he also insisted that this was not his role to exact any of this as a human being. The task of judgement belonged only to God. And that God would exercise this judgement with mercy. Like the psalmists, Cugoano's preaching did not ask God to provide him with the means and opportunity to exact vengeance. But revealed the pain and injustice of the world at the same time as throwing all this responsibility upon God to call it to account and receive the repentance of the perpetrators.

This is truly the hard-edged hope, the good news of redemption that comes with authentic repentance and restoration. The strength and courage that characterize his rebuke are breathtaking, given the context of both church and society in his day. For twentieth-century Christians, no longer familiar with the operation of God's judgement with mercy, this is a bracing message, but one that lands heavily in the debates about climate change, systemic injustice, persistent prejudice and inequality. To preach the judgement and mercy of God has become controversial, and difficult to do, not least because God's mercy addresses us as hearers at the point of our power to act, and our capacity for mistakes or betrayal or, to use the theological word, sin. Not only do we not really want to be addressed in this way – for that way lies accountability and potential exposure – but there is a combination of psychological strands that operate together to make us even more reluctant to be addressed by a merciful God.

What I mean by this is that not only are we addressed as people with the power to act, but we are addressed as people in need. Both powerful and needy. Hard to reconcile ourselves with either. Third, when those two attributes operate together, we discover our own identity not as victims, which is morally preferable and easier to inhabit, but as perpetrators. The things we have done and the things we have left undone.

It is a brave preacher who can really unpack these themes from the gospel without lapsing into judgemental assumptions or trespassing into territory that can hurt more than heal the divisions we live with.

The paradox of mercy and truth-telling

Contemplating the mercy of God brings us into close proximity with our power, our need and our sin. Otherwise, the mercy wouldn't be needed in the first place.

Rowan Williams paints a vivid picture: 'Where we are and who we are is the furnace where the Son of God walks.'[3]

In this poetic image, 'Where we are and who we are is the furnace where the Son of God walks', is a picture that captures somehow the paradox of mercy and truth-telling I have heard in the preaching of this particular preacher, Cugoano, and the paradox I am reaching for. It puts into words the sacrifice of God in Christ being burned for love of my burning soul.

It's not only when I am at my most powerful that the presence of mercy is required, but when I am at my most intimate. When I experience mercy being shown towards me, it is a choking relief. I have somehow been understood, my mistakes are seen as that – mistakes – and my intentions have not been wilfully misinterpreted. It makes it much easier to say sorry truly – much easier to admit that I want to be better. Something unlocks, something that was tight is loosened, something that was anxious is calm, something that was causing me to hold my breath to see if I could get away with it is now breathing freely.

There is a *false kindness* in the assurances of contemporary sermons which essentially say that being made in the image of God, a fundamental Christian principle, means that all we say and do is fine – whatever you need, whatever feels right – you are just fine as you are.

And there is a *false strictness* in the kind of sermon that fruitlessly and repetitively talks about sin and our begging for God's mercy and little else.

Both this false kindness and false strictness are methods of avoiding the path to freedom that is on offer in a life shaped by the mercy of God as revealed in the gospel from which we preach.

The Jewish philosopher, Gillian Rose, baptized towards the end of her too-short life, wrote a powerful book when she knew that she had not much longer to live. *Love's Work* is a message from the frontline of suffering and mercy: a message from the frontline of living while dying.

The quotation that she uses as part of the inspiration for her reflections is one from a nineteenth-century Russian Orthodox monk, Silouan, breathtaking in its simplicity and challenge: 'Keep your mind in hell and despair not.'[4]

This is preaching for the twenty-first century. Honest preaching in the face of huge and complex challenges that, even in its honesty, insists that despair is not an option. Because we preach a gospel of hope that is irreducible. Preaching that acknowledges there are contemporary kinds of hell. But hell that has been harrowed by Christ, in the act of divine mercy that was his death. And so I am not lost there; I am, like the prodigal son, found there. And I then have ears to hear, and a voice to preach the message from the God of mercy and truth. That whenever truth is preached, mercy is essential, to enable a fragile humanity to hear the good news from which it has become so estranged. The opportunity for preachers is immense in this context, because those who have ears to hear will hear.

Contributors

Matt Allen is the Blackburn Centre Lead Tutor at Emmanuel Theological College, overseeing the teaching of preaching and practical theology. His current doctoral research is in homiletics. Matt is on the Editorial Board of *The Preacher* magazine, has co-authored a book on preaching and preaches in a variety of contexts.

Mark Amos is Chaplain at The Abbey School, Reading. He has opportunity to speak in various contexts in school life, including assemblies and chapel services, and remains passionate about teaching in the classroom. He is completing doctoral research on how intimacy might be understood in the divine–human relationship.

Bill Braviner is an archdeacon in the diocese of Leeds. Originally from Tyneside, he has lived and served all over England. He thoroughly enjoys preaching, and hearing a diversity of voices in preaching, and has worked to promote accessibility and inclusion of disabled people across the church for many years.

Kate Bruce is an RAF chaplain, writer and regular preacher. She leads and contributes to retreats and conferences, and has taught preaching in different contexts over many years. Since 2020 she has been writing and researching on the theme of equipping preachers to focus on the women of the Bible.

Chris Campbell is the Rector of Ashwell with Hinxworth and Newnham, three rural parishes in North Hertfordshire. Chris has a passion for making the Bible come alive through storytelling, enjoys preaching to all ages, and draws inspiration from the natural world around her.

Kat Campion-Spall is an Anglican parish priest currently serving as Rector of the Bristol Harbourside Churches. Kat, influenced by feminist biblical interpretation, listens carefully for, and brings to light, the voices that have been silenced by received interpretations of the Scriptures.

Esther Elliott is a Church of Scotland Workplace and Community Chaplain in Edinburgh. She is also a Reader at St Mary's Episcopal Cathedral in Edinburgh. Previously she preached regularly in an Anglican parish in Nottingham and taught preaching, doctrine and mission for ministers in Derby Diocese.

Isabelle Hamley is an Anglican priest, author and broadcaster, with a passion for the Old Testament. She has been a parish priest, university chaplain, Old Testament lecturer and chaplain to the Archbishop of Canterbury, and currently works as Principal of Ridley Hall, Cambridge.

Mariama Ifode-Blease is a priest in the diocese of London, where she runs a charity and serves at St James's Piccadilly. Her preaching challenges social structures and affirms the invitation from Jesus Christ to the Table of Love. She is the author of *Inequality and Flourishing: A Theology of Education* (SCM Press, 2022).

Claire Jones is an ordained Church of England minister and co-leads Emmanuel Church, Woodley with her civil partner Rose. As an inclusive evangelical, she preaches primarily to invite anyone and everyone to hear and respond to the good news of Jesus Christ.

Jonathan Lawson is Vicar of St Gabriel's Church in Newcastle upon Tyne. He has served and preached in many different contexts from retreat houses to cathedrals, and ministered for ten years as a university chaplain. He has a particular interest in vocation and spiritual direction, and is the co-author of *Hearing the Call* (SPCK, 2014).

Rachel Mann is a priest, writer, broadcaster and theologian. She has written 14 books, including the acclaimed *Fierce Imaginings* (Darton, Longman & Todd, 2017), and writes regularly for the *Church Times* and *The Christian Century*. She is Archdeacon of Salford and Bolton in Manchester Diocese and is a member of the Faith and Order Commission. She broadcasts on BBC Radio 4 and Radio 2.

Mark Nam is a British-born Chinese priest in the diocese of Bristol. He is founder of *The Teahouse*, which raises the profile and participation of Chinese-heritage clergy in the Church of England. He is passionate about empowering diverse voices to lead in the areas of worship and preaching.

Catherine Okoronkwo is Vicar of All Saints and St Barnabas churches in Swindon and is the Bishop of Bristol's Adviser on Racial Justice. A poet and writer, she is interested in the use of the creative arts in ministry, mission and justice advocacy. Her poetry collection *Blood and Water / ọbara na mmiri* is available from Waterloo Press (2020).

Andrew Rudd is a Reader in Frodsham, Cheshire. A published poet, he was recently poet-in-residence at Manchester Cathedral. In preaching, teaching, retreat leading and spiritual direction he seeks – impossible task! – to find words for what cannot be put into words.

David Runcorn is a retired Anglican priest living in Devon. He loves preaching and longs to help people understand the Bible better. He is the author of a number of books and is still involved in teaching theology and working in areas of (lay and ordained) ministry support and development.

Michael Sadgrove was a parish priest and theological educator before spending nearly three decades in cathedral ministry. He was Dean of Durham from 2003 until his retirement in 2015. He has written on biblical and pastoral themes, on the Christian heritage of the North East where he lives, and has also published a book of sermons.

Liz Shercliff teaches, writes about and researches preaching. Her books include *Preaching Women* (SCM Press, 2019); *The Present Preacher*, with Matt Allen (Canterbury Press, 2021); *Out of the Shadows: Preaching the Women of the Bible*, with Kate Bruce (Canterbury Press, 2021). She teaches preaching for the College of Preachers, Luther King Centre, Emmanuel Theological College, and the Nazarene Theological College.

Karen E Smith is a Baptist minister who taught church history and Christian spirituality at Cardiff University and served as pastor of a church in South Wales. Now retired, she is an Honorary Senior Research Fellow of Cardiff University, and continues to publish in the area of Christian spirituality and Dissenting history.

Kt Tupling is an Anglican priest, Diocesan Disability Adviser and Oxford University College Chaplain. She is co-founder of the online community *Disability and Jesus*, with whom she co-authored *Pilgrims in the Dark* (2018) and has written for Grove booklets (*Worship and Disability* (2018) and *Being Disabled, Being Human* (2022)). She is a narrowboat owner and real ale drinker.

Catherine Williams is a spiritual director and writer. She contributes to various spirituality resources and is the lead voice on the Church of England's *Daily Prayer* App (Aimer Media Ltd). Licensed to the Bishop of Norwich as a Public Preacher, Catherine preaches regularly in a variety of contexts.

Lucy Winkett is Rector of St James's Piccadilly, formerly Canon Precentor of St Paul's Cathedral. Her latest publication is *Reading the Bible with Your Feet* (Canterbury Press, 2022). She is a broadcaster and writer, and is a long-standing contributor to Radio 4's 'Thought for the Day'.

Year C, the Year of Luke

(Year C begins on Advent Sunday in 2024, 2027, 2030 etc.)

Advent

First Sunday of Advent 1 December
Principal Service **Straining Our Eyes for God's Kingdom**
Jer. 33.14–16; Ps. 25.1–9; 1 Thess. 3.9–end; **Luke 21.25–36**

Staring at the sea

Early one summer morning, we parked the car on the edge of a road, and hiked out across bogs and moor, laden with binoculars and cameras, in search of otters. Across tufts of grass, up and down hills, to a discrete corner of an island which felt like the edge of the world. Now we stood on the bank of a windswept peninsula, hair whipping around our faces and, despite it being July, buttoning our coats tighter, silently wishing we'd brought gloves.

The cold blue of the sea frothed and foamed; shades of cobalt, sapphire and azure, melting and merging into one another. Shadows drifted. We watched. Not just the sea, but the craggy shoreline too. Staring more intently than we had ever done before; eyes straining for a shape, a splash, a fleeting glimpse … a sign.

It felt almost overwhelming; there was too much to see; too much sea, too much sky, too much shoreline … As we turned to scan the horizon, would we miss the very thing we wanted to glimpse? Or if we kept our gaze in one spot, would we never know what was happening behind us? Our guide gave us tips, from the need to keep one eye on the lurking gulls in the sky, to the way to differentiate otter poo from that of mink.

But it was cold and damp, and we'd been watching for hours, and those potential signs seemed just to frustrate our novice searching even more. Patient watching is hard work and it's easy to feel like giving up.

Advent watching

Today is the start of Advent, our special time of watching. A time to be sentinels, keeping vigil with the prophets. A time for standing and scanning the horizon of the world, peering into the immense dark ocean, with only the vaguest hope that something might catch our attention. But what are we watching for?

Not for the signs that Christmas is coming, for those are plain for all of us to see: in the onslaught of marketing emails, the lights going up, and the shelves that have been filling with mince pies for weeks. Instead, for the signs of the inbreaking of God's kingdom; those glimmers of God's work happening in unexpected places, and God's perspective being found in unexpected people.

Like otters on the coast of Skye, those glimmers aren't always going to be easy to find. The world is vast and troubled, and we often wonder if God could ever be present in the vast choppy oceans. And even if God is, we might be looking the wrong way.

Where is God in that?

Our Gospel reading from Luke is set just a day or two before Jesus is arrested. The disciples have walked with him and will soon watch as the man they loved and followed is taken away from them; whipped, scorned and hanged upon a cross. In a few days, they will stand far off, trying to stay safe from the authorities, watching as hope descends into chaos, wondering where God is, in the darkness of the Passion.

Jesus knows what happens, he knows that things are not going to be easy, that it will look like everything has gone wrong and that hope is impossible. So, he captures the feeling of that time, with vivid images of some future time; a time when there will be distress among nations, confused by the roaring of the sea and the waves. A time when people will faint from fear and foreboding of what is coming upon the world, and the powers of the heavens will be shaken. A time when everyone will wonder where God is.

God is there if you look

But even in such a time as *that*, Jesus tells them, the kingdom of God comes near. Jesus, our guide, points to the future horizon and assures the disciples that even in the darkest of all times, you can stand and lift your heads with hope. 'Heaven and earth will pass away, but my words will not pass away,' Jesus tells them; God will be there if you look.

Because of this, the disciples, with us, are warned to be on their guard; so that hearts are not weighed down with the worries of this life. To continue scanning the horizon, alert and awake to the restorative possibility of God. Because even if it may look chaotic and hopeless, the days are surely coming, says the Lord, when God will fulfil God's promise.

Sometimes that will be hard. Sometimes we might feel cold and damp, our attention will wander, we'll lose hope in our watching and we'll want to just give up and go home.

But each Advent Jesus emboldens us to stay awake; to reinvigorate our patient vigil on the top of the cliffs, and to foster a prayerful attentiveness in our lives. Because sometimes, when you watch hard enough, you suddenly see the ripple of water, and the sleek brown head of an otter, and you know that the waiting was worth it.

Chris Campbell

Hymn suggestions

Earth was waiting, spent and restless; Longing for light, we wait in darkness; People, look East; Ye servants of the Lord.

First Sunday of Advent 1 December
Second Service **Advent Hope**
Ps. 9 [*or* 9.1–8]; **Joel 3.9–end**; Rev. 14.13—15.4;
Gospel at Holy Communion: John 3.1–17

The first Sunday of the Advent season is seen by some people as the beginning of the countdown to Christmas Day. It is certainly a time to prepare to celebrate the coming of God in Christ, but also to look forward to the final coming of God as judge at the end of time. For the people of old, and perhaps for us, too, the Day of the Lord – the time when God will put things right in the world – is difficult to imagine. Yet, the prophet Joel assures us that on the 'Day of the Lord' we will know God's nearness.

A loss of hope

Every 17 years, in some places in the eastern United States, in early spring, there is the appearance of the periodical cicada, popularly known as the '17-year locust'. They emerge suddenly – in their trillions – from under the ground, and they live for about four to six weeks. Actually, these very large and noisy grasshoppers do not harm people or plants, though just having them swarming about is a very unsettling experience.

Having experienced swirling dark clouds of cicadas, I can only imagine how terrible it must be to live through an invasion of destructive locusts. Describing the circumstances of God's people, the prophet Joel said that after the cutting, swarming, hopping and destroying locusts, the crops were ruined, vines withered and the joy of the people had withered away, too (Joel 1.4–12).

A call to return

Realizing that the people were fearful and with little hope, the prophet urged them to turn to the Lord 'with fasting, with weeping, and with mourning' (Joel 2.12), remembering that God is 'gracious and merciful, slow to anger, and abounding in steadfast love, and relents from punishing' (2.13). If the people so turned to God, the prophet envisaged a new day dawning – a time when they would experience God's spirit being poured out on them all (2.28–29).

Reading these promising words of the prophet today, the choice to return to God seems an easy one. Surely, God's people would simply turn immediately in trust to God. Yet, for those whose lives have been shattered by trouble, hope is not so easily restored. If you have experienced loss that left you drinking deeply from a cup of despair, or accompanied a friend along the dark path of depression, you may know how difficult it is to go on hoping and believing in the love of God. While the prophet promised that the Day of the Lord – a day when God would intervene and make things right in the world – would indeed come, the people of old could not imagine such a day. Sometimes, perhaps, we can't either.

The valley of decision

Realizing their despondency, the prophet assured the people of God's love for them and then offered a vision of the Day of the Lord. At first, the prophet's words seem foreboding as the prophet claimed that 'multitudes, multitudes' of people would gather in the valley of Jehoshaphat (literally the valley of judgement), where 'the sun and moon are darkened, and stars withdraw their shining'. Surprisingly, though, the prophet suggests that the valley of judgement is also a valley of decision. While there is no claim that all trouble and difficulty will be removed from the people, they are assured that they may place their hope and their trust in God who is for them a 'refuge' and a 'stronghold'.

God is with us

Writing to a friend, from his cell in a Gestapo prison on Advent Sunday, in 1943, Dietrich Bonhoeffer spoke of all the difficulties and dangers he faced in prison. Then, he reflected on an Advent hymn that seemed to sum up the Advent hope. The last two lines claimed:

> Darkness now must fade away,
> For faith within the light must stay.[5]

In a world of turmoil and trouble, at times we may find it difficult to hope in God. Yet, Scripture promises that while at times we may feel that we struggle amid the darkness of despair, we can have confidence. For we may be sure that whatever problems we face, with God as our stronghold, we can discover light even amid darkness. God has come to us and still comes to us now as a present help in every kind of trouble. The Advent hope is that the Lord God will surely also come again in glory. Thanks be to God!

Karen E. Smith

Hymn suggestions

All my hope on God is founded; Come, thou long expected Jesus; Hark, the glad sound, the Saviour comes; The light of the morning is breaking.

Second Sunday of Advent 8 December
Principal Service **Potholes and Speed Bumps**
Baruch 5, *or* Mal. 3.1–4; *Canticle*: Benedictus; Phil. 1.3–11;
Luke 3.1–6

I'm not sure I like Advent very much. The lectionary becomes challenging, pointing me to things I find difficult. Advent calls us to seriousness. Not *miserable* seriousness, but commitment. In a relationship there may come a time when it gets *serious*. People start planning for the future, for involvement with another person that might be costly …

Advent calls us to be serious about the spiritual dimension of our lives. That's different for each of us. It might be about understanding more about what we believe – maybe with deeper reading. It might be cultivating compassion – finding new ways to be kind to others. It might be developing our practice of silence and prayer. All these are ways of getting serious with God.

World context

What a very odd reading we have from Luke! Half of it is a list of rulers and places, and half is a quotation from the book of Isaiah.

Before he tells us the story of John the Baptist, Luke wants to give us a big picture, a world context. As in a theatre programme, here are some names to keep in mind. Here's the cast list, and here's the setting. And we recognize some of them, don't we? Here's Herod, here's Pontius Pilate. They will reappear at the end of the final act. Luke sets us up for that.

But Luke gives us this list for another reason. Nowadays we might say, 'While Charles III was king, and so-and-so was Prime Minister …' Yes, but is that the real news? Luke drills through the politics and says, 'No, it's not there, look here!' The main event is happening elsewhere.

The word of God doesn't come to these kings, these powerful people, but to this man John, in the desert, on his own, by himself.

Because the wilderness is where it all begins. What's a wilderness? It's a place of nothing, no significance, a place without people. And that's where the word of God comes, where we least expect it. Where there are no distractions, no agenda. Out on the edge.

For Luke, this kickstarts the story of the gospel. It begins in the desert, with places and people of no significance – mangers, shepherds and a baby.

But it's also a story which will happen on a world stage. That word, that voice, will meet Herod, Pontius Pilate, the life of politics and empire. Change is going to come. But not in the way anybody expects.

Luke comments on this with words from Isaiah: 'The voice of one crying out in the wilderness: "Prepare the way of the Lord."'

Isaiah was speaking to people in exile, refugees from their own country. He was thinking about preparing a way for God's people to get back to the land from which they came, to get back home.

Luke wants to map this onto *his* story, his experience of Jesus. In Luke's story all kinds of people – out on the edge, out on a limb, in no place – are invited back, brought home, to belonging in the kingdom of God.

If God is going to bring us back home, then God needs the infrastructure to do it. A great highway through the desert. And so, the road bumps are being smoothed, the dips and potholes filled in, so that Emmanuel, God with us, can speed into the whole world, bringing joy, peace and freedom.

Great levelling

In Mary's great song, God pulls down the mighty, has mercy on the lowly, and lifts up the humble. This is the great levelling, the kingdom of God: 'Every valley filled and every mountain and hill shall be made low.' So that on this vast level playing field, the whole world can see the salvation, the glory of God.

Good news

This kingdom of God, which John preaches, is good news – amazing news – for those deprived of medicine or clean water, those deprived of food or homes by violence. The gospel claims that this is so, and challenges us to bring that hope to others.

Potholes and speed bumps

If my life was a road, there would be a lot of *potholes*. Gaps, spots of emptiness, darkness, anxiety, trouble. And these can obstruct what God wants to do in my life. God takes the valleys, the potholes of my experience and fills them in, to make a level, stable surface for the life of God to travel.

But also, there are plenty of *speed bumps* – resistances, aspects of my life and personality that get in the way, where my journey stops God's journey. And here, 'every mountain and hill shall be made low'.

This road-mending is a good picture of our spiritual work. Silence, and conversation with God. These practices work on the surface of the road that is my life. They build a highway for God to come, for love to come again.

Prepare the way. Advent preparing is work we do in darkness. We do it without full understanding, but it draws us closer to the light. We make a way believing that God will 'ride in', bringing goodness, joy and peace.

'Prepare the way of the Lord!'

Andrew Rudd

Hymn suggestions

Wait for the Lord (Taizé); Make way; On Jordan's bank the Baptist's cry; Hark a herald voice is calling.

Second Sunday of Advent   8 December
Second Service   **The Last Prophet**
Ps. 75 [76]; Isa. 40.1–11; **Luke 1.1–25**

God's people had waited a long time. Day by day, year by year, they waited; waited for the promises of God to be fulfilled, waited for the voice prophesied by Isaiah to be heard, waited for the pains of exile and occupation to be healed, waited for a new exodus of liberation, of restoration, of freedom truly to fulfil their calling to be the people of God.

Faithfulness or familiarity?

Amid their waiting, they were called to be faithful. The lamp of God did not go out; the worship of God did not cease; the story of God continued to be told. They committed themselves to live out the law, to adhere to Torah. They participated in the daily round and the annual cycle of Temple and synagogue, of new moons and Sabbaths. But is it possible that faithfulness had lapsed into familiarity, that responsiveness had lapsed into routine? How else are we to understand a priest who is surprised to meet God in the Holy of Holies?

Perhaps that's a bit harsh. Who wouldn't be surprised to be confronted by an angel? Who wouldn't experience fear at what this might mean? It is, after all, an awe-full thing to fall into the hands of the living God! Why should Zechariah, or Elizabeth, think that they would be used by God in this way, to fulfil promises for the whole people of Israel? An inconspicuous priest; blameless, yes – but not especially blessed.

Unlikely people

God had a history of using the unlikeliest of people to bring his promises to birth, but despite the examples littered throughout the story of God's dealings with his people, those same people were not always ready to recognize God's action or his call, even when it seemed inescapable.

Despite God's faithfulness, seen famously in the gift of a child to Abraham and Sarah in their old age, to fulfil the promise that from them would come descendants more numerous than the stars, and despite the appearance of the Archangel Gabriel to bring God's promise that the waiting was drawing to its culmination, still Zechariah could not find the faith to embrace that promise and believe. His question is along the lines of 'How can it be?' It's a question born of anxiety, of fear.

But it *can* be – for, as the Archangel will reassure another questioner before too long, 'nothing will be impossible with God' (Luke 1.37). Zechariah and Elizabeth, though old and barren, will indeed bring to birth the long-awaited voice that will comfort God's people, to herald the advent of the long-awaited Messiah. No longer will they be a people in waiting. No longer need they be a people driven by fear or enduring disgrace; soon they will be a people liberated by love, and led by hope.

Unlike Zechariah, Elizabeth seems to have been able to open herself to this promise from God much more readily, perhaps because the promise was incarnate within her, growing to fruition inside her own body. Within six months, she would feel her child's first prophecy when he leapt in exultation at the approach of the long-awaited Messiah in his own mother's womb. Perhaps Elizabeth was ready to respond without having to rationalize, ready to stand under God rather than first wanting to understand God.

What will this child become?

By the time of the fulfilment of the angel's promise to Zechariah, people will be asking of the child to be born: 'What then will this child become?' (Luke 1.66). As herald of God's kingdom, John will be the last of the prophets of the old covenant, and the first prophet of the new. In calling people back to God, in opening hearts and minds to God's possibilities, in preparing the way for Jesus and in speaking truth to power, John will disturb the comfortable and comfort the disturbed. He will recognize Jesus, point to Jesus, lift up Jesus and make way for Jesus. But for Zechariah and Elizabeth, that's in a future yet to be revealed.

We wait

Like Zechariah, like Elizabeth, like countless others, we too wait. In this Advent season, we remind ourselves to prepare the way of the Lord in our own lives; not just to ready ourselves to celebrate once again his birth at Bethlehem, but to ready ourselves to meet him when he comes again so that our response need not be one of fear, but of hope.

Let us pray that we may never be so dulled by the practice of our religion that we fail to respond to the presence and promises of God in our lives. Let us pray that our faithfulness may always be to his call, to our discipleship, rather than merely to our routines and our rhythms. May we be ready to encounter our Lord, not just in a Christmas crib, nor just at the day of judgement, but also day by day, as he comes to us afresh with his comfort: 'Do not fear' – and his challenge: 'What will *you* become?'

Bill Braviner

Hymn suggestions

Do not be afraid; Will you come and follow me; Be still, for the presence of the Lord; Wait for the Lord, whose day is near (Taizé).

Third Sunday of Advent 15 December
Principal Service **Foreboding and Faith**
Zeph. 3.14–end; *Canticle*: Isa. 12.2–end, *or* Ps. 146.4–end; Phil. 4.4–7; **Luke 3.7–18**

Advent can be a time of foreboding. As the days grow darker and colder, so can the prospects for our world. 'Things fall apart; the centre cannot hold.'[6] Those who can read the signs of the times no longer whisper behind closed doors. The widening gap between privilege and poverty, the inflated bonuses and wealth of reckless risk-takers who played casino with our finances and plunged our economies into disarray, cuts in public services, all this is embittering a growing underclass of have-nots. It raises the real threat of social unrest. In France, they have a warning: *quand la banlieues brûlent* – 'when the suburbs start burning', not least because of the impacts on the young of huge and inescapable hopelessness.

The rhetoric of wartime which some leaders employ plays into these alarms because survival requires a collective will, a wartime spirit across our peoples. But the enemy is not someone or somewhere else. It is in our midst; we are all part of this environment in which the pursuit of material gain, easy credit, the uncritical cult of growth, and the expectation of an easy, untroubled life have almost become human rights at the expense of hard-won virtue and spiritual values. It is a high price to pay. When greed begets envy and envy resentment, and resentment despair and despair hatred, we should fear for the future of our society and its capacity to be strong and united enough to resist the shocks of crisis.

Advent speaks

How does Advent speak into this wintry atmosphere? By setting our human crises in the larger context of the divine. *Krisis* in Greek means 'judgement'. The root meaning is separating or distinguishing things from one another, so judgement is making a decision based on insight and discernment. This is a central theme in Advent. Last judgement means the final settling of accounts, the righting of the wrongs of history, and the establishment of God's just reign over all things. The Psalmists rejoiced as they looked forward to YHWH's coming to judge the world and the people with equity. The day of God's enthronement would be the vindication of his truth before the world and therefore its salvation. But Advent also looks for

God's coming in our ordinary days, 'now in the time of this mortal life in which thy Son came to visit us in great humility'.[7] That word 'visit', gratuitously omitted from the modern collect in *Common Worship*, is all-important because it intentionally carries an ambiguity: *visit* us and stay awhile among us as the guest who brings blessing, but also *visit* as in bringing visitation upon us, herald a crisis, announce a coming judgement. Advent is both: *krisis* is mercy and judgement.

John the Baptist

This season brings a dose of reality to our fantasy and illusion. It deflects us from the lazy optimism that says, come what may no harm will befall us. Christmas can play into it as if we can hide from crises in the warm glow of Yuletide. But our Gospel reading about John the Baptist is of a man who knew *krisis* in the uncompromising harshness of the desert. 'The voice of one crying out in the wilderness, "Prepare the way of the Lord, make his paths straight."' 'Out of the crooked timber of humanity, no straight thing was ever made,'[8] said Immanuel Kant. But God can and will straighten out the human heart, says John, just as he makes the rough places plain. At one with Elijah in his hatred of all that was false; and with Moses in his love of all that was good and true; and with the Messiah himself, in his summons to turn and embrace the kingdom of God. In the desert of these times, we need a John the Baptist to point us towards a future worth living for.

Bearing witness

How should the church speak to this crisis? 'Do justly, love mercy, walk humbly with the Lord' is a good place to start. And then? Don't we need to restore trust in our global institutions so that we can begin to reconstruct a society based on good faith, a notion of shared common wealth, and wise humane values that restore social and spiritual capital? The church can broker conversation about how this could happen. And as an aspect of bearing prophetic witness, shouldn't we intercede more urgently for the world and for humanity?

This calls for imagination because it requires us to ponder what God thinks about our predicaments and what it would mean to be delivered from them. The answer to midwinter forebodings is to pray the Advent words of Psalm 80 in faith and hope: 'Restore us, O God of hosts; let your face shine, that we may be saved.'

Michael Sadgrove

Hymn suggestions

On Jordan's bank, the Baptist's cry; Sing we the praises of the great forerunner; O come, O come, Emmanuel; Thy kingdom come, O God.

Third Sunday of Advent   15 December
Second Service   **Fools on the Road**
Ps. 50.1–6 [62]; **Isa. 35**; Luke 1.57–66 [67–end]

What do you think the most beautiful passage in Scripture is? For me, it is Isaiah 35. The vision of the people of God, ransomed and healed, safe and walking with God in a desert blossoming with new life. It is the kind of passage that could be dismissed as pie in the sky if you don't read carefully, but a passage of utter realism when you do.

New life demands dealing with the past

Isaiah starts with the vision of new life and exhorts readers to let the vision of tomorrow transform today's reality. The manner of transformation is not entirely comfortable: God comes with vengeance, recompense and salvation. The idea of judgement is not particularly popular today, but it is an Advent theme. In Scripture, judgement is an essential companion to promises of peace and justice. Dealing with injustice, pain, violence and conflict goes hand in hand with making a different world, and that involves judgement on everything that deals death. Before new life can blossom, sin needs to be dealt with – decisively. Creating something new cannot be based on ignoring or dismissing the past, but only on dealing with it, naming its brokenness. It cannot be an instant zap that bypasses our intellectual and mental faculties and habits, but an unveiling of truth, facing up to our responsibilities.

God of love and justice

God in Isaiah is neither a cuddly God of intimacy nor a distant, angry God of judgement. It is a God who holds justice and love, tenderness and power together closely. It is a God who loves his people and a God who leads them into costly holiness. In the whole book, Isaiah moves swiftly between visions of power and love, judgement and healing, hard truth and tenderness. These are things about God we often like to keep separate – we often want a God of judgement to deal with others who have hurt us, and a God of love to deal with our own shortcomings; we want a God of power to change everything instantly, but a God of love to respect our free will. Isaiah says it isn't either/or, it is both/and. The God who is far, holy, fearsome and awesome is also the God who is near, caring, tender and loving.

A fool's hope

Isaiah's picture of transformation holds clues to the character of God and the vocation of humanity. He pictures a road for God's people, a place of safety. A road involves a journey and movement on our part. The future isn't only God's work, it is ours too.

It is a road for God's people – and God's people are not the strong, the perfect, the righteous, the wonderful, those who've got it together. They're the broken, the ransomed, the healed and even, the fools! I love the little aside, 'No traveller, not even fools, shall go astray.' It's OK to be part of God's people and get it wrong. The point is that it is those who know their need of God, their need for healing, redemption and direction who walk on the road. They are the people who have let God's truth shine over them and accepted and welcomed God's healing. It is a road for you and me.

A road and a city

I am always fascinated that it is the desert that blooms and is transformed. Most of us don't want to stay in the desert. We don't want a road, we want teleporting out! But the people stay in the desert, and see the desert transformed. Faith and walking with God are not a pass to another reality, but a transformation of what we know. Then the new city appears – Zion, the Holy City, the vision of a new day. It is a picture of a fully transformed world, a fully transformed human community. But the transformation can only happen by walking the road: through truth, justice and transformation, for ourselves and others around us, a path that holds healing but also judgement, a path that will allow us to come face to face with the truth of who we are, the truth of the world, yet know the power of God's redemption and grace.

The invitation of Advent

This is the path we tread in Advent. Advent is this time when we acknowledge the truth of the world as it is, the continuing truth of the world that Christ was born into – Roman oppression, insalubrious birth, refugees, children killed by power-hungry rulers, and a world of selfishness and greed. But Advent is also a time to look ahead to what God is doing – a future more glorious than any of us can imagine, a future that begs us to allow God to change and transform our present. And so, Advent calls us to examine our response to Christ, our willingness to let him work within us, our willingness to let his light shine in our personal darkness, our willingness to shine the light on the dark corners of the world we inhabit, so that he can bring healing and new life, and his power and love work within and around us.

Isabelle Hamley

Hymn suggestions

Jesus, remember me (Taizé); Longing for light, we wait in darkness; My hope is built on nothing less (Cornerstone); Come, thou long-expected Jesus.

Fourth Sunday of Advent   22 December
Principal Service   **Leading Us to the Incarnation**
Mic. 5.2–5a; *Canticle*: Magnificat, *or* Ps. 80.1–8; Heb. 10.5–10;
Luke 1.39–45 [46–55]

The Advent journey

Today we draw near to the end of our Advent journey, on the final Sunday before Christmas Day. The picture that has been building up over Advent comes to a climax in this wonderful story from

Luke's Gospel about two cousins, pregnant women, greeting each other in reverence and joy.

There is a progression of themes in Advent, which are particularly evident in our Collects and readings over the four weeks: first patriarchs, then prophets, then John the Baptist, and finally this week Mary; and all these themes come together in this encounter.

Stories old and new

The story of Elizabeth and Zechariah echoes the story of Abraham and Sarah, an older couple, past childbearing and still longing for a child, who are surprised and blessed by God with a son – for Abraham and Sarah, Isaac; for Elizabeth and Zechariah, John. The parallels are clear between these two couples, and so the story of the patriarchs is infused in this scene, in which John the Baptist is present as a child in the womb of his mother.

Mary's song of praise, her Magnificat, is closely aligned with that of another mother, Hannah. Hannah prayed for a son and gave birth to Samuel, whom she gave to the Lord's service, and Hannah's prayer of praise and thanksgiving to God was clearly in Mary's mind as she sang her Magnificat. You might remember that wonderful story of Samuel as a boy in the Temple with his master the prophet Eli. Samuel hears a voice calling him in the night and thinks it is Eli, but discovers it is in fact the voice of God. Samuel became a great prophet and anointed both Saul and David as kings. So here in the words of Mary we have a thread that runs from the prophets and through the establishment of the line of David.

Mary herself reminds us of the great unfolding story of God's love for humanity, passing through the Old Testament into the New, as she harks back to Abraham. 'He has helped his servant Israel, in remembrance of his mercy, according to the promise he made to our ancestors, to Abraham and to his descendants for ever.' Mary sings.

The beginning of the end

And what's the other story we remember about Abraham and his son Isaac? That Abraham took Isaac up the mountain to sacrifice him to God – which, incidentally, was not unusual behaviour in other religions in those days, offering human sacrifices to appease angry, bloodthirsty gods. Abraham took Isaac up the mountain to sacrifice him to God, and God told Abraham not to do it. That encounter was the beginning of the end of this kind of sacrificial religion, which was made complete when God became human and lived among us.

From sacrifice to love

Our reading from Hebrews is talking exactly about sacrifice, and setting it against doing God's will. It tells us that Jesus abolishes ritual sacrifices, the rules and regulations of religion, to establish something new – call it a religion if you like, but a religion which is not about appeasing an angry God with ritual offerings, but rather responding to God's love by doing God's will.

This is what Abraham starts when he doesn't sacrifice his son but listens to the voice of God. Abraham, through his son Isaac, is the father of the people who will become the Israelites.

This is what Mary sings of when she proclaims that God's mercy isn't with those who are proud of how well they have followed the religious laws, or with those who are powerful or rich, but rather with those who are faithful. Not with those who believe themselves to be great, but with those who know themselves to be lowly.

So this encounter between Elizabeth and Mary somehow encompasses the whole of the Old Testament as these two women and their unborn children lead us towards the incarnation.

Greeting our Saviour with joy

By the Fourth Sunday of Advent, we have often given up any pretence of keeping this special season, even though there are still a few days left. Advent disappears into our cultural celebration of Christmas in the lead-up to 25 December. But perhaps we can think of ourselves in the position of John the Baptist in this story. He celebrates in the presence of God incarnate, he jumps with joy to greet his saviour, even though Christ is not yet born.

Perhaps today and for the final couple of days of Advent, we can joyfully celebrate that Christmas is coming, while we anchor ourselves in the great and wonderful story of God's people that leads us to Christ's incarnation.

Kat Campion-Spall

Hymn suggestions

Tell out, my soul; Long ago, prophets knew; Thy kingdom come, on bended knee; Come, thou long-expected Jesus.

Fourth Sunday of Advent   22 December
Second Service   **Shame**
Ps. 123 [131]; Isa. 10.33—11.10; **Matt. 1.18–end**

Running away

When I was a young boy, I ran away from school – or, to be more precise, I pretended to walk to school one day, but instead hid. There was a search and the police were called, and it is only as an adult that I have come to realize how much anxiety I must have caused my parents. But there was a back story. Isn't there always? I ran away because I was very scared and frightened. A day or two before, my mother had told me that she had seen one of the single masters at school kissing a woman, and this seemed like a juicy bit of gossip to a young boy. I told lots of people and then explained to my mother what I had said. She told me I would probably get into trouble for spreading this gossip, so I ran away. Shame is a powerful thing.

Cock and bull

Today is a day when many will be getting ready for Christmas. A day for carol services, crib services and nativity plays. Lots of tinsel, tea towels and carols. The fact that it is still Advent, a time of longing and waiting, will have passed most people by. As will, I suspect, the true nature of this story of the birth of Jesus. It is so familiar to us. But it is scandalous. I have been heavily influenced by Ignatian spirituality, and the gift of entering into passages such as these imaginatively; it has the ability to bring Scripture alive and to go deeper into it. In today's Gospel reading from St Matthew, we are presented with a story almost as a matter of fact. But can you imagine the consequences? Even today, as a man, going home to tell your parents that your betrothed is pregnant, but not by you, is not a great story to tell. We can only imagine their response if they were still alive and indeed if he ever told them. It's all there in verse 19: 'Her husband Joseph, being a righteous man and unwilling to expose her to public disgrace, planned to dismiss her quietly.' Joseph knows this is not a good look: he knows this can bring shame on Mary, and he wants to protect her. But the way of God is different.

Read the whole story

It fits my character, but I was taught to notice what is cut out of (or not used in) readings, particularly from the Bible. Before today's chosen reading are verses 1–17 of the first chapter of Matthew's Gospel. You can see why this reading is not often read, as it is the genealogy of Jesus. The late Father Raymond Brown was very eloquent about the importance of this passage, for it sets up the whole context of the Gospel. Matthew includes some very surprising people in the genealogy: women for a start, like Rahab, a prostitute, and Bathsheba, the mother of Solomon, named only as the wife of Uriah, whom David murdered so that he could marry Bathsheba. Indeed, all the women mentioned in the genealogy have scandal or notoriety attached to them. Shame is here from the very beginning.

Shame

The word shame can have different meanings. We might break something and say, 'That's a shame.' But we also use it to suggest some form of ostracization: 'Shame on you', like what happened to me as a boy. Shame is a very powerful construct, created by individuals, families, religions, communities and nations. What was once commonplace, say, something like racism, is now seen as shameful by many, and institutions are now named and shamed as 'institutionally racist'. The story of Jesus' life on earth starts in shame and ends in shame. Dying on a cross was a shameful way to die, preserved as a punishment for the worst sort of people. Being born out of wedlock was also shameful, particularly when the male parentage was so very indefinable. Imagine the birth certificate entry for Jesus' father!

Hope

This child Jesus is also named in today's Gospel as 'Emmanuel', 'God is with us'. How extraordinary to find God in this shameful place. But is that not the gospel story, particularly for Matthew? God enters into shame so that no one can feel outside the scope of God's grace. There is reconciliation then in God, and Isaiah's words today of harmony among those of difference ring true, for God in Jesus breaks down division that comes through shame and allows all to feel of worth. Nothing is too shameful for God. Radical stuff, rarely captured I might suggest in crib scenes with clean straw and a sweetly smelling stable. Where's all the shit, I wonder?

Jonathan Lawson

Hymn suggestions

God is working his purpose out; Away in a manger; Who would think that what was needed; When God Almighty came to earth.

Christmas and Epiphany

Christmas Day   25 December
Set I   **Born in Us Today**
Isa. 9.2–7; Ps. 96; Titus 2.11–14; **Luke 2.1–14** [15–20]

When Karen Anvil joined the excited crowd at Sandringham on Christmas Day 2017, she had no idea that she would be lucky enough to capture a perfect photo of members of the Royal Family. Prince Harry's engagement to Meghan Markle just a month previously was still hot news, and the quick snap of them both smiling alongside William and Kate soon became iconic, earning Karen – an ordinary working mum – £40,000 from media outlets over the next year.[9]

Sharing the news of major world events is a competitive business, and for professionals it takes planning, skill and a bit of good fortune to be in the right place at just the right moment to capture it. But when the Son of God was born – the axis on which all of history would turn – there was no paparazzi waiting in the wings. There had been no carefully timed press announcement, no meet and greets planned, and certainly no scheduled interviews with the new parents. Instead, the news of a baby called both Saviour and Messiah was announced in the darkness of night to a field of shepherds on shift.

An ordinary occupation

There is always some debate at this time of year as to the precise status of shepherds in first-century Bethlehem. It used to be common to suggest that looking after the sheep was a lowly occupation, the work of despised outcasts. This interpretation allows the story to illustrate the radically inclusive good news of Jesus, offered first to those considered the dregs of society. But more recently, attention has been drawn to the generally positive portrayal of the role in the Hebrew Scriptures, particularly as the early career of King David. Shepherds feature as a down-to-earth, relatable image for the guidance and protection of God, and those entrusted to be leaders of his people.

You might be relieved to hear that we can safely leave the debate to continue in the hands of historians and biblical scholars – although I hope they too take a break for Christmas, because what Luke most wants to tell us is not what the shepherds *were* but what they *became*. These ordinary folk, on an ordinary night, became witnesses to a moment with global and eternal significance. No one had to instruct them or pay them to share what they'd seen: the story of the angels in the sky and the baby in the manger came tumbling out to anyone else who was out and about on the streets of Bethlehem that night. It was too good not to share.

A wonder to witness

Much of what we know about Jesus is recorded for us because those who were there at the time spoke of what they'd seen. Those closest to Jesus were important sources of these stories: it's often suggested that Luke got some of his material from Mary, for instance. But we can imagine many others telling their snippets of stories too: onlookers to miraculous healings, people who sat in the crowds as Jesus taught, and even the young man who fled naked when he saw Jesus arrested. Nameless and often peripheral to the events, these ordinary people shared their extraordinary stories and played their part in handing down the good news about Jesus from generation to generation.

Being present for a typical historical event involves a common geographical and temporal location; you've got to be in the right place and time to experience it. But the birth of Jesus isn't a typical event. While Luke is clear about when and where Mary was delivered of the child, by faith we also recognize the truth that Christ is eternally born in everyone who believes in him. He is the eternal Word of God, forever breaking into our world as the Holy Spirit overshadows us and faith is conceived.

As the shepherds became witnesses as soon as they had seen the baby in the manger, so we too become eye-witnesses to the birth of Christ every time we spot signs of his life bubbling up in our world. When in moments of prayer our despair is washed over by peace, we witness the birth of Christ. When by the impact of Christian activism, injustices are overthrown by righteousness, we witness the birth of Christ. When through the love of a church community a person on the margins finds their home in God's family, we witness the birth of Christ.

Unlike Karen Anvil, we're unlikely to make any great fortune by sharing what we've seen. But for a world straining for a glimpse of real love, real hope and real peace, we can paint a vivid picture of the Saviour we've found, not just in the manger but in the extraordinary moments that make up our ordinary lives. Even more wonderfully, our friends need not worry that they've missed the moment: we can invite them to come and see for themselves.

Claire Jones

Hymn suggestions

O little town of Bethlehem; While shepherds watched their flocks by night; Go, tell it on the mountain; Come and join the celebration.

Christmas Day   25 December
Set II   **Good News Alert: Do Not Be Afraid!**
Isa. 62.6–end; Ps. 97; Titus 3.4–7; **Luke 2.[1–7] 8–20**

Our world is swimming in information. Indeed, it can be very difficult to distinguish between fake and actual news, not least because social media generates endless plausible-seeming information which is readily shareable.

You may have seen a meme on social media which states: 'Do not be afraid' is said 365 times in the Bible; according to the meme there is 'reassurance in the Bible for every day of the year'. It is a very powerful idea and sounds amazing: God is so attentive to our needs that he has ensured that you can read your Bible every day (saving in a leap year!) and hear him say, 'Do not be afraid.'

Trustworthy news

Sadly, however, it is a made-up 'fact'. 'Do not be afraid' is actually used about 80 times. If the meme is fake, the good news of God is not. And what good news it is! As our reading from Luke for Christmas Day reminds us, first, this good news begins with a proclamation of reassurance: 'Do not be afraid!' It is not whispered but proclaimed from the heavens by God's messengers, the angels, who show forth the glory of God. Second, it is news proclaimed to ordinary people, to shepherds; it is good news for all the people. Finally, this good news is both simple and incredible: the saviour of the world has been born. Glory to God in the highest!

This is not just good news; this is the greatest news that has or ever will be shared in the world. It is all the more intriguing, then, to consider how God shares this news. Imagine if PR advisers had existed in ancient Judaea and God had engaged them to manage his good news story. I reckon they would have offered God rather different advice on how to get it out into the world. While a PR adviser might have approved of God's decision to deliver the news with appropriate fanfare – after all, God's angels effectively light up the sky near Bethlehem with hosannas – I suspect they would have told God that if he wanted to achieve maximum impact he was doing his 'launch' in the wrong place.

At the very least, they might have advised God to launch his news story near a large urban centre or a place of power: somewhere like Jerusalem or ... if you really want to catch the attention of the powerful and make a splash ... Rome. Equally, a PR adviser would likely have told God not to get his good news story out to peasants like shepherds; if you really want the news to be shared and heard, use those who have influence and a large following – kings and emperors, politicians and priests; the influencers of Jesus' time.

News in context

From the perspective of our media-grabbing, modern 'influencer-shaped' media world, then, it might seem that God's approach is all wrong. However, part of the power of the Christmas story lies in how it subverts expectations of power and authority. God reveals a deeper news, far beyond the understanding of modern media strategies.

The good news of Jesus Christ, both back in the day and now, is sent first into the midst of those who need it. It is not sent to those who can exploit it for their own ends. The shepherds in the fields who hear God's good news would have lived with levels of precariousness we can barely imagine. Their job was to be out with the flocks in the lonely places in all weathers, where wild animals may come and night can play tricks on the mind; where there is time and space both to dream and to imagine terrible things. They are rightly terrified when they see the angel. Yet, the angel's words – 'Do not be afraid' – speak into more than their immediate terror.

Good news for ordinary people

The shepherds could be any of us. They are ordinary folk facing real-life challenges and everyday worries and fear. They are not grand kings or influencers. Indeed, in their role, they are exposed to the precariousness of the world. On the cold nights in the hills of Judaea, they have the solidarity of one another and no other safety net. They are ordinary people, rather like us, who long for good news.

God's good news extends far beyond the imaginings and plans of a modern PR strategy. It is not meant as a viral campaign but to invite people, both ordinary and powerful, into the truth: in Jesus Christ, God is with us; as a helpless babe, he knows our human condition from the inside. If sending the good news to shepherds does have symbolic resonance – Jesus himself sees himself as a shepherd of God's flock – it also reminds us about what kind of God we serve: one whose first and primary call is to look after the vulnerable flock exposed to the world's dangers. God sends good news to people who long for salvation and safety, who need to hear once again, 'Do not be afraid …'

Rachel Mann

Hymn suggestions

While shepherds watched their flocks; It came upon the midnight clear; The first nowell; Once in royal David's city.

Christmas Day 25 December
Set III The Squalid Stable
Isa. 52.7–10; Ps. 98; Heb. 1.1–4 [5–12]; **John 1.1–14**

It was a stinking, filthy, dank sort of a place; the sort of place which animals make their own, with their own strong scent. It was the sort of place nobody who didn't have to would dream of going into, let alone spending time there.

But there was nowhere else; everywhere was full because of the census, nothing available for a couple who'd had a long journey, whose child was obviously going to be born very soon. But people shouldn't be out in the open in her state – let them bed down in the stable if they like. Better than nothing, I suppose …

So it was that God became flesh and was born in a filthy, stinking hole of a stable. The King of Kings had to make do with a feeding trough as a cot, and the only people who seemed to realize that something special had happened were a few peasant shepherds coming down off the hills after seeing a vision. Nobody else seemed to care, or even realize, that this young woman had given birth in that awful place. They certainly didn't spare a thought that this baby might be anyone important.

Worthy of God?

All of this hardly sounds like the way people would expect to hear of a god becoming human, and yet it fits perfectly with our experience of God, once we get to know him. He is not interested in coming to us as some sort of all-powerful, all-conquering superhero, leaving no one in any doubt as to who he is. Our God finds his power in weakness, his strength in humility, and his lordship in being a servant.

Our God doesn't only have a *message* for the poor and the lowly, the outcast and the homeless, the worried and the weary – no, our God becomes one *with* them. In a stinking filthy stable, surrounded by the sounds and smells of the animals, lying in a feeding trough, gazed upon by dirt-poor shepherds, God comes into our world as a helpless baby. He comes in weakness that we may see that real power lies in weakness. He comes in humility that we may see that true greatness lies in humility. He comes in poverty that we may see what it is that truly makes us rich. He comes in servitude that we may see the nature of his lordship. He comes with a message of good news, a message of God's love for all, a message for everyone.

Emmanuel – God with us

There we have the wonder and the glory of the Christmas message – because in the incarnation, the Word-becoming-flesh, we see revealed perhaps the greatest truth that we can know: that no matter who we are – how lowly or poor, how much of a disappointment to society we are, what our background is, or what we have done – God comes to us, in the earthy reality of our lives and our situations, to be one with us.

We don't have to somehow earn our right to reach God, work hard at discovering the way to enlightenment, or be a respectable member of society so that he'll take notice of us.

No: God comes to us. God seeks us out.

Finding Jesus

Where do you let God find you this Christmas, and where do you find him? Among the presents under your tree? In your Christmas dinner, or your left-over turkey sandwiches? In the joy of children when it's Christmas Day at last?

We can and should find God in all those things – he is everywhere – but we find him also in the quiet moments of Christmas, in the thoughtfulness behind the gifts, in our pondering on the birth of Christ for us, in the hope that the message of peace is touching hearts and lives all over the world.

But above all, let us pray that we find Jesus in the place in which he became human for us, in the ordinariness of life and in other people, especially those on the edges. Let us pray that we see something of Jesus in that lonely person who lives in our neighbourhood, in that homeless person we pass in the street, in the person seeking asylum and refuge, in the many people who warrant not even a second glance for most of us. Let us find God in our neighbour.

Let us open our eyes to see God in those around us, those whose lives we can be a part of, and act accordingly. Let us show forth in our own lives the message of God's love, and shine its light into the lives of those around us. Let us allow that love to be born among us today and every day, and so glorify our God who is in the business of coming among ordinary people in their ordinary lives and transforming them with his love.

Love came down at Christmas to bring peace on earth, goodwill to all.

May we live in, and live out, that love.

Bill Braviner

Hymn suggestions

O come, all ye faithful; O little town of Bethlehem; Silent night; Hark, the herald angels sing.

Christmas Day   25 December
Second Service   **Making Choices**

Morning Ps. 110, 117; Evening Ps 8; Isa. 65.17–25; **Phil. 2.5–11**, or Luke 2.1–20 (*if it has not been used at the Principal Service of the day*)

The mind of Christ

Sometimes, when we see a great heroic act or an act that we might deem foolish, we ask, 'What were they thinking?' or, 'What was going through their mind?' We wonder what drove them to make the decision or take the course of action.

Here, Paul invites us to ask, 'What was in Jesus' mind when he made the choice to become like us?' and challenges us to model our thinking similarly.

Paul also challenges his audience with the assertion that Jesus existed even before becoming a human being. Jesus was in the form of God and equal to God, and from that reality chose to be born as a human. He was the spoken word of Genesis, bringing all of creation into being. He could have remained as he was, within the glory of the Godhead.

Making a choice

Jesus, who is fully divine, makes a choice. He is not coerced into being born a human being, it is his willingness to embrace humanity. He chooses to pour his divine self into his human self. He is no less divine, and now he is also fully human.

He is the Word (of Genesis creation) made flesh. God, among us. The glory of the Godhead, concealed for a time. He chooses not to come in might and power, in military authority and leading an army, but to be born as a human baby and all the vulnerability that entails. He chooses to live an ordinary life in an ordinary family, learning an ordinary family trade.

He chooses to spend time on harbour sides and marketplaces, at wedding celebrations and funerals, in conversations with lawyers, women and tax-collectors.

Jesus chooses to wash feet and feed hungry people.

He challenges his disciples to stand out from the crowd by not being like the rulers who lord it over their people, but, instead, the disciples are to lead by serving.

He chooses forgiveness over retaliation.
He chooses the ordinary over the extravagant.
He chooses solitude over platitudes.
He chooses the lost over the popular.

Death

Jesus chooses to die. Again, we hear the question: 'What was he thinking?'

To many of Paul's audience, this was a cultural challenge. They lived among military might and the histories of heroes who commanded armies. A Messiah who comes to save his people by dying is no hero. Jesus holds nothing back.

He could have reclaimed his divine authority and summoned armies of angels. He who made all of creation could have commanded the same created order to protect him. He who saved others could have saved himself.

Instead – in the same way that he set aside his ordinary clothes and chose a towel in order to wash his disciples' feet – he chose to set aside divine privilege and authority in order to serve each one of us.

And it is this same Messiah who is to be lifted higher than any other and celebrated throughout time and space by every human being. Whose name will be spoken throughout every generation. Whose outpouring of himself and the choices he made will be the subject of conversations, theological debates and life-changing decisions.

Who reveals the glory of the Godhead as the humble servant of humankind. Who shows us the mind of God in his love for us.

An invitation

In this scriptural poem Paul holds up a mirror and invites us to take a look: if this is the mind of Christ, if these are the choices he makes, if this is the way of the true hero, how are we like him?

Are we a community of people who live in humble and loving service, or do we compete with each other for power and status?

Can we set aside that which we cling to and be open to new possibilities? When we make our choices, what is going through our minds? What are we thinking?

Do we, in our words and actions, remind people of Jesus?

Are we willing to empty ourselves into God's calling?

Are we prepared to be humble and not arrogant?

This Christmas, can we let go of expectations and privilege, in order to bring others into God's presence? Choosing to live humbly as Christ's community of believers, that we may serve each other and everyone we meet, in order that Jesus' name might be known and his glory shine in people's lives.

Kt Tupling

Hymn suggestions

What child is this? Of the Father's love begotten; Meekness and majesty; You laid aside your majesty.

First Sunday of Christmas   29 December
Principal Service   **Growing Up with Jesus**
1 Sam. 2.18–20, 26; Ps. 148 [*or* 148.7–end]; **Col. 3.12–17**; Luke 2.41–end

In today's readings, we have stories of faithfulness, generosity and growth. On the cusp of a new year, we are encouraged to explore growing up with Jesus and ponder the love, service and sacrifice he calls us to, both as individuals and as a church.

Faithfulness: Samuel and Jesus

Samuel was given to God by his mother Hannah. Being granted the gift of a child by God Hannah dedicated Samuel to the Lord and he served at the temple at Shiloh with the priest Eli. In a corrupt generation of priests, Samuel stands out for his faithful and committed service. We hear that he continues to 'grow both in stature and in favour with the Lord and with the people'. His ability to recognize the call of God will lead Samuel to anoint and proclaim the boy David as King of Israel.

We also have the familiar story of Jesus, aged 12, in the Temple, astounding the teachers of the law with his wisdom and knowledge. Jesus is surprised that his parents haven't realized what he's about. He is about his Father's business – not his father Joseph the carpenter, but his father in heaven. He is about heavenly business, discussing theology with the experts.

Two boys, then, being faithful to their calling. Scripture reminds us that God uses the little to further the kingdom. You are never too young to love and serve God. Fidelity is not dependent on age. Are we sufficiently encouraging of young people? Do we recognize and celebrate the gifts they bring and their equality before God, and as members of the body of Christ? Are we prepared to learn from them?

Generosity: Hannah, Mary and Joseph

These passages aren't only about young people and the hope they bring. We are also given insight into parents in these scriptures. Hannah has longed for a child and when one is granted, she gives him back to God; an incredible thing to do! She sees her son only once a year when she delivers his new robe. Her dedication, generosity and sacrifice led to fruitfulness in abundance: three more sons and two daughters. It's a surprising truth that the more we give to God the more we receive in return. God has promised that that will be so: 'Put me to the test ... see if I will not open the windows of heaven for you and pour down for you an overflowing blessing' (Mal. 3.10). Try it and see! Upping our generosity would be a good New Year's resolution.

And so to Mary and Joseph. We feel for them as they search for their lost son who has been missing for three days. We lost one of our children once on Blackpool seafront when he was a toddler. We lost him for 15 minutes. He just disappeared, and we were frantic. Mary must have been sick with worry and she gives Jesus a piece of her mind when she finds him: 'Child, why have you treated us like this?' Such a human response. Jesus, once he's put his side of the story, is obedient and they return home together.

Mary yet again tucks what's happened away in her heart and ponders it along with all the other strange and mysterious things that have happened with her young son. This is not the last time that Jesus will disappear for three days while doing his Father's business. I wonder if Mary remembered this incident in the light of the crucifixion and resurrection and made the connection.

Growth: Jesus and us

How curious that we should have this reading of Mary and Joseph losing Jesus so soon after Christmas. It's a reminder for us that the infant Jesus, 'meek and mild', 'wrapped in bands of cloth', doesn't stay long in the manger. He grows up and moves into his calling and ministry. We read that he 'increased in wisdom and in years, and in divine and human favour'. Jesus will also go through rejection and humiliation in order to fulfil his Father's will, and obtain the salvation of the world.

It's very easy for us to lose Jesus. We often try to keep him under control rather than follow where he leads. But Jesus grew. He couldn't remain in the manger for ever. We too are called to grow with Jesus, to grow in wisdom and to deepen our relationship with God and with one another, as God leads us into new and unexpected places. We may not find Jesus where we thought he'd be or where we've found him in the past. The work of the kingdom calls us onwards, inwards, upwards and outwards.

So, then, as we approach a new year, let's celebrate the faithfulness of young people. Let's take time to consider and review our generosity to God and to one another. And let's allow the infant Jesus to grow up within us so that we too may exercise a mature, committed and generous faith, open to change and transformation.

Catherine Williams

Hymn suggestions

Of the Father's heart begotten; Unto us a child is born; Take my life, and let it be; Take this moment, sign and space (Iona).

First Sunday of Christmas 29 December
Second Service **We Begin Again**
Ps. 132; **Isa. 61**; Gal. 3.27—4.7;
Gospel at Holy Communion: Luke 2.15–21.

There is something rather disarming about hearing the voice of Isaiah so soon after Christmas. You may be thinking that your work was already done. You have cooked, served, washed up, dished up, wrapped, unwrapped, hosted or visited. The shepherds, too, have gone back to their flock, the magi have returned by another way home, and Mary has indeed given birth to the saviour of the world. Surely the work is done? Surely, I have done my bit, you may be saying. The truth is that the celebration of the incarnation was, and is, just the beginning. And in Isaiah's prophetic voice, we hear the call to begin again.

A people in exile return

This part of Isaiah (chapters 56–66) is often referred to by scholars as the 'third Isaiah'. It is about the ancient Israelites' return from exile, which has been referred to in earlier chapters. So, in that story of exile and return is a question about home, and what home now looks like when you have been away for so long. What we see is that things cannot be as they used to be. God is not content with a return to the status quo. Separation, loss and coming back mean that we need to begin again. We need to find a new way of seeing and being. We begin again and find a new voice and a new vision for ourselves and for the world.

New priorities

When we return from a place where we did not want to be, be that physical, mental or spiritual, how do we regroup? How do we find healing and restoration? Isaiah offers us a challenge that feels too much to bear. It is not us that is at the centre of the story, but the 'oppressed' to whom we need to bring good news; the 'broken-hearted' who need binding up; and the 'captives' to whom we need to proclaim liberty. We somehow need to see their pain, their sorrow and their grief as well as our own and have the courage to *still say* that there is hope, that there is light and that there is a promise of something better. The call to begin again has to be on our lips, even if we feel we do not have the strength or words to follow that call.

New hope

After all that has been broken and lost comes the need for restoration, and that, Isaiah suggests, can only happen through God. We read: 'For I the LORD love justice, I hate robbery and wrongdoing.' There is a sense that the flight and fight can be tethered to a greater story and promise. God is not absent in our grief and sorrow. God is not asleep when we suffer. While it is clear through our lived experience that we may not often feel as if we see justice in the world, we have a God who is in front, beside and behind us *when we seek justice*. We find that we are asked to begin again and rebuild using a framework of equity, and that can be hard for us as humans to do. In a social media age, to begin again is to relinquish our thirst for humiliation, revenge and self-righteousness.

New purpose

In a world that is battling the climate emergency, and coming to terms with the consequences of human-led actions on our environment, how will we hold justice at the heart of our restoration of our planet? When we see the ashes of burnt forests, grassland and communities, where will the 'garlands' be found, and who will be empowered to bring them? We find echoes of this passage in Luke, as the Gospel writer sees Isaiah's prophecy being fulfilled in Jesus as the Messiah. We can also see Jesus' life and actions reflecting the words and hope evident here. To begin again is to recognize that words are the beginning of a journey into action that can change lives and transform our world. What we say matters. How we interact online matters. Because we have a new purpose after the periods of exile in our lives. Restoration is not easy, and rebuilding is not an exclusive activity. The call to begin again is about our own lives as individuals and as communities, and also about how we work to bring about a world that has more hope and less pain.

Mariama Ifode-Blease

Hymn suggestions

Joy in the morning (Tauren Wells); For I'm building a people of power; All hail the power of Jesus' name; God of freedom, God of justice.

Second Sunday of Christmas   5 January
(For Epiphany, see p. 292.)
Principal Service   **Another Helping**
Jer. 31.7–14; Ps. 147.13–end, *or* Ecclus. 24.1–12;
Canticle: Wisd. 10.15–end; Eph. 1.3–14; **John 1.[1–9] 10–18**

Unwrapped

Like a good Christmas turkey, the Prologue to John's Gospel is unwrapped from its foil to provide another meal that continues the feast on the Second Sunday of Christmas. John's poetic masterpiece offers much to chew on as he introduces the significance of Jesus' life with its mind-blowing mysteries and stunning surprises. In the optional verses of the reading, John takes us back to the very beginning, to the basic building blocks of God and creation. 'In the beginning was the Word.' Throughout the Christmas season, we have been ingesting the intriguing idea that the one who comes from God, who is God, who created all things, enters the world, as a human being, in human history. The meatiest verse sees God's expression, expressly and expressively, come home to roost as the Word becomes flesh to make his dwelling among us.

Even multiple sittings with multiple helpings cannot make it possible to fully pick the bones of the life of the one who changes everything, the one in whom there is life. As John will go on to show, through Jesus all heaven breaks loose; Jesus makes the unseen one seen. The shiny veneers that we use to enfold this story remind us that what truly feeds must be more than a reflection of ourselves. What we find in Jesus unlocks our biographies, unravels our certainties and unwraps our identities, again and again.

Empowered

A theme common to the readings from Jeremiah 31, Ephesians 1 and John 1 is the parenthood of God. In Jeremiah 31.9, the Lord affirms his fatherhood of Israel and declares Ephraim to be his firstborn. In Ephesians 1, 'the God and Father of our Lord Jesus Christ' destined those chosen in Christ to be adopted and receive the full rights and privileges of an heir. In the heart of the reading from John 1, Jesus, God's Word, comes into the world but is not accepted. Even among his own people, those whom God has called his children, God's son is not known. Yet to all who receive Jesus, who believe in his name, Jesus gives the power to become children of God. Did you catch that? Jesus gives the power, that is, the authority and right, to become children of God.

At Christmas, we have been celebrating the mind-blowing idea that the God of all the universe became a child. The divine became dependent – a tiny scrap in the hands of normal folk like you or me. John may not tell us of pregnant virgins or honoured shepherds, but he has his own surprise up his sleeve when he says that Jesus empowers us to become children. The very presence of God's Word made flesh is life-changing, intimating that if God comes to us born of humanity, then we can be empowered to become children born of God.

Re-originated

'You can choose your friends, but you can't choose your family' is the common form of an expression inspired by a line from Atticus Finch in Harper Lee's *To Kill a Mockingbird*.[10] As the Word of God is made flesh it seems that Jesus makes it possible to choose your family. To do so means becoming a child. I can think of many reasons why becoming a child is not as attractive an offer as it sounds. It doesn't surprise me that people rejected Jesus and spurned the opportunity to become God's children. Becoming a child seems to fly in the face of all I have experienced of life and the world. It minimizes what I already feel I know and understand. It questions who I think I am. But here in this Christmas story is God the Son who is close to his Father's heart. He does not aspire to individuation and independence but is able to form his identity based on who truly loves him and who invites us in him to know ourselves to be children of God.

Whomever our earthly parents, whether known or unknown, beloved or estranged, for joy or sorrow, in the person of Jesus we are invited to see our true beginnings as human beings as being not at birth, nor in the womb, nor at conception but in the One who was in the beginning. The one who handles dust and mud, who forms and fashions human flesh, who shapes and sculpts human souls, who holds all human history, and who can heal all human hearts. Through Jesus, we discover that whoever we have been, whoever others have told us we are, whoever we have been made to feel like, the furthest, deepest, ultimate truth is who we are in God. In Jesus, we can see God in the flesh, so that through Jesus, in our flesh, we might see God.

In my small-minded judgements, in my self-serving kindnesses and in my shallow-rooted love, I do not come close to the Father's heart. But there is one who has made him known, in whom there is the power to become a child of God. I can come to him for another helping again and again.

Matt Allen

Hymn suggestions

In the bleak midwinter; Noel (Tomlin); Joy to the world; O holy night.

Second Sunday of Christmas   5 January
Second Service   **God Hears**
Ps. 135 [*or* 135.1–14]; **1 Sam. 1.20–end**; 1 John 4.7–16; *Gospel at Holy Communion*: Matt. 2.13–end

Imagine a woman walking into this church. She is clearly bowed down and troubled. She walks to the front and there she can hold back no longer. All restraint gives way as she pours out her prayer in a torrent of bitter pain and unrestrained weeping. She cries out to God. 'If only you will look on the misery of your servant' (1 Sam. 1.11). That is where the great historic books of Samuel began. With a barren woman called Hannah praying in the Temple for the gift of a son. Her prayer was answered. In our reading today she is back in the Temple, with her three-year-old son, to give thanks and to fulfil a promise she made.

Storytelling

In that ancient world, stories were heard not read. There were no books and very few scrolls. Storytelling was an oral art and a good storyteller had a variety of ways of keeping attention, leaving hints and guiding hearers as to what might be going on.

Sometimes the clue was in the person's name. The name Samuel means 'God hears'. So, every time Samuel's name was called, spoken or heard, the people were being reminded – 'God hears'. 'God hears!' And so are we. Throughout his long ministry as a faithful leader and prophet God heard Samuel and he heard God.

Sometimes it was a play on words. A pun. This is harder to pick up when reading in a different language. For example, we simply cannot tell that in Hebrew the word for 'ask' sounds just like the name 'Saul'. Twice we are told that Hannah named her son Samuel because she asked for him/Sauled him from the Lord. So, in a story about Samuel, we suddenly keep hearing the name Saul.

Storytellers do that – slip in a word or comment from left field. Why has Saul turned up? Perhaps it was meant to leave hearers scratching their heads. But those first hearers would know that although Samuel would be a towering leader of the nation, he would be replaced by Israel's first king, the king people insisted on 'asking' God for. His name was Saul and the story that unfolded from that coronation was not a happy one, for him or the people. Be careful what you ask for, what you 'Saul' for.

Another story device used here is repetition. To make your point just keep repeating it. Nine times in this short reading the focus of Hannah's faith and action is repeated. Everything that happens is directed 'to', 'for' or 'of' the Lord. There is no mistaking what we are being told. God is the centre of this story and people. As God always is.

From tears to hope

When the barren Hannah was weeping before God, she made a promise. If granted a son by God, she vowed to dedicate him to God's lifelong service. Here she is fulfilling that vow. She leaves him at the Temple. No parent can easily imagine doing that. It is also true that desperate people will promise *any*thing. It is so hard not to try and bargain when we are deeply in need. But the storyteller is wholly positive about Hannah. All that follows suggests that Hannah is making a remarkable offering, born out of costly and profound faith. And God gives generously and willingly to his people through her gift of Samuel.

Through Samuel, a whole new era of faith and life begins. Not many are called to such great sacrifices. But we are all invited to take our place in this ancient story of gift, faith, offering and new beginnings.

Hearing, trusting, believing

The story reminds us – God hears. In a teasing, indirect way, the story reminds us that life can take uncertain turns, that what we ask for is not always wise, and that best-laid plans can let us down badly. But we can still ask of God – we can 'Saul' him. And God hears and will lead us in new ways and paths.

Hannah's presence at the story of that epic saga is often treated like a touching vignette, a little aside telling us where the great characters first emerged from. In fact, her story is the key to interpreting all that follows. Her faith, prayers and actions model everything. She reveals to us the God who hears. In her own vulnerable need, she lives her faith in the vulnerabilities and uncertainties that life often finds us in.

Finally, Hannah is our evangelist. She tells us that the life that is truly ours is for living to, of and for the Lord. Wholly given to God.

And that which is wholly given becomes wholly gift in return.

David Runcorn

Hymn suggestions

My soul magnifies the Lord (Magnificat); Take my life and let it be; We have a gospel to proclaim; In the bleak mid-winter.

Baptism of Christ (First Sunday of Epiphany)
12 January
Principal Service   **'Well, So That is That'**
Isa. 43.1–7; Ps. 29; Acts 8.14–17; **Luke 3.15–17, 21–22**

'Well, so that is that.' W. H. Auden, on taking down the Christmas tree once again.[11] We're past twelfth night. We're perhaps missing the decorations, the lights, the colour. But there's another big day coming up in the rural calendar at this time of year: Plough Monday, the Monday after twelfth night. Which is tomorrow, when (once upon a time) the holiday was finally over and everyone went back to work. January meant spring ploughing, hence Plough Monday, marked by the blessing of ploughs in church and the procession around the parish to collect for the 'plough lights' that burnt in front of the altar as a prayer for a good harvest.

Ah yes … That's that, another Christmas done and dusted, time to go back to work, the unwelcome realization that it's Monday morning and ordinary time again. It's a peak time of year for the winter blues, and more serious depressive illness and suicide. Sometimes the cold and dark of January are just too much. We should hold in our hearts people, perhaps among our own families, friends and neighbours, who are simply overwhelmed by hopelessness and fear, or simply the disappointment that yet again the festivities didn't deliver on their promise.

But there is a wisdom in the ritual of Plough Monday. It was a way of crossing safely a necessary threshold, not leaving behind the warmth and conviviality of Christmas but allowing it to shed light on daily life. For Epiphany is a season of *reception*, a time to ponder the mystery of the incarnation and make it our own. We call it the manifestation of Christ to the Gentiles, but it's surely his manifestation to *all* of us at every level of our being, especially, the 'gentile' part of ourselves that has yet to welcome him, receive him, honour him.

And although three wonders mark this holy season, the magi, the turning of water into wine at Cana in Galilee and the baptism of Christ that we celebrate today, I want nevertheless stay with the crib awhile. And I want to remind us that the magi made *two* journeys, not one, and their second journey was at least as important as the first. Only this time, there was no star to guide, no precious gifts to carry, and no child's welcome at the end of it: just the heavy homeward tread of men who had lands to govern and issues to deal with. They too had to say, 'That is that' and begin their return journey. This was their Plough Monday so to speak, leaving the vision behind, going back to work, going back.

And yet this is the whole point. For we want to believe that the magi went back touched and changed by what they had experienced. They had seen a birth and realized that it portended a death – *theirs* – a death to the old world, with its old ways and old habits, and a *metanoia*, a turning towards a new way of being and living, *no longer* at home in an old dispensation among an alien people clutching their gods. Far from leaving the vision behind, they took it with them into reaches of life where it had not found a home before.

In today's reading, the Spirit falls on those who have newly believed, just as in the gospel the Spirit fell on Jesus as he was newly commissioned for his ministry. In both stories, there is transformation wrought by an epiphany, a revelation of God to us as grace and truth and wonder and glory and love. We believe that this wondrous coming changes the world. One test of this will be in the details of human existence: how we go about the routines of daily work, the choices we make about our relationships, the perspectives we bring to the issues of our day, the resources we draw on in times of pressure and pain and in the face of death.

The real test of how well we have celebrated Christmas is how well we make the journey through Epiphany: not the journey *to* the crib, but the journey *away* from it, going back to our ordinary days. Plough Monday invites us to sing and dance our way back into the new year and the craft of living the human life. Is that the needed antidote to our January blues? And when it's time to pack the crib away for another year, it's not before it has lodged in our hearts and has travelled with us into whatever awaits while the order of time runs its course.

Michael Sadgrove

Hymn suggestions

Awake, awake: fling off the night; When Jesus came to Jordan; Hail to the Lord's anointed; Teach me, my God and King.

Baptism of Christ (First Sunday of Epiphany)
12 January
Second Service   **Freedom in Christ**
Ps. 46, 47; **Isa. 55.1–11**; **Rom. 6.1–11**;
Gospel at Holy Communion: Mark 1.4–11

For many, ministry is hectic. Making space to be still and spend time with self and God can be an incredible challenge. To be intentional in protecting our Sabbaths is important. However, I often find that when I'm preparing for annual leave, I become more tense and anxious as I switch on my 'out of office' notice on my email. Why? Well, because I know that I will return to a significant pile of emails which will take me time to respond to.

In today's world, our 'To-Do' lists are ever-increasing and in the busyness of life our friend Jesus is often pushed to the sidelines and reduced to being on the outside of our lives and hearts. In lifestyles consumed and controlled by *doing*, rather than *being*, we lose sight of what is important for our spiritual life. Isaiah sums it up in this way, 'Why do you spend your money for that which is not bread, and your labour for that which does not satisfy?'

A new life in Christ

In Paul's letter to the Romans, he writes to introduce himself to new Christians in Rome. The question he reflects on in the Romans 6 passage is: what did Jesus' death and resurrection mean for the new believers in Rome – for us? In a world full of distractions, driven by consumerism and materialism, we find ourselves drifting through lives with little anchoring or purpose. Paul wrote that just as Christ was raised from the dead, we too might walk in newness of life. Without Jesus in our lives, we find ourselves 'dead' in our sins. With Jesus in our lives, we receive the Holy Spirit who enables us to live a new life. That is, having Jesus at the centre of the world, rather than in the margins. Our desires change. Because to continue living in sin is to remain imprisoned to our fleshly inclinations, the dazzle of this world. It is impossible to continue living unchanged if God's grace has touched our hearts. No longer are we caught up and knotted by the shackles of our world; rather, we seek fellowship with the Source of Life. In fact, we do not really begin to live until we live for God.

The invitation of grace

In living a resurrection life, the invitation of grace calls us to trust God's protection, presence and concern (Ps. 46). How do we choose to live? How do we choose to love? Time and time again, Israel was worshipping idols and, in our generation, we too often worship the idols of this world: busy schedules, social media, keeping up 'appearances' and such like. God reminds us that rather than worshipping these things, we should worship him, spending time in prayer, Scripture and fellowshipping with other believers. Being in a living relationship with God offers us eternal hope and future. Jesus came into our broken lives to save us from our impoverished and skewed focus, clinging on to things that deaden the spirit. Isaiah 55 reminds us of God's great blessings because of all Jesus, the Messiah, accomplished on the cross. Who does God invite to his joyful feast? All who are thirsty, poor and hungry. All who know that things aren't quite as they should be because they're not living in grace the abundant life promised to us. God invites all of us to his feast. And we are led to respond to that great invitation: redemption is offered to all who believe and will receive from the waters of eternal life.

No matter what is going on in our lives, we can be assured of his provision. If at the heart of our relationship with Jesus is transformation, we cannot go on living in sin. Are we living a life liberated by all that Jesus did on the cross? Are we saying 'yes' to the hope offered in the gospel? In reflecting on these questions, as we lean into our understanding of who God is, we stretch and grow, offering ourselves to the transformation that can happen by the power of the Holy Spirit. Are we ready to get rid of our old self?

Catherine Okoronkwo

Hymn suggestions

In Christ alone; I believe in Jesus; Such love, pure as the whitest snow; My hope is built in nothing less.

Second Sunday of Epiphany   19 January

(For the Week of Prayer for Christian Unity, see p. 294.)
Principal Service   **God's Overwhelming Generosity**
Isa. 62.1–5; Ps. 36.5–10; 1 Cor. 12.1–11; **John 2.1–11**

Here we are firmly in the season of Epiphany. The season began with the visit of the magi to the infant Jesus and it continues with episodes from the life of Jesus in which the glory of God is revealed. Today we have the first of Jesus' miracles in the wedding at Cana. Jesus turns water into wine. He makes the ordinary extraordinary in an act of overwhelming generosity.

Today's readings from Isaiah, the First Letter to the Corinthians and John's Gospel tell of this overwhelming generosity of God. Here is a God who gives gifts in abundance and calls people to join in inaugurating the kingdom: the reign of God.

God's generous love

In our passage from Isaiah the people of Israel have returned from exile. Rather than being jubilant at their freedom, they are bowed down and exhausted. They've run out of energy and are not quite sure what to do next. The prophet calls. He is so filled with excitement at the message he brings that he can't keep it in: 'I will not keep silent,' he says. He rushes around telling everyone: 'I will not rest.'

God has promised to vindicate the Israelites. They are going to be God's beautiful crown, 'a royal diadem'. They will be held in God's hand and given a new name. No longer will they be called 'forsaken' and their land called 'desolate'. Instead, they are to be renamed: 'My Delight is in Her', and the land will be called 'Married'. God is renewing the covenant relationship with the people of Israel, telling them again that they are loved for ever. The marriage of God and God's people is recalled with all that that means: faithfulness, commitment, one flesh and eternal love. Here is God's overwhelming generosity. The wedding imagery is about the celebration of the whole community over this relationship of love between God and the people.

Jesus' generous provision

That celebratory theme is carried through to the Gospel when John records another wedding, this time at Cana. It starts as an earthly, all-too-human event at which people overindulge so that the wine runs out, potentially a social embarrassment for the host.

But all is not lost because Jesus is on the guest list. Heaven and earth meet and a miracle occurs. Plain ordinary water becomes the very best wine. God again is more than generous. Six hundred litres of wine are provided (that's a lot of wine!). John makes it equal to the amount expected in the heavenly banquet at the end of time. The fingerprints of heaven are all over this occasion.

This is the first of Jesus' miracles and he isn't sure that it's the right time to reveal his hand: 'My hour has not yet come,' he says to his mother. But Mary has faith in him and encourages him to act. The wedding is transformed and God's glory is revealed.

The Spirit's generous gifting

Paul writing to the Corinthians encourages them to proclaim Jesus as Lord, and when they do he reminds them that it is by the power of the Holy Spirit that they recognize Jesus' kingship in their lives. The Holy Spirit is at work in anyone who recognizes that Jesus Christ is Lord of heaven and earth. The Spirit gives a variety of gifts to God's people: wisdom and knowledge, faith, prophecy and prayer, healing and miraculous works. These and other gifts are given to us by God. All of us are gifted by the Spirit and called to use our gifts to build up one another to be Christ's witnesses in the world. We can feel confident to do this because the God who calls us loves us completely, is wedded to us and will never let us go whatever happens.

Sometimes we need to be Mary to each other, encouraging one another to exercise our gifts. Sometimes we need to stand back so that others can come to the fore. And like Jesus at the wedding, when God wants us to do something new in his name, we might feel it's the wrong time. But God's love and grace are overwhelmingly generous – there is always more to draw on. When we feel inadequate the Holy Spirit is there to comfort and encourage us, filling the gaps and giving us confidence and ability to undertake the task at hand.

Our generous response

As we continue to embrace this new year let's remember who we are in God's sight. We are the ones in whom God delights. We are God's beloved, God's bride, with whom God wishes to remain united for eternity. Let's take time to think and pray through how God might be calling us to respond to such overwhelming generosity and love. The gifts we have been given are to be used for God's glory. Let's encourage one another to grow in faith and godly character, to be the servants of one another and the gospel. Everyone is important, and every gift is valuable. The more we work together, the more risks we take with God, the more we will experience and be able to witness to God's overwhelming generosity for the world.

Catherine Williams

Hymn suggestions

All hail the power of Jesus' name; To Cana's wedding feast; Spirit of the living God; How great is our God.

Second Sunday of Epiphany   19 January
Second Service   **Here I Am**
Ps. 96; **1 Sam. 3.1–20**; Eph. 4.1–16;
Gospel at Holy Communion: John 1.29–42

The reading from Samuel comes at a crisis point for God's people. The storyteller is in no doubt. This is his diagnosis of those times. 'The word of the LORD was rare in those days; visions were not widespread.' This is serious. The people are out of sight and sound with the heart of their faith. In the Bible, the greatest crisis in any age is always God.

The silent God

What is a world like in which God seems to have withdrawn? Does it go strangely silent? Maybe it is noisier than ever? When God goes missing, we do not hear *nothing*, we hear *every*thing. There is a clash of conflicting noises with no way of discerning the message or meaning in it at all. It is a kind of tinnitus.

I am hearing impaired and one of the things about getting new aids fitted is that you don't just hear what you *want* to hear more clearly – *everything* is louder. A door slamming is like a gun going off. The toilet flushing is like Niagara Falls. You have to learn all over again how to listen.

Hearing is not the difference between sound and silence. It is the difference between noise and signal. In the midst of the noise in our life – and there is lots of it and some of it may be quite important – we need to learn to hear the signal, the guiding word for us and what is before us.

In the night

The setting of this story is the Temple, the centre of Israel's faith. The meeting place between God and his people. There we find the high priest Eli. He is now very elderly and has almost lost his sight. We will learn elsewhere his sons are corrupt. The scene is a sad one. He represents the lost, worn-out, failed faith of his people.

But the storyteller adds a detail. In the gloom of the Temple, out of sight and sound of God, he says, 'the lamp of God had not yet gone out'. This would have been the lamp burning before the holiest place, a symbol of God's presence and of the people's faithful vigilance. Faith has declined but is not completely extinguished.

Man and boy

Someone else is there. He is called Samuel. The storyteller sharply contrasts him with Eli.

Eli is very old. Samuel is a boy.

Eli is asleep in a side room. He is out of the action. Samuel is lying in the Temple in front of the Ark of the Lord. He is present. Available. Vigilant. This is faith on active service.

Eli represents things that are ending. In Samuel, something new is beginning. But it is yet to be revealed.

Here I am

In the darkness, lit only by that flickering lamp, a voice calls: 'Samuel.'

Remember, the word of the Lord was rare. This boy had never heard God speaking before. He doesn't recognize the voice and thinks Eli is calling. This happens several times until Eli finally realizes it is God and teaches Samuel how to respond.

In these ancient stories, the first words a character speaks often reveal who they are in a significant way. For example, Saul's first words were, 'Let us turn back.' And that, as man and king, was his tragic flaw. He never saw anything through. He kept giving up.

What are Samuel's first words? 'Here I am.' It is repeated four times. That describes Samuel throughout his long and faithful ministry. He will be utterly present – to God and to the people of God. Through him, the word of the Lord will be heard again in the land and the Temple. Faith will be renewed and vision reawakened.

Here *we* are

What does this story say to us? Do you recognize Israel's world? In the noisy and frightening uncertainties of our present world, it is no easier to hear clearly. But the lamp has not gone out for us either. Nor will it. We follow the light of the world.

Samuel teaches us how to respond. 'Here I am.' 'Here we are.' That means learning to be present. This is not easy in difficult times because we would rather not be here at all. We can and do spend a lot of time wishing we were somewhere else. But there is nowhere else. Being present here, now, is all we need. This is where we need God – and this is where we will find him. The writer Etty Hillesum put it like this: 'There is a really deep well in me and in it dwells God. Sometimes I am there too.'[12]

Becoming present requires us to stop. To find somewhere quiet and to sit still. A few minutes each day to pause, settle, breathe in and say, 'Here I am.'

This is not just for us, but for our world too – for everywhere that is lost and burdened and needs the sight and sound of God to guide. So here *we* are. In a quiet moment now, present and listening, let us make Samuel's response our own.

(*brief pause*)

'Speak, LORD, for your servant is listening.'

David Runcorn

Hymn suggestions

I, the Lord of sea and sky; Be still, for the presence of the Lord; O Jesus, I have promised; Lead, kindly light.

Third Sunday of Epiphany   26 January
Principal Service   **Personal, Political, Holy**
Neh. 8.1–3, 5–6, 8–10; Ps. 19 [*or* 19.1–6]; 1 Cor. 12.12–31a;
Luke 4.14–21

A manifesto and an icon

This passage from Luke's Gospel always catapults me right back to my religious studies A-level class at sixth-form college. We were a small group, some Christian, some not. All of us heavily involved in politics and campaigning. We were in an area with a rich coal-mining history and had just lived through the UK miners' strikes of 1984–85. We were boycotting South Africa and were about to see the release of Nelson Mandela. We studied this passage as the Nazareth Manifesto. A political declaration of what we were committed to and putting energy into, the end of poverty, injustice, oppression, and the release of falsely imprisoned captives.

Luke's Gospel starts in this spirit. Mary, Jesus' mother, proclaims her manifesto that God casts down the mighty, lifts up the lowly, fills the hungry and sends the rich away. So begins a spirited pile-on of the work of the Holy Spirit in people. Zechariah, Simeon, John, Elizabeth all with words of something new and good and holy about to happen. Jesus arrives in the narrative and his first adult public act is to choose a reading from Scripture. Words evoking the spirit of his mother and the Spirit of God. After this, Luke's Gospel continues in this spirit. Over the next few pages, Jesus will be revealed as someone who is committed to liberation for the poor, the sick, those in captivity of all kinds and those who are on the receiving end of injustice.

During the space of the Gospel, Jesus will also be revealed as someone who stands within a particular strand of history, a prophet within a nation and culture full of prophets. So, the image of Jesus publicly reading words written by the prophet of the restoration to guide people who had been restored to a land and culture after years of exile is very powerful. Almost an icon to stand alongside the manifesto.

The people and the community

This small bit of Luke before us is a space which could be very full. We could cram into it lots of history, future events, imagery, connections, meanings and interpretations. If you ram in a lot of stuff, though, you lose sight of the most important thing, the poor, the captives, the blind and the oppressed. These are the true occupants of the space that Jesus concerns himself with. These are people, not theories, concepts or ideas. Jesus begins his ministry by standing up among people he knows and who know him and talking about people. Presumably, speaker and audience alike could put faces and names to those described as poor, captive, blind and oppressed. That's the way of religious services, they are centred in community life. In Luke's Gospel Jesus' ministry will also end with people from another community he was a part of. People who are also living with fear. They also will get a revelation of who Jesus is and what makes him tick.

One of the really interesting things about this story, as Luke tells it, is that the time it takes to read the story is the actual time of the whole event. Furthermore, if read as today, within a church service followed by a sermon, the context is the same. This mirroring of time and space can help bring the message home. Jesus was all about people, particularly the poor, the captive, the blind and the oppressed. Just pause for a moment and put faces and names to those descriptions. Faces and names from within this community. Faces and names of people you know, people you see in the street, people who have been in this building.

Holy acts of recognition and responsibility

As the Gospel of Luke goes on, Jesus puts these words into action. He liberates people, heals people and fights for justice. Also, as the Gospel unfolds, the poor are identified as worthy hearers of the good news, as recipients of God's kingdom (6.20), as a sign of Jesus' ministry (7.22), and as invitees to the kingdom feast (14.13). And so, the disconnecting begins. The poor, along with the captives, the blind and the oppressed increasingly become attached to concepts rather than communities. The flesh and blood, concrete daily actions which liberate and bring health and wholeness to real people somehow get downgraded in what it means to live the gospel and follow Jesus.

However, if we steer from the front, take our cue from the beginning, the prophetic tradition in which Jesus stands up and speaks up suggests that to intentionally recognize the demands of the poor as the responsibility of one human to another is to recognize, obey and worship God. That is what following Jesus really means. We live in a world where creation is being destroyed by selfishness and folly, where injustice, greed and oppression destroy people. People on our own doorsteps and in our own homes and communities as well as people far away. To act to reverse that is personal, political and holy.

Esther Elliott

Hymn suggestions

Inspired by love and anger; God of freedom, God of justice; Beauty for brokenness; Sent by the Lord am I.

Third Sunday of Epiphany   26 January
Second Service   **Remain as You Were Called**
Ps. 33 [*or* 33.1–12]; Num. 9.15–end; **1 Cor. 7.17–24**; *Gospel at Holy Communion*: Mark 1.21–28

You are probably familiar with the works of Vincent van Gogh. You will have seen his *Starry Night* or his *Sunflowers* perhaps. When my children were at primary school, copying the *Sunflowers* painting was part of the art curriculum. You may know something of van Gogh's story. He suffered from mental illness, cut off his own ear, and sold very few paintings during his lifetime. I wonder whether you have ever wondered, though, how it is that he is now so famous that one of his paintings sold for $83 million in 1990. To my shame, I never asked myself the question, until I read the story of Johanna van Gogh-Bonger, Vincent's sister-in-law. She was so convinced by his brilliance that after the death of Vincent and her husband Theo, Vincent's brother, she vowed to make van Gogh's work famous. From the age of 28, she worked on bringing his work to the world. By the time she died in 1925, van Gogh was world-famous. She achieved both the biggest-ever exhibition of his work and the first-ever exhibition to feature extracts from letters written by the artist. Johanna van Gogh-Bonger was innovative and determined. She made van Gogh known.

Committed to the message

You are probably also familiar with the letters of St Paul. You will have heard some of his writings, including today's Epistle reading. Most people are familiar with a passage he wrote about love because it is so often used at weddings. Paul had a clear vision, and he was determined to bring it to the world. He travelled and spoke in major cities around the Empire. When he died, the churches he founded were being persecuted by the Roman emperor. Yet his story and his teachings are still known. Paul's vision was of a new commonwealth, where everyone was equal.

Remain in the condition you were called

In the extract from Paul's first letter to the Corinthian church that we read today, one message is clear. In fact, it's crystal clear, because Paul says it twice. Paul writes: 'Let each of you remain in the condition in which you were called.' And later, 'In whatever condition you were called, brothers and sisters, there remain with God.'

First, he addresses religious practice, then social status. He suggests that those who are circumcised should remain so, and those who are not circumcised don't need to be so. One is easier than the other, of course, but nevertheless the principle is clear. Stay as you are. Second, he says, if you were a slave when you were called, don't worry about it – though if you can gain your freedom, do. The point is, we are free in Christ. We belong to the Lord, not to other human beings. Paul's principal aim is to show how God's new community, the church of Jesus, is to be. First, it is to be diverse. Christians are not to try to look like each other. We are not to impose our own religious practices or ideals on other people. Neither circumcision nor uncircumcision is better. All are one in Christ.

Be free if you can

The issue of slavery seems to be slightly different. Paul may be saying that if it is possible to gain your freedom, do so. Slaves were owned. In the Roman Empire, and particularly in Corinth, there was no expectation of men to be either monogamous or even sexually continent.[13] Ownership of slaves meant exactly that, slaves belonged to their owners, body and soul. Slaves were routinely victims of abuse, including sexual abuse, and in the eyes of church members whose background was Jewish, this made them unclean. They would not be seen as worthy of taking part in worship. Paul says if it is possible to be free, be free. Nevertheless, free or not, you are just as worthy as anyone else in the congregation.

All bought with the same price

The church in Corinth was as diverse as the city itself.[14] In it were Jews and Gentiles, slaves and slave owners, abusers and abused. How were they to worship together? By realizing that all were bought for exactly the same price. All belong to God through Christ. No one is superior and no one is inferior. All are called, and all are to remain with God.

Serving the purpose of God

Johanna van Gogh-Bonger's story is inspirational. She had a vision, she was innovative and determined, she devoted her life to it. I am not an artist or an art dealer, but I am a Christian. In the words of a chorus, 'I want to serve the purpose of God in my generation, I want to serve the purpose of God while I am alive.'[15] Will you join me?

Liz Shercliff

Hymn suggestions

I want to serve the purpose of God; God has called us for his purpose; The Spirit dwells within us all; I am redeemed.

Presentation of Christ in the Temple (Candlemas)
2 February
Principal Service   **Bucket List**
Mal. 3.1–5; Ps. 24.[1–6] 7–end; Heb. 2.14–end; **Luke 2.22–40**

I wonder if you have a personal bucket list: a list of once-in-a-lifetime moments or experiences that you particularly want to fit into your time on earth.

Jack Reynolds was still ticking things off his list when most of us would be putting our feet up. At 104 years old, he became the oldest person to get his first tattoo. He broke another record by taking a rollercoaster ride for his birthday when he was 105. A year later, he marked his birthday by going on a zip wire. At 107, Jack managed to get himself a cameo part on the soap opera *Hollyoaks*, making him the oldest person to perform as a supporting artist on TV. He died in 2020, aged 108, a truly amazing man. It's certainly never too late to have new experiences![16]

Faith-filled lives

Our Gospel reading today introduces us to two people, both assumed to be of riper years. Anna we know is 84, and Simeon is assumed to be older too, because it's implied that, were it not for the Holy Spirit's promise to him, he might well have expected to die by now.

We don't know much about Simeon. Luke doesn't mention his family, his hobbies, or how he made a living. Just that he was a devout believer, the Holy Spirit was upon him, and he had a hope. Simeon was waiting, praying and longing for the time when God would intervene once and for all in his people's fortunes, when he would comfort his people and dry the tears from their eyes, when God himself would come to them. To see that day with his own eyes – to catch a glimpse of the promised work of God in the world – was the only thing on Simeon's bucket list.

This was not just wishful thinking: the Holy Spirit had revealed to Simeon that he would indeed see the promised one come. Imagine the anticipation that filled each day, as Simeon wondered if it would be today. As he grew older and older, might he have been tempted towards disillusionment, to doubt, to just beginning to wonder if this would ever really happen? Still, Simeon hoped.

Anna's life seemed barely to have begun when it was struck with grief. Assuming she married young, she was probably in her twenties when her husband died. What hopes must have died with him that day, what plans for their future, what dreams and ambitions seemed impossible now without him? The bucket list was scrapped, or at least radically changed. For Anna, the next 60 years or so were spent not in the expected domestic bliss but in the Temple, praying, fasting, worshipping God. Anna set all her hopes on God. She found all she needed in him: being with him, learning from him, enjoying his presence, and bringing before him the longings and hopes of her people.

Peace at last

On the day that Mary and Joseph brought their young baby into the Temple, Simeon and Anna's hopes were finally fulfilled. Here, they saw and recognized – with Holy Spirit-inspired vision – God's rescue plan, not just for their own people but for the whole world. The insiders and the outsiders, Jew and Gentile, old and young, men and women, poor and rich, everyone.

Simeon's exclamation of praise has become deeply embedded in our liturgy as the Nunc Dimittis, named after the Latin translation of the first few words. Used to mark endings, the words speak of a life now complete, a life truly fulfilled, because 'my eyes have seen your salvation'. The life that can end in peace, no matter how many rollercoasters it has travelled, is the life of one who has seen Jesus the saviour.

One goal

Meeting Jesus for ourselves changes everything. We won't get to cradle the baby in the Temple, but we can know him as the Spirit brings Scripture alive to us; we can meet him in the bread and wine of the Eucharist; we can hear him in the quiet of contemplative prayer. Whatever it looks like for us to see Jesus, it's only in encounters with him that we can be free from the pressure to find meaning and make something of our own lives. It's Jesus who is the source of adventure and purpose, true excitement and joy.

Of course, if breaking records at 105 is your style, you go for it! But whether your life is remarkable or very ordinary, only one goal really matters: to see Jesus. To know him, to love him, to share him with others. Make that your goal, however old you are, and you can be sure of a life well lived, now and into eternity.

Claire Jones

Hymn suggestions

Light of the world; Open the eyes of my heart; Longing for light, we wait in darkness; Take my life and let it be.

Presentation of Christ in the Temple (Candlemas)
2 February
Second Service   **The Promised Presence**
Ps. 122, 132; **Hag. 2.1–9**; John 2.18–22

Taking apart

When my children were small, we owned a set of colourful stacking cups. It was surprising to me that this simple, classic toy would prove to be such a favourite. I remember my son wanting us to play with them together. He would stack them one by one, according to their size, balancing the final cup precariously at the top before he took great pleasure in knocking them over, often pausing beforehand to add to the drama. This unsophisticated game was filled with laughter and would be repeated, time after time. As much as my infant son appreciated the patterns of the colours, the challenge of the building, and the amusement of seeing it all tumble down, even my basic understanding of human attachment points to the conclusion that what he enjoyed most was that I was spending time with him, interested in what he was doing, and keen to have fun together. The multi-coloured tower he could create stood as a totem of his father's engaged presence with him. Whether what he had built rose high or lay scattered around in pieces meant nothing. Having someone there at play, who delighted in what he was able to do and shared it all, meant everything.

Taking action

These readings for the Second Service of Candlemas do not invite us to see the infant Jesus presented in the Temple; instead, they speak of temples destroyed and rebuilt amid mixed emotions. In John 2, against the backdrop of the Temple, Jesus refers to his body as a temple when speaking elliptically about his resurrection. In the reading from Haggai, we are invited into a key part of the backstory of the Temple in Jerusalem whose ultimate meaning and purpose is revealed in Jesus.

In the final decades of the sixth century, we encounter Haggai among the people of Judah under the governorship of Zerubbabel. It has been 15 years since the people had returned home from exile. However, this was not proving to be a return worthy of the prophecies of Isaiah, Jeremiah and Ezekiel, where it might seem that Israel would be reunited around a restored Jerusalem with a Temple fit to be the source of the river of life. Indeed, little progress had been made since the people returned and the Lord's house lay in ruins. In chapter 1, Haggai comes with a wake-up call and God stirs the spirits of his people into action.

Building up

In chapter 2, Haggai has returned to rally the people and address an issue with the rebuilding project. The problem is simple: in comparison to Solomon's Temple, this one was underwhelming. Frankly, it was 'as nothing'. There were some older folks in the community who knew this based on first-hand experience. No one could pretend that this temple construction was anything but an imperfect project.

The prophet comes not with empty speech but with a timely reminder about what ultimately gives meaning to the Temple. The word of the Lord comes through Haggai in a form that echoes the ancient promises of God to Moses, and to Joshua: 'Take courage!' 'I am with you, do not fear.' The source of courage, the source of comfort is the promise of the presence of the one whose mighty hand has worked throughout history. The presence without which the Temple means nothing.

Shaking up

As a child, I enjoyed making glitter pictures where you paint with glue and then pour glitter all over the paper. Mid-project it can look a complete mess but when it is shaken up the picture is revealed. As the word of the Lord comes to the people through the prophet, there is promise of future action. God is going to shake things up. God will shake the nations and that which is treasured by the nations will be revealed. As God shakes things up, what is unmissable is that everything belongs to God and the splendour of God's dwelling place is entirely and only within God's gift, in God's timing. What God is about is the stuff that matters, the stuff that sticks.

Candlemas offers one last hurrah for contemplating the infancy of God incarnate and looking forward to what will unfold in the life of Jesus. The people of Haggai's time were promised a future that belied their unpromising construction. The Temple in Jerusalem would play its part in the greatest shakedown in history when God would reveal the true Temple, the true desire of all nations.

Right now, we may be disappointed by our imperfect projects or over-invested in things that will not last. Focusing on what is being taken apart, built up or shaken up in the present may lead us to forget the one who is present. Instead of looking to any totem of the engaged presence of the Father, we can gaze eye-to-eye with the person of God the Son who, with his Father, would send the Spirit upon living temples throughout the world. Only God is in charge of God's story and God is one who is at play across all of time. Which means everything.

Matt Allen

Hymn suggestions

My hope is built on nothing less (Cornerstone); Love divine, all loves excelling; Blessed be the name of the Lord; Come, thou long-expected Jesus.

Ordinary Time

Fourth Sunday before Lent (Proper 1)   9 February
Principal Service   **Ego**
Isa. 6.1–8 [9–end]; Ps. 138; 1 Cor. 15.1–11; **Luke 5.1–11**

Fire!

When I first started in my current ministry, I had a good go at setting fire to the church. It was an accident, you understand: a bin caught fire in the clergy vestry one evening and I burnt my hands putting the fire out. The day ended with my two hands bandaged up, and with me in quite a lot of pain. If you have ever suffered from a burn, you'll know the pain as well as the seriousness of the situation. In today's reading from Isaiah, we have the prophet's mouth touched with a 'live coal' – ouch! – and he is purified, so that he can speak God's word. The whole passage is full of drama: there's smoke, a throne and seraphs in attendance. This is a bit more than Parish Communion, and it gives a strong sense to Isaiah, as I imagine it would to anyone, of unworthiness.

'Here am I; send me!'

The Bible is littered with stories of people being called by God. Frequently, the recipient of the call feels frightened by the call and tries to avoid it or runs away: Jonah is for me the greatest example of that. But the call of Isaiah is very different. As mentioned above, the sense of being unclean is very clear, but once that uncleanness has been taken away, Isaiah's response is very definite: 'Hear am I; send me!' For those of us who are Christians, this has echoes of Gabriel speaking to Mary, when Mary replies: 'Here am I, the servant of the Lord; let it be with me according to your word' (Luke 1.38). When God is calling, there is always a need to surrender ourselves to him. No wonder most of us run away.

Failure

Always read the small print, especially with God. The rest of this chapter of Isaiah and what follows makes explicit that although the prophet has been granted this incredible vocation and a gift of speech, no one is going to listen to him. He will have the ear of the king too, but the king won't take his advice either. After all this, Israel will be invaded, the country laid waste and all the trees will be chopped down and all that will be left is stumps. This is what Isaiah's calling consists of. Not a great CV! But out of one of those stumps will come a shoot (Isa. 11.1), the stump of Jesse. It's not all about us.

Ego

Today's Gospel story is quite humiliating for the disciples. They have fished all night and caught nothing. If you enjoy imaginative prayer, you might imagine what you would say to a man who then suggests you go out in your boat again, having fished all night and caught nothing. I have a feeling that we have the polite version of events here. But there is a word that leaps out at me. Jesus says, 'Put out into the *deep* water.' The deep. A place of depth. How often is church life all about the surface of things? Where is it that we encounter the depths? That place of mystery. Darkness. Danger. For it is here that the catch is made, and it is staggering in quantity. Again, we have to surrender. The fishermen do what Jesus suggests and, when they do, there is abundance. Letting go of pride is quite a sacrifice.

Getting it wrong

I visited a parishioner the day before I wrote this, and they talked about the experience of returning to church after many years. One of the things they said was how important it was that the Eucharist begins with the confession, the acknowledgement that we get things wrong. In the reading today from St Paul's First Letter to the Corinthians, he is explicit in sharing what he had got wrong. His story of persecutor turned believer is a remarkable one, and I sense an important one for the modern era: a reminder that through God's grace, we can be changed and transformed if we allow ourselves to be. We are called to be instruments of God's love, and an instrument has to be surrendered to the one who plays it, wholly and unconditionally, for it to make the music it was created for. The stories in today's Scripture readings reveal that whatever our stories, our failures and our mistakes, God can use them if we let him, to bring abundance and hope. Dare we believe that? Can we also have the courage to say, 'Here am I; send me'?

Jonathan Lawson

Hymn suggestions

I, the Lord of sea and sky; I heard the voice of Jesus say; Will you come and follow me; Let all mortal flesh keep silence.

Fourth Sunday before Lent (Proper 1)   9 February
Second Service   **The Power of Naming**
Ps. [1] 2; Wisd. 6.1–21, *or* **Hos. 1**; Col. 3.1–22;
Gospel at Holy Communion: Matt. 5.13–20

A reasonable sermon?

This reading is uncomfortable. The book of Hosea speaks of judgement, punishment and hope. Hosea, the prophet of the northern kingdom, speaks across the reigns of five kings in the eighth century BC. He is told by God to take an unfaithful wife, Gomer, a picture of unfaithful Israel forsaking God. Gomer's three children are named as symbols of God's judgement and rejection of his people. The chapter ends on a powerful note of hope concerning Israel's fate, looking forward to a time of redemption and restoration. A very reasonable and faithful sermon could examine the twin bells of judgement and hope tolling out across this text, pointing to the love and constancy of God. But, as I said, this reading is uncomfortable.

Unheard voices

Let's not make an unseemly dash for a comforting sermon. There are some unheard voices here. Gomer, Hosea's 'wife of whoredom', remains undeveloped as a character. The text is not interested in her backstory. She is a sign and symbol: Gomer the whore, a picture of unfaithful Israel. Her children fare no better.

The power of naming

Hosea is commanded by God to give symbolic names to Gomer's three children. The text assumes a world view in which women and children have no agency or power. Here we might want to pause and ponder: 'Sticks and stones will break my bones, but names will never hurt me.' Really? Neither Gomer nor her children have any say in this naming. Jezreel's name recalls the ancestry of the house of Jehu – referring to the murders in the valley of Jezreel recorded in 2 Kings 9 and 10. The boy's name is a reminder of murder and a promise of God's judgement coming on a house conceived in bloodshed. Nice name.

More painful still is the naming of Gomer's daughter 'Lo-ruhmah', meaning 'not loved, not pitied'. This girl has no choice over this. How does such a name shape the growing child? The dominant reading points to this naming symbolizing God's rejection of his people because of their unfaithfulness, but inside this symbolic name is a child, bearing the weight of 'no love' in her identity. The theme of powerlessness here is heartaching. How many identities are damaged by narratives imposed, stories of harm – where the name 'unloved' is written by the actions of others? Children who are abused, neglected or bullied, subjected to trauma, will undoubtedly be shaped by their experiences, often naming themselves in the process: 'not good enough', 'worthless', 'stupid', 'ugly'. The name 'Lo-ruhamah' is perhaps more common than we might imagine, in the sense of an internalized belief system connected to feelings of worthlessness.

Lo-ruhamah's brother is named 'Lo-ammi'. This is a name with rejection at its heart: 'I am not yours.' Read with the grain of the text it points to God's rejection of Israel for infidelity. If we read against the grain, pausing again to explore the themes of powerlessness and labelling, we see a child set up to fail. Reading from the underside says, 'we see', 'we notice' and 'we hear'. This is a message of hope and redemption for those who have been trampled on.

Searching for hope

Where do we witness children today being labelled and used, rendered powerless? Reflection on the terrible stories of child abuse within the church, of powerful 'prophets' acting with impunity, will enable us to see more clearly. Recognizing the awful costs etched into the lives of survivors of abuse will sensitize us to silencing power dynamics – in Scripture, in our institutions, and all around us. Reading with the grain of the text can blind us to the assumptions lying before us, hidden in plain sight. Imagine reading this passage as a woman or man who carries the internal name 'not loved' or 'rejected'. Imagine how it would be for the dominant reading to simply be, unchallenged. Such a message would be silencing, crushing and lacking in any sense of hope.

So where is the hope for any who find they carry names they never chose? It's hard to look at God's renaming in this book as a source of hope, given that God is portrayed as giving the name in the first place. Read from the child's perspective, it feels like a form of divine gaslighting. The reading today *is* uncomfortable. It should be. If it isn't we are not reading it with empathy and an ear for the powerless.

Hope beyond the horizons of this text

The theme of redemption in the text, however problematic, points us beyond its horizons, to the Christ who came in love, to the Christ who sees the hurting and brings us home. Here is the source of all hope for those who are silenced, abused, misused at another's whim, mocked with names of another's devising.

In Christ and with Christ we are called to act as agents of reconciliation and healing, joining with him in the work of revealing the true names of all his children – 'Worthy', 'Seen', 'Heard', 'Known', 'Beloved'. Herein lies the hope, in commitment to the holy work of renaming.

Kate Bruce

Hymn suggestions

We cannot measure how you heal; I bind unto myself this day; Will you come and follow me; Beauty for brokenness.

Third Sunday before Lent (Proper 2)   16 February
Principal Service   **Blessings and Woes**
Jer. 17.5–10; Ps. 1; 1 Cor. 15.12–20; **Luke 6.17–26**

Blessings and woes, but first, healing. We read that the crowd had come to 'hear' Jesus and be 'healed' in that order. As ever, Jesus is not defined by expectations. He flips the desired order, making sure that the embodied comes first.

Non-standard kingdom

Those who had 'unclean spirits' or 'diseases' would have found it particularly difficult to access community and religious life. They would have been seen as sinners rather than saints and pushed to the margins of society. But this would not be the way of things in Jesus' upside-down kingdom. In fact, before anything else, Jesus wants to enact the fact that these people are first in the kingdom of God and thus the site of the presence of God.

We don't know the personalities and positions of everyone in the crowd that day. There would have been those looking for something in Jesus that would bring about a change in their circumstances, whether personal or political. There would have been, too, those who were not friendly towards this latest itinerant peasant prophet and were looking for a way to catch him out or condemn him. Jesus has a word or two for them: not a word of blessing but of doom; not 'well done' but 'beware'. The word he uses for this is 'woe'. One way of seeing this is to think of 'woe' as 'whoa', like 'whoa there, horsey'. In other words, 'stop', 'listen', 'warning'. Whoever we are, we need to stop sometimes and check in to see what Jesus would say to us. Are we willing to hear him say, 'Whoa there (*insert own name*)'?

In need of a doctor?

I wonder if Jesus is saying that when we come to him, we shouldn't only expect some quality teaching. In our connected world, good advice isn't hard to come by. Jesus is not the latest social media influencer dishing out well-polished platitudes. When we come to Jesus, we won't receive a quick-fix plan. No, in him we receive more than that. In fact, we receive a new person in our lives. And in this person, we even begin to receive healing. That might mean too that we acknowledge that there's something wrong, and that can be difficult. Sometimes we can think we're getting along fine all by ourselves. We can even think that we're the ones who can sort the world out because we have it all together. It's easy to get into fix-it mode, seeing the disease as something that needs sorting in others and not in ourselves. But, 'Whoa there (*insert own name*)'; wait a minute, is that what Jesus is saying?

When we locate ourselves in the story, whoever we are, we might receive Jesus most when we identify as those who are sick and need a doctor. Yes, there is something to learn in terms of our receipt and embrace of those who are sick, but there is also something to learn in terms of recognizing that we can be counted in that number. There is no them and us in terms of who needs a doctor in this scenario. We all need this doctor. We all need Jesus.

And when we go about life recognizing this, we no longer have to see the sickness in others. In other words, we no longer have to judge others as those that need fixing. Yes, those whom I see each day need a doctor – this same doctor, Jesus. But so do I. I, therefore, relate to others as one in the same boat, with the same, albeit different, needs. And this realization of the nature of life with others is what it is to take hold of the kingdom of God.

Come to Jesus

The kingdom of God requires no qualifications, no special talents and no particular status. Who is without these things? Me, you, all of us. That doesn't mean that we are not gifted, unique, loved or special, but in the ordering of the kingdom of God, we are no more of these things than anyone else. In fact, the only things we can bring at the point of access are our troubles, our sicknesses, our possessedness. Blessed are those who come to Jesus like that. We have access to God, which is amazing. But really it requires us to know that we're not beyond the need of a doctor. Woe to me if my actions suggest to others that I don't think I need one.

Are you troubled or sick? Come to Jesus. Are you getting along OK? Come to Jesus, there is still something to receive from him. Blessed are those who need a doctor; woe to those who don't.

Mark Amos

Hymn suggestions

Lead me, guide me along the way; When I needed a neighbour; Jesus Christ is waiting; Come to Jesus (rest in him).

Third Sunday before Lent (Proper 2)   16 February
Second Service   **Turning Back – Moving Forward**
Ps. [5] 6; Wisd. 11.21—12.11, *or* Hos. 10.1–8, 12; **Gal. 4.8–20**;
Gospel at Holy Communion: Matt. 5.21–37

It's not often we hear somebody preach with this much passion. When Paul writes to the church in Galatia, in one of his earliest letters, the intensity of his feelings has not lost its force, even after all these years. He is passionate, grief-stricken, about the way this church in Galatia seems to be throwing away the new life they have discovered. He is passionate about trying to help them to move into the fullness of that life. We can learn a lot from the depth and strength of that passion!

Turning back

They are turning back. It's what we do, isn't it? It almost seems to be the human condition. We discover a better view of reality, experience something that makes us full of happiness, and establish a good practice which helps us live – and then it slips away, and we lose it. Like New Year resolutions that barely make it two weeks into January, our intentions turn back, again and again.

These Galatian believers had started as pagans and then found their way into the Jewish understanding of the world. We would recognize them as converts to Judaism. But then as Paul taught them, this Judaism was beginning to morph into following Jesus, the Messiah. It was gradually turning into what we might call Christianity. These people had discovered Christ, the risen one, and their lives had been transformed. Unfortunately, other people were teaching them that Christ wasn't quite enough – they needed a lot of culture and tradition to understand Christ properly. They needed to keep the law, the Torah.

And, to be fair, it made a lot of sense! It's quite hard, to keep the experience alive, to live in a daily renewal. How good to have laws, codes and texts to fall back on. It's hard to keep enthusiasm alive. How much easier it is to puzzle over texts, sort out ideas and live as much as possible in the head.

Paul gets angry

This is the point where Paul gets really cross. As far as he is concerned, they are throwing their lives away. They are puzzling over the finer points of the Torah, and having great Bible studies. They are obsessed with 'calendar piety', they are becoming good bookish *church* people, but, to Paul, they are turning away from the living Christ!

And, shockingly, Paul seems to equate their over-religious bibliolatry of the Torah with their old pagan ways! It's just as bad! They are using religion to turn back from Christ.

Christ is present in lived experience. This body, community and presence of Christ are born in our lives. It is the most wonderful thing, so why do we turn back?

Knowing God, and being known by God, is a simple, transcendent relationship. It is completely satisfying. But it can also be terrifying. So often we substitute religion for relationship, compulsion for conversation. When we could be free, we voluntarily become slaves.

Moving forward

But Paul calls them brothers, sisters. They are family to him. And that's not because they have been really good, or engaged in piety, but because they are uncircumcised Gentiles – that's why they are part of God's family. Christ is being formed in them.

To Paul, the people of Galatia seem to be slipping back. That matters because of their potential. Paul has a passion to see, in these people, the fullness of Christ. And that is what speaks to us, too. With all our limitations, with our propensity to miss the point and wander from the path, can we begin to see that Christ may be formed in us?

Paul sees this body coming into the world. To him it is not a vague, mystical phenomenon, but the physicality of the body of Christ. And if you expect Paul to be patriarchal and exclusive, it may come as a shock when he reaches for the only possible image: the profoundly feminine language of childbirth. My pains, my anger, my longing for you, he says, are labour pains as I push and struggle to bring you to new birth. As, in your community, the body of Christ is formed in the world.

The passion of possibility

Paul is filled with the passion of possibility. I have seen what this life could be, he says. I have seen this body of love and I will endure all the labour pains necessary to bring it to birth again.

Could we share that passion? Could we see that happening in our communities? Is our church a place of pieties, observance, rituals and practices, and conformity? Or is it a labour ward? A place in which even the conflicts and difficulties are heralding the joyful news that, once again, here among us, Jesus is born.

Andrew Rudd

Hymn suggestions

Abba, Father, let me be; There is a longing in our hearts; The Spirit lives to set us free; All I once held dear.

Second Sunday before Lent   23 February
Principal Service   **The Power to Bring Calm to Chaos**
Gen. 2.4b–9, 15–end; Ps. 65; Rev. 4; **Luke 8.22–25**

The power of water

We've all experienced the power of water at some point in our lives. Perhaps it was walking under a waterfall on holiday. Perhaps it is that moment when a pipe has burst in our house. Perhaps it is when the sea comes in a little more quickly than you have expected. Perhaps it is being caught in a sudden rain shower when you haven't got your coat. Perhaps it is the news of devastating floods washing through communities, or tsunamis sweeping through villages and towns. Water out of our control can be terrifying.

For these seasoned fishermen, the storm took them by surprise and made them afraid. They must have experienced the sudden squalls the lake was known for. On this occasion, something was significantly different for them, and they feared for their lives.

Often in the Bible, the sea is used as a metaphor for life itself and the chaos that may surround us at any point. In the book of Revelation, when it says there is 'no more sea' it is a metaphor for no more chaos and disarray. Revelation imagines a time when we know what it is to live peacefully in the presence of God.

Notice how it was Jesus' idea to get in the boat and cross the lake. Did he know that there was a storm brewing? If he did know, then he could have avoided sailing through it, and taken the disciples by a different route. Sometimes, Jesus takes us through the storms, rather than avoiding them.

The power of Jesus

In the midst of the storm on the lake, while the disciples are panicking, Jesus sleeps peacefully. He has fallen asleep before the storm starts – and it is reassuring to know that Jesus gets tired in the middle of the day and needs to rest! It is a reminder of his humanity, as we are about to see his divinity unfold. He is, at this moment, the living embodiment of what it is to be peaceful in the presence of God. No matter the extent of the chaos and tumult around him, Jesus sleeps.

His disciples come to him in fear that they are on the point of death – and at the same time in the certainty that if Jesus was awake they would be safe. Sure enough, Jesus stands up and commands the chaos to become calm, the tumult to be tamed, and peace to be restored. The disciples have what they asked for, and now they are confused.

The power of presence

The disciples in the midst of the storm can do nothing to save themselves. However, they have Jesus with them (even if he is asleep). They turned to him when all seemed lost and they were convinced that only death awaited them. Somewhere in that cry of 'Master, we are going to drown!' was the unspoken plea 'Help us!' There was an assumption that Jesus could intervene and bring rescue. In the simple act of waking him up, there was trust. Jesus was present and therefore Jesus would do something.

However, Jesus' act of power over chaos leads to confusion. Who is this that the wind and the waves obey him? We might ask the disciples, what did you expect would happen when you woke Jesus up? We have the benefit of hindsight in our ability to connect Jesus who speaks words over creation as the very word of creation in the poetry of Genesis. The one who commanded the wind and the waves into being is the one who now commands them to be peaceful. The disciples at that moment were yet to make that connection.

The power to change lives

Here we have an invitation to encounter Jesus amid our own periods of chaos and tumult. Life can be overwhelming, like being caught in the middle of a great storm, and we share the experience of the disciples in the boat when we fear that all is lost. We may pray faithfully that something will change, but it may feel as though Jesus is fast asleep and unaware of our prayers and the chaos. At this point, we could simply give up praying and await the inevitable. Or we can persist and shake Jesus awake, trusting that by his very presence something will change. And then we can witness the life-changing power of Jesus to bring calm to chaos as he meets us in the storms of life.

Kt Tupling

Hymn suggestions

Will your anchor hold; Be still, my soul; Inspired by love and anger; Eternal Father, strong to save.

Second Sunday before Lent   23 February
Second Service   **Beginning Now**
Ps. 147 [*or* 147.13–end]; **Gen 1.1—2.3**; Matt 6.25–end

'In the beginning when God created …'

These famous opening words appear to be looking back to a past action. A job completed. But at the bottom of the first page of our Bibles, tucked in the footnotes, is another way of translating that verse. 'In the beginning when God *began creating*.' Both statements are true. God is the original source of everything. But his work of creation is not finished. Life is still evolving. We are still becoming. We will never reach the end of God's creating imagination. At some point, though, that second way of reading got lost in the small print and so is never read aloud.

But what if our Bibles started with the footnote option instead? When God *began creating* …' There is suddenly an energy – here and now. A creating present. Do you sense it? It means that something that began back then is still at work. Everything that was in the beginning is still continuing. Beginning now. It always is. God is with us. How might that change our life and faith?

Soup of nothingness

What was in the beginning? The storyteller says, 'The earth was a formless void' (Gen. 1.2). The Hebrew words here are *tohu wa bohu*. Its meaning is not clear. 'Shapeless flux' is one attempt. My favourite is 'a soup of nothingness' (*The Message*) because cosmologists often speak of soups of gasses to describe the beginnings of stars and planets. Creation does not start with nothing. God fashions us out of this formless waste.

This ancient creation poem is thought to have found its final Bible voice during Israel's exile in Babylon. God's people were far from home. Their land, Holy City, Temple and faith were reduced to *tohu*. Shapeless rubble. Even their God had apparently been defeated by foreign gods. They were trying to pray in a strange land and language. Does this sound at all familiar? In recent years much of the familiar shape, content and securities of life have been shaken – for many, lost completely. The message is that God does his creating working with what is *tohu wah bohu*. He still does.

In this unfolding creation story, chaos takes order and form, emptiness finds substance, 'nothing' finds meaning. What is untranslatable finds halting words and expression. God needs no other material to do the work he loves most. This is very good news!

'... a wind from God swept over the face of the waters'

Translations often speak of the Spirit hovering and brooding over it all. But the image here is not a sheltering, maternal one. The mood is wild. The world of quantum physics borrows words like 'shaking', 'bending', 'rippling' and 'jittering' to express the energy and movement at the core of matter. The same mix of hovering and wildness combines in Deuteronomy 32 where God's care of his Exodus people is imagined as an eagle with her young 'in a howling wilderness waste' (Deut. 32.10). 'As an eagle stirs up its nest, and hovers over its young ... it spreads its wings, takes them up, and bears them aloft on its pinions' (Deut. 32.11). Why is the parent bird stirring up the nest? To make it uninhabitable! To force their young to take flight. To tip them into the life that is theirs to be. All is vibrating and trembling on the winds. Wings are outstretched to overshadow, protect and uplift. There is a deep stirring. Something is about to happen.

'Let there be'

Now God speaks. 'Let there be.' A world is about to come into being. What tone of voice do you hear God speaking in here? Are these declarations of an absolute authority? Effortless power working a preordained plan? Or is God wondering aloud what to create next? Is this divine imagination playfully improvising? The priest and scientist John Polkinghorne once suggested that creation has more the appearance of an improvisation than the performance of a predetermined script.[17] How might we imagine God speaking to our world today? What is he willing that we may become? What kind of voice is he speaking with?

Day by day

The account of creation now unfolds on a firm, rhythmic cycle. Perhaps it was a song?

> Let there be
> and there was
> and it was good
> and there was evening and morning
> a first day

Imagine this cathartic song, slowly taking hold of the exhausted imaginations of exiles in a far country. It subverts the despair and hopelessness. Out of the formless *tohu* of loss, faith is steadily, unexpectedly rekindled. Hope is awakening. New meanings – tentative and vulnerable – becoming possible. There is no way back, but, quite improbably, there is a future in all this. We must let it take hold of us too. It is beginning now.

All is being shaped and reshaped in the endless, playful, imaginative wisdom of God.

David Runcorn

Hymn suggestions

Thou, whose almighty word; Breathe on me, breath of God; Come to us, creative Spirit; From the highest of heights to the depths of the sea (Indescribable).

Sunday next before Lent 2 March
Principal Service **A Shining Face**
Ex. 34.29–end; Ps. 99; 2 Cor. 3.12—4.2; **Luke 9.28–36 [37–43a]**

The icon painter

White flashes. It's the very last thing that she paints. The icon painter prepares the board, making a background of gold leaf. She builds up the figures in the traditional colours and, when all that is done, puts these white flashes on the picture. Splashed on the folds of people's robes, in the details of their faces, and even the cracks in the ground.

These flashes of light are where this world bursts into transcendence. The cracks where the light gets in.

I wonder, do these flashes represent another world that shines through a thin place? Or could it be that the glory is always here, but is hidden from us? Unless, that is, our *seeing* is *cleansed*.

The hidden beauty around us

Often, as we walk around, we miss a great deal of this world. We don't even notice the incredible beauty that is here. Surely that beauty is the presence of God. It is there in the depth of every moment, but we miss it, until, in the words of Scripture, our 'eyes are opened'.

Tulips on a windowsill, caught by early morning light.

A pebble dropped into water, so that all the unexpected colours appear.

Noticing a tiny grasshopper, its little mask of a face, its jointed legs – a wonder that is almost too small to see.

A world of wonder that is often right in front of me, but I miss it.

Transfiguration

Our Gospel story today has a word for this. These moments of seeing are *transfiguration*. This is not transformation into something new, but transfiguration. Something that has been hidden or unnoticed becomes visible, becomes light.

Become light

Almost all religions seem to feel the need to depict the moment when holiness becomes visible – look at stained-glass windows! It's as if there could be a light shining from people: a halo, an aura, a dazzling, shining face.

And nowhere more than on this hilltop, this story of the transfiguration. It seems to be a strong memory of the church. It's in Matthew, Mark and Luke, and then referred to in the Second Letter of Peter.

This story sets Jesus alongside the giants of Jewish tradition. Alongside Moses who represents the Torah. Alongside Elijah who represents the prophets. That's parts one and two of the Jewish Bible. Part three is Wisdom. Could it be that this story is placing Jesus as the *Wisdom* of God? And then everything else vanishes, and Jesus remains.

Not a superhero

This is not meant, in any way, to be like Clark Kent shedding his everyday identity and becoming Superman. Rather, this is a *vision* of what things are really like *all the time*. And it isn't just a theological challenge, but a personal one.

Certainly, this *was* a vision of Jesus, but the Bible makes it very clear that this is not *just* about Jesus, but about the experience of every one of us.

It is a glimpse of a possibility, that we – you and me – can *become* light, or rather the light that is in us already could shine out.

Metamorphosis

This word the Gospel writers use for *transfigure* is *metamorphosis*. It's the word we use for tadpoles becoming frogs, or caterpillars becoming butterflies.

It's a big change – a change of form certainly, but not into a different being.

In potential, the butterfly was in the caterpillar all the time.

In potential, the tree is in the acorn.

In potential, what is within each one of us is more wonderful than we can imagine.

The DNA of Christ is in us …

I think that, deep down, we know this. Sometimes we say that love is blind, but I think that love is not really blind – love gets a glimpse of who we could be, who we are. Because who we are is beautiful, shining.

The task, the challenge, is to accept that in ourselves and to spot that in others. If I can glimpse how special and unique you are …

If I can recognize even a glimmer of the beauty of God within you, then it changes things. How can I belittle you, or disrespect you? How can I ignore you, or pull back from you if you are shining with the light of God?

'You are the light of the world,' says Jesus, but if that light is hidden under a basket, what use is it? How can we recognize this light in one another and in every person we meet?

Andrew Rudd

Hymn suggestions

Lord, the light of your love (Shine, Jesus, shine); Longing for light (Christ, be our light); For the beauty of the earth; Christ, whose glory fills the skies.

Sunday next before Lent   2 March
Second Service   **Storing Up in the Hump of Faith**
Ps. 89.1–18 [*or* 89.5–12]; Ex. 3.1–6; **John 12.27–36a**

Ships of the desert

Have you ever watched a camel?

I did once; tall and proud, neck arched like a bow. Shaggy in parts, particularly the tufts on the top of the hump, smooth in others. Long face with small, deep-set eyes, dark eyelashes and an extra eyelid, that blinks and flicks, to stop the dusty sand from getting in. Great oversized lips that flap, and chew and pucker, and hang. Hooves wide, to stop them from sinking into the sand.

Have you ever watched a camel?

Perfectly adapted to the harsh environment of the desert. Able to go days without needing to drink; although not, as is a popular myth, because their humps are full of water. Instead, they are incredibly efficient consumers of water, in part due to their unique oval-shaped blood cells. Their prominent humps (either one or two, depending on the species) are stores of fatty tissue, not water, which is used as a source of nourishment when food is scarce.

Camels are the perfect beast for a long, dry season, where you need sustenance stored up in advance.

I wonder how we cope with long, dry seasons. How adapted we are?

Troubled souls

Our reading from John's Gospel begins, 'Now my soul is troubled.' Jesus has entered Jerusalem, with a mighty procession, great joy and enthusiasm. He has come into the city like a king, with palm branches waving, singing and chanting of psalms.

But despite all the celebration, he knows what is about to happen. He begins to speak openly about all that will come to pass, predicting his death to Andrew and Philip. He tells them that his soul is troubled. There is an approaching sense of gloom; of the darkness that will overtake the light; that times will be hard. Jesus knows that in such times it can be difficult to keep faith.

Perhaps there is something that resonates in that with you today. Perhaps you can pinpoint times in your own journey when the circumstances of your life have made your faith more difficult. Times when your prayer life has felt as dry as a desert, and where the words of praise in worship have felt dry on your tongue. Perhaps you even have that impending sense of gloom now; you feel as if you have run out of faith, as you look on helplessly at situations of trouble in the world, the church or your own life.

Storing up faith

In order to ready ourselves for such times, let us look at Jesus' words and the life of camels. For we hear Jesus say, 'Walk while you have the light, so that the darkness may not overtake you ... While you have the light, believe in the light, so that you may be children of light.'

Jesus is encouraging the troubled disciples to walk in the light while they can so that when they come to the inevitable times of darkness, they will have something to rely on. Likewise, the voice from heaven is for their benefit; a sign they can hold on to when times become dark. Like a camel at a desert oasis, the disciples are being encouraged to drink deeply of the waters of faith now, in order that they can be sustained by those stores in the difficult times.

For us too, although maybe not as dramatic as a voice from heaven, it is our moments of real encounter with God, when our prayer life goes well and we have a clear understanding of our walk with God, that then sustain us in the times when we feel bereft and adrift from the divine.

Journeying into Lent

On Wednesday we enter the season of Lent. Often, we can equate this to a wilderness season; a time of fasting and abstinence; mapped on to Jesus' trials in the wilderness. But if it is a time of 'giving up', it is only of the things that might get in the way of our spiritual cramming. Because in this most holy of seasons, there is an encouragement to take time and space to do the work of 'storing up'. In whatever way works best for you, think now about what you need to do with God; perhaps time in prayer, in fellowship, or dwelling in both God's word and God's creation. Plan now, for Lent is a time of doing the things that you need to sustain you in your faith and to keep you walking in the light.

Through this, we fill up our own reserves, like fat in a camel's hump, so that in the difficult times and the dry times, we have something to draw from. And we discover, too, that as we set ourselves apart to be renewed and refreshed by Christ's life-giving waters, we are reinvigorated in God's call to peace, love, generosity and kindness; becoming sustained to go out and share those things in the world around us.

So, as we look towards Lent, how full is your hump, and what will you do in the weeks ahead to build up your reserves?

Chris Campbell

Hymn suggestions

As the deer pants for the water; As water to the thirsty; I heard the voice of Jesus say; The Spirit lives to set us free.

Lent

Ash Wednesday 5 March
Writing in the Dust
Joel 2.1–2, 12–17, *or* Isa. 58.1–12; Ps. 51.1–18;
2 Cor. 5.20b—6.10; Matt. 6.1–6, 16–21, *or* **John 8.1–11**

John's Gospel records a shocking story. If we were watching this on television, there would be a warning before it began: 'Viewers may find some scenes disturbing.' A woman has been interrupted having sex and dragged before Jesus in the middle of a crowd, by religious leaders who are demanding her stoning. The story is commonly known as 'The woman caught in adultery'. But it is misnamed. By the time this story ends, the focus of judgement will be somewhere else. This is a story of men caught in hypocrisy – including the adulterous *man* who no one seems to notice has gone missing.

Setting up Jesus

The woman was being used. Goodness knows what it took to plan all this. How do you 'catch' someone in adultery? And there she is, forced to stand dishevelled and terrified, facing brutal death in the name of religion. But she was there to set up Jesus. Will he obey the law?

Interestingly, many of the earliest Bible versions omit this story altogether. Even modern versions put it in brackets with a coy comment in the footnotes. What is it that makes this story so controversial? Is it in any way untypical of how Jesus behaved? Did he not constantly shock by whom he forgave and showed love to, especially the marginalized and the victims of abusive, judgemental religion and by his treatment of women in that patriarchal culture? How did Jesus react? This tense dramatic scene, on the edge of brutal violence, is now simply and vividly recounted and his silence and his movements are recorded as carefully as his words.

Jesus reacts

As the religious leaders confront Jesus …

He bends down. He averts his eyes. I like to think this was respect for the woman. He refuses to gaze on her brutal exposure and humiliation.

He writes with his finger in the dust. But they keep on demanding an answer from him. Do you obey the law? She must be stoned.

He straightens up – in contrast to the twisted behaviour of those around him. He is straight-speaking too: 'Let anyone among you who is without sin be the first to throw a stone at her.'

He bends down and *writes* in the dust again. I imagine the action suddenly freezing. Hypocrisy is exposed. Accusers are silenced. The trial collapses. The judges leave – the eldest first. The crowd disperses.

Now he straightens up again and faces the woman. Everyone else has gone. His words, though recorded for us, are for her alone: 'Neither do I condemn you.'

Writing in the dust

But what *did* Jesus write in the dust? I'm with those who think he was just doodling. It's a good tactic when severely provoked. Pause. Breathe deeply. Take time before responding. Was he struggling to contain his anger at an abusive, judgemental religion that so distorts the face and heart of God? Furious at the hypocrisy and the brutal exploitation of this vulnerable and powerless woman? As the lead judge kept shouting at him, was Jesus praying, 'God help me not to punch that mean, vindictive face'?

But what *might* he have written? And what might he be writing now in the dust on our foreheads, or at our feet, this Ash Wednesday?

We are dust

We hear four words spoken directly to us in this service: 'Remember you are dust.' Who makes anything of dust? Well God does – as only God can. Dust clearly does not embarrass or frustrate him. Rather it inspires him. He creates whole worlds out of this dust.

He created our humanity out of dust, and leaned over and breathed his own breath into the nostrils of the creatures of dust, that is, you and me. He still does. It is not that God does not take sin seriously – he does. But that story reminds us he has a very different way of responding to it. 'Neither do I condemn you.'

There is quite a lot of cruelty, judging, threatening and stone-throwing in our world too. But what if here, at our feet, bent down and silent in the face of our shouty concerns and demands, he is writing other things, here in the dust? Can you think of some? What about, 'I have come to give you *life*'? Or, 'Look, I make all things new.'

Remembering dust

So here, on this Ash Wednesday, we remember we are dust. But we remember what becomes of dust in the imagination and desire of God. Let God speak his words of creating again in this world. In humble joy let him write with his finger, in the dust of our being, with all its imperfections, these reminders of his uncondemning love.

This fragile and broken world of ours needs no reminding – you are dust. But today we renew our hope in what God can fashion out of dust in his mercy and love. This Ash Wednesday let us imagine Jesus bending over and writing in the dust of your life and mine his words of eternal life.

David Runcorn

Hymn suggestions

Give thanks with a grateful heart; My song is love unknown; Breathe on me, breath of God; Such love, pure as the whitest snow.

First Sunday of Lent   9 March
Principal Service   **The Weakness of Jesus**
Deut. 26.1–11; Ps. 91.1–2, 9–end [*or* 91.1–11]; Rom. 10.8b–13; **Luke 4.1–13**

'You just don't understand!' It's the cry of every frustrated teenager to their dumbfounded parents at some point in those tricky years. On some level, they're right. Every generation of young people faces different pressures, shaped by developments in technology, a changing economic climate and shifting expectations laid upon them. No wonder so many feel alone and misunderstood.

Nevertheless, human nature remains constant, and the underlying struggles and strains of growing up are shared from age to age and across borders too. It's often when emerging from adolescence to adulthood that we're able to see our parents as fellow humans with both feelings and fallibilities, rather than the alien beings they once seemed!

A very human story

The narrative of Jesus' time in the wilderness might at first feel alien to our experience. Christians are generally comfortable with the idea of God speaking to us in some way, but far fewer tell of personal conversations with the devil! Unusual though this story is, at its heart it is a story about the common human experience in which the Son of God had a share.

The writer to the Hebrews, speaking of Jesus, tells us that 'we do not have a high priest who is unable to sympathize with our weaknesses, but we have one who in every respect has been tested as we are, yet without sin' (Heb. 4.15). The events in the wilderness are often described as the three temptations of Jesus since the devil lays before him the opportunity to attain attractive things by sinful means. But the experience of human weakness began before the devil picked up a stone and suggested Jesus turn it into bread.

Let's look a bit more closely at why Jesus was vulnerable to the devil's enticements.

Weak in the wilderness

The story takes place immediately after Jesus' baptism, with its divine affirmation of his identity as God's beloved son. We can imagine Jesus riding high after the event, fired up and ready to go out and do all that the Father had called him to. But rather than getting stuck in where the action was, Jesus found himself in a place where there was no crowd, no crisis and apparently no one in need of his new ministry. The wilderness is a lonely place, and those whose vocation is bound up in serving other people can find loneliness particularly hard to bear. Memories of the expectant crowds responding to John's preaching on the banks of the Jordan just days earlier would make the silence all the more overwhelming. Without the stimulation and support that comes from relating to other people, we become open to self-doubt and discouragement. Left alone with his thoughts for almost six weeks, Jesus was vulnerable, because Jesus was human.

It wasn't only human contact that was missing in the wilderness; Luke tells us that Jesus went without food for those 40 days too. As embodied beings, our physical needs are never far from our minds, and when those needs are not being met, it gets increasingly difficult to continue with normal tasks and decision-making. Some of us struggle to recognize when this is happening: I can be 'stuck' in unproductivity and lack of focus for several hours before I realize that I'm just a little cold or thirsty. But after nearly six weeks without food, Jesus would be well past the point of discomfort. Weak in body and mind, he was at risk of confusion and disorientation, as well as anxiety and depression. Without energy for his body, Jesus was vulnerable, because Jesus was human.

Above all, Jesus' greatest vulnerability wasn't social or physical, but spiritual. Notice that he didn't end up in the desert by accident; he hadn't taken a wrong turn on the way to the nearest town. No, it was the Holy Spirit who led him there, even 'drove' him there (Mark 1.12). This strange and difficult action of the Holy Spirit clearly made an impact: Jesus would later teach his disciples to pray, 'lead us not into temptation'. I wonder if this unexpected and even unwanted leading of the Spirit left Jesus desperately craving the kind of certainty he'd experienced at his baptism. When God seemed obscure, Jesus was vulnerable, because Jesus was human. But in all this, he didn't sin.

In time of trial

Temptation can strike us at any time, but it's wise to be aware of our own particular moments of vulnerability. Social isolation or anxieties, physical suffering and spiritual darkness can all leave us open to thoughts and actions we would otherwise recognize as damaging. That Jesus – unique as his experience was – truly does know our human fragility can give us confidence to turn to him in our weakness. In him, we will find comfort and support from the one who has been there, and it is him who is able to meet all our emotional, physical and spiritual needs. In clinging to Jesus, we find power to resist temptation, and most importantly, endless grace for when we don't.

Claire Jones

Hymn suggestions

What a friend we have in Jesus; Everyone needs compassion; Forty days and forty nights; Seek ye first the kingdom of God.

First Sunday of Lent   9 March
Second Service   **Lord, Have Mercy**
Ps. 119.73–88; Jonah 3; **Luke 18.9–14**

Last Wednesday – Ash Wednesday – we entered into Lent, with the words:

> Remember that you are dust, and to dust you shall return.
> Turn away from sin and be faithful to Christ.[18]

Lent is the penitential season that leads to Holy Week and Easter. This First Sunday of Lent provides a moment for us to consider our frailty as human beings, our propensity to go astray, to get things wrong, and to be less than we can be.

It seems to be part of the human condition to go astray and end up doing things we shouldn't. St Paul hits the nail on the head in Romans when he writes, 'I do not do the good I want, but the evil I do not want is what I do' (Rom. 7.19). That's true for us as individuals, as the church and as the family of God throughout creation, from Adam onwards. Sin seems hard-wired into the human condition and never more so than when we watch with horror the violence and misery that pervades our news every day. We find ourselves between a rock and a hard place. Lord, have mercy.

Turning to the Lord

Turning to the Lord in penitence is where we find hope and deliverance. It is in and through Jesus that we find resources to 'get over ourselves' and our flawed human natures. Jesus is our head, our source, the firstborn of creation and the blueprint for humanity. If we wish to seek wisdom about how to live our lives then it is to Jesus that we should look: his life, his teachings, his death, his resurrection, his eternity.

We have a snapshot of that teaching in our reading from Luke. Jesus tells the parable of the Pharisee and the tax-collector. In it, he is teaching the wisdom of God seen through the topsy-turvy spectacles of the kingdom. Grandiose posturing before God, self-congratulation, self-promotion, religiosity or celebrity status will not ultimately win the day. It is in turning and returning to the Lord that we will be saved. It is humility that brings us to our knees and keeps us in touch with the earth that makes the difference.

Showing steadfast love and genuinely casting ourselves onto the mercy of God – whose heart beats with grace and forgiveness – is the touchstone of restoration. Lord, have mercy.

God makes the first move

Penitence doesn't begin with us. It is God who makes the first move. In the death of Jesus on the cross, the sin of humanity throughout time, all the evil, violence and fear, past, present and yet to come, were taken up into God and blown apart, washed away, rubbed out – gone. On the cross Jesus holds together the old creation with its sin and death and the new creation – restored, reconciled and made whole and at one with God. Such amazing self-giving love makes it possible for you and me to be reconciled to God and to one another. It's the act, projected back through time, that makes God change his mind and not destroy the repentant Ninevites in the reading from Jonah.

Therefore, whatever we do we can never step outside the love of God, because the price for that sin has already been paid in full, come what may. We are liberated, we are free, Jesus presents us before God as holy and blameless to be loved unconditionally and for ever. This is extraordinary grace that none of us deserve. We have been revived and raised up with Christ, to be partakers in his eternal resurrection life. This is truth which, like the tax-collector in the parable, drives us to our knees in gratitude, humility and penitence. Lord, have mercy.

Ongoing repentance

Most acts of worship in the Church of England contain an opportunity to confess our sins and hear the words of forgiveness. It is the only place we can go regularly, week by week, to come before God and make a fresh start. It's the place where we remember that we are loved because Jesus presents us clean and holy before God. Forgiveness is a deep, holy and much-needed gift that the church offers to any and to all.

Confession is first and foremost about confessing Jesus Christ as Lord. Marking out over and again that the truth of God is what motivates and drives us. When we forget that then we go our own way and live by our desires and not the grace of God. Then we justify ourselves like the Pharisee in the parable. It is not through anything we do ourselves but by God's grace that we are forgiven and transformed. The Holy Spirit dwelling within us brings more and more into the light to be redeemed, turning us to deeper and more steadfast Christ-like living.

So in the first week of Lent, it's a good time to remind ourselves that God loves each of us just as we are and that, through God's grace, we are acceptable, precious and part of the new creation. So, let's come in humility, let's come in gratitude, let's come in love as we turn again to the Lord.

Lord, have mercy.

Catherine Williams

Hymn suggestions

Dear Lord and Father of mankind; Lord Jesus, think on me; There's a wideness in God's mercy; Such love, pure as the whitest snow.

Second Sunday of Lent   16 March
Principal Service   **Beware Foxes**
Gen. 15.1–12, 17–18; Ps. 27; Phil. 3.17—4.1; **Luke 13.31–end**

Jesus and his disciples have begun to make their way towards Jerusalem. This journey will take around six months, before finally entering Jerusalem on Palm Sunday. That is the direction of travel. But along the way, Jesus attracts the resentment of religious leaders, and in today's passage we observe such an encounter.

Mixed motives

The passage begins with the Pharisees warning Jesus to leave because Herod wants to kill him. We know that the Pharisees resent Jesus; in fact, we know that they want him dead. Why on earth, then, are they warning Jesus about Herod's intention to kill him? Why are they helping him? It does not add up.

It could be that they are genuinely concerned about Jesus' safety, but that is unlikely. The likely explanation is that they are attempting to strike fear into Jesus so that he will go. Up until this point, they have been offended by Jesus' counter-cultural teachings. It is more likely that the Pharisees are trying to get him to leave, under the guise of friendship and being his confidant, when really they are not.

Have you ever come across someone who has supposedly told you something for your own good, but in reality were serving their own self-interests? This is the kind of thing that manipulative people do, and the Pharisees are being manipulative. Sadly, this type of manipulation can happen inside the church just as much as outside it.

Beware of foxes

Jesus had a mission to accomplish and work to do. But here, the Pharisees are seeking to derail him, by manipulating him through fear. Jesus knows this and responds, 'Go and tell that fox for me, "Listen, I am casting out demons and performing cures today and tomorrow, and on the third day I finish my work."' Jesus is not going to permit anybody or anything to distract him from his mission and work.

Jesus' use of the word 'fox' is significant. He is not saying that Herod is as sly as a fox as we would understand it, he is actually insulting him. Under the Israelite holiness codes of the time, a fox was considered an unclean animal. Jesus is saying he refuses to allow himself to be controlled by a vile creature like Herod. Jesus will not allow Herod to distract him, strike fear into him, hinder or influence his life in any way.

Jesus' response to Herod differs from that of his cousin John the Baptist. Luke mentions the beheading of John in chapter 9. In the corresponding account in the Gospel of Mark, we see how John the Baptist allows himself to get caught up in the 'affairs' of Herod, quite literally, because John confronts Herod about lusting after his own brother's wife. Unlike Jesus, John allows himself to become consumed with Herod's affairs, which enables Herod to manipulate, control and eventually destroy him. This is what foxes do if we do not learn how to handle the 'Herods' in our life.

Embrace the hen

Jesus introduces another creature – one that might be regarded as the opposite of a fox – a hen. He says, 'How often have I desired to gather your children together as a hen gathers her brood under her wings, and you were not willing!'

Jesus wants to brood over Jerusalem with a hen's devoted love and protection. Following Jewish tradition that describes God as a mother – a mother eagle in Deuteronomy, a mother bear in Hosea, or a nursing mother as in Isaiah – Jesus describes his relationship to Jerusalem in this way. In contrast to tyrants and foxes, Jesus offers the image of a mother hen, gathering her chicks under her wings and nurturing them to become the people of God. This mother hen is willing to put herself between the fox and her brood. She is vulnerable to violence but willing to risk her own body to save her chicks.

Being a chicken

In a world of crafty foxes and treacherous rulers, a brooding mother hen is a wonderful picture. Who would have thought that a chicken could be an image of courage and love? It is not easy to be a chicken. Chickens are often targets for the strong and manipulative, as we've seen with King Herod and John the Baptist.

While Jesus was able to avoid the fox that was Herod, a greater predator awaited him in Jerusalem. Jesus knew that his journey would culminate in his death. And yet, like the mother hen, he used his love and his own body to protect the ones he loves.

Thankfully, we know that the hen's sacrifice was not the end of the story. Her love remains, and we are here today as a witness to the power of that mothering, brooding, sacrificial love. With a mother hen like Jesus, we do not need to fear the foxes of this world. We do not need to fear death.

Mark Nam

Hymn suggestions

Great is thy faithfulness; And can it be; Meekness and majesty; Hide Me Now (Reuben Morgan).

Second Sunday of Lent   16 March
Second Service   **Because He's Worth It**
Ps. 135 [*or* 135.1–14]; Jer. 22.1–9, 13–17; **Luke 14.27–33**

Jesus is rarely alone in the Gospels and, when he is, it is clear that he needs some quiet time. He needs time to pray and to replenish. In the Gospel passage today, the crowds feel relentless. One wonders if Jesus talks about the cost of discipleship to thin out the crowd and give some people pause for thought. What Jesus says is rather abrasive. It is almost as if we have to choose between him and our earthly family and friends, and that feels a bit much, frankly. There seems to be a stark reality facing us, namely that our walk with Jesus will cost us. Jesus is preparing us for that, and Jesus is saying that he's worth it.

God, the cross and us

The foresight Jesus shares with those who were following him around centres on a cross that is unnamed but plural by definition. One person's cross may be another's minor irritation. For Jesus to identify a cross that needs to be carried not only foreshadows his own suffering and dying but also paints a picture of the one who will physically help Jesus with his own load, Simon of Cyrene. To have at once a human portrayal of cross-bearing in Simon and the Son of God's own journey of suffering in Jesus underlines the fact that we have a God who understands the weight of all that we can bear in this life, and who is not absent from our grief, pain and loss. We believe that Jesus took on our suffering in an act of selfless giving, affirming God's love for humanity. God in Jesus was saying that we were worth it. We are worth it. Something in us as a human race was worth that level of sacrifice. The Christian faith is characterized by cross-bearing, and we have to believe, too, that Jesus is worth it.

Preparing for the long haul

The tower would have been a familiar landmark in the landscape of the bigger towns and cities of the first century. It signalled sturdiness and watchfulness and, as a structure, had to be able to hold the weight of at least one individual. To build a good tower meant giving the time and resources worthy of the enterprise. It was a construction that was not something that should collapse. The analogy here is not so much that we need to be as immutable as a tower, but rather perhaps that the care and attention it takes to build it must also be applied to the Christian walk. We are in it, or at least are meant to be, for the long haul. The considerations of what would be needed for its construction and maintenance could also be applied to the thoughts about following Jesus. To follow was not simply an empty act for show because of Jesus' charisma, popularity and the attractiveness of 'group think'. More was needed to stay the course. More was needed to last beyond the initial allure.

A new way of living

Preparedness echoes, too, in the example of the king getting ready for war. This would have been another familiar story for Jesus' listeners, who would have known of the great kings of the Hebrew Scriptures. It is not Jesus advocating war, but rather underlining the challenge of giving ourselves entirely and wholly to a new belief system and a new way of seeing the world. This is a new way of living. The followers of Jesus would have been coming with their own fixed ideas of what 'winning' was and what being successful in their society looked like. They would have had firm ideas about who was at the top of their society, who was at the bottom, and who should be on the margins. As the king relies on his possessions to win the war, there is a subtle question here about what we depend on. The call to give up all our possessions strikes a chord because it feels utterly outrageous in our material-obsessed world, but Jesus says that he is worth it. As New Testament scholar Eric Franklin writes: 'Discipleship may be a response to grace, as Luke's story emphasizes, but it makes demands which mean that it should not be entered upon lightly.'[19] This is serious stuff. The call to discipleship is not an easy one but God is saying that we are worthy of that call, and of God's love. We may not feel worthy of God's love, yet we are reminded that in the abandonment of our possessions, we will have something else to depend on. We will have Jesus and, through him, God. We are reminded that this is expansive, nurturing and restorative love, which is outside of our possessions, beyond what we have bought and what we own, and greater than any battle we could ever face.

Mariama Ifode-Blease

Hymn suggestions

When I survey the wondrous cross; The old rugged cross; He will carry me (Mark Schultz); This is our God (Phil Wickham).

Third Sunday of Lent 23 March
Principal Service **Repentance and Salvation**
Isa. 55.1–9; Ps. 63.1–9; 1 Cor. 10.1–13; **Luke 13.1–9**

In every sector of society, there are words and expressions, sometimes considered buzzwords, which circulate in every generation. Here are some I've come across. In business: synergy, dynamic, innovative. In education: differentiated learning, best practice, growth mindset. In ministry: creativity, wholeness, visionary. In my years of ministry, rarely have I heard people speak on repentance. But Jesus often spoke of our need to repent, to turn away from anything which dishonours and causes a disconnect in our relationship with God.

Cost of the cross

A few weeks ago, we journeyed with Jesus to the Mount of Transfiguration, where Moses and Elijah talked with Jesus about all he would accomplish in Jerusalem (Luke 9.31). In this conversation, they discussed Jesus' death, resurrection and ascension. From this incredible encounter, Jesus was on a journey towards suffering, rejection and death. Jesus and the disciples were going to experience their own struggles. Jesus and the disciples – like us – had to confront the cross because it is only here that resurrection becomes possible. In Luke's passage, Jesus reminds us that in preparing for the cross, a day of reckoning is at hand. His disciples, and us today, are called to 'repent' so that we may receive the salvation of God which Jesus offers. To enter into the grace, peace and presence of God, we need to seek and thirst for God, we need to praise God with 'joyful lips' and meditate on him (Ps. 63). The good news is that God invites us to accept the salvation of Jesus and enter into an 'everlasting covenant' (Isa. 55.3).

Turn towards Jesus

Repentance is a call to turn *towards* Jesus. Isaiah states, 'Let them turn to the LORD, that he may have mercy on them, and to our God, for he will abundantly pardon' (Isa. 55.7). Repentance is about surrendering to God's grace. Repentance is a response to all Jesus did for us on the cross.

We all find ourselves tempted in different ways and we all have our wilderness moments or seasons, yet we know that 'God is faithful, and he will not let you be tested beyond your strength, but with the testing he will also provide the way out so that you may be able to endure it' (1 Cor. 10.13). Do we trust God who is always on our side? Do we believe God is constantly seeking us in love?

Repentance and reconciliation

As we seek to serve God in our communities, in a broken and dysfunctional world, the time for repentance and reconciliation is now. Jesus never denies that sin leads to judgement and death, but he does encourage us to see the graciousness of God. Repentance is about changing our lives to reflect God's will. It is this decision, to repent and follow Jesus, which will produce fruit for the kingdom. For this reason, it's important that when we share the gospel with others we speak about sin and our need for repentance. Jesus came to save sinners. In our knowledge of who God is in our lives, and all he has done for us, we are given the opportunity to touch other lives so that they too know the Divine whose ways are higher than our ways (Isa. 55.9).

Catherine Okoronkwo

Hymn suggestions

My chains are gone (Chris Tomlin); Amazing grace; Be still, for the presence of the Lord; Who breaks the power of sin and darkness (Phil Wickham).

Third Sunday of Lent   23 March
Second Service   **God the Still-point in All Our Dreaming**
Ps. 12, 13; **Gen. 28.10–19a**; John 1.35–end

Today's story of Jacob and his dream of a ladder is like an overheard scrap of gossip about family life. Not only do we start listening part way through, but for some reason the reading as the lectionary gives it to us stops halfway through a sentence. But Genesis itself is a 50-chapter-long story of a family, of births, deaths, love, sibling rivalries, tragic events, miracles, homes and journeys. More than anything, it's a tale of how individual people develop and hold on to a sense of themselves, their identity and values while staying close to their family and friends. It's the human version of the first couple of chapters of the book where the created world develops out of the formless void.

The family story

Like many family stories over time, the main characters get typecast and get a personal brand. Jacob is no exception. He's seen as a clever con-artist, always on the take and forever wrestling with the people around him and himself, until he comes good. At this point in his story, he's on the run because he's just pulled off a massive con, lying and disguising himself to steal his dying father's blessing from his brother. His brother is furious. It will take many years for Jacob to face the realities and consequences of being this sort of person, to own the harm he has done and try to offer repair. Many years and another dream of angels until he feels at peace enough with himself to take on a new name and way of life. Many years until, on his deathbed, he can unknot the effects of that moment where he stole the single blessing that was on offer. As he dies, he liberally blesses all his sons and so the story develops from being about a family to being about tribes.

Jacob's dream

Back to Jacob in his young adult scammer phase. Here he is, settling down to try to get some sleep in some random place in the open air, knowing his brother is really, really angry with him, knowing his father is close to death and knowing he probably won't see his mother again for a long time. With all that emotional churning going on I'm not surprised that he has a vivid dream that stays with him. It's a dream with lots of activity, lots of characters endlessly moving, perhaps picking up his anxiety about getting away really quickly. It's also a dream about things going up and down, perhaps picking up those family patterns and power dynamics he is running from. After all, his life thus far has been a tale of trying to outwit his brother, the favourite, and become the person in the family in the ascendency with power and control. But notice: God is standing still. There's some debate over the translation of the text, whether God is standing beside Jacob or standing above the ladder; whichever is right, God is standing still.

God the still-point

In all his scamming and running, God comes to Jacob as his still-point, his lodestar, his way marker, his moral compass. God comes to Jacob as that thing, a feeling as well as a knowing, deep within, which provides a point of stability and rootedness, a sense of what is right and what is wrong, a sense of identity and confidence in who you are, where you have come from and how to make decisions about the future. God is standing still and calling Jacob back to remember who he is and where he has come from. 'And the LORD stood beside him and said, "I am the LORD, the God of Abraham your father and the God of Isaac."' And then God reminds him of the promises, the future his family has believed in. It is no surprise then, as Jacob wakes up, that he takes a stone, a rock, a static unmoving thing of solidity and permanence, and the very stone his head, his thoughts, have been resting on, and sets it up as a symbol of his dream. He's not ready yet to live out of this space, but he's ready to acknowledge it before moving on.

There are often times in life when because of something we have done, or something that has happened to us, we run away, perhaps physically make a run for it, or metaphorically. Sometimes it's transformational, we leave nasty stuff behind and become happier and healthier. Sometimes not so much, because we have forgotten we have taken ourselves with us, or forgotten to check where we are running to, or forgotten something else. That's not really the point. The point is that in our running God is our still-point, calling us to an inner place of certainty in who we are and what our values are. When everything around us is moving, when the power dynamics of life around us are forever going up and down, God is our still-point. When we pause for breath, we catch a glimpse of the alternative reality that creates. And God remains that still, patient constant until we are ready to wrestle ourselves into freedom.

Esther Elliott

Hymn suggestions

O God of Bethel, by whose hand; Be still, my soul; Great is your faithfulness; O God, you search me and you know me.

Fourth Sunday of Lent 30 March

(For Mothering Sunday, see p. 98.)
Principal Service **The Truth We Find**
Josh. 5.9–12; Ps. 32; **2 Cor. 5.16–end**; Luke 15.1–3, 11b–end

It would seem entirely appropriate to talk about reconciliation in this period of Lent, at this time of wilderness wandering. We are, after all, meant to be engaged in a period of self-scrutiny that leaves us less smug as Christians and humbler. Sometimes, however, that level of self-examination can be hard to take, not because we cannot bear the truth but rather because we are asked to do something about the truth we find.

Open minds and stretched hearts

In his Second Letter to the Corinthians, Paul is talking about a transformed reality. Because of Jesus' death and resurrection, we can start afresh and have a new perspective. This new world view extends from Jesus Christ to one another. We can see that 'there is a new creation … see everything has become new!' This is a tall ask. Are we meant to just grin and bear it when someone cuts through the queue at the supermarket or pushes past us on public transport? Are we simply to ignore some sarcastic comment or veiled attack on social media? What is clear is that more is being demanded of us than we sometimes can give. We are being called to see others also as being part of this new creation. We are being called to open our minds and stretch our hearts because the truth we will find is that Jesus is in others as much as he is in us, even if we have to work rather hard to see this sometimes. And this seeing brings us closer to a greater understanding, to generosity and to reconciliation.

Being the door, not the doormat

It is important to remember that the call to reconciliation is not simplified by seeing more of ourselves and more of others. Rather, it is made all the more complicated because of what we see and how we are then asked to process and deal with this. The truth we find and that Paul highlights is that to engage with reconciliation at any level, we need to take issues, people, causes, concerns and our strongest emotions back to Jesus. Jesus is the mitigating factor, and it is Jesus who can help us respond when we start counting the trespassing against us. We are not asked to be doormats, but instead to be the door to the possibility of transformation of our negative and worst experiences through the grace and love of God as offered by Jesus Christ.

The truth we find is that God wants to be our divine Creator and to be closer as people of God for a greater purpose. As scholar Lois Malcolm reminds us,

> All this comes from God, who has reconciled us to Godself and has not given us a special status to lord it over others – or to be immune from life's suffering – but a ministry or a service (diakonia) of reconciliation. And this diakonia is grounded in the fact in Christ God was reconciling the entire cosmos to Godself – not judging them and calculating their trespasses against them – and entrusting us also with a message or a word (logos) of reconciliation for everyone (2 Corinthians 5.18–19).[20]

An ambassador's reception

I wonder if you remember that famous advert for chocolate which was always framed around an ambassador's reception. The premise was that the chocolates were so good that they were used for occasions such as these. The ambassador is presented as someone of exceedingly good taste. As on earth, so it is in heaven. The truth we find in this passage is that God has chosen us as God's representatives on earth to transmit some of the excellence of the love of God. God's love has no equal. It is exquisite, it is a daily treat, it is simply divine. As such we have an inherited closeness to God from the gift of Jesus' death and resurrection. Our job is to maintain that closeness through the ups and downs of life, and through the episodes even when we feel distant. Through the good times and bad we have to keep coming back to God to see the truth of who we are. Ultimately, we are reminded that the truth we find is that God's love is not just for us, but for all.

Mariama Ifode-Blease

Hymn suggestions

Love divine, all loves excelling; Amazing grace; I love you, Lord (Goodness of God); I am guilty (Lauren Diagle).

Fourth Sunday of Lent 30 March
Second Service **Where is God?**
Ps. 30; Prayer of Manasseh, *or* **Isa. 40.27—41.13**; 2 Tim. 4.1–18; *Gospel at Holy Communion*: John 11.17–44

The question everyone asks

Where is God? Where is God in the mess of the world we live in? Where is God when our lives go wrong? Where is God amid deep evil? The question is one that people of faith – and none – have asked for centuries. How do we keep faith when everything around us seems to say that God is indifferent at best and absent at worst? How do we keep faith in a God of love, when what we see tells a different story?

Very few people of faith get through life without asking this at some point. You certainly can't read the Bible, or the writings of great Christian writers, without coming across the question. If we look at the world and our lives honestly, we just *have* to ask.

The task of faith is precisely this discernment of where God is. It is good and healthy to ask the question because our vocation as people of God is to wrestle, like Jacob, with the reality of God, ourselves and the world. It is our vocation to learn to see God when God's presence is hidden, or surprising, or unexpected.

Israel in exile: wrestling with God's absence

The question is central to one of the great books of Scripture, the book of the prophet Isaiah. The book chronicles the wrestling of Israel and its prophets with a sinful world, where disastrous political decisions have catastrophic consequences and Israel is taken into exile.

Israel's faith was based on a promise, a promise linked to place, to land, to a city, to a people and a nation. Exile seems to negate the promise. Exile takes away everything that Israel thought was theirs before God – and some more. The stunningly beautiful language of Isaiah, in the passage we read, highlights the tension between faith in Almighty God, who created the stars, and the reality of exile. The people of Israel cry out in the words, 'My way is hidden from the LORD, and my right is disregarded by my God.' It is a question heavy with doubt and pain, with fear of abandonment, and doubts that justice will ever come.

The question is typical of lament, the language of the people of God when life collapses and shadows lengthen. It is a question of deep crisis, and it waits for God's answer. The people had been waiting a long time, and so the conclusion that God had abandoned them was logical and warranted.

God's underlying presence

And yet. And yet, the question is only a launch pad for the glorious response that restates the love and care of YHWH for his people. Throughout chapter 40, Isaiah reaffirms God's power and care for the world as Creator, but creation is not a one-time event. It is God's continual work in giving and sustaining life to creatures who have no intrinsic power of their own.

Isaiah then uses beautiful metaphors of the natural world to reassure the people that even though they feel that they have come to the end of their strength, God, the Creator of all things, will renew them and care for them, and they will 'soar like eagles', and their strength will be renewed.

The statement is therefore both pastoral and political. It is pastoral in reassuring the exiles that they are not alone and that energy and power are available to them. And it is political, as an invitation for Jews in exile to live their lives according to God's direction, which opens up a life of new possibilities. The people are invited to look beyond what they can see, and live according to a different rule, in a different reality.

Thinking outside the box

It is always a challenge to imagine our life beyond the systems in which we live it out, to perceive that what we see on the surface is not the whole story and that God is at work and more powerful than the forces that crush and maim around us. Isaiah is inviting the people of God to be bold and reimagine or reconstruct life in terms of God's promise, rather than Babylon's actions. The vocation of the people of God is always to live a life that may not make sense, because it is lived in ways that contradict the claims of systems and empires around us, in ways that challenge stories that are told about the power of humanity and the absence of God. The people of God are called to proclaim the presence of God, and the fact that this presence may not be overpowering in the ways that worldly powers expect, but instead that God comes in stealth, in unexpected places, and in unexpected ways, in a crib and on a cross. The power of God is ultimately the power that reveals the powerlessness of the ways in which a broken world is structured, and unmasks the possibility of something new.

Isabelle Hamley

Hymn suggestions

O God, our help in ages past; Be still, my soul; Strength will rise as we wait upon the Lord; Lord, you hear the cry (Lord have mercy).

Mothering Sunday   30 March
Here is Your Mother
Ex. 2.1–10, *or* 1 Sam. 1.20–end; Ps. 34.11–20, *or* Ps. 127.1–4; 2 Cor. 1.3–7, *or* Col. 3.12–17; Luke 2.33–35, *or* **John 19.25b–27**

Here we are on the Fourth Sunday of Lent. Once called 'Mid-Lenting' in some traditions it's also called 'Laetare' from the Latin for 'Rejoice'. It's the root of the word 'laughter'. We've reached the point where we take a little break from our Lenten fasting and draw breath before we rush into Passiontide, Palm Sunday, Holy Week and Easter.

It is also, of course, Mothering Sunday. In medieval times folk gave thanks for their 'mother church' on this day – sometimes their parish, sometimes their cathedral. From the seventeenth century onwards, it became a Sunday when young people in service went home for the day to visit their families.

From the 1920s onwards, Mother's Day in America and Mothering Sunday in the UK began to be developed and promoted as a day on which to give thanks for mothers. This was especially important following the First World War when so many lost children to warfare and disease. So, it's a rich day, with much more to it than buying a card for your mum (though that's important too!)

Hebrew mothering

Mothering is a gift we can all experience and exercise whoever we are. The act of mothering can be done by any of us to anyone of any age. We can 'mother' as individuals and as communities. The readings set for today contain good examples of mothering and help us to focus on three qualities: care, courage and compassion.

In the book of Exodus Pharaoh carries out ethnic cleansing. All Hebrew baby boys are to be drowned in the Nile. But one Levite mother takes tremendous care to conceal her baby boy for three months. She then takes the enormous risk of placing him in a water-proof basket in the crocodile-infested Nile and trusting his future to God. Desperate times demand desperate measures and tremendous courage. Pharaoh's daughter, finding the baby, is moved by his crying and identifies him as a Hebrew. In her compassion, she takes an enormous risk to save the baby. The baby's sister is watching out for him – caring what happens – and in a stroke of courageous genius, intervenes to suggest that her mother might help to raise the baby. So, Moses is raised by his mother, under royal patronage, ensuring that he is absolutely safe. Not only that, his mother gets paid for raising him. All three women are exercising amazing mothering in this story, showing care, courage and compassion. But did you notice? God is also mothering, weaving an imaginative, brilliant and compassionate rescue that will lead eventually to the liberation of the Israelites.

Christian mothering

Jump forward hundreds of years to the crucifixion. In our Gospel reading Jesus is on the cross, looking down on his mother Mary and the beloved disciple who is not named here but traditionally acknowledged to be John. Care, courage and compassion feature heavily in this story too. All three show extraordinary courage in the face of this horrific episode of torture and slow execution.

From the cross, Jesus creates a new family. Mary and John are brought together as parent and child to care for one another in the years ahead, bridging the gap left by a son and a friend. Jesus shows the possibilities for a new future beyond this terrible event. It takes immense courage to watch someone you love suffer and die. It takes immense courage to die as an innocent on behalf of the world, and in that moment to have sufficient care and compassion to look out for those you leave behind. These biblical examples of 'mothering' are perhaps beyond the scope of most of us. But the mothering qualities of care, courage and compassion that make such a difference in peoples' lives take place every day in communities all over the world. They take place in this community too.

Our mothering

So, how's your mothering going? Where are you showing those qualities of care, courage and compassion? How might we do more of this as a Christian community? Caring for those in need in our parish and beyond, having the courage to call out injustice and making ourselves unpopular for the sake of those whose voices go unheard, walking alongside the suffering and broken, with compassion to bring consolation and hope for the future. Economically, environmentally and politically it all seems bleak at the moment. But so it was for the Israelites and those first followers of Jesus. Let's not allow our feelings of powerlessness to hinder our capacity to exercise care, courage and compassion.

On this mid-Lent Mothering Sunday pause and give thanks for those who have mothered you down the years, and pray that the Lord may fill you with the gifts of care, courage and compassion as you seek to follow Jesus Christ faithfully in the power of the Holy Spirit.

Catherine Williams

Hymn suggestions

For Mary, mother of our Lord; For the beauty of the earth; Let us build a house; God, you hold me like a mother.

Fifth Sunday of Lent (Passiontide) 6 April
Principal Service **Out of Control?**
Isa. 43.16–21; Ps. 126; Phil. 3.4b–14; **John 12.1–8**

We all have weaknesses and flaws. Here's one of mine: I like to feel I am in control. I want to be in charge of my diary and responsibilities despite having a PA. I like to know what time a meeting is so that I can plan how long it will take to get there (often meaning I turn up half an hour early). I prefer to be in the chair in a meeting because I can then set the pace. All of these things can be good in their proper place. However, my longing to be in control is often exposed by the realities of life. In my experience, being alive in a world like ours means that at the moment you feel in control something comes along to throw you off course. Needing to be in control can be self-defeating.

Passionately out of control

On this Passion Sunday, we are invited to turn our gaze towards Holy Week and the Passion of Jesus Christ. The Gospel reading set for today draws us intimately into the events on the cusp of that world-defining and world-changing week. It also challenges us to reflect on how we respond to situations over which we have no control.

When I read about Jesus, Mary of Bethany and Judas on that evening in Lazarus' home, a week before Good Friday, my heart quickens with a kind of anxiety. I have this sense that I'm caught up in events beyond any of our control. If I were witnessing scenes from a play, I would be tempted to shout 'stop', for this is the moment which foreshadows the painful events to come and signals their inevitability. What we see in Lazarus, Martha and Mary's home is the beat before the action unfolds. We cannot control the action or stop it. All we can do, at this point, is seek to become participants in the drama of salvation.

Out of control and responding well

Passion is an evocative word. It has connotations of love and desire, as well as of being out of control and of passivity. Passion means to 'undergo' and has implications of pain and suffering. A passionate person can, then, be someone undergoing a strong emotion – something they cannot quite control, like the first flush of love – but also can mean they are caught up in events and situations they do not control.

I think this way of understanding passion and Passiontide helps us go deeper into today's Gospel. First, consider the contrasting behaviour of Mary and Judas. Mary's actions reveal her profound, albeit mostly unconscious grasp of the situation facing Jesus. Her offering of a perfume suitable for anointing the dead indicates her recognition that Jesus is about to walk a painful, death-filled path. She offers all she has as she seeks to be in solidarity with Jesus and embrace the costly path Jesus will lead his followers on. At the centre of the action, Jesus recognizes her gesture as an offering of love. Mary bathes Jesus' feet, prefiguring his foot-washing of his disciples' feet on Maundy Thursday.

Judas, in contrast, responds to the drama of passion unfolding around Jesus with merely economic and self-centred considerations. He is irritated. He says that this expensive perfume might better have been sold to help the poor. Perhaps, initially, we have some sympathy: is he not reminding us of a greater justice? We learn, of course, that what Judas says is all talk. In reality, he is concerned with the impact on the community purse which he controls. Jesus rebukes him, saying, 'You always have the poor with you, but you do not always have me.' Judas' grip on God's unfolding work of salvation is flimsy in comparison to Mary's.

Let go of control

As I read this passage, then, I sense that Jesus is at the still turning point of the world. He is in the eye of the storm – perhaps is the eye of the storm – and undergoes the loving offering of Mary with grace. Soon enough he will be handed over to those who will torture and kill him. He will lose agency and control. For now, he receives the passionate offering of Mary as a token of her commitment to God; he rebukes Judas' inattention to what really matters.

How will we respond to God? Passiontide invites us to become fuller and more faithful participants in the loving and saving work of God. It beckons us towards the model of Jesus himself. We are not called to maintain iron control over events or our lives. Rather, we are invited to respond to the redeeming work of God with trust and passion. We are called to offer all we have, trusting that God's abundance – even as it faces the bleakness and ugliness of human violence – will exceed our wildest imaginings.

Rachel Mann

Hymn suggestions

My song is love unknown; There is a green hill far away; All my hope on God is founded; Hail, thou once despised Jesus.

Fifth Sunday of Lent (Passiontide)   6 April
Second Service   **Lay Down Your Ark**
Ps. 35 [*or* 35.1–9]; **2 Chron. 35.1–6, 10–16**; Luke 22.1–13

'You need no longer carry it on your shoulders.' For those without a home, for those struggling to find a place in the world, for those in conflict, these words might feel like an unimaginable dream. Whatever we're carrying – and we're all carrying something – this,

'You need no longer carry it', is a liberative message. Some people can worship even while carrying heavy loads. Indeed, those with the biggest weights often have the most powerful songs of praise. For others, the idea of worshipping while that weight sits there, unyielding, choking and bruising, can be unbearable. Whichever of these describes us, I'm sure we would all want to lay our burdens down for a while.

Carrying the presence of God

The Ark mentioned in our passage contained the presence of God. For years, it went on the move with the people whether they were in conflict or peace. It then landed in the Temple, the focal point of worship for the community of God. Josiah led a people that had been through great troubles going back generations, and under recent monarchs things had been going badly. They were a community in need of renewal. Josiah wanted to put the house back in order. The Ark had probably been taken out of the Temple to protect it while the Temple was given a clear-out. All the false gods had been removed so that worshipping life could be re-established. The Ark being returned symbolically meant that God was coming back to be at the centre of the community.

The instruction to put the Ark down would have been a word of life as though God was saying, 'I'm going to dwell again with you; lay down your burden; lay down your Ark; you no longer need to carry it on your shoulders.' Some of us might need to dwell in the presence of God today. We've been working hard, maybe with a lot of good stuff, maybe with the presence of God on our shoulders. However, it's time to lay the Ark down, to bring our heavy load into the presence of God, even as that load contains the presence of God. It's almost as if we've been on a long hike carrying a sumptuous lunch that we prepared earlier on our backs. It's been with us, but we haven't been able to open it up and enjoy the flavours. Then we stop in a quiet spot, next to a gentle stream and open up the backpack. Maybe today, here in this place, we can lay our burdens down and open up the presence of God.

Take it easy

The idea of being with God for a while with our burdens off our shoulders has great appeal. But it takes time to get used to the presence of God, particularly when we've been carrying so much for so long. It's a good thing that there's no hurry. God isn't going anywhere. There's a kind of message that implies that we need to come to God quickly before the opportunity disappears: 'Turn to God before it's too late', 'Commit your life to God now', and that kind of thing. But that's a false message. God's invitation, God's presence, is not going anywhere. God is patient. Are you ready for the presence of God? Yes? Great, the door is open. Enter in and breathe. No? That's OK. Tomorrow is fine, or the next day.

Notice each other

In a wholly different moment, Jesus, Josiah's namesake, says, 'Bear one other's burdens.' It seems that people are still carrying things. And it seems as if we have a role to play in sharing the load. And this too links somehow to the presence of God. As we bear each other's burdens, we carry with us the presence of God, not in an Ark but in our connections, our friendships and our presence with each other. But we needn't think that we have to bear the weight alone. The presence of God is with us, ready and willing to take our burdens off our shoulders, even if they're the burdens of others.

As we go out into the world and offer a word of peace, a smile, or an act of justice, we acclimatize each other to the presence of God. The presence of God is no longer confined to an Ark. It is everywhere that we put our feet. We will meet it in those we encounter, wherever that happens to be. And the presence of God is rest, joy, comfort and peace. It is where we can lay our burdens down. It is the place where we can say, 'You need no longer carry it on your shoulders.'

Mark Amos

Hymn suggestions

Be still, for the presence of the Lord; Down by the riverside; Peace doubting heart, my God's I am; The Lord is my shepherd.

Holy Week

Palm Sunday   13 April
(For Palm Sunday All-Age, see p. 356.)
Principal Service   **Looking On from a Distance**
Liturgy of the Palms: **Luke 19.28–40**; Ps. 118.1–2, 19–end [*or* 118.19–end]; *Liturgy of the Passion*: Isa. 50.4–9a; Ps. 31.9–16 [*or* 31.9–18]; Phil. 2.5–11; Luke 22.14—end of 23, *or* **Luke 23.1–49**

Public executions were common enough, but this one was somehow different. There were three men to be crucified: two well-known criminals and Jesus. He was not a criminal – not a thief, nor a murderer. In fact, Pontius Pilate, the Roman governor, could find no grounds on which to accuse him. Those of us who travelled with Jesus knew he was guilty of no wrong, unless you claim that loving without measure is a punishable offence.

The journey towards Jerusalem

Jesus knew his opponents were out to silence him and he had told us that he would 'undergo great suffering and be rejected by the elders, chief priests, scribes, and be killed and on the third day be raised'. We were alarmed at such talk, especially when he said that he would be 'betrayed into human hands'. Yet, in spite of our warnings, he 'set his face to go to Jerusalem'.

Jesus entered the city, riding on the back of a colt, and he was welcomed by people who spread their cloaks on the ground. Those of us who were disciples joined with other followers, saying, 'Blessed is the king who comes in the name of the Lord!' It felt like a victory parade, and we imagined that, at last, the kingdom of God would be established on earth. Some of us even hoped that, with Jesus in charge, we might have a special place alongside him.

On entering Jerusalem, I was shocked when Jesus began to weep. To my shame, while I had been thinking about the possibility of status, influence and power, Jesus was grieving over people who refused to recognize the things that make for peace. This deep lament of love was for those who had rejected him, and he knew they would soon be baying for his death.

The arrest and trial

The authorities were looking for a way to silence Jesus. One evening, after we shared a meal together, he warned us that one of us – one of his very own – was going to betray him. We could not imagine such treachery, but later Judas appeared with the Temple authorities to secure Jesus' arrest. First before the high priest, and then before Pilate, Jesus was accused of blasphemy, then of sedition. Realizing he was a Galilean, Pilate even sent Jesus to be questioned by Herod, but neither of them could find a valid charge against him. The hostile crowd, however, was adamant that he should be executed, and shouted, 'Crucify him, crucify him.' To satisfy them, Pilate released Barabbas (someone convicted of insurrection and murder), and Jesus was handed over to be crucified.

The execution

His tormentors heaped insults on him, beat him, and took him to a place called Golgotha (literally, The Skull). There, the crowd jeered and mocked saying, 'If you are the King of the Jews, save yourself!' In the midst of their taunts, Jesus prayed, 'Father, forgive them; for they do not know what they are doing.' Among the jeers, the sound of women weeping was heard. They may have heard Jesus in the Temple or were professional mourners showing their pity in the face of death. Jesus told them not to weep for him but for themselves and their children. Amazingly, even as he faced death, his great sorrow was for those who seemed unable to recognize God's coming among them.

From noon until about three in the afternoon, darkness descended. As we looked on from a distance, we heard Jesus cry out, 'Father, into your hands I commend my spirit,' and he died. For a moment, the crowd was silenced. Perhaps they could not believe that in the midst of such suffering, he could pray so confidently to God. Then, in an extraordinary outburst, a Roman centurion praised God and proclaimed Jesus' innocence. Other spectators to the execution returned home beating their breasts. Was this a sign of penitence? Had they realized that by his suffering and death, the one whom they had rejected had opened a way into the future for us all?

The cross: a symbol of love

To those of us who were followers of Jesus, the grief over the loss of our teacher and friend was almost too much to bear. Yet, strangely, in the forsakenness of the cross and the darkness of death, our eyes were opened to God's vulnerable, suffering love. It is difficult to explain, but even as we stood and looked on from a distance that day, we knew that God held in love every person in the world. In this divine embrace, the cross which had been intended as an instrument of death was transformed into a symbol of God's limitless love.

Karen E. Smith

Hymn suggestions

Were you there when they crucified my Lord; From heaven you came (The Servant King); How deep the Father's love for us; And can it be?

Palm Sunday 13 April
Second Service **Speaking Truth to Power**
Ps. 69.1–20; **Isa. 5.1–7**; Luke 20.9–19

This is the beginning of the holiest week in the Christian calendar: Holy Week. Over the coming days we shall hear again the story of God's great love for us, demonstrated in Jesus' sacrifice on the cross and his being raised from the dead. It is a story of great drama, which reveals how destructive humanity can be. The murder of love.

Preaching

There is an art to preaching. Many books have been written about it. I wonder what makes a good sermon. Story is often an element, as is humour; and depth, wisdom and spirituality play a role. But there is also something prophetic in preaching – of telling truths that are hard to hear. But how to tell those truths? I have met many a person scarred by preaching, where they felt harangued for not being a good person. Such preaching rarely seems to bear much fruit. Yet, there are times when hard things need saying. The world is clearly not as it should be, and sin is ever present.

A love story

I would suggest that today's reading from Isaiah is an extraordinary example of effective preaching. It is set up as a love song, sung to his beloved who is God. It was probably sung at a feast, where you could imagine those present have been partaking of that which comes from a vineyard. I think that's worth pondering. Those crowded moments, when everyone is on a roll at a celebration, and one of the crowd gets up to sing. My imagination suggests that rapturous applause or shouting follows, as he tells his story. The story is about a vineyard, and so the context is one that the hearers know well. It is well looked after, on a fertile hill, guarded by hedge and wall and containing 'choice vines', but it yields 'wild grapes'. What is the owner to do? You can again imagine suggestions from those gathered, and the shouts of adulation as judgement is being passed on this vineyard, until that final crushing conclusion in verse 7. For this story, this love song, is not about some unknown group of people, it is about the very people who are listening. The land of Israel, the people of Judah.

Drama

Once you understand the context, this is an incredible bit of drama. Those present are lured into a false sense of security: a fun story, about a context they know all too well, and they are invited to pass judgement on a situation that turns out to be a judgement on them. I bet the person who told the story disappeared pretty quickly afterwards! But it is clever rhetoric. It takes people to a seemingly safe place and then twists the story around to reveal some hard truths they wouldn't otherwise be able to hear. Nathan does much the same with King David in 2 Samuel 12.1–14.

Holy Week

It is perhaps not surprising then that when Jesus tells a story about a vineyard in today's Gospel reading, a story that has obvious echoes of Isaiah's story, people are shocked by it (Luke 20.16). This coming week after all tells a very similar story to Isaiah's story. It is a story that is all about love and generosity. It is also a story about how human beings destroy that which is given to them: where the destructive nature of humanity becomes all too clear.

Be changed

Things that happen when we are under the influence of alcohol can feel different from when we're sober. I am guessing that a lot of wine was consumed at the Passover feast Jesus shared with his disciples on Maundy Thursday, which might explain why the disciples fell asleep in the Garden of Gethsemane. As Jesus is arrested, as the night's horror unfolds, and as his disciples sober up, the dark reality of what is happening must have become very real. Isaiah in his love song today has a similar effect, and as his hearers sobered up and reflected on the song that they had heard, the hope would be that they are changed and transformed, to reflect on their responsibility and their stewardship of what has been given to them. Effective preaching, it seems to me, should always invite a response. It needs to shake us out of complacency, to help us reflect on who we are and what we do with what God has given us. But there is a subtle art to that, and Isaiah today gives us a wonderful example of how to do it.

Jonathan Lawson

Hymn suggestions

Christ is our cornerstone; My song is love unknown; Judge eternal, throned in splendour; Christ is made the sure foundation.

First Three Days of Holy Week   14–16 April
Carrying the Cross

(These are the readings for Wednesday of Holy Week but the sermon may be adapted for use on any day since the first three Servant Songs are read on Monday, Tuesday and Wednesday.)

Isa. 50.4–9a; Ps. 70; Heb. 12.1–3; John 13.21–32

The Servant Songs

In his first 39 chapters, Isaiah builds up the expectation that God will fulfil his promise of restoration, and salvation, to his people. In chapters 40–55, he introduces 'the Servant of the LORD', through whom God will accomplish all this. He includes four poetic passages, known as the Servant Songs, which describe this person. We've just heard the third of these.

Justice

The first song, Isaiah 42.1–9, tells of the servant as the ideal Israelite who lives as God intends, and who brings justice to Israel and the nations, the Gentiles – to the whole world.

In a world where, still today, so many of us find we put our faith in money, status, property, connections, prospects, and so many other idols, how timely is it to be reminded of where, and in whom, our faith should be. The servant, says this first song, will be a person of justice, compassion, faithfulness and stamina for God's kingdom. There's a Holy Week calling for us all!

Herald

The second song, Isaiah 49.1–7, tells of the servant as messenger, herald and prophet of God's voice; characteristics emphasized with images of a mouth like a sharp-edged sword and a polished arrow, cutting to the heart of the matter.

Isaiah tells us how God had plans for him from way before he was born, how God had been preparing the servant's ministry from the beginning, before time itself. Even though at times it would seem that the servant's ministry was useless or unsuccessful, God's will would be unfolding, God's mission advancing – and not just for Israel. That would be 'too light a thing'. No, the calling of the servant is for the whole world, to be a light to the nations, so that salvation may reach to the ends of the earth. I wonder whether our increasingly nationalistic world hears that call.

Obedience

And then in Isaiah 50.4–9, we hear the third of the songs, which speaks about the obedience of the servant, which contrasts with Israel's disobedience (dissected in chapters 1–12). In contrast to the way God's people have lived, the servant's tongue will be guided by God, his ears be open to God, his will submitted to God, and his hope be in God.

This obedience to God will come up against the vested interests of the world and of people, of course. It will lead to rejection, violence and suffering. But throughout, the servant will remain faithful and true to God, and so will ultimately be vindicated.

Vindication

And then the fourth of the songs, in Isaiah 52.13—53.12, tells of both the ordeals and the vindication of the servant. He will be lifted up, and offer himself for our salvation. And of course, we who know the stories of Holy Week, of the Passion of Christ, can hardly be left in any doubt as to who this Suffering Servant really is. From the earliest days of the church, Christians have understood that this person is Jesus. The Messiah. The Christ.

Fulcrum

Jesus' life and Jesus' ministry were not some sort of intervention by God in response to what was happening in the world. Rather, they are the fulcrum on which history turns. This life, this ministry, this salvation, has been part of God's plan and God's calling since the beginning.

Since things went wrong in the garden of Eden, God's promise of salvation has been proclaimed. In the call of Abraham, the call of Moses and the call of all the great prophets, this promise remained. In Jesus, it is fulfilled.

Even though he was rejected by many, despised by the very people he came to save, 'a man of sorrows, and acquainted with grief' (Isa. 53.3, KJV), this promise from God could not and would not be thwarted.

Through the suffering of the Servant, through his Passion and death, new life was wrought and made possible, and shone out in the resurrection for all to see and experience.

I have plans for you

Just as God had a plan and a calling on the life of the Suffering Servant, so also God has had plans and callings on our lives since before time. These plans may well involve journeys on which we will encounter hardship and suffering. Jesus told us we would have our crosses to carry. But in Jesus, we are assured of the ultimate promise, that we can enter into the new life of the kingdom; not just as a future hope, but as a here-and-now reality.

The road we travel might indeed be a Via Dolorosa – a hard road of sorrows – but it's a road with only one end: an empty tomb and a new set of possibilities in God. With Jesus, therefore, we move towards the cross, knowing that he leads us on into his future – and where he leads, we must follow.

Bill Braviner

Hymn suggestions

Glory be to Jesus, who in bitter pains; My song is love unknown; O sacred head, sore wounded; Sing, my tongue, the glorious battle.

Maundy Thursday   17 April
In the Upper Room: a reflective sermon

Ex. 12.1–4 [5–10] 11–14; Ps. 116.1, 10–end [*or* 116.9–end]; 1 Cor. 11.23–26; **John 13.1–17, 31b–35**

Today on Maundy Thursday I want to invite you to be part of the story we all share. To go back and imagine yourself into the story, imagine the thoughts and feelings of everyone there, the smells of the food, the sounds of people eating, chatting, serving. The growing gap between those who understood what would unfold and those who did not.

Jesus and the disciples gathered in the upper room.

The air was close, it was warm in the year already. The smell of food was wafting from below – lamb cooked tenderly, bread baked carefully. On the table, bitter herbs and reminders of the Hebrew journey in the desert. A reminder that all gathered were part of a story, the story of a people and their walk with the God who delivers.

So they gathered to share a meal, not knowing it was the last. The last supper before the cross, before the resurrection, before new ways of being. Life still made sense, in the way it had for centuries. The boundaries between life and death were clear, and they thought they understood the ways of God.

Remembering the apostles

Simon, called Peter. The fisherman. The man with a temper, the man with enthusiasm, the man who loved Jesus and the man who denied him; the man who died for him, eventually, too.

Peter's brother, Andrew; the one we only remember as one of the Twelve, Peter's brother. Who was he? He was called too.

James and his brother John, the sons of Zebedee; sons of thunder. Banter and joy between them. They wanted to be first, on earth and in the kingdom of heaven. But the first will be last, and the last will be first. There is no hierarchy at the table of Jesus.

Philip and Bartholomew; faithful, obedient followers.

Thomas, the twin. Thomas, who did not find faith easy. Thomas, who was rooted in the world yet was first to declare of Jesus, 'My Lord and my God'.

Matthew the tax-collector; reviled and despised by good society. Not a good man, they said. A cheat, greedy, colluding with the Romans. Matthew was called, loved and transformed. Matthew treasured the story of Jesus and passed it on.

James the son of Alphaeus, Thaddaeus; do we know them? Do we remember them? There is more we don't know about these friends of Jesus than there are things we remember. Forgotten and invisible, like so many of the people we walk by every day. Like the countless witnesses to the faith whose love persists, whose love leads them to live faithful lives, known and recognized mostly by God. We stand with a great cloud of witnesses from the many years of our faith, unknown and unremembered, yet held in the memory of God.

Simon the patriot, who loved his country, looking for a Messiah, a deliverer, an action man. Someone to lead a rebellion, so that, at last, things would change. Watching his leader stoop and wash feet. The most un-leaderlike leader you could imagine.

And Judas Iscariot. The betrayer. The enemy. The other. The one who did not belong, surely. The odd one out. The one we dare not identify with. Surely, we are not like him. Surely we would never have done what he did. And yet … he was human. Fallible and mistaken. Was it a momentary weakness? A character flaw? Who knows? Jesus washed his feet, too.

The ones we always forget

And there were probably others. The ones we always forget. Women who followed, who served at tables and supported, silently, often invisibly.

Mary and Martha, Jesus' friends, who wept with him at the grave of Lazarus, listened as he taught, and welcomed him in their Bethany home.

Mary Magdalene, ever grateful, who had been freed from some unknown spirits. Mary Magdalene, first to proclaim the resurrection.

Mary the mother of Jesus, silently treasuring and pondering the life of her son. Did she remember then the prophecy made to her in the Temple, that a sword would pierce her soul? Did she silently beg her son not to stir up trouble, not to anger the powers that be?

Joanna and Suzanna, who shared their wealth and resources, and supported the disciples who had left their work and livelihood to follow Jesus.

Maybe servants, too. They would have been expected to wash feet. Did Jesus wash their feet too?

And all those who are not remembered at all. The children that would have been part of the household, sharing in the Passover meal. The youngest child asking the questions, and the wisest man giving the answers – why Passover? Why a lamb? Why bitter herbs?

Because. Because God loves the world. Because God delivers. Because God's grace is on offer, and he washes feet, even the feet of betrayers. Because God never forgets, and God always reaches out. The disciples remembered Passover, just as we remember them. The disciples knew little, as we know little. But they loved, and trusted, just as we are called to, on the eve of an Easter not yet in our grasp.

Isabelle Hamley

Hymn suggestions

Brother, sister, let me serve you; I stand amazed in the presence of Jesus the Nazarene; All to Jesus I surrender; Meekness and majesty.

Good Friday   18 April
Principal Service   **The Stone Rejected**
Isa. 52.13—end of 53; Ps. 22 [*or* 22.1–11, *or* 22.1–21];
Heb. 10.16–25, *or* Heb. 4.14–16; 5.7–9; **John 18.1—end of 19**

'There they crucified him'

Where was 'there'? The question matters. Jesus was not crucified *any*where. He was crucified *som*ewhere. In ancient times crucifixions would have been public spectacles. They were intended to warn and deter. For that reason, the authorities favoured somewhere just outside the city walls, near one of the main gates. The agonized victims would be hanging there beside one of the busy trade routes that linked Jerusalem to the wider world. It would have been busy, noisy and international, especially on that festival weekend. That is why the declaration above Jesus' cross was written in three languages.

'There they crucified him'

Like every growing city, there were quarries by the roadside outside Jerusalem to meet the endless demand for building materials. As the rock was steadily cut back into hillsides the quarriers would occasionally come to stone that was flawed or fractured, perhaps from an earthquake. They would cut round it and continue back into the good seam. This meant that over time the quarry floor would be littered with pieces of damaged rock, rejected by the builders, a motley assortment of blocks, contorted lumps, columns and blocks, standing alone.

'There they crucified him'

In that quarry outside Jerusalem, it seems one of those rejected, flawed stones rising up off the quarry floor had attracted the name 'The Skull'. Most probably because it looked like a human head. 'There they crucified him', by the place of the skull, on that first Good Friday. We know that in the early years after the death of Jesus until persecution made it impossible, the Christians in Jerusalem gathered by that stone every Easter Day. It would have been a very dramatic place to worship and remember.

Years later, St Peter was almost certainly remembering The Skull when he wrote to believers in his epistle, 'Come to him (Jesus), a living stone, though rejected by mortals ... and like living stones, let yourselves be built into a spiritual house ... "The stone that the builders rejected has become the very head of the corner"' (1 Peter 2.4–5, 7).

Rejected

What Peter is saying is so very counter-intuitive. It is not even common sense. If you are wanting to build something it is not very wise to use material that professional builders have already assessed and rejected as unsuitable. Still less would you make such a rock your cornerstone. If Jesus, the rejected stone, is the foundation stone of life, God is building something very new. With very unexpected materials. And when we are called to become part of that building, we are being shown a completely new way of knowing ourselves and knowing God. A new humanity is being built upon his loving sacrifice. All that has been previously rejected and left behind as worthless is being seen in the new light.

By any normal measure, anything built on such flawed foundations will look foolish and irrelevant, be easily mocked and despised. Well, many to whom Peter was writing knew all too well what that was like. In that world, they were the rejected – the poor, marginalized, of little worth, value or importance.

Chosen

To them, Peter makes an unexpected invitation.

Come to Jesus. You too are like stones in the quarry, left behind in this world like so much worthless debris. Odd shapes and flawed pieces no one has any use for, or can see any beauty in. Discarded after the powers that have made their choices according to their own measures of need, image and importance. But the gospel reverses all this. You are, in fact, 'of great value', says Peter. Imagine people hearing that said to them; people would never have heard anyone speak to them with such respect and honour before.

'There they crucified him'

I remember a counsellor speaking about the cross. He worked in some of the deepest places of human darkness and pain. He told stories, drawing as he went until the lower board was cluttered with various bent and broken figures. 'Where is the cross in this?' he asked, offering a marker. Well, the cross is often pictured on top of a hill, isn't it? Several of us put the cross above all this pain. 'No,' he said. 'It is here.' And he drew a large rough cross down below, right in the midst of broken humanity. *There* they crucified him. It matters where. It is where this world needs him most.

The place of rejection becomes a place of acceptance.
The place of threat becomes a place of welcome.
The place of judgement becomes a place of forgiveness.
The place of hatred is actually a place of love.
The place of death will become the place where real life begins.
There they crucified him …

David Runcorn

Hymn suggestions

When I survey; What a friend we have in Jesus; Christ is made the sure foundation. Were you there when they crucified my Lord?

Easter

Easter Vigil 19–20 April
Free at Last!
(A minimum of three Old Testament readings should be chosen. The reading from Exodus 14 should always be used.)
Gen. 1.1—2.4a *and* Ps. 136.1–9, 23–end; Gen. 7.1–5, 11–18; 8.6–18; 9.8–13 *and* Ps. 46; Gen. 22.1–18 *and* Ps. 16; **Ex. 14.10–end**; 15.20–21 *and Canticle*: Ex. 15.1b–13, 17–18; Isa. 55.1–11 *and Canticle*: Isa. 12.2–end; Baruch 3.9–15, 32—4.4 *and* Ps. 19, *or* Prov. 8.1–8, 19–21; 9.4b–6 *and* Ps. 19; Ezek. 36.24–28 *and* Ps. 42, 43; Ezek. 37.1–14 *and* Ps. 143; Zeph. 3.14–end *and* Ps. 98; Rom. 6.3–11 *and* Ps. 114; Luke 24.1–12

What is Easter?

It is sunrise and springtime, a feast and a dance; music and song; best wine and a wedding; perfume and paradise, eyes wide open; names known; souls with wings; ashes to fire; a palette of colours; a garden of flowers, endless holiday. 'Rise heart, thy Lord is risen!'[21]

The Bible has its own magnificent treasure house of images. Resurrection is the warrior's triumphant return from harrowing hell. It is the first day of the week, the beginning of a new creation. It is the first fruits of the harvest of the earth. It is our own resurrection foretold, last things first here and now. It is the death of death, the last enemy. It is the banquet of God's Messiah. It is the last Adam's triumph in which our humanity is restored. It is glory, salvation and love; joy and life and crown.

But there is one picture of resurrection that the New Testament returns to again and again. We read the story in our reading from Exodus. 'The Israelites walked on dry ground through the sea ... Thus the LORD saved Israel that day from the Egyptians.' The deliverance of the Hebrews from their Egyptian slavery is the defining metaphor of Easter. And that is because this story was already the defining event in Jewish history that formed Israel as a people and shaped their identity. Down the ages at the Passover seder, the memory has been kept alive. 'Why is this night different from all other nights?' 'Because on this night the Lord brought us out of Egypt with a mighty hand and outstretched arm, to give us our land and our freedom.' It's the theme of some of the oldest songs in the Scriptures. If the ordeals and agonies of Egypt were Israel's passion, the Exodus was her resurrection. In that saving event, God took a people to be his own, made his covenant with them, and promised that he would never leave them nor forsake them.

The events of Jesus' Passion and resurrection took place at Passover time. Whether or not the Last Supper Jesus celebrated with his disciples was a Passover meal, this Exodus story would have been hanging in the springtime air. Only now, in Jesus, a greater event than the Exodus is here. St Paul writes, in the words of the Easter Anthems, 'Christ our Passover has been sacrificed for us: so let us celebrate the feast.'[22] So since earliest times, the celebration of Easter has always been shot through with the stories and images of that great night of deliverance, when the sea fled before the awesome power of God, when mountains were convulsed and the earth trembled for fear, and a people went free.

We must follow this imagery where it leads us. The time of Exodus, the prophets said, was a kind of honeymoon when Israel learned to be God's and give him what he claimed: their absolute loyalty and allegiance: 'I am the LORD your God, who brought you out of the land of Egypt ... you shall have no other gods before me' (Ex. 20.2–3). So, Easter is not the end of the story but its beginning, when all the promises and possibilities held out to us in the coming of Jesus are realized. For those who are baptized this night or at daybreak, it is their exodus: dying to the old life, rising to the new, embracing the risen Christ as Lord, walking into his sunrise of wonder. And the initiation vows we each renew at this service mark us for ever as an Easter people whose song is alleluia and whose watchword is hope.

Today we gaze into the mouth of the empty tomb, perplexed, afraid, yet also hoping against hope. We see the strange work God has done, this exodus from the grave, and do not fully understand what this may mean. But we believe that the rolled-away stone opens a door of promise to a broken world. For Christ, the alpha and omega, the first and the last and the living one, holds the keys of death and hell. A new creation is pledged where pain and sorrow are banished and God's kingdom of light and life and love is here, and we are free at last. What zest that expectation adds to our daily prayer, 'Thy kingdom come'!

Yes, that is bread for tomorrow. But Easter says: live it now – live in that light, live in that love, and let the risen Jesus offer the exodus we long for:

> Unfold! unfold! Take in His light,
> Who makes thy cares more short than night,
> The joys which with His day-star rise,
> He deals to all but drowsy eyes;
> And (what the men of this world miss)
> Some drops and dews of future bliss.[23]

Michael Sadgrove

Hymn suggestions

Sing choirs of heaven! Let saints and angels sing; Awake, awake, fling off the night; I will sing the Lord's high triumph; The day of resurrection!

Easter Day   20 April
Principal Service   **While It Was Still Dark**
Acts 10.34–43, *or* Isa. 65.17–end; Ps. 118.1–2, 14–24 [*or* 118.14–24]; 1 Cor. 15.19–26, *or* Acts 10.34–43; **John 20.1–18**, *or* Luke 24.1–12 (*The reading from Acts must be used as either the first or second reading.*)

'Early on the first day while it was still dark ...'

How strange of God to do this most amazing, world-changing work in the dark. Before the first light of day. Before anyone could see *anything*, let alone witness the resurrection. Before any human hand or faith could claim any involvement. Matthew says there was an earthquake but it does not seem to have woken anyone up.

Somewhere on the edge of the sleeping city is a garden with a tomb in it. Two days before it had been sealed with a large stone. Now, as night turns to day, it is plain something strange has happened. The heavy stone has been rolled away. The tomb is empty.

Empty

There it is, just waiting for someone to discover it, apparently. What God chooses to reveal or conceal is always a mystery to our human agendas. The resurrection would have been such a photo opportunity, don't you think? And why miss out on such a media opportunity? Think of the vivid power of those interviews with eyewitnesses. 'So how did you feel as you saw Jesus bursting out of the tomb?' It would have been so compelling.

Mary finds it first. She has come to complete the anointing required for the dead before their mortal remains are finally committed and sealed in the tomb. There had not been time to finish this work on the Friday evening. She had come as soon as she could.

The men have come and gone home in bewilderment. This was still so soon after the appalling trauma of watching Jesus crucified. All of them would have been emotionally stressed and exhausted.

But there is a further trauma. The empty tomb. The body gone. Mary can only assume the body has been stolen. She checks again. Now there are angels in the tomb. 'Why are you weeping?' they ask. It is a strange question to ask someone standing by the grave of a loved one. You would think the answer was obvious.

Loss

So it is that the first experience of resurrection is one of loss and emptiness. But there is no other way. We will not come to it by any familiar ways of human understanding. This is non-sense. Arguments for the resurrection do indeed suggest grounds for faith but they cannot compel it. The empty tomb didn't convince the first disciples. Where was the body? It must have felt like yet another cruel twist in a story that had already left them frightened, traumatized and uncomprehending. 'The world is breached by an enclave of non-death' is how the Orthodox theologian Olivier Clément describes that empty place that is for ever at the heart of the Christian faith.[24]

Turning

'Turning' is the key action in this story. It is the key to all Christian discipleship. It changes everything.

Mary turns, away from the tomb. Someone is standing there. She knows him so well, but now does not recognize him. She thinks he is the gardener. 'Why are you weeping?', the stranger asks. That question again. But faith comes to birth where it is needed most – in the very heart of our *in*comprehension and helplessness. This will be a familiar theme in the stories that follow. The risen Jesus is not for recognizing by human choice or will. It is for him to reveal himself. Faith is invited and received as a gift. What is really encouraging is that he is already present even when not recognized.

But there is a deep irony in her confusion. In one sense she was quite right to think Jesus was the gardener. Notice how John has set the scene.

> They are standing in a garden.
> It is the morning of the first day.
> Jesus is the new Adam.
> This is the beginning of a new creation.
> He begins, as the first Adam did, by naming his creation – 'Mary'.

Now Mary turns for a third time. But this time it is in astonished and joyful recognition.

Breached

The world has been breached. It still waits to be discovered, as it did on that first morning. But life is streaming through it. It is our discovery to make too. Christ is risen!

Like Mary, there is only one journey to make. We must come to this place. We too must bend and look into the place of death and find it empty. That much we can do. And then with our own mix of bewilderment, grief, searching and questioning we must *turn*.

This is the first day. New life is beginning.

By ancient tradition, Christians renew the promise of their baptism on Easter Day:

> 'I turn to Christ.'[25]
> And when we do.
> He is there,
> waiting to greet us.

David Runcorn

Hymn suggestions

Light of the word, you stepped down into darkness. Led like a lamb to the slaughter; Christ the Lord is risen today; Thine be the glory.

Easter Day 20 April
Second Service   **I Am What I Am**
Morning Ps. 114, 117; Evening Ps. 105, *or* 66.1–11; Isa. 43.1–21;
1 Cor. 15.1–11, *or* John 20.19–23

By the grace of God, I am what I am

Grace, nothing but grace. Resurrection grace. Easter Sunday grace.

In our reading from his letter to the church in Corinth, Paul tells us that his experience of the resurrection is, before anything else, an experience of grace. To have this privilege, to meet the one who went through the deepest darkness of death, the one who was raised, and appeared; the one who is now always accessible, always beside us – that's grace. It comes to us, says Paul, without worthiness, or merit, without striving. It is pure gift and grace. The resurrection is the grace of God in us. It is an expression, an experience of love. For where else can grace flow from, but the love of God?

Identity

This grace, this risen life, is the bedrock of Paul's identity. 'By the grace of God, I am what I am.' So, if Jesus is risen from the dead, that resurrection is now the source of my life. This risen person, whose love is stronger than death, stands beside me and speaks peace. But more than that, this risen Christ resides within me. Christ is a grace in which we stand, a presence, so all-encompassing and subtle, that even my own actions no longer belong to me, but arise from the risen one within. No longer I, but Christ. And as Paul discovers who he really is, does anything resonate with us? Does he have anything to say about our identity?

Maybe, on Easter Day, this can take our thinking and understanding to a deeper level. This is not just a story about the past. This is no longer a question of our wonder at something that happened long ago, or even amazement that such a transcendent event should happen. Paul's words bring the resurrection into *now*.

Now

We, even now, are placed as witnesses of these things. We, in the twenty-first century, are able to participate in Christ, in the crucifixion, the burial, the resurrection. And all this happens in our contemporary, everyday lives. In us, Christ draws near, Christ is recognized, Christ takes residence and abides. Christ is risen – he is risen indeed!

This presence, this reality, is not just something to be found in sacred experience or heroic action but is a part and parcel of everyday life. One of the great gifts of the Jewish heritage is a compendium of prayers. There is a different prayer of blessing for every conceivable action or occasion: eating, opening a door, going out, coming in, even going to the toilet! This was an everyday practice which affirmed the reality and presence of God in each moment of our lives.

Paul's vision of the risen Christ leads us to the same recognition. We too can know the risen Christ as an all-pervading presence. This is expressed beautifully in the Celtic spirituality of St Patrick's breastplate: Christ within me, Christ around me, Christ, when I sit down, Christ, when I lie down ...

A grace-filled life

Paul frames this everyday experience as a grace-filled life. In this continuous gift, this presence of the risen Christ, we stand. And, he asserts, if I recognize this reality, if I understand, even for a moment, that this relationship or task or conflict or predicament in which I find myself is already filled up with the grace of God, that can be transformative. It will lead me into gratitude, it will rein in my ego. I find my identity. Not I, but Christ, who lives within me.

Paul is someone who knows, in his own direct experience, the reality of the resurrection. He knows – not just that Jesus is risen but that somehow that event energizes his own life. Somehow, he has died and has risen into a different life. And in that life he finds confidence and identity: I am what I am – not I, but the grace of God.

The name of God

What a bold, even reckless thing to say. To take on, as Paul does here, the name of God. For when Moses asked God, 'What is your name?', God's answer was just this: 'I am what I am.' I will be what I will be. I am not constrained by anyone else's idea of my identity.

To Paul, this degree of freedom can be ours. The very nature of God is at work in us by grace. And all of this is a continual enactment of the resurrection. Jesus has burst into life. Jesus has overcome everything that might keep us bound or imprisoned. The grace we receive is the sign of that undeserved, joyful presence of the risen one.

Grace, nothing but grace. Resurrection grace. Easter Sunday grace.

Andrew Rudd

Hymn suggestions

Now the green blade riseth; This joyful Eastertide; Hail the day that sees him rise; All I once held dear.

Second Sunday of Easter   27 April
Principal Service   **I'll Leave You with This ...**
Ex. 14.10–end; 15.20–21 (*if used, the reading from Acts must be used as the second reading*), *or* Acts 5.27–32; Ps. 118.14–end, *or* Ps. 150; Rev. 1.4–8; **John 20.19–end**

I'll leave you with this ...

There are five words that every stand-up comedian needs to know. Five words that are guaranteed to grab people's attention. Five words that need to be used wisely: 'I'll leave you with this.' These words cue the hearer in for the big finish, the grand finale, the cherry on the icing on the cake. They create a chance to leave a lasting impression and go out with a bang.

Because John 21 is an epilogue, here in John 20 we're reading the final chapter which happens on the day of resurrection. Jesus is grabbing the reader's attention one final time with a line that packs a punch.

Gathered in a room

After Mary encounters the risen Jesus in the garden, the disciples are gathered in a room. The whole faith community is there, the women and men (apart from Thomas, as we see later). Perhaps huddled together exchanging stories of Jesus while harbouring a queasy sick feeling about it all and sharing one overriding emotion – fear. The doors are locked, we are told, for fear of the religious authorities. But what have they really got to hold on to? Two of their number have seen some folded linen in an empty tomb and one of them has embraced a man in a garden who claimed to be Jesus. The evidence is anecdotal and flimsy. Yet there is something compelling about the way the witnesses share what they have seen. Behind locked doors, this community stares at the walls trying to make sense of it all.

Peace and the Spirit

Then, Jesus came and stood among them. The disciples' fear dissolves as they recognize him. After they see his hands and his side, they are overjoyed. Here is Jesus with a captive audience, the nascent church, and he has their full attention. He could say anything at this point. (I would be tempted to go for something along the lines of 'I told you so'.) However, for his big finish, his 'I'll leave you with this', Jesus says, 'Peace be with you. As the Father has sent me, so I send you.' Then 'he breathed on them and said to them, "Receive the Holy Spirit."'

Jesus, undeterred by crucifixion, unhindered by death and unobstructed by locked doors, could conceivably offer just about anything at this point. His parting gift however is peace and the life-giving breath of the Spirit. The disciples may have had a sense of déjà vu. Back in John 14, Jesus had promised the coming of the Spirit, offering a peace different from that offered by the world.

Bearing the wounds

The drama of this appearance demonstrates the uniqueness of Jesus' offer. The risen Jesus bears the wounds of crucifixion. Only with the marks of suffering can he be recognized as the Jesus they know. Only with the visible signs of trauma in his body can he reach them in the flesh. What he offers is not respite but resolution that has come at a cost, which cannot be erased or elided.

The peace Jesus offers is totally unlike the types of peace the world offers. It is unlike the famous Pax Romana where peace is won through domination and sustained by subjugation. It is unlike the fragile compromised peace brokered by Jewish leaders under Roman rule making them anxious of the inconvenient truth.

The peace Jesus offers is not the kind of peace that takes no prisoners, nor the kind of peace offered in exchange for retreat, nor the kind of peace that means being squeezed into a corner, staying in your lane, or silencing the cry for justice. It is a peace won through love, submission to God's will, and non-violence. It is a peace resting on humility, service and taking the lowest place. It is a peace that blows off the cobwebs, sweeps nothing under the carpet, and speaks in the flesh to those who are afraid and troubled.

When the world's peace ebbs, Jesus' peace flows. When the world's peace is changeable, Jesus' peace is world-changing. When the world's peace suffocates, Jesus' peace is breath itself.

Sharing the peace

The peace Jesus gives comes to those who ultimately recognize him as 'Lord'. As his Spirit-filled people, they are to be the bearers and carriers of his peace. The community are to take the lead as his witnesses. How Jesus' followers share his peace and wield his peace through the forgiveness of sins will be crucial. It is as though Jesus is saying, 'I'll leave *you* with this.'

Later, Thomas arrives and we can imagine him saying, 'So, did I miss anything?' In the famous exchange that follows a week later, Jesus begins by offering his peace – a peace that comes through his presence, that flourishes by the breath of the Spirit, and which includes those who are not even in the room. This is the risen Jesus we celebrate in the Easter season. He doesn't say, 'I'll leave you be.' He doesn't say, 'I'll leave you to it.' He says, 'I'll leave you with this.'

Matt Allen

Hymn suggestions

Crown him with many crowns; My peace I leave you (Taizé); In Christ alone; Peace, perfect peace.

Second Sunday of Easter   27 April
Second Service   **Trauma and the Next Steps**
Ps. 16; Isa. 52.13—53.12, *or* 53.1–6, 9–12; **Luke 24.13–35**

Trauma and a panicky conversation

The walk to Emmaus is an archetypal story of Christian faith. One possible way to read it with new insight is to use some of the language and concepts of trauma studies. We are used to calling the two people on the road to Emmaus 'disciples', but let's work with naming them as people who have experienced a set of events that have been traumatic. They have experienced the death by crucifixion of someone they loved and believed to be a prophet. They've also experienced their friends finding his tomb to be empty and saying far-fetched things about him coming back to life. Painful, frightening, confusing events, yes, but also violent events which are threatening and overwhelming to them as individuals and to their community. Seen this way, this is a story of how grace and love enable the next steps, those beginnings of feelings of wholeness and well-being after a trauma.

I realized as I was thinking about this sermon that I have always pictured these two characters as friends walking side by side having a blether, with their voices slightly lowered so that no one around them picks up the topic they are talking about. Actually, it's highly likely that the tone of their conversation was more panicky, and they were going round and round, telling the details of the past few days over and over again to try to make sense of them. Like anyone after witnessing a violent event, they were in shock and disorientated. Interestingly, the original Greek word we translate with the bland word 'discussion' is only used in one other place in Luke's Gospel. It's in chapter 22 when Jesus tells the disciples at the Last Supper that one of them will betray him – 'then they began to ask (discuss with) one another which one of them it could be who would do this' (v. 23). I can't imagine for a moment that was a cosy chat, so I suspect the use of the same word here means this isn't a cosy chat either.

A quiet and gentle presence

As two overwhelmed, raw and panicky people leave the site of the traumatizing event, grace and love quietly and gently become present alongside them. Jesus simply comes near and goes with them. And when the time is right, He breaks into their frantic going round and round of the story and tells the story a different way. He reweaves, reorders, and recrafts the story by putting it in a bigger framework. But this intervention doesn't have an immediate effect and they continue with their frantic, looping, dissociated conversation. Time passes and the natural need for rest and food takes over. As the meal arrives Jesus makes a very simple ritual action. He takes bread and blesses it, and something in their memory sparks to life, something is recalled, and they recognize the presence of grace and love right there with them. Just as quickly as the recognition arrives, Jesus vanishes. They have experienced something profound which is a step to helping them reimagine reality in the light of their trauma. There are many steps like this to come. Grace and love will reappear again and again, speaking words of peace, opening minds to understand things differently, and offering a mysterious and profound capacity to witness to the truth of what has happened.

The undemanding God

Told this way this story offers some wisdom for people experiencing trauma and for those who walk alongside them and try to help. Most importantly though I think it says something about the nature of God. God is simply there. They don't need to do anything to find or reach Jesus. Jesus walks alongside them listening to and understanding at a very deep level what is going on for them. This divine presence doesn't demand anything from them. They aren't put under pressure to forget what's happened, or to find a way of escaping from it, or to recover from the experience. There's the beginning of an offer of a way to understand and make sense of the experience, but no pressure on the disciples to do that. Then there's this glorious image of Jesus disappearing. The moment the disciples recognize him, recognize the presence of God, of grace and of love, he vanishes, is taken away. He withdraws and retreats. Again, nothing is demanded of them; recognition is enough, and they are given time and space to reflect, feel and gather themselves.

After the duty and demands of keeping Lent and celebrating Easter, this is a fabulous image of God. Divine presence, grace and love quietly and gently alongside us, not needing anything, not demanding anything, not requiring a response or a reaction. Grace and love that are sturdy enough to simply hold it all. God simply being with us, even at our most panicky and anxious and overwhelmed.

Simply standing alongside us bearing truthful witness to the effects of the misuse of power, violence and death. This divine presence comes to us in moments which, over time, build into patterns and stories of remaking, reimaging and re-creating.

Esther Elliott

Hymn suggestions

I heard the voice of Jesus say; I want Jesus to walk with me; Now the green blade riseth; Here, O my Lord, I see thee face to face.

Third Sunday of Easter   4 May
Principal Service   **Resurrection Promise**
Zeph. 3.14–end (*if used, the reading from Acts must be used as the second reading*), *or* Acts 9.1–6 [7–20]; Ps. 30; Rev. 5.11–end; **John 21.1–19**

When I lived in Streetly I would often run in Sutton Park and I particularly enjoyed getting out in the morning and watching the sunrise as I pounded the woodland paths. The brilliance of the sunrise often reminded me of the glory of God's resurrection story. Two weeks ago, the stone was rolled away, the tomb was found empty, and Jesus was seen alive. Two weeks ago, we celebrated Jesus' resurrection. Have you experienced Jesus' resurrection? How has the resurrected Jesus showed up in your life? What difference has he made?

For Christians, the resurrection of Jesus is a big deal. It is the heart of the gospel message we proclaim every day. It is the promise of the eternal hope we have in our friendship with Jesus, 'Weeping may linger for the night, but joy comes with the morning' (Ps. 30.5b).

Do you love me?

The resurrection of Jesus compels us to reflect on who Jesus is and what he means to us. In the passage from John 21, we are confronted with the question. Three times, Jesus asks, 'Simon son of John, do you love me?' and three times, Simon Peter answers, 'Yes, Lord; you know that I love you.' Jesus responds to Peter each time with a command to love his sheep. He says, 'Feed my lambs ... tend my sheep ... feed my sheep.'

When we consider the words 'feed' and 'tend', there is a quality of provision and protection. Simon Peter was being asked to watch over, to take care of and to have a concern for the people of God, the new community of believers.

This conversation was about Jesus passing on the baton. In starting with the question, 'Do you love me?' Jesus reminds Simon Peter that at the heart of the resurrection message is sacrificial and costly love. If we understand God's immeasurable love for us, we too will be inclined to love others.

If we remember, Simon Peter denied Jesus three times (John 18.15–27). And, Jesus asks Simon Peter the same question, not once but three times. Simon Peter gives the same answer, 'Yes, Lord; you know that I love you.' Jesus not only restores that relationship but creates a new one between himself and Simon Peter because now he entrusts him with the care of 'his sheep', those whom God loves.

We are loved by God. How many of us need to hear, understand and experience this God-love in our relationship with Jesus Christ?

Alive in Christ

The interaction between Jesus and Simon Peter drew him towards freedom, to a place where he could be more fully alive. I can imagine the feelings of guilt and shame Simon Peter felt about denying Jesus when he most needed his friends' support. Perhaps, these feelings that may have overwhelmed him at times may have prevented Simon Peter from living an abundant life. In Jesus restoring this relationship, he offers Simon Peter the gift of becoming more fully alive. This is the power of the cross.

The resurrected Christ shows up in the details of our lives; from the empty tomb moments of heartache and heartbreak, the darkness of the crucified Jesus gives way to the light that emerges from the empty tomb. When we discover and experience the resurrection of Jesus, we are able to look to the eternal, where we will sing with the angels:

Worthy is the Lamb that was slaughtered
to receive power and wealth and wisdom and might
and honour and glory and blessing! (Rev. 5.12)

Catherine Okoronkwo

Hymn suggestions

All my hope on God is founded; I know my Redeemer lives; Lord, for the years; Thine be the glory.

Third Sunday of Easter   4 May
Second Service   **What's Your Immediate 'Go-to'?**
Ps. 86; **Isa. 38.9–20**; John 11.[17–26] 27–44

What's your immediate 'go-to'?

When things go pear-shaped, when you are in difficulties of whatever nature, on dark and demanding days, what is your immediate 'go-to'? Chocolate? Exercise? A good rant? A glass of red? An outburst on social media? I wonder if we can honestly say that prayer is our immediate 'go-to'? Both the psalm and the reading from Isaiah remind us of the importance of turning to God in the midst of trouble. The act of reaching out to God shapes us.

Ousting the false images

In Psalm 86, King David, who is facing powerful enemies, says much about the character of God. God is 'good and forgiving', 'abounding in steadfast love'. There is none like God who is 'great and [does] wondrous things'. Does God need reminding of the divine nature? No. Perhaps David is trying to flatter God into action? Or maybe in his prayer, David is reminding himself of the nature of God, strengthening his trust by rehearsing aloud what he knows of God.

Sometimes I notice that though we might speak of the loving nature of God we can act as though God is out to get us, and not in a good way. False images of God come along and jostle with the true image, often leaving us afraid and unsure if we can really trust. This can lead to a kind of paralysis; our fear separates us from awareness of the God of love who is always present to us. A useful exercise is to remind ourselves of what we do know about God – pushing the false images aside – in order to reach out.

Stating intentions and making demands

In his psalm, David reorientates himself, stating what his intention is towards God: 'I am devoted to you', 'to you do I cry all day long', 'to you, O LORD, I lift up my soul', 'in the day of my trouble I call on you'. We could summarize the psalm as saying this is what God is like and therefore this is what we will do.

David is very clear and direct with his requests to God – even demanding! 'Be gracious to me', 'gladden the soul of your servant', 'give ear, O LORD, to my prayer', 'teach me', 'give me an undivided heart'. Notice he implicitly names his vulnerability; he needs teaching and his heart is divided. He doesn't hide from his weakness. His prayer is so human. On the one hand, he claims to be devoted to God. On the other, he names his divided heart. Like the rest of us, David is a bit of a muddle, a bundle of contradictions, yet he knows when the chips are down he can trust God.

God is no fair-weather friend

The reading from Isaiah reveals another king reflecting on his need for God. King Hezekiah has been extremely ill – to the point of death – with some kind of infection. The text makes reference to a boil, but I imagine it was a little more than that!

Hezekiah is reflecting back on his illness, his cry to God and his recovery. As he faced his own death, he experienced grief at leaving life behind. He acknowledges that God has the power over life and death, able to cut us from the loom of life. In his pain, he cried to God through the night: moaning, weary and oppressed. Sleepless and bitter, still he turns to God.

We don't have to come to God all neat and tidy, scrubbed up in Sunday best, with polite and holy words. I don't imagine Hezekiah held anything back as he railed at God through the night, bitter and afraid.

Interestingly, as Hezekiah reflects on his experience of a near-fatal illness, he states, 'Surely it was for my welfare that I had great bitterness.' Rather than being a destructive experience, he regards his suffering as shaping him. He knows God is with him. God is no fair-weather friend.

Resolving to make God our immediate 'go-to'

Today we stand in the light of Easter. For Hezekiah death meant Sheol, the pit of destruction, the end. The final full stop on his story. We come to the subject of death from a different perspective. In the company of Christ, death is not the final bitterness, shrouded in grief without hope. We stand in resurrection light. There is always hope, always tomorrow. Death is a semicolon.

Hezekiah praised God for the extension of his mortal life. We can praise God who meets us in this life – on sunny and dark days – and walks with us through the valley of the shadow of death into new vistas of possibility. On that basis, when things go pear-shaped, let's resolve to make God our immediate 'go-to'.

Kate Bruce

Hymn suggestions

What a friend we have in Jesus; Great is thy faithfulness; The Lord's my shepherd; In Christ alone.

Fourth Sunday of Easter   11 May
Principal Service   **Hear and Follow**

Gen. 7.1–5, 11–18; 8.6–18; 9.8–13 (*if used, the reading from Acts must be used as the second reading*), Acts 9.36–end; Ps 23; Rev. 7.9–end; **John 10.22–30**

Some people have very distinctive voices. When you hear certain people on the radio you know immediately who they are even though you can't see them. The voices of our closest family and friends can stop us in our tracks. When my children were babies, I could pick out their cries immediately, even at a distance. I could preach through almost any noise in church, except one of my own children crying. That makes me wonder: would we recognize Jesus, our brother, our friend, if we heard his voice?

Jesus' voice

Have you ever stopped to wonder what Jesus sounded like? We have an idea of what he may have looked like. Recently there have been a number of facial reconstructions using digital imaging and 3D modelling. There are thousands of painted images of Jesus created down the centuries, some more likely than others. We know Jesus was a Palestinian Jew. He was dark-skinned and spoke Aramaic. But what did he sound like? Was his voice loud or soft, gruff or gentle? When he sang, was he a tenor or a bass, or a baritone?

We also know that people listened to Jesus, and he drew big crowds. He was a gifted preacher and teacher. He read and taught with authority. He was a great storyteller who could hold people's attention and make them think. His voice contained within it the power of blessing. It could calm a storm, heal the sick and bring his dead friend Lazarus back to life. His voice had the power to call people to turn their lives around and follow him.

Hearing Jesus' voice

In John 10 Jesus responds to the question asked by saying, 'My sheep hear my voice. I know them and they follow me.' He suggests that people will know who he is if they listen. Peter, one of Jesus' disciples, recognizes in Jesus the voice of the Messiah and follows. In the reading from the book of Acts, we find Peter in Joppa where Tabitha, a much-loved and saintly woman, has died. Everyone is distraught. Peter kneels down, prays and then uses the authority of Jesus to call Tabitha back to life. By the power of the Holy Spirit God's work in Jesus is continuing through his disciples.

Listening for Jesus' voice

The church traditionally holds this day as Vocation Sunday, recognizing that Jesus is still calling. Many of us worshipping today are here because we've heard Jesus call us to follow him and we've responded to that call. But how do we hear and how do we know it's Jesus? People hear the call of Jesus in many ways. Some literally hear Jesus speaking to them, though in my experience that's quite rare. More often people are aware of Jesus calling them through passages of Scripture, hymns and songs. Sometimes people are moved to respond to Jesus due to the beauty and wonder of creation. Sometimes Jesus uses other people to speak his message of love and acceptance to us.

Recognizing Jesus' voice

We are all children of God, made in God's image. Through our baptism, we are members of the body of Christ. At the very core of our being, we recognize the voice of Jesus, though we may not always be aware that it is him speaking. He knows us even when we don't know him. We can know it's Jesus' voice even though we don't know what he sounds like because we become aware of something deep within us responding to his call. Our soul leaps, just like John the Baptist leapt in Elizabeth's womb when he encountered Jesus within Mary. We sense that something unusual, possibly something of God, is occurring. When that happens it's usually good practice to check out our experience with someone wise, who can be trusted.

Responding to Jesus' voice

The call of Jesus is sometimes a call to something difficult or demanding that requires courage. Something that we have to grow into, that teaches us to turn to God for help and guidance. It will be something that we sense is right. Those around us, who know us well, will agree and encourage us to do it. The call of Jesus leads to new life and healing, forgiveness, order and peace. The call of Jesus is a calling into the truth which sets us free.

In John 10 Jesus says that when we follow him, we will be with him for eternity and nothing can snatch us out of his hand. It is into the hands of Jesus that the sheep – God's people – are placed. Jesus says that the sheep he holds are safe, and because he and God the Father are one then to be safe in Jesus' hands is to be safe in God's hands: safe not just for now but for ever. We will continue to be called and carried, and nothing, not even death, will make Jesus let us go.

There's so much to look forward to as we respond to the call of Jesus and allow him to be our shepherd, our saviour and our friend. Jesus continues to call us throughout our lives. He calls us further on and deeper in. His call doesn't cease. Keep listening for, recognizing and responding to Jesus' voice of love. Hear the voice of Jesus and follow.

Catherine Williams

Hymn suggestions

The King of love my shepherd is; The Lord's my shepherd (Stuart Townend); Will you come and follow me; I heard the voice of Jesus say.

Fourth Sunday of Easter 11 May
Second Service **God of Surprises**
Ps. 113, 114; Isa. 63.7–14; **Luke 24.36–49**

Surprised by rumours ...

This resurrection appearance is one in a whole sequence of surprises which we have been journeying alongside through this Easter season so far.

Early on the first morning (Easter Sunday) the women find an empty tomb and have a perplexing conversation with angels who question the sensibility of looking for the living among the dead. Then Peter runs to the tomb to confirm the women's story and finds the tomb empty – exactly as the women had described. So if Jesus is not in the tomb, where is he? Next, we hear of travellers returning to Emmaus from Jerusalem that same evening and encountering a stranger on the road who unfolds Scripture, breaks bread in their home and – on disappearing into thin air – turns out to have been Jesus whom they knew to be dead.

We enter the narrative at the point where the travellers have abandoned their evening at home and hurried back to Jerusalem with their news that Jesus appears to be alive and well and was last seen in Emmaus. Together with the 11 disciples, and other followers, they gather in a room in Jerusalem to share their stories and their bewilderment. How can someone crucified, who has died and was sealed in a tomb, now be walking, talking and eating?

Surprised by presence ...

Jesus stands among them as they are discussing the impossibility of the empty tomb and the stranger on the road. Now the room is full of people who are no longer bewildered, but afraid. 'Peace' is the first word spoken by Jesus in this confused gathering. 'Peace be with you.' Jesus speaks, and their first assumption is that he must be a ghost. Jesus invites them to touch him, to handle his hands and feet, inspect for themselves the crucifixion wounds, to be clear that this is no trick. The disciples seem to hesitate, wondering still if this is an apparition. So Jesus challenges them – can a ghost eat food? He eats a piece of fish given to him by the disciples. Jesus speaks, and he eats. He goes on to unfold Scripture.

The previous three years of life together with Jesus in his ministry is encapsulated here in this moment, here in this upper room in Jerusalem. Three years of conversations, three years of food and fellowship, three years of teaching and understanding Scripture. It is a pattern that they have lived for three years. This is no ghost. This is Jesus.

Surprised by Scripture

It was not enough that these disciples had the experience of encountering the risen Jesus. They needed to understand – and evaluate – these events with their intellect too. So Jesus takes them back through his teachings, and how Scripture is being fulfilled through his ministry, life, death and resurrection. To fully understand where this encounter sits within the big picture, the history of the Jewish people and the story of God's love, grace and mercy throughout time. None of this should have come as a surprise, had they been paying attention, and yet here Jesus patiently explains his place in the prophecies of old.

Not only that but the ministry which flows from his resurrection is also foretold in their Scriptures. And these disciples and followers are to be the message bearers and witnesses in the season to come. They are the messengers promised in history. They are the very people who will be entrusted to proclaim the good news of repentance and forgiveness, according to the will of God the Father, who will commission them by the power of the Holy Spirit. The hopes and dreams of their prophetic ancestors are about to be fulfilled by this bewildered group of disciples.

Surprised by the commission

Those disciples, and the disciples of today, are called to be witnesses. To testify to what is seen, heard, experienced and understood of the love of God through the death and resurrection of Jesus, by the power of the Holy Spirit.

We are called to unfold Scripture to others.

We are called to encounter Jesus in the ordinary and the extraordinary.

We are called to speak and live the messages of repentance and forgiveness.

We are called to be people of peace, which the world cannot give but which is spoken over us by Jesus himself.

We are called to bear witness to Jesus, who was promised to us throughout the Old Testament, who died and rose again, who shapes our vision and our values, who loves the world.

Kt Tupling

Hymn suggestions

We have a gospel to proclaim; Jesus, stand among us; Be still, for the presence of the Lord; Go forth and tell.

Fifth Sunday of Easter   18 May
Principal Service   **What Does Love Look Like?**
Baruch 3.9–15, 32—4.4, *or* Gen. 22.1–18 (*if used, the reading from Acts must be used as the second reading*), *or* **Acts 11.1–18**; Ps. 148 [*or* 148.1–6]; Rev 21.1–6; **John 13.31–35**

Love, love, love – we sing or speak of it in many different contexts. Shoppers sometimes claim to love chocolate, cars, clothes, holidays, and so on. Even a football team was recently described in glowing terms by a journalist, who then asked, 'What is not to love?' While we may enjoy a concert or sporting event, I imagine most of us know that liking a pleasurable meal or a new purchase can never be equated with genuine love. In fact, it may be that love can't be adequately defined; perhaps it can only be described. If that is true, have you ever wondered what love actually looks like?

Love in action

The story of Peter's interaction with Cornelius provides a striking picture of love in action. When challenged by the risen Lord, Peter had claimed not once but three times that he loved him and that he wanted to serve him (John 21.15–19). Later, Peter and the other disciples heard the command of Jesus to be 'witnesses in Jerusalem, in all Judea and Samaria, and to the ends of the earth' (Acts 1.8). Yet, I don't think they had imagined that this commission to share the good news might mean that they would share food with Gentiles. Peter and the other apostles had been brought up to obey the Jewish food laws, and even as followers of Jesus they continued to keep those traditions which had always shaped their spiritual lives. As Peter later reported to the apostles in Jerusalem, even when commanded in a dream to 'kill and eat', he had stood firm, responding, 'By no means, Lord.' Yet, when prompted by the Holy Spirit, he soon found himself proclaiming the message to the Gentiles, and rejoicing as they were baptized and accepted as brothers and sisters in Christ.

When the apostles heard that Peter had been staying at the home of Cornelius, a centurion, they were shocked. It was one thing to proclaim the good news of Jesus to Gentiles, but quite another to stay with Gentiles and sit at table with them. However, as Peter recounted his experience, perhaps they realized that genuine love will always draw us out from ourselves and enable us to reach out to others in ways that we would never have imagined. I wonder, too, if those same apostles recalled again how Jesus not only urged them to 'love one another' but – while sharing a meal together – demonstrated to them what love looks like.

The command to love

It was, no doubt, an unforgettable experience for the disciples. After arriving in Jerusalem, one evening as they gathered for a meal Jesus suddenly got up from the table and began to wash their feet. They had all protested, but he had insisted that he was giving them an example of what they were to do for others. Later, he again told them that they were to 'love one another' as he had loved them.

At the time, I imagine the disciples thought that they could easily follow this 'new commandment'. After all, they associated with like-minded people, and they avoided those who were different or disagreed with them. What is not to love? It was not until later that the apostles discovered that loving others challenges us to turn out from ourselves and to reach out to others. Indeed, if our love reflects the love of God, it will not be restricted by boundaries such as culture, race or tradition, but will lead us to embrace those who are beyond our comfort zones and not like us at all.

A picture of self-giving love

Sr Denise Bergon was head of a Roman Catholic school in France during the Second World War. She risked her own life trying to protect Jewish children. Many years later, those who had been brought to the school recalled her generosity and care. They said that Sr Denise told them that for their own safety, while they were at the school, they must pretend to be Catholic, though she also told them that they should 'never be afraid of their own religion'.[26] Given the dangerous circumstances, Sr Denise could have made many excuses for not hiding Jewish children. Given this was a parochial school, she could have impressed on all the children a desire for them to sincerely confess the Christian faith. Yet, perhaps realizing that genuine love is always offered freely, without restrictions and without demanding a response, she simply cared for them. In so doing, she demonstrated in word and deed what Jesus meant when he said, 'By this everyone will know that you are my disciples, if you have love for one another.'

What does love look like? Perhaps it is impossible to fully describe it. But I have an idea that if we, like Peter, are open to the Spirit's challenge to let go of some of our long-held views, we might just catch a fresh glimpse of the height, depth and breadth of God's love.

Karen E. Smith

Hymn suggestions

There's a wideness in God's mercy; A new commandment; Brother, sister, let me serve you; Great God, your love has called us here.

Fifth Sunday of Easter   18 May
Second Service   **Not that Kind of Messiah**
Ps. 98; **Dan. 6.[1–5] 6–23**; Mark 15.46—16.8

The victorious hero

The story of Daniel in the lions' den appears in every child's Bible. It has everything you need in a good story: a morally upright hero, treacherous enemies, betrayal, suspense and, of course, a happy ending for the hero where it all comes right. Teaching a class of eight- and nine-year-olds RE recently, we watched a video about the Bible, and the child presenting it said this was his favourite Bible story because it showed that when we pray, God listens. We talked about it in the class, which included several children who have arrived in the UK in the last couple of years as refugees from Afghanistan, Syria and Iran, among other places. The idea of an oppressive king controlling people's religious observances, and the brave hero sticking to his guns and not betraying his beliefs, really captured their imaginations, but also felt quite close to home. The children especially liked the happy ending for Daniel – his God saved him. When I asked what the story is about, and what Christians might learn from the story to help us in our lives today, they said if we do good, if we pray, if we're brave, God will help us.

The defeated victim

But our reading from Mark takes us down a rather different path from the more simplistic, moralistic story of Daniel. This time the stone seals in not a brave hero but a defeated victim – a broken dead body. The danger has already been faced, and this time the oppressors, the treacherous enemies, the betrayers – they have won. The hero has been killed. Was he even a hero in the first place? Why didn't God help him?

As much as my class of children loved the story of brave Daniel being saved from the oppressive regime, for each of them who made it to safety in the UK there will be many innocent children and good, brave, faithful adults who have not had a happy ending. And this question, of why bad things happen to good people, is one that humans have wrestled with for millennia. Because bad things happen to us, and however faithful we are, however much we pray, sometimes it seems as if God isn't listening, God doesn't help us. A few verses earlier in Mark's Gospel we see Jesus on the cross and are told, 'Jesus cried out with a loud voice, "Eloi, Eloi, lema sabachthani?"' which means, 'My God, my God, why have you forsaken me?', which itself is a quote from Psalm 22. For every Daniel, there is someone else who isn't snatched from the jaws of the lions, however hard they pray.

Another Daniel?

And yet we know that Jesus could have chosen a different path. We're now in the season of Easter, but we always begin our journey of Lent remembering Jesus' temptations, which make it clear to us what kind of Messiah Jesus could have chosen to be. We're reminded of this on Good Friday as he hangs on the cross and is taunted: 'He saved others; he cannot save himself. He is the King of Israel; let him come down from the cross now, and we will believe in him' (Matt. 27.42). Jesus could have been a Daniel, the lions' jaws miraculously sealed, surviving the ordeal with 'no kind of harm'. But Jesus didn't choose that path.

There's a parallel in our two readings, between the king and the three women, going at dawn to remove the stone. King Darius is expecting to find the mauled remains of his trusted adviser behind the stone that sealed him into the lions' den; Mary, Mary and Salome go to anoint the broken body of their beloved friend and teacher, which lies behind the stone that seals his tomb. They are all surprised. King Darius, because the one he expected to find dead, by the grace of God is alive. Mary, Mary and Salome, because the one they *knew* was dead is, they are told, by the power of God, alive.

Choosing the path of the victim

We know that both through the deliberate actions of others and through random circumstances, people suffer and die. People who are loved, people who are good, people who are faithful and who the world is worse off without. Jesus chooses not to avoid their fate, but to go with them, to walk the path of the victim, tortured and murdered. While the story of Daniel gives us hope, when life doesn't turn out like that for us it can leave us feeling as if it must be our fault, as if God has abandoned us because we've done something wrong. But the story of Jesus' death and resurrection gives us a much deeper hope that whatever depths of suffering we must endure, Jesus goes there with us, even to death. And even death cannot separate us from the love of God.

Kat Campion-Spall

Hymn suggestions

Beauty for brokenness; Now the green blade riseth; O love that will not let me go; We cannot measure how you heal.

Sixth Sunday of Easter 25 May
Principal Service **God the Home-maker**
Ezek. 37.1–14 (*if used, the reading from Acts must be used as the second reading*), *or* Acts 16.9–15; Ps. 67; Rev. 21.10.22—22.5; **John 14.23–29**, *or* John 5.1–9

Homecoming

A couple of years ago I got a call from the armed police stationed at Edinburgh Airport. Someone had got off a long-haul flight, come through border control, walked straight up to them and asked to speak to the chaplain. They were refusing to say anything more to the police, so as airport chaplain I made my way over, absolutely intrigued. The start of the conversation was awkward, mostly caused by my inability to pick up the signals from the police that they were concerned this person wanted to confess to a serious crime and they were worried for my safety. But eventually, I sat down to listen, albeit with two armed guards outside the door. Quite simply, this was someone who was at a point in life where they wanted to come home to Scotland for a bit; to breathe the air, to stand on the soil and to re-root themselves. And for that person, this was somehow a sacred thing, a thing of the soul and spirit. They were not a church-goer, but they wanted that sacredness acknowledged and spoken of out loud. I listened and, when asked, said some words which seemed to form a deeper moment of prayer. Although, of course, the whole encounter was prayer of a sort.

The stuff of home

Home. It's a word that comes with a lot of stuff. In a literal sense. We put our stuff, our physical belongings, in our homes, the things we need, the things we treasure and all the stuff in between. Home is a word that comes with a lot of stuff metaphorically as well. To feel 'at home' is to feel at ease, comfortable, to be safe and secure. Home is where we have a private life and a family life, a place where we live alongside those who love us. Home is a place, a sanctuary that we retreat to for peace and to get used to new things. We value being able to die at home. We make a big deal out of the moments when we take a baby home for the first time, or when a family member comes back from a trip. Home, as a sports venue, is a place where you get an advantage. We can be homesick, or homeless, we can lose our home or long to go home. We can put all of our hopes into building a home somewhere. Or we can reject that whole idea and claim that 'home is where the heart is' or 'wherever I lay my hat that's my home'.

In recent memory, home has also been a place we've been legally obliged to stay in to save lives. A place, for some of us, to work from. A place perhaps we've not been able to get back to. And just recently, because of the war in Ukraine, it's been brought home to us, if you will, that homes can be bombed and fled from and left behind as well as opened up and shared with strangers in the direst of needs. Houses can become homes. Homes can also become just houses and even prisons, the sites of horrible things that happen behind closed doors like loneliness, violence and coercive control. Homes can be hard places where we face our deepest needs and experience some of the hardest things in life. Home, as I said, carries a lot of stuff.

God the home-maker

In the middle of this Gospel reading Jesus makes an astonishing statement. He talks about God making a home with people. Someone asks him how God will be revealed in the world and Jesus' response is to say, by making a home with people. It's an extraordinary image and an extraordinary choice of image. Here is Jesus talking to his friends the night before he is arrested, knowing that the authorities are out to get him, trying to get them to understand what is about to happen. The first image of God he reaches for is that of a home-maker. Not a fighter or a powerful ruler. Not a friend or a support or a comforter. Perhaps it was the experience of being in Jerusalem, a religious home, that sparked his imagination.

God makes a home with us. God doesn't just live among us, God makes a home among us. God doesn't just prepare a place for us in heaven, God makes a home among us while we are living daily life in the here and now. Moreover, God doesn't just give us a home or help us to feel at home, God makes a home with us. We are not done to or for, we are done with. God makes a home with us. Whatever home means to you at the moment, God is right there. God desires and God promises to build a home with us with all the love and commitment that takes and with all the joy and the comfort and safety that brings. As we face into our deepest needs and experience some of the hardest things in life, God is right there. When something new knocks on our door and we welcome it in and entertain it, God is right there too. When we are being most honestly and truly ourselves, God is still building a home with us, like the people who enjoy spending time with us and love us just as we are. God builds and makes with us; the places we treasure, the places that hold our treasures, the places where we do the most ordinary of daily things, the places we call home.

Esther Elliott

Hymn suggestions

Let us build a house where love can dwell; O God, our help in ages past; Be still, my soul, the Lord is on your side; I bind unto myself today.

Sixth Sunday of Easter 25 May
Second Service **The Story and the Song**
Ps. 126, 127; **Zeph. 3.14–end**; Matt. 28.1–10, 16–end

For music lovers, the story behind a song can be as important as the lyrics or music itself, shedding light on the inner experiences and motivations of the artist as they composed it. Many congregations have heard of the tragic deaths of Horatio Spafford's daughters, before singing his hymn 'It is well with my soul', and fans of Fleetwood Mac will know well of the relationship break-ups within the band that formed the backdrop for 'The Chain'.

When the prophet Zephaniah calls the people of Israel to 'sing aloud' (Zeph. 3.14), he's imagining a song born out of the dramatic story that he's been telling over the course of the book. It's a story with such an astonishing twist and glorious conclusion that generations since have sung its glories: this is a salvation story.

A final twist

You could be forgiven for thinking there's not much good news in the three chapters of Zephaniah. From the opening declaration that God will 'sweep away everything from the face of the earth' (1.2) to the final verdict that 'in the fire of my passion, all the earth shall be consumed' (3.8), the prophet's writings contain intensely vivid pictures of God's judgement on his own people and their enemies. Zephaniah's concern is the sheer extent of human sin, insisting that all the earth is affected and all people are implicated, and as such God's true justice requires judgement by absolute destruction.

This is the story we hearers are meant to know as we approach this end point of the prophet's writings; this is the background from which these concluding lyrics explode. After the apparent irrevocability of judgement, the real finale is unveiled: by God's grace, his people will be restored to a new and flourishing life with him.

Free at last

The glorious hope of which Zephaniah sings is both a freedom from the old (3.15) and a promise of the new (3.16–20). In freedom from their old guilt, God's people find the hope of justification. Zephaniah doesn't try to explain how the Lord of fierce judgement now turns that judgement away, but from this side of the life and death of Jesus, we can marvel at how justice and mercy came together at the cross. Many of us, even after coming to faith, struggle with a lingering sense of guilt and shame. But we can be fully assured that 'There is therefore now no condemnation for those who are in Christ Jesus' (Rom. 8.1).

Freedom from the old also means God's people will no longer be bound by fear. God's judgement on his own nation had often taken the form of invasion and attack, and the threat of powerful armies around them was ever-present. Yet in this vision of a restored, redeemed future, there is no longer a need to sleep with one eye open because God himself will turn away enemies and take care of the oppressors (Zeph. 3.19). The fears that keep us up at night may be somewhat different to those of Jerusalem in Zephaniah's day, though war is still a concerning reality in our time. But we too can sing of that day when we'll be free from nagging thoughts, from lurking anxieties and from wearying 'what ifs', beginning now as we take everything to God in prayer.

Transforming presence

Free from the past, God's people can look ahead to the promised future: the hope of God's presence in their midst. Earlier in the book, God's arrival in judgement is described as something to be feared, but now the presence of God in healing and salvation is the foundation of the peaceful new life they will enjoy. The presence of God will always bring about change and restoration. Those who have suffered and been excluded will no longer be figures of shame, but lifted up and celebrated as they find their place in God's purposes. Even as we sing together of God's presence among us, both now and in eternal fulfilment, God also sings songs of joy over the people he loves and has rescued, delighted to gather us close to himself once more.

Sing aloud, Zephaniah implores us. Our songs can and must include our cries to God to make right the injustices that still rage around us, but it's right that our hymn books should be overflowing with the glorious hope that we have. These promises, which have been fulfilled in part through the history of God's people, will one day be fully realized. Then we will know complete forgiveness, freedom from fear, the comfort of God's presence, and our own transformation from glory into glory. That's a chorus worth repeating.

Claire Jones

Hymn suggestions

When I was lost you came and rescued me; Glorious things of thee are spoken; Rejoice, the Lord is king; Be still, for the presence of the Lord.

Ascension Day 29 May
Principal Service **Set Free to Serve**
Acts 1.1–11 (*must be used as either the first or second reading*), *or* Dan. 7.9–14; Ps. 47, *or* Ps. 93; Eph. 1.15–end; **Luke 24.44–end**

'We try to cling on to the things that matter to us, but they will all be taken away in the end. The wisest thing we can do is learn to let them go or give them away.' Those words were shared with me by a person who comes to see me for spiritual direction. He had found himself at a crossroads in his life and career and his words were hard-won, emerging from some pretty tough experiences and changes in his life. He had worked all his life to achieve; now, he felt it all slipping away. How was he to react?

It might seem curious that I share my directee's challenging words as part of a sermon for Ascension Day. However, as I reflect on the abiding power and meaning of Jesus' ascension, those words of my friend strike me as curiously apt. For part of what's going on in the story of Christ's ascension is an invitation, made to those first disciples, to let Jesus go. Tempted though they might be to try to cling on to their friend, their Lord and their saviour, he cannot and will not stay. His time to ascend to the Father has come. Though he has told them that he will not leave them bereft and abandoned – the Spirit will be sent to equip them – can they believe? The wise and holy path is to let their saviour go.

Setting Jesus free

My reading of the emotional dynamics at play on Ascension Day may strike some readers as a little too much of a stretch. I accept that it is difficult to read the disciples' psychological reactions into the text Luke provides. Yet, Ascension Day is, without doubt, a kind of crossroads in the lives of those first followers of Jesus. They have been through so much with him. They have been called and found in him the lodestone of their lives. They have witnessed miracles and undergone trials and temptations. At Jesus' point of greatest need – his arrest and crucifixion – many of them ran away. Peter denied him. In the crucifixion, they thought that the one in whom they'd placed their trust for salvation was lost for ever, only for them to receive him back in resurrection on Easter Day. I cannot imagine the shock, perhaps even the fear they felt at receiving Jesus back again. How their hope must have swelled. And now they must say goodbye to him once again. I imagine Jesus' closest friends and followers gathered as he ascended to heaven longing to hold on to him … to have the Son of God, the very Life, Way and Truth to be with them just for one minute more. It would be such a human reaction, wouldn't it? Yet, the wisest, most hopeful and holy thing for them to do, at the moment when they will be left behind, is to let Jesus go.

Setting the apostles free

Why is it so wise and hopeful to rejoice in the Lord's ascent to the Father? Well, in the first instance, because it is time. Jesus' work on earth is done. All that God wishes to accomplish through Christ's earthly ministry has been brought to fulfilment. Those first followers of Christ, whether they like it or not, are in a place where they are called to recognize a new season of ministry and life; a new season which they are called to step into.

For Jesus says, 'I am sending upon you what my Father promised; so stay here in the city until you have been clothed with power from on high.' In his physical departure, space is made for a new flowering of love, power and mercy; that which already has been accomplished can be sent out through the work of those who follow Jesus. The Holy Spirit will anoint and clothe Jesus' followers with power.

Setting all God's people free

This idea brings me back to those words of my friend: 'We try to cling on to the things that matter to us, but they will all be taken away in the end. The wisest thing we can do is learn to let them go or give them away.' These words can sound rather sad and depressing. My friend echoes that idea we hear in the funeral service: we brought nothing into the world and we can take nothing out. Yet Ascension reveals the holy and positive horizon held within the idea that we are called to 'let go'.

As Jesus' disciples we are called to let go because, ultimately, Jesus 'lets go'. He does not cling to his earthly ministry but ascends to the Father's throne. He lets go of his earthly clothing. Those who are called to be his church on earth are invited to step forward and be clothed with power to serve. And – joy of joys! – we do not need to be afraid, for God will equip us with the Holy Spirit.

Rachel Mann

Hymn suggestions

All heaven declares; Crown him with many crowns; Jesus shall reign; Thine be the glory.

Ascension Day   29 May
Second Service   Transforming Heaven

Morning Ps. 110, 150; Evening Ps. 8; Song of the Three 29–37, *or* 2 Kings 2.1–15; **Rev. 5**; *Gospel at Holy Communion*: Matt. 28.16–end

Where's Wally?

From childhood, I was a fan of the *Where's Wally?* series of books.[27] Fellow 'Wally Watchers' will know that there is much more to each page of the books than locating the protagonist. Each scene is constructed to draw you into a diversity of domains for you to discover details you might have easily disregarded. Sometimes, Wally addresses the reader, informing them of his adventures. However, most of the time the stories have an invisible narrator who serves as your guide, ushering you into each enveloping scene. My daughter has a book of the same style, except that instead of searching for Wally, you are looking to find a blessing of unicorns (yes, that is the collective noun for unicorns) hidden among various crowd scenes.[28] The narrator is similar to the one in the *Where's Wally?* series, except that the narrator offers more insight into the seven unicorns' personalities, characters and emotions. Knowing more about who they are helps you to understand where they are likely to be found. Unlike Wally, who is often situated collaterally amid his surroundings, these unicorns can noticeably transform each place by their presence.

Where's Jesus?

Ascension might be an occasion when people find themselves asking, 'Where's Jesus?' The reading from Revelation invites readers to expand our interest beyond the location of Jesus and to note the impact that he has on his surroundings. Beginning in Revelation 4, John of Patmos writes his words of prophecy based on an experience 'in the spirit' where he has gone through a door into heaven. John, our narrator, paints a scene which is immersive and captivating. The reader encounters the dazzling one who is seated on the throne and meets the 24 elders around the throne. Next, the enigmatic and mystifying four living creatures sing 'Holy, holy, holy …', and the elders respond to their song by confirming in their praise that only God who created all things is worthy 'to receive glory and honour and power' (Rev. 4.11).

For those looking for Jesus, he makes his appearance in Revelation 5. Here, the resurrected and ascended Jesus is depicted as the Lamb of God. In the Johannine material, only John the Baptist has referred to Jesus as the 'Lamb of God who takes away the sin of the world' (John 1.29). In Revelation 5, this extraordinary achievement of the Lamb is confirmed by the acknowledgement that he alone is worthy to open the scroll. The elders sing of how the blood of the Lamb who was slain has ransomed saints for God out of 'every tribe and language and people and nation'.

Changing the picture

An extraordinary thing happens in the heavenly scene John describes. Following the song of the elders which praises the works of the Lamb, John sees millions of angels who burst into song declaring that the Lamb is worthy 'to receive power and wealth and wisdom and might and honour and glory and blessing'. The Lamb is worthy of the same worship due to the one who sits on the throne. This astonishing refrain is confirmed and echoed by 'every creature in heaven and on earth and under the earth and in the sea', to their song the four living creatures add their 'amen' and the elders fall down in worship. This is new. Something has happened in this picture because of the works of the Lamb of God in human history. A shift has taken place, Jesus has changed the picture of heaven. Jesus changes heaven.

In 2009, a poll conducted by a national British newspaper indicated that 5 per cent of people believe that they have seen or heard an angel.[29] I can't claim any great spiritual or religious experience, but I would put myself in that 5 per cent. Just over a decade ago, during a church service, something unusual happened. As we sang one powerful and moving song based on these chapters in Revelation, it felt as if the place somehow changed. From the front right-hand-side corner of the church, there was a kind of shimmering radiance, like when heat makes the air look blurry. Colours seemed brighter and the music felt thick in the air. The sound of our singing became amplified, sounding fuller and richer for about a minute. I think that we heard the angels sing – the agreement of earth and heaven as we praised the Lamb of God as God.

I do not understand the mystery of how the life of heaven touches earth. I do believe that Ascension reminds us that the God of heaven came to earth to transform both earth and heaven. Jesus, the Lamb of God, is worthy of our praise and he calls us to be those who can hold something of the two together. This means that we ought to make a difference wherever we are based on who we are, considering whether, indeed, we collectively might be described as a blessing.

Matt Allen

Hymn suggestions

There is a higher throne; Worthy is the Lamb who was slain (Riddle); Holy, holy, holy, Lord God Almighty; And can it be.

Seventh Sunday of Easter
(Sunday after Ascension Day) 1 June
Principal Service **The Business, Not Busy-ness, of Faith**
Ezek. 36.24–28 (*if used, the reading from Acts must be used as the second reading*), or **Acts 16.16–34**; Ps. 97; Rev. 22.12–14, 16–17, 20–end; John 17.20–end

Ascension Day is like handover day, the day you move to a new job, and wonder how your successor will do. On Ascension Day, Jesus hands over to his followers, and in our reading from Acts, we see how they get on. At first sight, it looks encouraging. Paul and Silas demonstrate power over an evil spirit, then put up with beating and imprisonment, and yet still praise God. 'What a great story,' you might think. Let's have another look.

Preoccupied with religion?

Paul, Silas and Luke are on their way to the place of prayer when a girl starts shouting after them. They are so preoccupied that they fail to see, fail to *really* see, their mission to the city. They are so busy going about the *busy*-ness of faith that they forget what really is the *business* of faith. According to Luke, Paul only sets the girl free because she is getting on his nerves. Perhaps they don't help straight away because who they see is a slave, demon-possessed, and a nuisance. Yet she is innocent. She is not to blame for her enslavement, nor her possession, and she is being a nuisance by telling the truth: 'These men are slaves of the Most High God.' Yet Paul frees her because she is getting on his nerves. He seems to have lost focus. He is concentrating on getting to prayer rather than on bringing the kingdom of God to the town. Once he remembers that the job of a follower of Jesus is to bring freedom to the captives, he is focused. He frees the slave girl from oppression.

Identifying with the oppressed

For the girl's owners, this isn't freedom. It's a loss of income. They incite a riot and have Paul and Silas arrested, flogged and thrown in jail. Again, we need to take another look. Elsewhere, Paul points out that he is a Roman citizen, and refuses to be beaten or imprisoned. But here, he chooses to let it happen. Because here it identifies him with the inhabitants of Philippi, conscripted Roman soldiers used to being flogged. Paul participates in God's mission to Philippi by identifying with people, even to the extent of suffering like them. It is probably no coincidence that later when Paul writes to the church in Philippi, he commends them for being his partners in his imprisonment. They do for him what he did for them.

The jailer is so determined to keep his prisoners secure he takes them to the middle of the prison. There was no way out. Except, they weren't ever really imprisoned. They pray and praise God even in jail. There's an earthquake, which opens the doors and loosens the chains. Everyone stays put and Paul reassures the jailer that they are all there.

Finally, Paul preaches

Finally, Paul gets to preach. It's a short sermon: 'Believe in the Lord Jesus, and you will be saved, you and your household.' Maybe at the beginning of the story, Paul was heading to the place of prayer to preach. It is remarkable, though, that his apparent preoccupation with religious duty seems to prevent him from noticing the needs of the girl. It is remarkable that when he sees her, and addresses her need, there is a response to the gospel. Not a good response, but a response. And once Paul has empathized with this slave girl, he realizes the importance of being alongside people. He allows himself to be treated like a Philippian. He and his companions recognize God's presence with them even in jail. An amazing opportunity to escape occurs. They choose to stay, Paul gives a short sermon and the jailer comes to God.

Showing how much we care

This story tells us something very important. It reminds us not to be so preoccupied with the *busy-ness* of faith that we forget the *business* of faith. It reminds us that sharing our faith in action opens the opportunity to share it in word. Ascension Day is the day that Jesus left the earth and handed over to the church God's mission to the world. It is our task to be Jesus to others. It is our calling to love both God and the world and to keep those two things in balance. Paul, in the end, demonstrates God's love for others in action, by being with them. Then he speaks, and people turn to God.

Our calling is first to notice what is going on and empathize with those who suffer. Perhaps more challengingly, it is to identify with them. Remember the story of Andrew Graystone, the Christian who stood outside a mosque so that people could attend Friday prayers in safety?[30] That is identifying with others. Finally, Paul got to preach – briefly. It is probably true that people do not care how much you know until they know you care. I believe that our primary calling is to show how much we care.

Liz Shercliff

Hymn suggestions

Heaven shall not wait; Rejoice, the Lord is king; A new commandment I give unto you; All hail the power of Jesus' name.

Seventh Sunday of Easter   1 June
Second Service   As Water on a Thirsty Land
Ps. 68 [*or* 68.1–13, 18–19]; **Isa. 44.1–8**; Eph. 4.7–16; *Gospel at Holy Communion*: Luke 24.44–end

A dry and thirsty land

The ground is dry and thirsty. Earth torn apart; separated by great, deep cracks, formed as the last bits of moisture seep out of the claggy clay soil. Ground baked as hard as rock. Ground so devoid of moisture that an impermeable crust has formed on the surface. Ground without life, ground that will take more than one short shower to renew and replenish.

It is the image of the ground that every farmer dreads in early June, but one we fear may become more frequent, as hot, dry summers increase, and crops find it harder to thrive.

It is also the image given to us by the writer of our passage from Isaiah.

A thirsty people

Dry ground and thirst are often used in Scripture as metaphors for a deep spiritual need, which only God can satisfy. Here, the hearers of the word are those in exile in Babylon; far away from the spiritual home in Jerusalem. They are a people who are worn out, and hopeless; struggling to imagine a new and better future, where God will act and bring them home. A people who have forgotten their relationship with God; not coming to God in praise, but only burdening the Lord with their offences. They are a people who are dried up and impervious to the gentle rain of hope.

But now, despite their sins and their disregard for God, a deluge of hope is poured out on to that parched ground. With it, we hear God's promise, that the one who had formed them in the womb would now come to help them. Isaiah tells us that God will pour water on to the thirsty, parched places; that there will be streams on the dry ground and the spirit of God will fall upon the people and their descendants. That the barren wasteland of their faith will turn into a lush and fertile meadow.

It is a prophecy we hear many times in the Old Testament; that the promise of blessing given to Abraham and his descendants back in the book of Genesis will be fulfilled. A promise confirmed, not just by Isaiah but by Ezekiel, Joel and Zechariah; that help and refreshment will come, through the outpouring of God's spirit on the people.

Waiting on the Spirit

On Thursday, we celebrated the Ascension. Coming 40 days after we celebrated Christ's bursting from the tomb, we watched; looking up with the disciples, as Jesus disappeared into the clouds, to take his rightful place at God's right hand. Now, with them, we wait. Because although Pentecost was the day that God's promise, given in Isaiah, was first fulfilled, it did not just happen once. The promise continues to be fulfilled today, and so, like the dry ground waiting for the rain, in this season between Ascension and Pentecost we long for the Spirit of God which refreshes, refills, and brings our lives to flourish.

A pleasant aroma

Have you ever noticed how good it smells after the rain has fallen? Many of us will know that wonderful scent when a soft sustained shower falls onto dry ground. Named by two Australian geologists in the 1960s, the smell even has a name, *petrichor*; formed from the Greek for stone, 'petra' (remember Jesus' naming of Peter, the rock), and 'ichor', the golden life blood, which flows through the veins of the gods in Greek mythology. The aroma is actually produced by a molecule being released by certain bacteria in the soil, and humans are particularly sensitive to it, perhaps developed because of how important rain is to our survival.

Likewise, we long for the Spirit, because of her importance to us. For she is the Spirit who is our lifeblood; running through the veins of faith, enabling us to grow, and building us up in love. It is the same Spirit who offers the gifts mentioned in our reading from Ephesians. The Spirit who equips us for all sorts of ministries in the church, building up the body of Christ, and fuelling our everyday Christian discipleship. It is the Spirit who also produces a good smell; the aroma of Christ. Just as the rain falling on the hard ground produces a recognizable and agreeable scent, so should the pouring out of the Spirit in our lives producing something that is both positive and recognizable. A fragrance that is pleasing to the Lord (as the burnt offerings of old) and by which he who has died, risen and ascended might be better known to those around us.

As a dry and thirsty land, we long for God's refreshing rain; Lord, make us ready for the coming of your Spirit.

Chris Campbell

Hymn suggestions

A mighty wind invades the world; As water to the thirsty; Have you heard the raindrops (Water of Life); May the fragrance of Jesus.

Day of Pentecost (Whit Sunday)   8 June
(For Pentecost All-Age, see p. 359.)

Principal Service   **The Power of Wind and Flame**

Acts 2.1–21 (*must be used as either the first or second reading*), *or* Gen. 11.1–9; Ps. 104.26–36, 37b [*or* 104.26–end]; Rom. 8.14–17; John 14.8–17 [25–27]

Wind and flame

Where I live in Bristol, on a sunny summer day, a couple of hours after dawn or before dusk, you'll likely see three or four hot-air balloons drifting over the city. And however commonplace a sight it may be, it always lifts the spirit. A hot-air balloon big enough to carry 12 adults would just about fit in a regular pulpit in its deflated state. Inflated it would be too big to fit in most churches. First, it is filled with cold air using a huge fan – like a strong wind. Then the air is heated with a flame that is hot enough to make the back of a passenger's neck feel rather uncomfortable. The power of the wind that fills it and the flame that lifts it transform the balloon from a flat pile of fabric to an extraordinary vehicle.

The disciples were probably feeling rather deflated that first Pentecost. Jesus had gone, and although he had promised he would send his Spirit, he hadn't given them a timescale – they were waiting, wondering what on earth to do next. They were gathered together, inside, feeling ... what? Directionless, powerless, fearful ...? Then came a sound like the rush of a violent wind, filling the house. A tongue of fire on each of them. Suddenly they were filled by the Holy Spirit and something changed. They were animated, they were confident, they were powerful.

Filled and lifted

Jesus' followers were filled, they were filled by the Holy Spirit and transformed, lifted. They became something new and extraordinary with the Spirit's power in them. They grew in confidence and courage, in presence and passion. They occupied their place in the world differently: they had a message of God's love for all people and they wanted to share it. Their preaching on that first day of Pentecost reached people from many countries; through the power of the Spirit, they could speak to them in ways they understood. They were changed from a fearful group meeting in secret to bold proclaimers of the gospel for all to hear.

Directed by the Spirit

Not everyone realizes that hot-air balloons can't steer. The pilots can take advantage of different air streams that travel in different directions by moving the balloon higher or lower, but basically they have to go where the wind takes them. It can be like that when we allow the Spirit to fill our lives. We don't always get to choose where to go! But we're carried along in the Spirit's power, to the places God takes us that we couldn't have imagined when we set off. The disciples on the first Pentecost must have had no idea that they would suddenly be preaching to huge crowds, no idea what was coming or where it would lead next. It was a step of faith and trust in God.

Uplifted by God's love

I once had the pleasure of a hot-air balloon ride. I saw people of every age stop and look up at us. People were running out into their gardens; children were chasing along paths to follow us. Because I knew how delighted my children would be to be waved at from a hot-air balloon, I decided I would wave at every person as if they were my children. And it felt like I was bestowing blessings on them as we flew past – something in them was touched by wonder as they on the ground made a real connection with us in the air.

Imagine if the church had that impact on people. If, when people encountered us, they were uplifted. If they felt joy and wonder at what we had to say. So how do we look as a church today? Are we deflated, fearful, gathered in secret, directionless? Or are we filled with the Spirit, flying high for everyone to see and hear the love of God that we proclaim?

We can soar

Imagine. Imagine if we were to greet every person like our best beloved, to love them as we want our own families to be loved, to bless them with the blessings that we pray our own children would receive. That's exactly what Jesus tells us to do. And filled by the Spirit, we can. It's not in our own power, it's not our own direction we choose, it's not our own message we proclaim. A hot-air balloon is just a massive empty sack without the power of the flame and air that fills it. However small, deflated or empty we might feel, we can be transformed and lifted by the power of the Spirit. We can soar.

Kat Campion-Spall

Hymn suggestions

Come down, O love divine; Come, Holy Ghost, our souls inspire; She sits like a bird; There's a spirit in the air.

Pentecost 8 June
Second Service **Changed from Greyness into Glory**
Morning Ps. 36.5–10, 150; Evening Ps. 33.1–12; **Ex. 33.7–20**;
2 Cor. 3.4–end; *Gospel at Holy Communion*: John 16.4b–15

Trapped in grey days?

Do you ever find yourself feeling a bit grey, a tad jaded, stuck in a rut? Has your relationship with God become more like a loveless marriage – the spark gone, the dynamism of first love faded to a routine ritual? Has that childlike wonder about God been snuffed out by a world-weary cynicism, the fire of faith now a smoking ember? Has the letter of the law – rote religion – killed the dynamism of faith; hardness of heart making us inflexible and cold? Does it sometimes feel as if you are just going through the motions? If that resonates with you today, listen up!

Consider the glory of God

Quite the opposite of grey is the word 'glory'. It's referenced twice in today's Old Testament reading and 14 times in the verses from 2 Corinthians.

The passage from Exodus references the glory of God, the *kabod* – the majesty, wonder and awe of God. This is the white-hot holiness of God which will pass by as Moses hides in a cleft of the rock, covered by the hand of God. This is the *Shekinah*, the blazing majesty of God, like the light from a welder's torch times a million. The glory of God is simply too much for a human being, even Moses, to handle. Yet in 2 Corinthians we read of the transformative effect of this glory.

Pentecost – the day of *kabod-doxa*

In the Epistle, the Hebrew *kabod* is now translated into Greek as *doxa*. For those who know the grey experience, *kabod-doxa* is required. Paul sees glory as having degrees of power; from the old covenant, the law of Mount Sinai, to the new covenant revealed in the flesh of Jesus Christ – the glory increases in intensity and dynamism. There is a challenge here. Have we allowed our thoughts about God to become stale and static? The readings today, set for the Day of Pentecost, remind us that God's glory is dynamic, that revelation is like fire, coming to transform our tawdry dull humanity, bringing life and energy, movement and hope. The glory of God changes those who bask in its reflection. This is the invitation of the Epistle.

Pray earnestly for the gift of the Holy Spirit

If the greyness of rote religion is your reality and you find yourself bound in routine emptiness, listen to Paul:

> Now the Lord is the Spirit, and where the Spirit of the Lord is, there is freedom. And all of us, with unveiled faces, seeing the glory of the Lord as though reflected in a mirror, are being transformed into the same image from one degree of glory to another; for this comes from the Lord, the Spirit.

This Pentecost, today, right now, let's pray earnestly for the gift of the Spirit, for the breath of God to blow over the void of our lives, summoning new life, freedom and hope. Let's tear aside the veil of defensiveness, cynicism, fear and stubbornness, turning to face God as we are. Let's trust in the love that always desires us, and will never turn us away, sinful though we are. Notice how the glory which emanates from God has such a transformative effect, changing us, as Paul puts it, 'from one degree of glory to another'.

Take a leaf from Moses' book

Dare we believe this? Are we fearful? Anxious that we will take that leap of faith and come crashing down? Take a leaf from Moses' book; he speaks to God with bold directness. It's almost as though he argues with God: 'You said this ... but I experience that ... yet you have also said ...' Perhaps he is also arguing with himself, calling himself to deeper levels of trust in God.

If today you are heartsick and weary – tired of yourself, tired of the failure of the church, tired of all the greyness of the petty round of day-to-day routine – *stop*. Tell God how you are – openly and honestly – and be open to the Holy Spirit who comes to give new life.

This Pentecost let's come to God holding the stained veil of our sin, seeking his face directly. Let's trust that there is faith to be found on the other side of failure and sin, not as naive as our first faith, perhaps a bit dog-eared and worn, but all the more glorious for this. God has not left or abandoned us – the Spirit comes to bring new life and transform us from greyness into glory.

> Almighty God,
> in Christ you make all things new:
> transform the poverty of our nature by the riches of your grace,
> and in the renewal of our lives
> make known your heavenly glory;
> through Jesus Christ your Son our Lord. Amen.[31]

Kate Bruce

Hymn suggestions

Love divine; Breathe on me, breath of God; Fall afresh; Spirit, fall.

Ordinary Time

Trinity Sunday 15 June
Principal Service **Love in Harmony**
Prov. 8.1–4, 22–31; Ps. 8; Rom. 5.1–5; **John 16.12–15**

Jesus said, 'Whoever does not receive the kingdom of God as a little child will never enter it' (Luke 18.17). I often wonder why we can't all just accept God with a childlike sense of awe and wonder; accepting the mystery *as* a mystery, without needing to pin down and pigeonhole God, getting him neatly into a box and keeping him there. I long for this childlike acceptance of mystery never more so than when I have to preach on Trinity Sunday!

God in a box?

The human mind simply cannot contain God, and therefore cannot understand God. As a little child, taught St Augustine, trying to fit God into the human mind is like trying to fit the ocean into a tiny hole in the sand. It's not for us to explain *how* God is Trinity – rather, to accept the mystery *that* God is Trinity because that is our experience of God. Fitting God into a mental box runs the risk of manipulating God for our selfish ends.

God reveals himself to us as Father, Son and Holy Spirit. This is, quite simply, who God is. God must be allowed to be God, and God will frequently surprise us.

God is God: who are we?

We are made in the image of God, who reveals himself as a *relational* being. The mystery of the Trinity is the mystery of *community* – community so perfect that the three persons are truly one God, in a constant reciprocation of pure, divine love.

We too are called to community. When God created Adam, he said, 'It is not good that the man should be alone' (Gen. 2.18). To everything else God made, he said, 'It is good'. But he couldn't say that about humankind until there was community. We *need* one another, we affect one another. What builds up one builds up all, and what hurts one hurts all, for in the end all are connected.

We are all part of communities, large and small, local and global, and we are called to work hard at making those relationships real, making them work, because community is what God created us to be.

We share so much, but it's our choice whether we join in as an *individual* with our wants and wishes paramount in our thoughts, or else we join in as a *part* of a living community of faith, genuinely interested in one another and our unity in God.

It can be *hard* to work at relationships, and it's always a two-way street: but holding on to what prevents us from being community, in however small a way, diminishes us all, because it kills off something *of* the community. The more we allow God to help us make community real, the more of God we'll understand and the more of one another we'll understand.

Embodying community

A commitment to the God who reveals himself as a community of love is the vocation of the church, and we must seek to embody that commitment. This requires several things.

It needs prayer, including the courage to ask for forgiveness and for the grace to forgive and be forgiven.

It needs people who don't look to be the ones in the right all the time; people who, above all, *want* and *work for* the common good.

It needs people who accept one another's diversity, and seek the harmonies within that, rather than pursuing a bland uniformity.

It needs people who are open to the guidance and the love of God, who allow themselves to be filled so full of that love that it overflows to the people around them, to the whole church. And that means real, honest love, which rolls its sleeves up and tackles the real issues, the real problems, the real truth. It's the love of God, seen in crib and cross, resurrection and renewal. When we are filled to overflowing with that love, it pours out into the world out there, which was the plan all along.

Communion

God reveals himself to us as Father, Son and Holy Spirit, and seeks to draw us into the life of that community of love. It's in this relationship that we see the importance of our *image* of God.

If God, if *truth* for us, were merely a set of *doctrines*, of beliefs, then faith would be reduced to little more than an intellectual exercise. That would be death, not life!

On the other hand, if truth were merely the way we *feel* about things, then our lives would have little meaning, and when we felt bad, we would realize the emptiness of a merely emotional approach to the spiritual life.

But if truth for us is a God of *mind and heart and spirit*, with whom we can grow in *relationship*, then we do have life; we enter *communion* with the God who loves us and has saved us, and we have the strength and the impetus to shed that love abroad in this community of Christ in which we share.

Bill Braviner

Hymn suggestions

Holy, holy, holy, Lord God almighty; I bind unto myself this day; Father of heaven, whose love profound; Can we by searching find out God.

Trinity Sunday   15 June
Second Service   **On Holy Ground**
Morning Ps. 29; Evening Ps. 73.1–3, 16–end; **Ex. 3.1–15**; John 3.1–17

The holy ground we least expect

'Remove the sandals from your feet, for the place on which you are standing is holy ground.' What do you picture when you hear 'holy ground'? Moses was standing on a dusty hillside, in a dry, hot, windy place with little water and little beauty, looking for lost sheep. It's a Monday morning kind of place. Hard at work. Busy. Not the kind of place we often look for God. Yet that place is the grand opening for Moses' first dramatic encounter with God. Far from temples, far from religious places. By the end, God promises

Moses that he and the people of Israel will return and worship him there, on that mountain. Somehow, in a few moments, that place changes. It becomes holy ground, a sacred place, where God can be found. Well, some of the time, at least. After all, God promises to Moses, 'I will be with you.'

Sacred spaces and sacred journeys

There is a basic tension that runs through the whole of Scripture. The tension between Monday and Sunday, between gathered worship and worship out there, in everyday life; between travelling with God, worshipping God anywhere, anytime, and stopping in and setting aside special places. We see that tension in images of the Temple and the tabernacle. The tabernacle was a portable sanctuary, a tent that went around with the Israelites, that symbolized God's presence going with them, everywhere. A presence that was awesome, scary, untameable. Dangerous. A presence that guided and cared – the presence that guided the Hebrews slaves out of Egypt and into safety, opened the sea before them and provided food in the desert. Yet a presence few dared to approach because it was at times unpredictable, or hard to understand. A presence so holy that people had to cover themselves as they became aware of their own shortcomings – as Moses does, covering his face before God. And the tabernacle went with them, always. They couldn't escape, they couldn't hide. God lived in their midst, knew them inside and out, and shaped their every moment. This is the tabernacle. God coming into human affairs, intimately living with his people. And this is what God promises to Moses in our passage.

God with us

God has seen the suffering of Israel and will do something about it. But not from the outside, not with great displays of power. No zapping Pharaoh from above. No heavenly strike button. Instead, God will go with his people, with Moses, step by step, victory by victory, mistake by mistake. Slowly and patiently, without taking over. But working together, discussing, fighting, wrestling with his people.

Moses starts by covering his face, but the shyness doesn't last long. God's presence isn't one that overwhelms, but one that enables. And Moses, who says he can't speak well, seems to be pretty good at arguing his case. He hears God out first, hears the plan. You will go to Pharaoh. Moses doesn't say yes! He goes, 'You've got the wrong guy. Not me. I am nothing, no one. Wrong qualification. Clear case of mistaken identity.' And God gives this great response: 'I will be with you.' Does that make it any easier to go to Pharaoh? Moses doesn't think so!

A place of wrestling and revelation

Moses argues, wrestles, complains. Holy ground isn't a passive place where Moses simply receives God's revelation or sits there feeling good about a vision. It is a place where he meets with himself, with his doubts and fears and inadequacies. With his dreams also, a place where the limits of his faith and trust are tested; and a place where he discovers that life may be bigger than he thought. That God may be closer than he thought. That faith isn't just belief or obedience, but true partnership. Moses argues with God, and in response God reveals himself further. Arguing and wrestling with God lead to deeper knowledge and experience of God. God reveals his name to Moses. God promises to be consistent, to be faithful, to be the God he has already proved himself to be in history, in relationship with Abraham, Isaac and Jacob. A God of faithfulness, justice and loving-kindness.

In this special place, Moses is equipped. He is not equipped to become a professional believer spending his life in sacred spaces – he is equipped to go out into the world, and walk with God as God delivers, redeems and restores.

Moses meets God on holy ground, and holy ground is both a Monday place and a Sunday place. It stands as an in-between place, between the steady, steadfast revelation of the God who does not change and can be relied on, and the ever-moving God who goes with us.

Sinai as a sacred space gives us a model: it is a place to be equipped and resourced to go out and work with God, and then return, tell the stories and meet again with the God who surprises us with new knowledge and understanding of the ways of God, of ourselves and our communities, and with his constant invitation to engage more deeply with the world God has come to save.

Isabelle Hamley

Hymn suggestions

Be still, for the presence of the Lord; The God of Abraham, praise; Glorious things of thee are spoken; You are holy, Lord, there is none like you.

First Sunday after Trinity (Proper 7)   22 June
Principal Service   **A Man on the Edge, and a Herd of Pigs**
(*Continuous*): 1 Kings 19.1–4 [5–7] 8–15a; Ps. 42, 43 [*or* 42, *or* 43]; *or* (*Related*): Isa. 65.1–9; Ps. 22.19–28; Gal. 3.23–end; **Luke 8.26–39**

An encounter with 'the other'

It is difficult to read this encounter in our modern context when we might shy away from the language of demons and possession. Nevertheless, this is a troubled and deeply overwhelmed young man who is out of his depth and out of control. There are conflicting identities within him, and his own is seemingly lost. In mind, body and spirit he is in turmoil. He lives on the edges – of society, of friendships, of family and community. He is naked and lives among death, with only tombs as his shelter. He is constantly reminded of the fate that awaits him imminently, for no one can imagine that a long and healthy life lies ahead of him.

Everyone is afraid of him, and more than likely feels helpless in his presence. People had tried to contain him and control him. Every time, by some super-human strength, he has escaped the chains which bound him. Nothing can be done for him or to him. He is beyond any human intervention.

As Jesus steps out of the boat on to the shore, the man rushes towards him shouting. What a sight it must have been. One imagines the disciples hurriedly heading back into the boat and urgently encouraging Jesus to do the same. They have only just come through a weather storm on the lake. Now they are faced with a human storm.

Jesus stands his ground and meets him.

What's in a name?

The identities within the man scream out in recognition of Jesus, addressing him directly by name and by title: Jesus, Son of the

Most High God. They know exactly who Jesus is, and they know exactly what Jesus has the power to do. The disciples are still trying to answer the question, 'Who is this man that even the wind and waves obey him?' The voices inside the man have no doubts about Jesus' identity and what this means for them.

In return, Jesus asks the man for his name, and the voices cry out, 'Legion'. They have taken his body, mind and spirit, and have now taken his name and his identity. The 'name' they give is a descriptor of their presence. Multiple identities which Jesus commands to leave. Their time of occupation is over. The man is to regain all that has been stolen.

Pigs lost – a life restored

Allowing the occupants permission to enter the pigs rather than being sent to a place of torture is perhaps an act of compassion on Jesus' part. Unclean spirits occupying unclean animals seems to fit the religious context of the time. The herd now experience the turmoil which had lived inside the man, who is now free. The pigs, in terror, rush off a cliff and drown. The man is saved, in body, mind and spirit. He is restored. He occupies his own space once more.

When the community come out to see what is happening for themselves, they no longer see a naked, screaming, chaotic man of whom they are afraid. They see a calm, clothed man who is engaged in conversation. Now the community's fear switches to Jesus. Who is this, that even 'demons' obey? Jesus is more powerful than anything they have encountered. Rather than celebrate a man restored, they lament a herd lost and request (strongly) that Jesus leave. If he's capable of this, what more might happen with him around? Rather than argue or persuade them, Jesus gets back into the boat and leaves, telling the man to stay and bear witness to what God has done for him.

Who is this man?

This is a question faced by almost everyone who meets Jesus. The chief priests and elders ask him publicly by whose authority he preaches and teaches. The disciples ask this question in a boat battered by a storm. The crowds ask each other whether Jesus is one of the ancient prophets come back. Pilate one day asks, 'Are you the Messiah?'

This is Jesus, who unnerves and disturbs, who restores and saves. Who gives back dignity and agency. Who encounters the most vulnerable at the edges and on the margins, and does not leave them there. Who has power and authority over all things, even over the 'demonic' occupation of human lives. Who commissions a once dangerous man to become a witness to the community who were afraid of him.

As we enter the Ordinary Time of the church's seasons, we remember that we follow and serve an extraordinary Jesus.

Kt Tupling

Hymn suggestions

Inspired by love and anger; Hills of the north, rejoice; Praise my soul, the king of heaven; My Jesus, my saviour.

First Sunday after Trinity (Proper 7) 22 June
Second Service **Never Go Back ...**
Ps. **[50] 57**; **Gen. 24.1–27**; Mark 5.21–end

To modern sensibilities, the Bible can read as a strange collection of writings. Such a judgement very much applies to today's passage from the book of Genesis. I cannot be alone in finding myself feeling a mixture of quiet bewilderment and, well, queasiness, as we read of the aged Abraham inviting his retainer to place his hand under Abraham's thigh as a bond of fidelity; equally, the transactions around 'finding' a wife – Rebekah – for Isaac absolutely do not fit our current ideas of consent and romantic love.

The promises of God

Nonetheless, this story has real power. It invites us to consider the faithfulness of God and how this faithfulness is always expressed as an invitation to move forward, like a pilgrim, and not turn back. As Abraham says to his servant:

> 'See to it that you do not take my son back there. The LORD, the God of heaven, who took me from my father's house and from the land of my birth, and who spoke to me and swore to me, "To

your offspring I will give this land", he will send his angel before you; you shall take a wife for my son from there.'

We might find the specifics of Abraham's narrative odd, but the invitation from God to all of us to keep stepping into God's holy promises is very real. Ultimately, God will be faithful.

At the same time, it does not take the skills of a professional psychologist to understand why Abraham might not wish his son to be taken back to the 'old country'. Abraham and his family have been called by God to be children of promise. They have, in effect, been given an awesome commission by God to trust that he will provide for them and lead them to the Promised Land. Perhaps, Abraham fears that should Isaac go back to his homeland, a homeland Isaac has never seen, he will end up being ravished by it and perhaps never leave.

Perhaps, like so many of us as we age, Abraham finds himself – in his dotage – spending time reminiscing about the days of his youth. Perhaps this sense of nostalgia only amplifies his fear that Isaac, should he go to Ur, will be deflected from his true inheritance: to carry forward God's promises into the Promised Land. All the hope founded in Abraham's line might be drawn to an abrupt end.

Steadfast love

If I find the servant's mission to find a wife for Isaac out of step with the mores of our time, I do not doubt the servant's humility and faithfulness. He arrives in Abraham's homeland and asks God to 'show steadfast love to my master Abraham'. He asks this not only because he is faithful to Abraham, but because God swore to Abraham that this is where a wife for Isaac shall be found.

The golden thread through this narrative is the characters' desire to centre everything on God as the giver of all good things. God is steadfast and has shown his love to Abraham and he will show his love to his descendants for ever. This covenant made by God with Abraham and his descendants flows both ways; as God offers grace, Abraham responds with trust. He responds with a seasoned love for the God who is faithful. Even the curious, perhaps bizarre, moment when the servant places his hand under Abraham's thigh is a token of fidelity: it is a signal that faithfulness and trust is at the heart of people of God.

Follow Jesus

The circumstances of life in which we find ourselves are rather different from those presented in the Bronze Age world of Abraham, Rebekah and Isaac. Nonetheless, we are children of covenant and promise too; we are called to follow Jesus as his pilgrim people. As I age, indeed as I increasingly feel as if my body is falling apart and I am plunging headlong towards my dotage, I am tempted to look back towards earlier stages of life with nostalgia. There have been times when I have thought, 'If only I had the firebrand faith and commitment I had back then.' However, while I believe that God does not begrudge us our memories and our talent for casting the past in rose-tinted hues, the truth is that we are called forward into new life and promise by God.

When we look back, as Abraham did in his old age, we are invited to do so not with longing for the 'Kingdom of Youth', but to recall the abiding facts of God's promises. Just as Abraham never forgets the promises made to him and his descendants by the living God, we are invited to look back on God's faithfulness to us in Jesus. We do this not to congratulate ourselves and feel complacent. Rather, we do so to ensure that we are inspired to pass God's faithful inheritance on.

Rachel Mann

Hymn suggestions

All my hope on God is founded; The God of Abraham, praise; Will you come and follow me; Faithful one, so unchanging.

Second Sunday after Trinity (Proper 8) 29 June
(For SS Peter and Paul, Apostles, see p. 321.)
Principal Service **The Cost of Following Jesus**
(*Continuous*): 2 Kings 2.1–2, 6–14; Ps. 77.1–2, 11–end
[*or* 77.11–end]; or (*Related*): 1 Kings 19.15–16, 19–end;
Ps. 16; Gal. 5.1, 13–25; **Luke 9.51–end**

Where was Jesus going? The opening verse from our reading from Luke tells us that Jesus was heading resolutely towards Jerusalem. This signals the beginning of 'Luke's journey narrative'. Journeying is one of the main ways Luke unpacks what it means to be a disciple of Jesus.

In this passage, Jesus encounters three individuals on his journey. In each of these three encounters, Jesus gives three sayings, or 'chreia', which are pithy little sayings that speak to the character of a person, to make an important point. As we examine each of these sayings in turn, let's see what we can learn about the nature of discipleship.

Discipleship: costly and inconvenient

The first person encountered along the road is very willing to follow Jesus. Without any prompting, he says, 'I will follow you wherever you go.' In response to this apparent willingness, Jesus highlights the cost and inconvenience of being a disciple. He says, 'Foxes have holes, and birds of the air have nests; but the Son of Man has nowhere to lay his head.' Being a disciple of Jesus means embarking on a journey that will involve being unsettled and possibly experiencing rejection.

In the following chapter, Jesus states that to inherit eternal life, we must love the Lord God with all our heart, soul, mind and strength, and also love our neighbours as ourselves. While we may think we are prepared to love and follow God, the latter half of this statement – to love our neighbours as ourselves – demands deeper consideration. Loving others requires time and effort, emotionally and physically. Loving in this way can be inconvenient, it can be costly, and sometimes will lead to rejection. When we claim to be disciples of Jesus, have we taken fully into account what loving others might entail?

Discipleship: putting aside social conventions

Jesus meets a second person on the road and says to him, 'Follow me.' This encounter differs from the first because here it is Jesus who takes the initiative. The respondent points out the commitments he has which will affect his ability to follow, in this instance the responsibility of burying his parents. Interestingly, there was no specific Mosaic command at the time to be responsible for burying one's parents. The sentiment being expressed here is likely one informed by the commandment to 'honour your father and mother'. It is, therefore, a social expectation or convention of the day, rather than a legal obligation.

Jesus responds by simply saying, 'Let the dead bury their own dead; but as for you, go and proclaim the kingdom of God.' Not only is being a disciple inconvenient and costly, but it may also require disregarding common social conventions and commitments of the day.

This gives us pause to reflect, to consider ourselves and all the things we hold dear or sacred. Are we willing to lay down some of the traditions and social conventions that have shaped our lives, in order to proclaim the kingdom of God?

Discipleship: not being distracted from the goal

Jesus' third encounter differs from the first two, as it does not appear in the other Synoptic Gospels. This exchange is found in Luke alone, and so we ought to pay special attention to it. Here, the person declares he will follow Jesus, but with the proviso that he is allowed to go back and say goodbye to his family. Jesus responds, 'No one who puts a hand to the plough and looks back is fit for the kingdom of God.'

Jesus is quoting a well-known proverb which is based on the demands of ploughing a field. If you are to plough a field with oxen, then – as with driving a car – you need to keep your eyes fixed ahead, to avoid veering off course. This metaphor connects back to the opening verse where Jesus has his sights set resolutely on Jerusalem. He will not allow anything to distract him. To look back risks inviting regret, fostering nostalgia and living in retrospect. But to follow Jesus, to be a disciple, is to keep your eyes fixed on the goal.

The journey of discipleship

The journey of discipleship is costly and inconvenient. The journey of discipleship may offend social conventions. The journey of discipleship requires letting go of the things that distract us. Notice that the passage does not tell us how the three people Jesus met along the road responded. The important question is, how will we respond to Jesus' invitation to follow him? In the words of the beautiful hymn 'The heavenly vision' (1922) – better known as 'Turn your eyes upon Jesus':

Turn your eyes upon Jesus,
Look full in his wonderful face,
And the things of earth will grow strangely dim
In the light of his glory and grace.

Mark Nam

Hymn suggestions

Turn your eyes upon Jesus; Guide me, O thou great Redeemer; I heard the voice of Jesus say; I have decided to follow Jesus.

Second Sunday after Trinity (Proper 8)   29 June
Second Service   **Not Just a Man**
Ps. [59.1–6, 18–end] 60; Gen. 27.1–40; **Mark 6.1–6**

For all its theological faults, the musical *Jesus Christ Superstar* encapsulates some real truths. When Mary Magdalene sings, 'I don't know how to love him',[32] she probably speaks for most people. And when she sings, 'He's just a man', she broaches the subject of incarnation. He *is* a man, but not just a man. Isn't this what Jesus' neighbours struggle with in today's Gospel reading?

Divisive Jesus

When Barack Obama was elected President of the United States in 2008, friends who knew him from schooldays didn't reflect on his leadership qualities or his political convictions. They remembered his love of comic books and basketball. He had been one of them. In his hometown, Jesus too had been one of them: 'The carpenter, the son of Mary and brother of James and Joses and Judas.' Jesus' effect on the villagers is not clear. They either took offence because of him, or they stumbled because of him. Whichever it was, it seems to have had a negative effect on Jesus. Confusingly, Mark tells us Jesus could do no work of power there, and then lists some works of power that he did. It just wasn't many. The neighbours seem to have been divided. Some believed, and were healed; some were dismissed, and Jesus could do nothing for them. They were just human, after all. Jesus, too, seems human. Where there is no faith in him, he can do nothing. What he does is in partnership with those who have faith. Jesus, it seems to me, is always divisive. Who is he? What would he do? In reality, we don't know. What does seem clear from the Gospels is that Jesus divides people because he was – is – more than just a man.

Just a man

This incident is a story worth telling, in Mark's estimation, because the neighbours are so convinced of Jesus' humanity. He is one of them. They know his family, they've seen him grow up, they're familiar with his family and his job. He's a carpenter who grew up among them. Let's not be too quick to condemn these village folk. What they say is true. Jesus is a human being. He has normal human experiences. He has brothers and sisters and a mother. This is not just a story of unfaithful friends or leery locals; what they say is true. Why does Mark include this tale in his Gospel?

I think it is because it points to the uniqueness of Jesus. When Mark was writing, Romans believed that human beings – Caesars anyway – could become gods when they died. This is a reverse story. God becomes human. So human, in fact, that those who saw him grow up know that he is human and have trouble believing he is divine.

Jesus does not try to explain himself, however. He simply points out that 'Prophets are not without honour, except in their home town, and among their own kin, and in their own house.' It isn't necessarily condemnation, just a statement of how things are. And perhaps it's also a statement of how things should be. Read almost any biography of a great leader, and you will find that when they go home to their families, their kids treat them like any other parent. They expect great orators to read them bedtime stories, senior religious leaders to put plasters on bumped knees and world-class footballers to play keepie-uppie in the garden. Hollywood star Angelina Jolie once said that it was her kids that kept her grounded.[33]

More than a man

It is not that Jesus does nothing here. He heals some people. He is more than a man. This season of Trinity offers an opportunity to dwell on the three-in-one God, each divine person distinctly different. Jesus, as well as being human, is God. He has not shed his humanity to become something other. The story of his ascension tells us that – he left his disciples bodily. Somehow humanity is now joined to God. Jesus is more than a man.

The main point of Mary Magdalene's song in *Jesus Christ Superstar* is not, of course, the doctrine of incarnation. It is that she does not know how to love this God-man, the Word become flesh. It seems that Jesus' childhood friends and neighbours don't know how to love him either. What the story seems to suggest, though, is that keeping an open mind allows Jesus to do miraculous works, while closed minds prevent him.

As Thomas Merton says, 'You do not need to know precisely what is happening … what you need is to recognize the possibilities and challenges … and to embrace them with courage, faith and hope.'[34] We are not so different from Jesus' neighbours. We do not know precisely who Jesus is. What is asked of us is courage, faith and hope.

Liz Shercliff

Hymn suggestions

Meekness and majesty; All hail the power of Jesus' name; One with God and one with man; Above the clash of creeds.

Third Sunday after Trinity (Proper 9)   6 July
Principal Service   Speaking Powerfully
(*Continuous*): 2 Kings 5.1–14; Ps. 30; *or* (*Related*): Isa. 66.10–14; Ps. 66.1–8; Gal. 6.[1–6] 7–16; **Luke 10.1–11, 16–20**

Speak friend

I live about ten minutes away from the Tolkien Trail. It is a fantastic local walk that sets off from Hurst Green, the village which is home to Stonyhurst school where Tolkien lived and taught when penning his compelling tales set in Middle Earth. One of the features of Tolkien's writing is his love of riddles and his ability to demonstrate how language can be provocative, puzzling, playful and powerful. In one of my favourite scenes from *The Fellowship of the Ring*, the fellowship arrive at 'The Doors of Durin' where they find 'Speak, friend, and enter' inscribed in Elvish. Gandalf is stumped by what to do to get the doors to open; he exasperates himself by speaking many complicated words and commands in all different languages of Middle Earth. The rising fear and anxiety among the group is eventually broken by Gandalf's laughter as he realizes how simple the solution is – that he 'had only to speak the Elvish word for friend' and the doors would open.[35]

Speak peace

In Luke 10, Jesus sends out the 72. They are invited to speak peace to the places they enter and to expect to find people who will welcome them and offer hospitality and friendship. However, they also experience the frustration and rejection of finding doors closed and not being welcomed. Towards the end of the Gospel reading, an interesting scene unfolds where those sent out return to report back to Jesus. What is striking is that those who were sent take joy in the submission of spirits to the name of Jesus. Jesus affirms that this is the case, but he chides them for rejoicing in the power they can demonstrate instead of rejoicing that their 'names are written in heaven'. Something is going on here to do with power and invoking the name of Jesus. Luke has something important for us to recognize here about the authority Jesus gives his followers and how it most effectively treads over the powers of evil. It is a theme found in both Luke's Gospel and in Acts.

Speak Jesus

In Acts, Luke tells the story of the church being birthed through the Spirit at Pentecost. There the apostles are empowered to be Jesus' witnesses and sent, ultimately, to the ends of the earth. They set about that task by ensuring that people know that the power by which they are doing things is not their own. Their actions are in the name of Jesus. In Acts 2, Peter challenges the crowd to 'repent and be baptized in the name of Jesus Christ'. In Acts 3, Peter invites the man at Gate Beautiful to stand up and walk in the name in Jesus Christ. It was the use of the name of Jesus that was stirring things up. In Acts 4 and in Acts 5 the Sanhedrin made their position clear to the followers of Jesus. They said: do not teach in his name; do not speak in his name. Action in the name of Jesus was unsettling for those in power.

Speak powerfully

Back in Luke's Gospel, the notion of doing things in the name of Jesus was first introduced by Luke just before our Gospel reading. In Luke 9, following the sending out of the Twelve, the disciples argue about which of them is the greatest. Jesus explains to them that the least of all is the greatest and that those who welcome a child in his name welcome him. For all the things that might be done by using the name of Jesus, the first example is extending a welcome to a child. It is about receiving and recognizing those who are overlooked or belittled. In no time at all, the 72, ministering in the name of Jesus, are seduced by the spiritual supremacy Jesus-given authority offers, taking great joy in seeing spirits submit to the power they wield.

Sometimes in the life of faith I recognize that I focus on the wrong things or I over-complicate matters. Even when well intentioned or well informed, I can miss the humble simplicity of the call of Jesus. Jesus sends his followers out offering peace, seeking persons of peace. There is power in the name of Jesus. He challenges us to respond in repentance and faith. However, the deepest joy comes not from witnessing displays of dominant power but from knowing friendship and fellowship with God. Actions done in the name of Jesus that speak most powerfully are those that open the door for all of God's children to know the same.

Matt Allen

Hymn suggestions

At the name of Jesus; Be still, for the presence of the Lord; Speak, O Lord; Guide me, O thou great Redeemer.

Third Sunday after Trinity (Proper 9) 6 July
Second Service **Food, Water and Love**
Ps. 65 [70]; **Gen. 29.1–20**; Mark 6.7–29

Food, water and love. What more could we want? I'm sure we can see deep value in each of these things. Indeed, we can over-spiritualize our needs sometimes. Not here. Rachel knows that sheep are her food, that they will need water, and that loving her family will probably mean that she needs to marry. That's how her world worked.

A knotty passage

But there are some properly knotty issues in our passage. The implication is that Rachel is a commodity. That she is very 'graceful and beautiful' does not undo the implication. There is also the suggestion that bloodlines – biological family bonds – are the most important thing going. So, what is the message for those of us who might want to question such priorities? Can we find a hero in Jacob? The rest of Jacob's story presents him as morally ambiguous at best. He occasionally manages to understand something of what it is to love but more often relates poorly to his wives and children.

The rest of the story is a proper saga, by the way: Jacob has to wait for Rachel, then Laban 'gives' him Leah instead, before relenting and giving Rachel to him; Leah is unloved but then blessed by God with a child, and it keeps going. So, can we find inspiration from Rachel or Leah? Quite possibly, but there is little in this particular passage.

Back to basics

Let's try returning to the three simple needs mentioned at the start: food, water and love. Having and sharing these things looked a very particular way in Rachel's world. It looks a particular way in ours too. Getting food is no neutral task. Food, if we have it, might end up on our plates, but it has taken a complex (and potentially morally ambiguous) journey to get there. Many have to rely on food banks because food is so very expensive. Food matters. In this story, there seems to be a connectedness to the earth from which food comes and there seems to be a respect for that.

Water, too, is a big deal here. It doesn't come easily, either for the livestock or for those whose communities depend on it. We may find that we can just turn on a tap, but the journey of water to get there cannot morally bypass the difficulties of that journey the world over. This ancient community knows the complexities of that journey. The well is very understandably at the centre of this story. It is the centre of life.

Developing bonds of love is also complex, just as it has always been. We have to work these things out within the mess: jostling, giving, sharing and receiving. There are hints of kindness in the story among the knots. The shepherds are hospitable to Jacob and answer his questions. They even helpfully point out Rachel. Rachel looks after the sheep: credit to her for doing such a thing. There is physical warmth through an embrace – intimacy among the complexity of familial life. Even as each of these instances has its risks, these small things express a simple humanity yearning for fulfilment in relationship. That yearning for fulfilment continues through the Hebrew Scriptures. We might yearn for fulfilment today: for food, for water and for love.

The living well

And then Jesus comes: the Lamb of God who takes away the sin of the world, who loosens knotty problems like bloodlines through his own blood. The coming of the Son of Man took seriously these simple needs of ours. Jesus also made do with the knotty circumstances of the world. He didn't stay aloof; rather, he associated with the fishing folk, the tax-collectors and the prostitutes. That is, he associated with food, water and love. He took people and their circumstances seriously. And he didn't forcefully sort out the chaos. He lived in it and with it, even as he began to unpick and subvert it. We too can take these things of the world seriously and be those who receive, give and share amid the stormy chaos of our lives.

And remember the well at the centre. Jesus comes as the living water; those who come to him will never go thirsty. Jesus is the well at the centre of life. He comes as the food of heaven, which we share in our communion together. He comes as the lover of our souls and commands us to love too. We would do 'well' to let him be the centre of our lives.

Mark Amos

Hymn suggestions

Jesus, lover of my soul; Come to the waters; How great the chasm (Living hope); Jesus, be the centre.

Fourth Sunday after Trinity (Proper 10)   13 July
Principal Service   **Following the Family Way**
(*Continuous*): Amos 7.7–end; Ps. 82; *or* (*Related*): Deut. 30.9–14; Ps. 25.1–10; Col 1.1–14; **Luke 10.25–37**

When we speak of inheritance, we probably think first of cash, property or other goods of material or sentimental value handed down after the death of a relative. But in more traditional societies, an inheritance is just as likely to be the family trade; in a fishing or farming family, for instance, children grow up being shaped by the knowledge, skills, culture and customs that enable them to step into the same way of life and pass it on.

God's people have always been promised an inheritance from him. At first, the promise centred around a geographical land, but it gradually became clear that God's riches are both more substantial and less tangible than a piece of earth: his children are given a share in his kingdom as heirs to the fruitful, abundant life that flourishes eternally.

So, when a young lawyer asks Jesus how to inherit eternal life, we should hear a question not about financial contracts and lump sums after a death, but a question about family values: how must being an heir to God's kingdom shape my life? How do I learn to live the family way?

A great gulf

The story Jesus shares in response begins with a man in desperate need: he's been attacked by bandits and left for dead. Naked and bleeding, he's a pitiful sight and it's obvious that he needs urgent help. First a priest and then a Levite witness the scene, both apparently good candidates for a compassionate response. But, as it turns out, they both fail to stop.

Their reasons could be various and sensible. Important appointments to get to, the fear of ceremonial uncleanness, the personal danger of aligning oneself with a man who seems to have violent enemies. Both priest and Levite have worship-leading responsibilities that if compromised would impact the whole community. This helpless, dying man poses all kinds of risks.

Where circumstance has created a gulf between the injured man and the passers-by, the response of the priest and then the Levite serves to increase it. They physically move to the other side of the road, creating as much distance between them as they possibly can. They widen the chasm for their own protection.

A different choice

Then the third man comes along, a Samaritan. As well as the many practical reasons not to stop, there is an even greater gulf between the Samaritan and the wounded man: the chasm of race, ethnicity and culture. The Jews and the Samaritans hated one another and went out of their way to avoid one another. The Samaritan would risk his friendships, reputation and good standing in the community if he were to help his enemy. This chasm is huge.

The Samaritan makes his choice. Rather than flee to the other side of the road, protecting himself by making the distance wider, the Samaritan chooses to close the gap. He crosses a great divide to come near to the Jewish man in need. The rest of the parable describes how the Samaritan goes to great lengths in his care for the injured man. He takes risks; he pays the price; he overcomes every obstacle.

It's the Samaritan who shows us what it looks like to be an inheritor of eternal life. He demonstrates that the family culture of the kingdom of God means crossing every chasm to show real and genuine love. It should come as no surprise because it's exactly what God has done for us in Jesus Christ.

A true story

The story of the good Samaritan is our story, but we are not the heroes. The truth is that we are that dying, bleeding man, helpless and in great need. There was a great chasm between us and God, because humanity turned away from God. Because we chose to live our own way and to put ourselves first, the gulf caused by sin separated us from God and we had no way to get across it.

But God did not turn away from us. God did not leave us to die. He didn't cross to the other side, but instead he came near to us in his Son Jesus Christ, and he took the risks, he paid the price, and he bridged the chasm between us. Through Jesus' death and resurrection, he overcame the obstacles of our sin to heal our wounds and welcome us into his family. This is the business of the kingdom of God because this is the character of God himself.

To be true inheritors of eternal life, we need to follow in the family way. It looks like taking risks, bridging gaps and crossing barriers of prejudice and difference to care for the people whom others ignore and exclude. It looks like helping people who will never be able to repay us, putting our own reputations and lives on the line for the sake of others. That's what we're called to do because that's what Jesus has done for us.

Claire Jones

Hymn suggestions

The church of Christ in every age; When I needed a neighbour; Beauty for brokenness; How deep the Father's love for us.

Fourth Sunday after Trinity (Proper 10) 13 July
Second Service **But, it's Tradition!**
Ps. 77 [*or* 77.1–12]; Gen. 32.9–30; **Mark 7.1–23**

Traditions can be both comforting and alienating. Imagine arriving in a new country and learning that you had not adhered to a particular tradition, making you instantly recognizable as an outsider. On the other hand, imagine the traditions that you have created with family and friends, warm and joyful ones, those that have been shaped by funny stories or accidental mishaps, and which are now cast in stone to be repeated year in and year out. The cry, 'But, it's tradition!' can signal an invitation into something collective, yet it can also offer a narrow reading of what is acceptable or not, making clear what or who does not belong.

There may be trouble ahead

In the Gospel of Mark, chapter 7, we see that Jesus' fame and reputation means that everyone, even the religious leaders, want to come and see him. The Pharisees who had 'come from Jerusalem' are keen, as you would expect, to highlight what is considered inappropriate behaviour. They notice that Jesus' disciples were simply not behaving as their Jewish heritage would have expected of them. You can hear the Pharisees cry, 'But, it's tradition!' And they were, of course, correct. It *was* tradition to cleanse oneself before eating, to eat only specific foods from the market and to wash the crockery and utensils. The Pharisees instantly pounce on this lack of adherence to tradition and seek to entrap Jesus. Was it Jesus who had told his disciples that they could behave in this way? And if so, why? What was Jesus trying to prove? What is clear is that Jesus was having none of it. 'But it's tradition' was not a phrase that Jesus would ever be using.

God is superior to our human traditions

Jesus instead draws the intellect and hearts of those around him, including those of the Pharisees, to the ancient text of Isaiah. Jesus knows that the listeners would have known Isaiah's writings, and this is his response to the challenge of the religious authorities. He says very clearly: I can see you and know you are out to get me. He says without fear: I can see you and I know that your hearts are not filled with love. I wonder how many of us have been in situations where we know that we are being set up to fail, or to be exposed, and when we also know that we have done nothing wrong. How do we, and how can we, respond? Here we see that the words 'But it's tradition' are the words that are really underneath the accusation of the Pharisees. Jesus responds with a challenge to the idea of tradition, namely that it must fall under the authority and superiority of God. We cannot build for ourselves traditions that we then worship, sidelining God, and then expecting others to do the same.

A new way of seeing

Jesus offers something totally radical in this encounter. He says tradition is one thing, but also asks how this tradition brings people together or tears them apart. He uses the example of the commandment to honour one's father and mother. As one scholar writes, 'According to tradition, once a person's property is vowed as a gift (korban) to the temple, that property cannot be released to support one's parents.'[36] Here Jesus highlights the contradiction between tradition and the requirements of the law. The plea 'But it's tradition' is also suddenly unpicked as Jesus confirms that what comes out of us through our thoughts, words and actions has a greater impact than the superficial choices we make for all to see. 'But it's tradition' is no longer valid as a cover for our behaviour. We can no longer rely on inherited practices to absolve ourselves of individual and collective responsibility. God in the person of Jesus exposes our core, the human heart, to scrutiny, to the light and truth that emanate from our divine Creator. This view of us from the inside out ensures that, while we may be exposed, we will not be exploited; while we may be seen, we will not be cast out of the love of God; while we may be judged, we will be enveloped by the grace and mercy of God, whose constant invitation is to be transformed. Ultimately, Jesus gives us a new way of seeing our relationship with God and our material world. God values us as created beings not because we follow traditions without question, but because we question ourselves in the face of traditions, and how those traditions bring us back to God who is love, and whose purpose for us is love.

Mariama Ifode-Blease

Hymn suggestions

Breathe on me, breath of God; Be thou my vision; How deep the Father's love for us; How can it be (Lauren Daigle).

Fifth Sunday after Trinity (Proper 11) 20 July
Principal Service **An Invitation into Deeper Freedom**
(*Continuous*): Amos 8.1–12; Ps. 52; *or* (*Related*): Gen. 18.1–10a; Ps. 15; Col. 1.15–28; **Luke 10.38–end**

A row about the washing-up?

How do you picture the scene in today's Gospel reading? I guess most people imagine a harassed and irritated Martha bashing pots about in the kitchen while her sister Mary sits like the model disciple at Jesus' feet. Then it seems as though Jesus has a pop at Martha for being overly focused on preparing a meal for others. Is this really a row about the washing-up? Would the one who came to serve really make such a criticism?

In praise of the contemplative life?

There is no shortage of sermons that claim this passage is suggesting that the contemplative life is better than the active, but that makes no sense. After all, Jesus' own life was marked by seasons of intense activity and times when he headed off for the hills to pray. Just what is this about?

Re-imagining the scene

Why do we assume that Martha and Mary are both in the house on this particular day? Well, the passage does say that Mary 'sat at Jesus' feet and listened to him', so it seems natural to assume she was under the same roof as her sister. But in Acts 22.3 we read that Paul was brought up 'at the feet of Gamaliel', meaning he was a student of Gamaliel. Sitting at a person's feet is a figurative expression meaning being a disciple of that person. Add to this the point that in the Greek we read that Mary *also* sat at Jesus' feet, meaning that Martha too was a disciple – a little detail dropped out of many translations. So, the picture of one sister sweating over a hot stove and the other one sitting serenely at the Lord's feet doesn't stack up. We read that Martha welcomed Jesus into 'her house'. What if Mary isn't home at all? Can we start to see another way of reading the passage?

Martha asks Jesus, 'Lord, do you not care that my sister has left me to do all the work by myself?' We assume this work is food preparation, but the word *diakonian* can mean ministry. Is Martha stressed that the local ministry has fallen to her while Mary is off doing something else? Jesus' response is to notice that Martha is 'worried and distracted by many things'. Does rustling up a small meal equate to such stress?

What if Martha's discipleship is expressed in the local community while Mary is off on mission – perhaps with the 72 – exploring a new vocation, expressing her gifts and calling away from the domestic environment and community.

Can we re-imagine this scene? In the house are Jesus and Martha. Mary is away. Martha is annoyed because Mary has left; she is asking Jesus to fetch her sister home to support her. Jesus' response is that Mary's ministry won't be taken from her.

Either way ...

However you choose to picture the scene – with the more common interpretation or in this arguably legitimate way – let's focus on Martha. It seems she is pressured, stressed, annoyed and distracted. Worry is looming – and dear Martha is having a tough time. We only get a snippet of the conversation. I cannot for a moment believe that after Martha expressed her troubles, Jesus ticked her off, supped his tea and left it at that. There must have been a much longer conversation. Perhaps that is an invitation to any today who feel under the cosh and have lost focus – step into honest conversation about that.

Mary, however, has found a new focus, a new sense of purpose, and Jesus says this won't be taken from her. Perhaps Martha has over-relied on her sister, in an unhealthy way. The answer to Martha's troubles is not to clip her sister's wings.

An invitation to new freedom

However we read the passage it seems clear that both these disciples are being invited into new freedom. The fruit of this can be seen in John 11 and 12, where Martha confesses her faith in Jesus in a statement like Peter's, that Jesus is the Messiah. In that passage Mary expresses her faith in her anointing of Jesus' body – a sensory creed.

This passage is not about praising the contemplative life. It is about two beloved disciples being invited into new life and possibility.

Maybe like Martha we are being invited to explore our stress and anxiety, to be honest about the things that press in on us, to reassess our focus. Are we holding others back by our needs and expectations? Perhaps we need to set people free?

Maybe like Mary we are entering a new expression of vocation. In doing this we might need to leave some things behind and reassess how we relate to key people. Some old patterns might need to change. Overall, the invitation is into deeper freedom.

Kate Bruce

Hymn suggestions

All to Jesus I surrender; Be thou my vision; From heaven you came (The Servant King); I, the Lord of sea and sky.

Fifth Sunday after Trinity (Proper 11)   20 July
Second Service   **Living the Dream**
Ps. 81; **Gen. 41.1–16, 25–37**; 1 Cor. 4.8–13;
Gospel at Holy Communion: John 4.31–35

Joseph seems to have grown up a bit of a spoilt brat; a real teacher's pet. He knew he was the favourite, and he played on it. Telling Dad about his older brothers' faults, enjoying his father's praise, not to mention the gifts. And then the dreams! Dreams of his own prestige, with his brothers, his mother and even his father bowing down before his greatness. It doesn't excuse what they did, but it does explain something of his brothers' motivation in wanting to get rid of him. Thankfully his brother Reuben saved his life, but could not stop him from being sold into slavery.

But God has a habit of turning apparent disasters into new beginnings.

A fresh start

Joseph ends up in Egypt, aged 17, far from home, as a slave. He's been sold to Potiphar, captain of the Pharaoh's guard. What is significant is that Joseph seems to have decided to make the best of his situation, and be the best he could be under God. Far from retreating into himself as many a spoilt teenager might have done, and wallowing in misery, he is inspired to get stuck into this new life and make the best of a bad job. It goes well. He ends up as the butler – but he also ends up as the target of his master's wife, and his refusal to give her what she wants lands him in prison.

Even then, Joseph keeps his commitment to doing the right thing and ends up basically running the prison – perhaps because the prison was in Potiphar's house, and the chief jailer would have known Joseph. But when Pharaoh sent his chief cupbearer and his chief baker to be imprisoned there, it was time for Joseph's God-given gift of interpreting dreams to come to the fore. It's good news for the cupbearer and bad news for the baker, but that seems to be that. The cupbearer is released and returns to his life, forgetting Joseph.

The big chance

And now, two whole years later, Pharaoh has dreams, which nobody can interpret, despite Pharaoh consulting everyone he can think of. It's only after this, when those of us watching the story unfold are screaming with frustration, that the cupbearer finally remembers Joseph, and Joseph is scrubbed up and brought before Pharaoh.

Here's Joseph's big chance. The greatness of which he'd dreamt all those years ago could soon be his. He has this gift for interpretation of dreams, and Pharaoh has exhausted all his other 'experts'. If Joseph can display his gift before Pharaoh and win his favour and his praise, then at the grand old age of 30, he'll be made for life. He'll be Pharaoh's honoured counsellor, his right-hand man. What an opportunity.

And yet Joseph doesn't grab at it. He doesn't boast to Pharaoh that he can discern the meaning of the dreams for him. Instead, Joseph reveals to Pharaoh the ultimate, invaluable truth that he has come to realize through all that has happened to him over the years, that the focus needs to be on God. He tells Pharaoh that it's not he, Joseph, who will give the interpretation but God.

The yoke's on Joseph

Joseph's teenage ego has been transformed and moulded into a humble, meek spirit. Not 'meek' in the sense of being cowed and timorous, but in the true meaning of the word meek – power under control. As Jesus would later invite us to do, Joseph had yoked himself to the Lord, and was using his gifts and abilities under God's guidance and in his service, harnessed for the vocation God had given him.

And it's this which leads Joseph not to seek personal glory and status but to offer Pharaoh God's interpretations of his dreams, which crystallize into a plan to safeguard not just the nation but the region from the impending famine.

Joseph doesn't even bid for a position running the food programme. But Pharaoh, amazed and impressed by Joseph, places him over not just the food programme but his entire household.

Joseph ends up with more greatness than he'd ever have dreamed of; but now he has the wisdom, the humility, the meekness, to hold that power under control, to exercise it under the guidance of God, and thereby to save countless lives – and, in the end, to regain the family that he'd once lost.

The yoke's on us?

The lesson for us is not something trite about simply embracing difficult or terrible times or enduring injustice so that God can teach us things. It's certainly not that we should try to do the right thing in the unspoken hope that it will ultimately be rewarded with honour and acclaim. Rather, it's that we should seek to keep the focus on God, seek genuinely to yoke ourselves to Christ, and respond to his call to remain faithful to the way of his kingdom, as agents of his kingdom, come what may.

Bill Braviner

Hymn suggestions

Be thou my vision; Guide me, O thou great Redeemer; Do not be afraid; May the mind of Christ my Saviour.

Sixth Sunday after Trinity (Proper 12) 27 July
Principal Service **Just Ask**
(*Continuous*): Hos. 1.2–10; Ps. 85 [*or* 85.1–7]; *or* (*Related*): Gen. 18.20–32; Ps. 138; Col 2.6–15 [16–19]; **Luke 11.1–13**

Why do we pray? Because we want to give thanks and extol the name of the Lord? Or, because we're desperate for help? There's a kind of Christian teaching that implies that we need to praise God before asking for help. After all, Jesus' prayer starts with the hallowing of God's name. It reminds us that God is Lord and not us. It puts us in an honorary frame of mind in response to our Creator.

It's OK to ask for help

But the God of love does not need our worship before being willing to help. There are good reasons to worship, but we needn't get bogged down in those reasons before asking for help. It might be helpful to train children to say 'please', but if we only give because someone says 'please' then we need to ask ourselves what we're about. Love gives freely.

I wonder if we can recover today a very real sense that we need help. Many of us will know that implicitly. But why? Just before Jesus tells us this prayer, he gives a quick recap of our story: we were dead in our transgressions. Pretty bleak, of course. But we know the story. Christ came, drew alongside us, walked our path, formed a community of love, shared our frailties and burdens, bore them to the grave, and undid the finality of death by being raised to life eternal. We could not do this by ourselves. But our help is right here in this same Jesus.

Dependency

It doesn't require an overly morbid sense of the human condition to know that we need help. After all, to be human is, in a sense, to be dependent. There is such a thing as negative dependency. We can make others dependent on us. We can be overly dependent. The risks for abuses of power are clearly there. But dependency is also a fact. Just as we needed help as infants, so too are we dependent on others as we grow older. There was never a time when we didn't need others and there never will be. Like it or not, there is something about being a creature that means we are dependent on others.

The radical egalitarianism of the Christian faith comes in the fact that we all need help. There is something about the Christian narrative that encourages an acknowledgement that we are dependent on God for help.

In Jesus, our help comes not only from a distant creator. It comes through a creature, a person, not unlike us. We receive help from a fellow human. Even this human was dependent on others. He was dependent on his family for food, care and warmth. He was dependent on his friends for friendship. He was dependent on the Torah for understanding. Before he could ever be hospitable, he was shown hospitality. That is as humbling as it is beautiful.

After Jesus tells the prayer, he seems to find it necessary to let his disciples know that it really is OK to ask for help. And he reminds them that when they ask for help, they ask it of one who loves and one who recognizes and accepts our neediness as creatures.

We are not alone in the world. We have a companion, a helper, a saviour. Because of this, we can pray. And because of this we can ask, plead, cry for help. And, it *is* worship to ask God for help. It does hallow God's name. It acknowledges the kind of God we pray to. It acknowledges a God who by very nature came close to us, even being willing to be dependent as we too are dependent.

What do we need?

What do we need help with today and tomorrow? Is our work too hard? Are our relationships too broken? Have we done something that we can't find a way of undoing? If so, ask God for help. Coming to a place where we acknowledge that we need help is difficult. But when we do, we become truthful with ourselves and those around us. We can't walk through this life alone. We are created for relationship. We are dependent beings. We need help just as we need to help.

It might be that we are accustomed in life to helping others. Amazing. That too is the gospel. But if we have abandoned our need for help, we might need gentle encouragement to remember our creatureliness again, including our dependency on others.

Lord, please help.

Mark Amos

Hymn suggestions

Meekness and majesty; What a friend we have in Jesus; I need thee every hour; Nearer, my God, to thee.

Sixth Sunday after Trinity (Proper 12)   27 July
Second Service   **Seeing Into the Life of Things**
Ps. 88 [*or* 88.1–10]; **Gen. 42.1–25**; 1 Cor. 10.1–24; *Gospel at Holy Communion*: Matt. 13.24–30 [31–43]

Wisdom means many things in the Hebrew Bible. It can mean practical skill, competence and good management. It can mean insight and discernment. It can mean knowledge of the natural world. It can mean learning the lessons of history and transmitting them to your children. It can mean being able to play music and write poetry. It can mean having a moral sense and an educated conscience. It can mean detachment from our drives, an inward stability of character. But above all, it's a *religious* quality. The wise sum it up as the fear of the Lord, committing your way to him. The wise know their place in the scheme of things, and in relation to God the Creator who is not only the source of wisdom but is Wisdom itself.

Awareness

Being aware means learning how to discern and 'read' the world and what God is doing in it. The Joseph story in Genesis is like this. It is one of the most perfect narratives not just in Scripture but in all of literature. Our passage comes in the middle of the story where Joseph is playing games with his estranged brothers: he knows who they are, but they have not yet recognized him. One of the story's themes is to portray Joseph as a wise man. He shows shrewdness and skill as a manager in Potiphar's house; when Potiphar's wife tries to seduce him, he behaves with integrity; he knows what is required when famine befalls; and not least, he has compassion for his brothers with whom he wants to be reconciled – but they don't, of course, know that yet.

Partial recognition

This part of the story needs to be read with the end in mind. Today's reading has a partial recognition: Joseph recognizes his brothers, but they have yet to recognize *him*. Scroll forward three chapters to one of the most moving scenes in the Bible, where he reveals himself to them and embraces them with tears, and after all that has come between them, there is reconciliation. And scroll on beyond that to the final chapter of Genesis where Joseph sums up this long, complicated story: 'Even though you intended to do harm to me, God intended it for good.' And the lovely little detail in the text, tells us that 'In this way he reassured them, speaking kindly to them' (Gen. 50.20–21).

Reading the signs of the times

Maybe reading the signs of the times is like reading dreams. Joseph can do both. But by the time the story reaches today's chapter, dreams have dropped out of the story, and the focus is on understanding what is going on in the events Joseph and his brothers are caught up in, in history, politics and human lives. You could say that Joseph's gift is that of being able to *interpret* what God is doing, make sense of it, discern good purposes running through what our forebears called providence, try to see what's required of the story's participants for the good of all involved.

Interpreters

The *interpreter* is a good image of what the church is for. One of its tasks is to help people understand and respond to what God is doing in the world and in people's lives: pointing to meanings, uncovering significance, not simply human significance but divine. It's what William Wordsworth called 'seeing into the life of things'.[37]

As Christian interpreters, we establish meaning in different ways. We do it when we bring the power of the gospel to bear upon human lives and transform them; or when we celebrate the liturgy and play at living in the kingdom of God as if it were already fully present. We do it pastorally in joy or in sadness, whenever we attempt to read the stories of people's lives in the light of the value God places on them. And we do it in our citizenship of the world by putting the questions of God's kingdom to situations where justice and mercy are unacknowledged or forgotten and victims have no voice of their own. In looking for 'divine significance', we are taking seriously our role as God's interpreters.

Can we not all be interpreters? And won't it come to us as naturally as breathing if we speak honestly out of our faith, and are ready to give a reason for the hope that is within us? To do what Joseph did, taking the long view and interpreting meanings is crucial. To help others glimpse how, in the changes and chances of the world, 'love is his meaning' is something each of us can try to do – and as we hint at how 'God meant it for good', make room for the life-giving purposes that God intends for the human family and for all God's beloved creation.

Michael Sadgrove

Hymn suggestions

Immortal, invisible, God only wise; Through all the changing scenes of life; Great is thy faithfulness; Immortal love, for ever full.

Seventh Sunday after Trinity (Proper 13)   3 August
Principal Service   **Abundant Living**
(*Continuous*): Hos. 11.1–11; Ps. 107.1–9, 43 [*or* 107.1–9]; *or* (*Related*): Eccles. 1.2, 12–14; 2.18–23; Ps. 49.1–12 [*or* 49.1–9]; Col. 3.1–11; **Luke 12.13–21**

A close friend of the family, whom we knew as Uncle Tony, spent his working life amassing wealth through his UN job. If there was overtime to be done, he did it. He rarely went on holidays and refused to spend his money on social activities. When asked, he'd say, 'I'm saving my money for my retirement.' That's how it went for the 30 or so years he worked for the UN and he did indeed make it to his retirement. However, soon after he retired he fell ill and within three years he was dead. All the money he made was never enjoyed. It always struck me how sad to have lived a half-life in the belief that he would have plenty of time to enjoy all his hard-earned money during his retirement years.

Rich towards God

Now let's be clear, money in and of itself is simply pieces of metal and paper. However, over time, society and culture have established that these pieces of paper and metal function as currency, representing value. Money is significant for us simply because we exchange it for what we value. Not surprisingly, then, what we do with our money shows what we value in our hearts.

Many of us spend our money on day-to-day living, entertainment, vacations, gifts for family and friends. We also might spend our money on supporting various charities that serve the most vulnerable of our society. And we may give money to the churches we attend regularly because we value the ministry of our churches.

Jesus says in Luke 12.34, 'For where your treasure is, there your heart will be also.' Thus, Jesus seems to be implying that the movement of our money reflects the movement of our heart. Put another way, we exchange money for the 'treasure' we value.

If we want to be rich towards God, we need to be careful to distinguish between the world's perspective and God's perspective. We are encouraged to value God more than money because when we value God more than material possessions, then we find that our relationship with God deepens and our faith grows. Money has the capacity to be both gift and burden, so being intentional about how we use our money is important. We are reminded that everything belongs to God and we are called to be 'rich towards God' because it is useless to 'store up treasures'. Our faith focus should be living lives drawn to, and immersed in, the abundance of knowing God, rather than acquiring things. Being 'rich towards God' means we long for a deeper relationship with Jesus, so much so that we are compelled to use our earthly riches to show how much we value God.

Greed or God

Luke 12.20 states: 'But God said to him, "You fool! This very night your life is being demanded of you. And the things you have prepared, whose will they be?"' This is why we have to be mindful when dealing with money because it can so easily lure us out of love for God, and away from treasuring God.

In this parable, the issue isn't that the rich man's fields prospered. The point is that God ceased to be his greatest treasure. If God had been his treasure, what would he have done differently? Perhaps, he would have said, 'Everything I have belongs to you, God. May my life be a reflection of your overflowing generosity and love. May I give to others from that abundance and gratitude.'

When we look at our lives, do we fully surrender all to God? Psalm 49 reminds us that trusting in our wealth and boasting of our great riches is futile. Rather, the fullest blessing comes from responding to the spirit of God, that invitation to be in a living relationship with Jesus Christ our Lord. The supreme treasure we have as followers of Christ is our relationship with God. In this relationship we are able to say, God, all that I have and all that I am is yours. In this relationship we are able to stand on God's steadfast love and 'give thanks to the LORD' (Ps. 107.1).

Abundant living

In the passage from Colossians, we read: 'Put to death, therefore, whatever in you is earthly: fornication, impurity, passion, evil desire, and greed (which is idolatry).' And isn't it true, very often, these are connected with the sinful use of money. By grace, we are forgiven and transformed not by what we do but by what God in Christ has done and is doing in our lives.

The antidote to greed is to be rich towards God. In kingdom currency, God-wealth is when we invest in others with the fruits of the Spirit: love, joy, peace, patience, kindness, goodness and self-control.

As we reflect on our financial affairs, as we reflect on where we spend our money, perhaps we can consider the ways we are honouring God in his mission on earth. Are we laying up treasures for ourselves or for eternity?

Catherine Okoronkwo

Hymn suggestions

How deep the Father's love for us; The hidden treasure; Treasure in earthen vessels; And can it be?

Seventh Sunday after Trinity (Proper 13) 3 August
Second Service **God Meant It for Good**
Ps. 107.1–32 [*or* 107.1–16]; **Gen. 50.4–end**; 1 Cor. 14.1–19;
Gospel at Holy Communion: Mark 6.45–52

Joseph says to his brothers, 'Even though you intended to do harm to me, God intended it for good', a luminous climax to a great story. It's Joseph's 'my Lord and my God' moment: 'you intended … God intended.' In conspiracy and catastrophe, everything has worked together for good.

When is it a true act of faith to say, 'It was for the best, and good has come out of it', and when is it just a thoughtless cliché to make us feel better about the bad things that happen? We should not say it when we hear of a child who has been abused, bystanders blown to pieces by a suicide bomber or a pensioner murdered in her own home. We condemn wickedness, and we do what we can to help its victims, but we are reticent about theorizing because we know that words can make things worse as well as better. In the face of what is wrong or just bewildering, we don't try to guess what God is doing in the tragic or baffling events of human life.

Yet the instinct to find meaning is also part of being human. Kierkegaard said that life has to be lived forwards but understood backwards.[38] And this is where Joseph helps us. These chapters of Genesis tell a story of how faith discerns in ordinary events, the everyday processes of cause and effect, a divine wisdom at work in the world. It is not necessarily apparent from the evidence: it's faith that makes the connections.

A few years ago, the philosophy of religion reached the side of the London bus, thanks to the British Humanist Association: 'There is probably no God. Now stop worrying and enjoy your life.'[39] The word 'probably' is the clue. It tells us that atheism is not so much a cool decision of unbiased reason as an act of faith, a wager: weigh up the evidence, then stake your life on it. Worry is only for religious people.

But what if it had said, 'God may possibly exist, so stop being frivolous and start living responsibly'? This is the dilemma posed by the seventeenth-century theologian and philosopher Blaise Pascal:

> God either exists or doesn't exist. But how do I decide to live in the light of that dilemma? Where does happiness lie? I must weigh up what I gain and what I stand to lose in this wager that God exists. If I win, I gain everything; if I lose, I lose nothing.[40]

Pascal's wager is that God exists, so we should live as if he does, even if we cannot be certain. As believers, our wager is that Christianity is true. But even if it turned out not to be, the Christian life would still be worthwhile and would still add to the sum of human happiness including my own. If I bet the other way, says Pascal, if I wagered that God did not exist and lived riotously and then found out on judgement day that I had been wrong, the cost would be eternal misery and loss. We may not do the last judgement calculus that way today. But arguably, we *might* still have been less content, and *might* have lived less satisfying lives, if we had not had faith.

So, suppose the London bus was right and faith turned out to be a fantasy? Would my life have been wasted? I have only this one life to live. I can't go back and start again, choose a different ladder to construct a life on and climb clear of childhood and adolescence. Whatever they are, we stake our life choices on these beliefs and values. It's a huge act of trust.

Indeed. And in the Gospels, to receive the kingdom 'gladly', as ordinary people did, is not at all the certainty of an intellectually coherent position. It is the belief that this is good news worth investing in, a wager that makes sense because the character of the man announcing it assures us that we can trust him. Perhaps Joseph's brothers began to see that 'God intended it for good' precisely because Joseph spoke kindly to them.

On this first day of the week we celebrate the resurrection, God's pledge that our hope in this good news and its bearer will not be disappointed. If ever it was true of an event that 'you intended harm but God meant it for good', it is the cross. On Good Friday that statement would be incredible. Yet resurrection makes it both possible and believable. There is still a wager involved in building our house upon the rock of Jesus and his kingdom. We don't yet know what the outcome will be. But to construct our life on this foundation gives it stability amid shifting sands. With the years the conviction grows that it was a wise decision. It was worth wagering that 'God intended it for good'.

Michael Sadgrove

Hymn suggestions

How shall I sing that majesty; God moves in a mysterious way; Put thou thy trust in God; Not far beyond the sea, nor high.

Eighth Sunday after Trinity (Proper 14)   10 August
Principal Service   **Treasure Seekers?**
(*Continuous*): Isa. 1.1, 10–20; Ps. 50.1–8, 23–end [*or* 50.1–7];
 or (*Related*): Gen. 15.1–6; Ps. 33.12–end [*or* 33.12–21];
Heb. 11.1–3, 8–16; **Luke 12.32–40**

Jesus has quite a lot of things to say about money and possessions. Repeatedly he tells us we cannot serve money and God; in today's Gospel, Jesus tells his disciples to give away their possessions. At the same time, Jesus does not prohibit his followers from seeking treasure. Rather – as so often with Jesus – he reverses the polarities: if our human instinct is to acquire, indeed pile up, possessions and money and call it treasure, in today's reading Jesus reminds us that the unfailing treasure is found in heaven.

Heaven: an elusive idea?

I don't mind admitting that I don't find the concept of heaven easy to grasp. We tend to rely on hand-me-down ideas about it. Indeed, I suspect most of us carry pictures of what it's like around in our heads, some of them derived from cinema and popular myth. If I asked you to picture heaven in your mind, you might find an image of angels playing harps on clouds popping into your head. If, like me, you're a movie fan, you might think of heaven as represented in the classic movie *A Matter of Life and Death*, in which heaven is a massively bureaucratic place in black and white.

Perhaps we might come to a richer grasp of why heaven represents real treasure, the purse which cannot wear out, if instead of picturing it as other-worldly, idealistic and immaterial we saw it as the most concrete reality in which God's reign is fully known. What if the kingdom of heaven is no flighty, flouncy thing, but the fullest, most grounded reality of God?

Heaven as solid reality

Christina Rossetti's short poem, 'Lay Up for Yourselves Treasures in Heaven',[41] presents a striking take on Jesus' invitation to seek the unfailing treasure of heaven. She begins with these two verses:

> Treasure plies a feather,
> Pleasure spreadeth wings,
> Taking flight together, –
> Ah! my cherished things.
>
> Fly away, poor pleasure,
> That art so brief a thing:
> Fly away, poor treasure,
> That hast so swift a wing.

Rossetti explores the concept of treasure in terms of flight and feathers; she suggests that so much of what we might consider treasure is actually mere pleasure and that such a thing is 'flighty' and weightless. In popular terms, 'treasure' is associated with gold, jewels and gems piled high. One might place them in a huge chest or a chamber (with perhaps a Tolkeinesque dragon on guard). Such treasure is weighty, this-worldly and tangible. It is about as 'this-worldly' and material as a thing can be. Yet, ironically, for Rossetti, the 'cherished things' are presented as winged and occupied and busily pursuing feathers.

Rossetti is discreet regarding what might count as her cherished things, yet these almost weightless things ('poor pleasure', 'poor treasure') she invites to fly away and depart. Perhaps like birds' bones, these cherished things have the appearance of solidity and yet are hollow. Perhaps their hollowness is what makes them capable of flight. Intriguingly, it is not pleasure or treasure itself that she disavows. There is no pious disavowal of pleasure as essentially sinful in this poem. Rather, the puzzle she presents is to suggest that flighty pleasure isn't true pleasure at all. She concludes the poem this way:

> Pleasure, to be pleasure,
> Must come without a wing;
> Treasure, to be treasure,
> Must be a stable thing.
>
> Treasure without feather,
> Pleasure without wings,
> Elsewhere dwell together
> And are heavenly things.

Real treasure in heaven

In this poem, Rossetti aligns herself with Jesus' priorities. In addition, she helps us see that 'heaven' is the most material, grounded and solid of things. It is present and available – as George Herbert describes it so elegantly in 'Prayer (I)' – as 'in ordinary'.[42] The extraordinary challenge for us – as much as for Rossetti or Herbert – is to draw closer to the material solidity of the true treasures of heaven.

Jesus always invites us to redraw the focus of our lives. He invites us to consider what is our true treasure. For us, as much as Jesus' first disciples, we are called to ask ourselves what our cherished things are and interrogate whether they create the illusions of solidity when they are weightless and fly away even as we grasp after them. What, in the end, are our 'cherished things', and do they have the lasting character of heaven? Rossetti suggests that true riches are wingless and stable. They are treasures in heaven, the most solid reality we can know. The stability and solidity on offer is not that of base materiality, but the consistent character found in God:

> Treasure without feather,
> Pleasure without wings,
> Elsewhere dwell together
> And are heavenly things.

Rachel Mann

Hymn suggestions

Seek ye first the kingdom of God; How firm a foundation, ye saints of the Lord; Immortal, invisible; Lord, enthroned in heavenly splendour.

Eighth Sunday after Trinity (Proper 14) 10 August
Second Service **Homecoming**
Ps. 108 [116]; **Isa. 11.10—end of 12**; 2 Cor. 1.1–22;
Gospel at Holy Communion: Mark 7.24–30

In the southern part of the United States, there was an old custom practised by many churches: on one Sunday of the year, members of the congregation along with others (those who had moved away or perhaps had not attended church services regularly) would gather for a worship service. After the service, there would be a 'bring and share' picnic meal, usually followed by hymn singing in the afternoon. The day was often filled with laughter and, at times, tears, too, as friends embraced and shared news. It was a time of renewal and restoration, and perhaps that is why the day was called 'homecoming'.

Returning home

The prophet Isaiah spoke of a kind of homecoming for the people of God. Having been dominated for many years by the Assyrians, he imagined that the day would come when the people would make their way home and Israel would be restored. He likened their return home to the deliverance of the Israelites escaping from captivity in Egypt and suggested that even as the Lord had opened the way for their ancestors by the parting of the Red Sea after the Exodus, so the Lord would, as it were, 'wave his hand over the river' and make a way for them to 'cross on foot' to their homeland.

Isaiah's vision of a homecoming was both geographical and spiritual: they were returning from an alien place to their land and, significantly, to their God. The pilgrimage, according to the prophet, would be an expression of the desire of the people to once again draw near to God. Though some had wandered away from God and even, at times, worshipped other gods, the journey home would be a time of repentance and restoration. On that day – the day of homecoming – there would be great joy and songs of gladness as the people offered their praise and thanksgiving to God.

An alien land

Over the years, the theme of journeying towards God has been used by spiritual writers who have often combined a story of a geographical journey with a spiritual goal. For instance, in John Bunyan's classic seventeenth-century work *The Pilgrim's Progress*, the central character, Christian, travels on a spiritual journey towards the celestial city. The narrative reflects a tortuous journey where Christian faces many hindrances, as well as temptations to end the journey, before he reaches his destination. Yet, he travels on claiming, 'Now I desire a better country.'[43] The theme throughout the journey is that he has realized that his old 'country' is somehow alien to the ways of God and he must walk carefully and diligently to the new 'country' if he is truly to discover his ultimate destination in God.

Coming home to God

Journeying home to God is a depiction of the Christian life that many people readily embrace. However, as the arduous journey made by Christian in Bunyan's tale reminds us, there are many obstacles to overcome along the way. In fact, before we can even begin the journey, or consider what it might mean to come home to God, perhaps we need to identify what we face which is alien to the Christian way.

Given the prevalence of cultural values, this is difficult to do. Yet, maybe there are ideas that we have assimilated from culture that have no true value. Perhaps we need to question the way we spend our time and money. Are there social norms that we have accepted as individuals, or even as a church, which are contrary to God's way of looking at the world? What about our views on power and control or care for the weak and marginalized? Do we admire power over weakness or value things that are of no ultimate worth? Almost certainly, if we are honest with ourselves, we have attitudes that do not accord with the teachings of Jesus, and so homecoming for most of us will entail a willingness to step out of our comfort zones.

It seems that these sorts of questions were asked by Isaiah before the people were encouraged to travel home to God. These are also the issues that Jesus raised with his disciples and the issues that – over many centuries – have disturbed the minds and hearts of spiritual writers yearning to make their home in God. As we seek to discern the way home, as individuals or as a community of faith, perhaps we can do no better than to pray (in the words of St Augustine of Hippo):

> Lead us, O Lord, and work within us: arouse us, and call us back; enkindle us, and draw us to you; grow fragrant and sweet to us. Let us love you, and let us run to you. Amen.[44]

Karen E. Smith

Hymn suggestions

Great God, your love has called us here; Be thou my vision; Who would true valour see; Guide me, O thou great Redeemer.

Ninth Sunday after Trinity (Proper 15)   17 August
Principal Service   **Lukewarm? As if!**
(*Continuous*): Isa. 5.1–7; Ps. 80.1–2, 9–end [*or* 80.9–end];
or (*Related*): Jer. 23.23–29; Ps. 82; Heb. 11.29—12.2;
Luke 12.49–56

Jesus uses lots of bold images in this Gospel reading: fire, baptism, conflict, division. It's a passionate passage and one that can take us aback. What's Jesus getting at?

Fire

Fire can signify destruction, and Jesus certainly came to destroy the power of sin and death, but fire is also closely associated in the Bible with holiness and refining. The fire that Jesus brings is to end the grip of evil on our lives; not to destroy us, but to fit us for the kingdom of God.

The refining fire of God's love is also the source of power and passion for the mission of God's church in the world, the fire in our bellies to rouse us to the work at hand. It is no accident that fire was manifest at Pentecost, as the rushing wind of God's Spirit infused his people and animated us for mission.

Baptism

Refining always involves the death of some things and the birth of the new. The refiner immerses the ore in fire to reveal the precious metal which is useful, beautiful and treasured.

Jesus spoke of his baptism and his immersion in the work that the Father had sent him to do in order to reveal the love of God to the world. Through his apostles, he promised that we too would be baptized into this mission. In our baptism, we not only die to sin and death, rising again to life and hope, but we embrace our commissioning into the *missio Dei*, the mission of God. We each accept our vocations, our ministries, in solidarity with God and his church; our lives are reorientated onto God's plan, to live not for ourselves only but for him.

Conflict

Embracing our part in the mission of God, being infused with the fire of God's love, means that we are by nature a passionate people. Passions produce positions, and positions often reveal conflict.

When Jesus speaks of bringing not peace but division, he recognizes that conflict is inevitable. He implicitly challenges the idea that peace is the absence of conflict. Being Christian, following Jesus, is not about calming everything down, smoothing things over and being 'nice'. It's not about maintaining 'the way we do things', nor about persuading everyone to conform.

Peace, for Jesus, can be about challenging injustice, exposing hypocrisy, naming corruption, showing up power. It can be about fresh perspectives coming up against accepted ways of seeing things (notice how Jesus' examples are all one generation versus the next).

As disciples, we each have our own faith journey, our own relationships, and we take that seriously; but we journey as a community of faith, and we must also take on others' faith journeys seriously. That takes working through, as a loving and honest community; travelling together, learning together and wrestling with issues together. There will always be conflict, as we each bring our understanding of what God is saying and add it to the mix.

Jesus' reminder about division and conflict is a challenge to us that issues must be faced, and that we have a responsibility to one another to deal with them; not avoiding conflict, nor squashing it by our power over others, but seeking to transform it into a means by which we find greater understanding, deeper relationship, real peace.

Jesus encourages us to embrace conflict, to approach dialogue not in order to defend our position at all costs, nor so that we can merely find something between our positions that we can live with, but in order to find a genuine 'third way' that emerges out of prayerful wrestling with what God is saying, a prayerful listening that helps us learn together. Then the conflict, which arises because we all care about the direction and the journey, leads us to a better understanding than we could have had alone.

Discernment

The key to our shared journey is our shared skill in discernment, reading the signs. Jesus was surrounded by people who knew how to read the weather and other natural signs – for farmers and fishermen, these were essential skills, and yet they didn't seem to pay the same attention to the signs of God's activity. All the promises and prophecies were there, being fulfilled in Jesus, right before their eyes; yet they refused to see what God was doing.

Jesus reminds us that we need to be good at spotting what God is up to. We need to be well versed in the Scriptures and the wisdom of the faith community down the ages. We need to be steeped in prayer, in listening to God, open to the guidance of the Holy Spirit and to what God might be saying through one another, and committed to seeking his will as we dialogue together in pursuit of community.

We need to be not lukewarm but passionate about God and the things of God, so that we might know the blessings of God.

Bill Braviner

Hymn suggestions

Dear Lord and Father of mankind; Brother, sister, let me serve you; Who would true valour see; Let us build a house where love can dwell.

Ninth Sunday after Trinity (Proper 15)   17 August
Second Service   **Which Bed Will You Choose?**
Ps. 119.17–32 [*or* 119.17–24]; **Isa. 28.9–22**; 2 Cor. 8.1–9; *Gospel at Holy Communion*: Matt. 20.1–16

Holiday essentials

It's the time of year when many of us are off on holiday. I don't really mind where I go on holiday, but some things are essentials: a good view, near to water, a decent shower and a comfortable bed. A good night's sleep (or seven) on my holiday is important; and an uncomfortable bed, be it too small, too bouncy, or having an ominous dent in the middle is probably the surest way to dampen my holiday mood.

Imagine knowing there are two rooms on offer. One has a super-king bed, with a firm divan base, cool, freshly laundered sheets, and a warm, but not too warm, down duvet, with a super-soft blanket. The other has a short, toddler-sized bed, a cheap, squeaking mattress, and one itchy blanket, which is simultaneously too short, too narrow and too thin. Which would you choose?

This is the analogy that the prophet Isaiah uses in our reading today. God has offered his people a resting place; a place of security, comfort and calm. But the people have chosen a different refuge. They have chosen a bed 'too short to stretch oneself' out on and a blanket 'too narrow to wrap oneself in'.

Gibberish faith

Isaiah is one of Israel's most prominent prophets and evangelists, writing this first section in around the seventh century BC, to a people that have 'made a covenant with death'. A people that has made their bed with a stronger power in the Middle East, probably an alliance with Egypt.

Having cosied up with the big boys, they don't think they need God any more. Which has led to God's words becoming like gibberish to them. They take a little bit – odd precepts, rules and lines – but it isn't the heart and soul of their being any more. They scatter a sprinkling of faith through their lives, 'here a little, there a little', but it's just a dusting. They have strayed so far from God's teaching that they can't even recognize true faith any more and just before the passage we heard tonight, we're told that even their priests and prophets have become drunkards who are 'confused with wine' and 'stagger with strong drink'!

God's 5* bed

But how different is it for those who have set God as the sure foundation; those who do rely on God as their cornerstone? They will never be stricken with panic, because they will know that their true resting place is with God.

Later in Isaiah, we hear how God 'gives power to the faint and strengthens the powerless', and how even when we grow tired, physically and mentally exhausted, those who hope in the Lord 'shall renew their strength', soaring on wings like an eagle.

Jesus says to us, in one of my favourite pieces of Scripture, 'Come to me, all you that are weary and are carrying heavy burdens, and I will give you rest.' When we choose to walk with God, we are choosing that super-king bed and premium quality duvet. We are choosing to lay down our heads in a place of refuge; where God will grant us rest, comfort and security.

Risky rest

Of course, at times, sometimes choosing to find our peace with God feels risky. The bed doesn't always feel instantly comfortable, and the world can offer more instant gratification. When we're feeling insecure and tired, many temporary comforts tempt us; be they a glass or two of wine, a tub of ice cream, the security of money, or the powerful protection of a popular but slightly dishonest friend or work colleague. But true comfort and security come from God; and when we seek it elsewhere, we stop being able to see that truth. God's promises become a jumble of words and we dismiss the safety of them as wishful thinking for those too naive to face up to reality.

And so, in our letter of St Paul to the Corinthians, we see the oblique contrast, between the church in Macedonia (hard pressed, under a severe ordeal of affliction and in extreme poverty) and the church in Corinth. Despite all their troubles, the church in Macedonia has made their bed with God and has responded to his grace with abundant generosity. The church in Corinth? Perhaps Paul with practised subtlety implies they are finding their security elsewhere.

Where are you making your bed?

So where are you making your bed?

As we go out into the week ahead, let us each find our repose with God, who provides all the comfort we need. Perhaps, if you're finding that rest hard to find, try saying compline, the office of night prayer that seeks to create a space for calm and quiet reflection at the end of each day. It gives us the chance to hand over everything that weighs on our minds to God, asking God to watch over us, as we sleep in God's bed.

May the Lord Almighty grant us a quiet night and a perfect rest. Amen.

Chris Campbell

Hymn suggestions

Before the ending of the day; Glory to thee, my God, this night; I heard the voice of Jesus say; When I am down (You raise me up).

Tenth Sunday after Trinity (Proper 16)   24 August
(For St Bartholomew the Apostle, see p. 335.)
Principal Service   **Be Expectant!**
(*Continuous*): Jer. 1.4–10; Ps. 71.1–6; *or* (*Related*):
Isa. 58.9b–end; Ps. 103.1–8; Heb. 12.18–end; **Luke 13.10–17**

Why did you come to church today? People go to church for many reasons. But I wonder why you've come today and what you are expecting to happen during this service.

In our reading from Luke's Gospel today a woman goes to the synagogue while Jesus is teaching on the Sabbath. We don't know why she goes, but Luke tells us that she has been crippled for 18 years: 'bent over', 'unable to stand up straight'. Her disability makes her an outcast. She is not a full member of the house of Israel, not one of God's Chosen People. She is not allowed to worship God in the synagogue. She's on the edge.

But that's all about to change. Notice that she doesn't seek out Jesus. She doesn't ask him for anything. But Jesus sees *her*. He calls her over. Before she even has a chance to say anything Jesus lays his hands on her, heals her and tells her she is set free. Free from her disability, free to stand tall, to recover her dignity. She is free to worship God, which she does immediately. She stands up straight and praises the Lord. Jesus calls her a 'daughter of Abraham'. He restores her inheritance as a child of the covenant, a child of the kingdom.

Being expectant

I wonder what she was expecting to happen in the synagogue that day. Did she expect to meet with the living God, be healed and be set free? Imagine for a moment what it's like to be bent double. You can't see much. You can't look anyone in the eye. Your field of vision is very limited. Did she long to stand up tall? Did she long to be healed and restored? Did she expect that to happen? What do you expect to happen when you come to church? Do you expect to meet with the living God, and be set free?

Challenging expectations

The leader of the synagogue is indignant that a healing has occurred. That was not his expectation. For him, Jesus has broken the law by healing on the Sabbath. Teaching was permitted on the Sabbath but not healing because healing is work. The leader of the synagogue tells the crowd that they should come to be healed on other days but not the Sabbath. We, and the crowd, can see that what he says is ridiculous. God is at work in Jesus in an extraordinary way which turns upside down accepted ways of believing and behaving. The Sabbath is God's holy day. The prophet Isaiah calls the Sabbath a 'delight', which is 'honourable' (Isa. 58.13). What more honourable thing can there be than making a person whole and restoring them to God? The Sabbath is the Lord's day and the Lord – Jesus – is doing the Lord's work. It's not the first time either. He healed the man with a withered arm on the Sabbath too. The religious authorities didn't like that either!

Changing expectations

This is the rub. Encountering the living God is challenging and in God's light the way we like to do things often needs to change. What we think of as the 'right thing' may require some rethinking in the light of God's new creation, God's better plan, to make all things new. Ruins rebuilt, streets restored, bones made strong, parched places watered. God straightens us up and encourages us to see with a new and wider vision. When we remain as inflexible as the synagogue leader, we fail to see God at work all around us, and our expectations diminish and ossify. What do you expect to happen when you meet with the living God?

Raising expectations

Following the death and resurrection of Jesus, our encounter with the living God is different from the terrifying encounter that Moses had on Mount Sinai. Coming into the presence of God is being part of 'the heavenly Jerusalem', God's new city, where angels rejoice and Jesus presents each of us to God. Like the woman in the synagogue, Jesus sets each of us free so that we can stand tall before God and know ourselves to be utterly acceptable and totally loved. God is a consuming fire who burns passionately with love for each of us. Nothing can happen to us that will stop God from loving us. Nothing will make him let go of us because of what Jesus has done for us on the cross. His sacrifice sets us free to enter God's presence and be God's beloved children for eternity.

So, when we come to church, let's expect to meet with the living God, who loves us with unending passion. Let's expect to meet with Jesus who sees us, calls us, feeds us and restores us. Let's expect to be filled with the Holy Spirit who comes to liberate, heal and empower us to change the world. Whether we expect it or not, God is here. Jesus sees you and calls you to meet with him. Be expectant today and every day for all that God will do in your life and the life of this church and community.

Catherine Williams

Hymn suggestions

Glorious things of thee are spoken; The splendour of a king (How great is our God); Amazing grace; Restore, O Lord.

Tenth Sunday after Trinity (Proper 16) 24 August
Second Service **Returning and Rest as Revolutionary**
Ps. 119.49–72 [*or* 119.49–56]; **Isa. 30.8–21**; 2 Cor. 9;
Gospel at Holy Communion: Matt. 21.28–32

The complicated and the run of the mill

Isaiah is a complicated text. Perhaps the word 'intricate' better suits its poetry and metaphors which are so deeply buried in our collective psyche and brought out every year for consolation at Christmas. But where its history and context are concerned, it's complicated. Dive in with some arbitrariness, as we are doing today, and it's like watching a mid-series episode of *Game of Thrones* before you've watched all the previous episodes. There are kings, armies and fighting, strange names and half-hidden backstories. Unless you are a real fan, deeply embedded in the world of ancient history or fictional history, it's hard to get purchase. Unless, of course, you pick a particular lens through which to focus the text. For Christians down the centuries that lens has been how Isaiah predicts the coming of Jesus. Sensible enough, when what really grabs attention in the text are the metaphors and poetry which are just crying out to be attached to Christ the saviour. But, of course, there is more.

Chapter 30 of Isaiah is not a keynote speech. It is a bit run of the mill. Isaiah as a prophet, priest and statesman is critiquing the policy of the local leadership in forming an alliance with Egypt as a way of stopping an encroaching invasion by the Assyrians. There is a power struggle going on in which Judah is getting entangled. You can't help thinking of the parallels with the power struggles between Russia, Ukraine and other states in Eastern Europe. That's complicated too, with lots of history and knotty relationships.

Isaiah: reminder of the extraordinary

Isaiah underpins his statesman role with a deep understanding of and care for the things of YHWH. First and foremost, he is someone who has living experience of glory. He knows the history and the politics inside out, but his heart is in the Temple. Isaiah is a contemporary of the other prophets, Amos, Hosea and Micah, who see within religion a call for social justice. He adds to their message a reminder of the extraordinary, of the astonishing closeness of God with us. So, Isaiah's counsel for the people at this point is to remind people to root themselves back into the Temple, into their historic and cultural spirituality: 'In returning and rest you shall be saved; in quietness and in trust shall be your strength.'

This is revolutionary advice for people on the brink of disaster who have lived with the fear and trauma of invasion, attack and conquest for a long time. Of course, they want to escape, to flee on the swiftest of horses, that's only natural. Perhaps, for many, Isaiah's words sound like a fierce belief that God will intervene somehow with miraculous force and saving power. All you have to do is believe and trust and God will save. I think Isaiah's counsel is far more sensitive and astute than that. You cannot know glory without knowing the depths and intricacies of the human spirit.

Return and rest

People in the middle of a traumatic experience lose a sense of themselves. Violence is something to live through and it has fragmenting power. People lose a sense of their bodies as they have known them, a sense of time with a past, present and a future, and a sense of being able to find the right words. People with PTSD, acutely so, but these are also common experiences in the hard things of life. A sudden death or nasty life event like redundancy can leave you shaking and not wanting to eat anything, rerunning the hearing of that news over and over in your mind and feeling as if you can't really find the words to express what you are going through. To people in this situation Isaiah says 'return' and 'rest'.

Taking a sabbath step back

Two words, two concepts which would mean so much to people steeped in the culture and history of Israel and Judah. Return, tell the stories. Perhaps you will remember things that give insight into your current situation. Like, for example, the very people you are now relying on for salvation are people who in the past have enslaved you. But the key is to return in a deeper way, remember who you are and where you have come from and re-root yourselves. Go home in that deep place within yourself. Rest, allow the world to be, just for a moment, without trying to influence it. Find some space of freedom away from that which binds and which frets, and for a moment find joy. To these people this is the language and practice of Sabbath, the practice of joining in the divine rhythm and purposefully creating a place of sanctuary and holiness, a temple in time.

At times of great stress, to take a sabbath step back is a revolutionary act. Isaiah knew that. It's the privileging of a space where everyone has worth simply because they are. Our systems based on transactions, oppression and the desire for power just for a moment do not hold sway. For a time, we dwell in the extraordinariness of creation, as created people who have inherent value simply because we exist. And God's glory fills the temple of the world.

Esther Elliott

Hymn suggestions

Be still, for the presence of the Lord; Holy, Holy, Holy; Through all the changing scenes of life; Come and find the quiet centre.

Eleventh Sunday after Trinity (Proper 17) 31 August
Principal Service **Tea Parties and Politics**
(*Continuous*): Jer. 2.4–13; Ps. 81.1, 10–end [*or* 81.1–11];
or (*Related*): Ecclus. 10.12–18, *or* Prov. 25.6–7; Ps. 112;
Heb. 13.1–8, 15–16; **Luke 14.1, 7–14**

You are probably familiar with Lewis Carroll's book *Alice's Adventures in Wonderland* where a young girl falls asleep and wakes in a world where everything is not as it seems. In this dream, Alice encounters a host of fantastical characters such as a white rabbit with a pocket watch, a grinning Cheshire cat who keeps vanishing, and the Queen of Hearts who keeps shouting, 'Off with their heads!' It is only when she stumbles upon the Mad-Hatter's Tea Party that Alice realizes everything is back to front and upside down in this strange new world. Today's Gospel reading is not quite as puzzling as *Alice's Adventures in Wonderland*, but when we consider Jesus' words we might be forgiven for thinking he gets things back to front and upside down too.

Jesus at a tea party

The passage begins with Jesus at a tea party, where it says, 'They were watching him closely.' Jesus has gained a reputation and the people are paying careful attention to his words and actions. And yet, as the narrative unfolds, we discover that it is in fact Jesus who has been watching them. Having observed how the guests chose the places of honour, Jesus tells them a parable about a wedding banquet. The parable is split into two parts – or two lessons – where the first half is written from the perspective of someone being invited, and the second half is from the perspective of someone doing the inviting. Jesus is addressing the guests and the hosts in turn. He is speaking to those without power, as well as those with power. He is speaking to all of us.

'Don't forget your table manners!'

In the first lesson, Jesus is saying that those who are great will be the least in the kingdom of God, and those who are humble will be the greatest. This is a topsy-turvy tale. Nowadays, it is only natural to assume that those who get ahead are the ones who push themselves forward. The successful ones in our society are adept at outmanoeuvring others.

This is in keeping with how things were in Jesus' time. Social status was key and had a bearing on every aspect of your existence, such as reputation, work, income, and who you could associate with. Where people sat during a meal in relation to their host was a sign of this status. And yet Jesus said, 'Sit down at the lowest place, so that when your host comes, he may say to you, "Friend, move up higher"; then you will be honoured in the presence of all who sit at the table with you.' Jesus' teaching was profoundly counter-cultural.

What's interesting is that Jesus' teaching would not have come as a complete surprise to his audience. His teaching was drawn from pre-existing Old Testament Scriptures. Proverbs 25.6–7 is almost identical where it says, 'Do not put yourself forward in the king's presence or stand in the place of the great; for it is better to be told, "Come up here", than to be put lower in the presence of a noble.' Jesus is not teaching anything new here. It is not as if the people didn't know what the right thing to do was. The issue is that they did know what to do, but they chose to disregard it anyway.

How many of us know what the kingdom of God looks like and yet still choose to give in to our own selfish desires and ambitions? Jesus' teaching is reminding us to remember our table manners!

'Don't forget to say grace!'

The second lesson contained in Jesus' parable is addressed to those who are in the privileged position to be doing the inviting: the hosts. Here, Jesus instructs the hosts to not favour those who are deemed worthy in the world's eyes – those who can pay them back – but instead to 'invite the poor, the crippled, the lame, and the blind … those who cannot repay you'.

It was customary in those days to only give gifts or return favour to those who were worthy in the eyes of society. But again, Jesus turns this thinking upside down and inside out by opening up the table to the least worthy in society, without any regard to worth. Jesus' teaching not only challenges notions of status but it also regards status and honour as something that is given, instead of being gained. This is a crucial difference. Status is a gift that is ultimately granted by God, not something earned through our own efforts. Jesus is painting a picture of God's grace for his hosts.

Jesus said all these things in the context of a 'wedding feast'. Elsewhere, Luke uses banqueting language to refer to the kingdom of God. The disruption of social order and social values is a foretaste of the coming kingdom. Whether we consider ourselves to be those invited to the table or those doing the inviting, we must always remember that in God's kingdom it is grace that begins the meal. It is grace that we share.

Mark Nam

Hymn suggestions

Oh, how glorious is thy table, Lord; Give thanks with a grateful heart; Behold the lamb; He brought me to his banqueting table (Kevin Prosch).

Eleventh Sunday after Trinity (Proper 17) 31 August
Second Service **The Best Man, Not the Groom**
Ps. 119.81–96 [*or* 119.81–88]; Isa. 33.13–22; **John 3.22–36**

Wedding responsibilities

It's a big moment for the best man. The minister turns to them and says, 'Can I have the rings, please.' Many a best man has been torn at this point, between pretending they have lost the rings and actually trying to remember which pocket they went into before the wedding began …

The best man's role is to ensure the groom arrives at the wedding on time, appropriately dressed and sober. Once the groom is at the front, and the rings have been safely handed over to the minister, the best man steps back. All eyes are now on the groom and the bride as they make their vows.

John the Baptist compares himself to the best man, with Jesus as the groom. The role of the best man is to prepare the groom for what lies ahead. To make the arrangements, sort out the suits, book the hotel rooms, ensure the groom is in the right place at the right time, write and deliver a speech which talks about the groom and their friendship – to be clear that the spotlight and focus is on the groom.

'All are going to him …'

We have the benefit of reading this in the context of the earlier chapters of the Gospel, where the writer is clear that John the Baptist is a herald and signpost for another who is yet to come. We understand John's words when he directs people to Jesus as the main feature, rather than to remain with John the Baptist who is the warm-up act. For the followers of John the Baptist, the fact that Jesus was a short distance away with a seemingly similar ministry of teaching and baptizing must have felt like competition. Perhaps in their commitment to John they felt a great sense of over-protection. Perhaps some of them enjoyed the prestige by association. Surely John the Baptist would feel envious of this competing ministry, and wish to retain his followers rather than lose them to a more popular rival.

John the Baptist disagrees. There is no envy here in his words, no sense of competition or ministerial ownership, no rights to exclusivity. There is joy that Jesus has come, as promised and as expected. The herald has served his purpose. The best man's plans have succeeded. The groom is here and ready to meet his bride. The guests, John the Baptist's disciples included, must now focus on the groom. The best man now steps back.

John the Baptist as a role model

We mostly focus on Jesus as our role model – how we should think, speak and act like Jesus in order that others may come to know him. Rightly so.

At the same time, John the Baptist teaches us a vital lesson in how to be the best man and not a version of the groom. There is a danger that in trying to be like Jesus, we can end up getting in the way of Jesus, and placing ourselves in the limelight.

We can name any number of church leaders over the years whose ministry has become centred on their personality and charisma, and less about Jesus. Whose preaching mentions the books they have written more than the Bible they are reading. Who trade on their name, rather than the 'name above all names'.

John the Baptist draws plenty of attention in the early phase of his ministry and immediately directs it away from himself and towards Jesus. He is clear that his ministry is about preparing people for the one who is to come. That he himself is not the Messiah, but the one to come most certainly is. That his God-given ministry is to point to Jesus and not to self.

Our lives as leaders and disciples

While we try to model ourselves on Jesus, we must not lose sight of the fact that we are to point people to Jesus. We are not the groom, Jesus is. It is he who has the words of eternal life, he who loves the world so much that he came to save and not condemn. It is Jesus' ministry entrusted to us, by the power of the Holy Spirit. It is Jesus' hands into which the Father places all things. It is Jesus whom people are called to believe and trust.

We are to be his heralds and signposts, not to be the ones casting a shadow over him with the spotlight on us. We are not the Messiah – he is. And we get to see the joy in Jesus' eyes as he looks at his people with love, as the groom who turns and his heart skips as he sees his bride on their wedding day.

Kt Tupling

Hymn suggestions

I will offer up my life; May the mind of Christ my saviour; All my hope on God is founded; Take my life, and let it be.

Twelfth Sunday after Trinity (Proper 18)
7 September
Principal Service   Giving the 'Useless' a Voice
(*Continuous*): Jer. 18.1–11; Ps. 139.1–5, 12–18 [*or* 139.1–7]; *or* (*Related*): Deut. 30.15–end; Ps. 1; **Philemon 1–21**; Luke 14.25–33

Useless

For about 2,000 years, the interpretation of this tiny letter has been more or less settled. Onesimus, whose name means 'Useful', has been useless to his master. In fact, it seems he has run away. During his flight, he has met Paul, become a Christian and is being returned to his master. The story provided, during the British abolition debates in the 1830s, a reason for slavery to be maintained. One man says:

> if it were a matter to be determined by my personal sympathies, tastes, or feelings, I should be as ready as any man to condemn the institution of slavery … But as a Christian … I am compelled to submit … to the authority of the Almighty.[45]

More recently, theologians have begun to ask who it is that is able to label others 'useless'. The answer, of course, is the powerful, those to whom others might be of use or service.

So then, is Onesimus useless?

Voiceless

Charles Colcock, a missionary in the 1840s in Georgia, preached from Philemon to a large congregation. He reports that when he 'insisted on fidelity and obedience as Christian virtues in servants ... one half of my audience deliberately rose up and walked off'.[46] After the service, some of those who remained declared that no such epistle existed, that this was not the gospel, and that Colcock was preaching to please 'the masters'. The issue was that the congregation was made up of slaves. From a position of white privilege, Colcock preached that slaves should be subservient.

I wonder whether rather than 'useless', Onesimus was 'voiceless'. The discussion between Paul and Philemon is between two privileged men about an enslaved one, whose voice is never heard. Or is it?

There is another, more hopeful, alternative. Paul twice calls Philemon 'brother'. He points out what they share – the goodness of Christ. Paul emphasizes that he and Philemon are equals, brothers. He speaks of Onesimus differently, however. He calls himself Onesimus' father, and he speaks on Onesimus' behalf. Onesimus is not, then, voiceless. Paul loans him his own voice, that of an apostle.

Gaining voice

Is Onesimus powerless? He is a slave. His usefulness is discussed by others. Paul *sends* him back and speaks *for* him. But there is more to the story. There would be no letter, no story, at all if Onesimus had not run away in the first place. Onesimus is a participant in his own freedom. Perhaps there is a challenge here for all of us who have, on occasion, said something like 'I couldn't' or 'I can't help it'. Perhaps before support and a way out comes action. Onesimus instigated events by running away.

Onesimus the brother

For most people, getting his job back would be a generous outcome for Onesimus. But Paul asks for more. He asks Philemon to accept Onesimus back, not as a slave but as a brother, his equal. The status he has given to Philemon, he asks Philemon to give to Onesimus.

We don't know who Philemon was exactly, but it isn't too difficult to imagine how an early Christian might feel being called 'brother' by the great apostle. Perhaps Philemon puffed out his chest a bit and thought, 'Wait till I tell the church on Sunday.' Then Paul asks Philemon to do for Onesimus what Paul has done for him. Follow my example, says Paul. There's the rub. Whoever someone is, irrespective of how important we might be, in Christ we are brothers and sisters.

Giving the 'useless' a voice

One of our tasks, as we comprehend all the good we share in Christ, is to be voices for the voiceless, for those that our society, our community and even our church call 'useless'. Lending others our voice can look insignificant – sitting next to the woman on the bus who is being abused because she wears a hijab; pointing out that not all teenagers are ... whatever the person you are talking to just said; writing to your MP about unjust laws.

Actions spring from attitudes, and we need first to check how we see others. I know that sometimes I talk about others as though I have the right to decide their fate, just as Paul and Philemon seem to do. I need to see others as valued brothers and sisters, who share with me in the goodness of Christ.

Liz Shercliff

Hymn suggestions

Brother, sister, let me serve you; One bread, one body; All are welcome; Whatsoever you do.

Twelfth Sunday after Trinity (Proper 18)
7 September
Second Service **You Search the Scriptures ...**
Ps. [120] 121; Isa. 43.14—44.5; **John 5.30–end**

'You search the scriptures ...'

To search the Bible seems like a really important thing to do. And sometimes this phrase is used to encourage people in their personal Bible study. But what Jesus is saying here, in John's account, is something quite different. There you are, he seems to say, sifting through the Scriptures to find some spiritual benefit, but you are missing the main event. The Scriptures are pointing you towards me, and you are missing it! Look up from the page – you won't find me there. Here I am in front of you!

Scriptures

And what exactly are these Scriptures that Jesus was talking about? It was clearly not a Bible as we know it. But already, in the time of the Gospels, the word 'scriptures' seems to have been used for a group of writings.

These writings were scattered. They were handwritten. Some were scrolls, and others were the more familiar little books called codices. How much access did a small Christian community have to these Scriptures? Maybe one cherished scroll or a Torah library in a synagogue cupboard? Might a group of Christians pass around a single, carefully copied-out letter from Paul or another apostle?

As John tells it, the audience Jesus is talking to would seem to be scribes and Pharisees, or others who could read. They were the leaders, the influencers. They represented the Jewish tradition. They were those who 'searched diligently' in the Torah to discover how to live: particularly how to live in the light of the eternal. That's how they learned about God.

A big mistake

And what is so wrong with that? Isn't that what these writings are for, to show us the way? Yes, and no, says Jesus. You are making a fundamental mistake. You are mistaking the writings for God. You are mistaking the questions for the answer.

The role of the Scriptures is not to be the place where we find eternal life but to be a signpost to the real source of that eternal life. To these people – and maybe ourselves as well? – the Scripture was a lifelong study. It was a Way, on which they travelled. They saw Scripture as the sole source of Truth for them to grasp. The words themselves were a constant source of life.

But all of these, Jesus claims, are actually to be found elsewhere. It is not these Scriptures, not any Scriptures, that are the Way, the Truth and the Life, but Jesus himself.

A shared life

Doesn't this sound arrogant? What Jesus says seems to be, as we might say these days, 'all about me'. But I don't think for one minute we should read his words as the ultimate ego trip! He is not saying, 'I am the answer for everything.' Something else is going on.

Jesus is showing us, by his incarnation, by his life, his compassion, what the life of God is actually like in this world. He is not saying, 'I am Superman'! This is not primarily a statement about his unique status. It is not about being God, but being fully human. He is drawing attention to his own life so that many can share it. He does not trumpet himself as a lone, heroic exemplar, but as a source. And if he has life, it is only to give it away to others.

Jesus is showing us that the life of God, the eternal life, is all about relationship, connection and love – far more than it is about words.

Signposts

The writings, the Torah, and the emerging documents of Christianity, every one of them acts as a signpost, a marker. They are fingers that point at Jesus himself. The law, says Paul, is a schoolmaster, a slave that leads the children to school. The law is designed to lead us to Christ.

This comment of Jesus might be painfully relevant to us, who love our books, and who wrestle with theology. This *searching the Scriptures*, this intense Bible study is, could be in the end, rather poignant, even tragic. We may spend hours with the Bible. We can come to great conclusions about theology and life, and yet at the same time refuse to come to him to have life.

Look up from your book, says Jesus, and look into my face. Don't spend your life following text, follow me. Don't make the Bible an object of worship, but listen to its witness and turn to face the Source. You are like walkers on the clifftop, spreading out the map, poring over every detail, absorbed in the names, the symbols and distances. You have become so absorbed that you never look out to the wide ocean, the light's glitter on the waves, the dynamic sky. You cannot even hear the waves or the cries of the seagulls.

So, Jesus stands before us with this invitation: God's invitation of unconditional grace and unconditional love. How can we respond to that love, without imposing our own conditions, walls of words that hold us back – however wonderful those words may be? May we become those who follow Jesus. Come to me, he says, and have life.

Andrew Rudd

Hymn suggestions

Jesus, be the centre; Will you come and follow me; Come, my Way, my Truth, my Life; All I once held dear.

Thirteenth Sunday after Trinity (Proper 19)
14 September
(For Holy Cross Day, see p. 337.)
Principal Service   **Lost and Found**
(*Continuous*): Jer. 4.11–12, 22–28; Ps. 14; *or* (*Related*):
Ex. 32.7–14; Ps. 51.1–11; 1 Tim 1.12–17; **Luke 15.1–10**

Losing and finding

I wonder if you can recall a time when you lost something very precious, or when you yourself got lost. With smartphones and satnavs, it's not so easy to get lost these days when we're out and about. But I can remember losing one of our children on Blackpool seafront when they were about four years old, and the absolute terror they and we went through before we were reunited. It was only about 20 minutes but it felt like for ever!

In Luke's Gospel, Jesus tells a parable about a sheep who wanders off, goes her own way and gets lost, and the man who leaves all the other sheep to search for just that one. That one in a hundred. Jesus follows up this parable with another, about a woman who loses a precious coin, a tenth of her silver pieces. She holds up a light, sweeps the house and searches high and low. She doesn't stop until she finds her coin.

Celebrating

In the parables, great celebration and rejoicing happen when that which is lost is found. The shepherd returns to his flock rejoicing. The woman throws a party for her friends and neighbours. 'Just so, I tell you,' says Jesus, 'there is joy in the presence of the angels of God over one sinner who repents.' The celebrating and rejoicing on earth over finding that which was lost is a reflection of the joy experienced in heaven when people return to God. There is misery in being lost, there is joy in being found. Many of you will know that the story that comes next in Luke's Gospel is the story of the prodigal son, who goes his own way, falls on bad times, struggles home and is welcomed with open arms by his loving parent.

God is always coming in search of us – coming to find us – waiting to rejoice over our homecoming, our being found. Whoever we are, God delights in us, and our being with God is cause for celebration. Cause for rejoicing.

Going our own way

There are times when we grumble like the Pharisees. There are times when we're dissatisfied with the way God goes about things. There are times when it seems very hard to trust either God or one another. There are times when the ways of God seem strange and our way seems better. There are times when we give up. There are even times when we cease to believe. But God doesn't ever give up on us. God always believes in us. God searches and seeks over and over and over again. For each of us. For you.

Worth searching for

The religious leaders and teachers in our reading resented the fact that Jesus chose to spend time with those on the edges, those rejected by society, those who made mistakes, and those who knew themselves to be lost. In contrast, Jesus teaches that we are all worth searching for. God longs to find us and spend time with us, whoever we are.

Sometimes we hide ourselves from God.
Sometimes we are not easy to find.
Sometimes we pretend we're not lost at all.
Sometimes we think we do not need God.

But God will never give up on any of us. God will never give up on you. God searches for that which is precious. Like the shepherd searching for the sheep. Like the woman turning the house upside down for her precious coin. When we lose our way, God comes to find us, bringing us home because God has solid, lasting, unrelenting love for each of us. For you. We are found through Jesus who on the cross draws everyone to himself because all are utterly precious and loved. All are worth dying for, and this sacrificial love breaks through the power of death and leads first Jesus and then each of us to new life.

Carrying home

There's a beautiful image in this reading: the picture of the shepherd carrying his precious sheep on his shoulders. It's a very intimate picture that conveys care, love and compassion. The shepherd holds the lost sheep close to himself and eases the hard or long journey home. Carried on the shepherd's shoulders the sheep is lifted high, has a great vantage point, and can see what's ahead. She knows when home is on the horizon.

I wonder … do we allow ourselves to be carried by Jesus in that way? Do we allow him to hold us close and lift us high? Do we feel secure with Jesus, knowing we are on the right path home? Do we allow ourselves to be found?

Carry us, Lord, when life is tough, when we've had enough, when it's all got too much, when we're tired, fragile and broken. Carry us, Lord, when we've gone our own way, when we've forgotten to trust and when hope has run dry.

Come to find us, Lord, search us out, lift us up, rejoice over us and carry us home.

Catherine Williams

Hymn suggestions

I heard the voice of Jesus say; Amazing grace; Faithful shepherd, lead me; Jesus is here (Chris Juby).

Thirteenth Sunday after Trinity (Proper 19)
14 September
Second Service   **Sustenance for Spiritual Life**
Ps. 124, 125; Isa. 60; **John 6.51–69**

In the last decade, I've taken up outdoor running and completed the Bournemouth Half Marathon in 2022. As a novice to running long distance, and in preparation for this feat, I pored over training programmes on the internet and consulted with friends who had achieved this distance and longer. Inevitably, many plans spoke about the importance of diet and nutrition to ensure a good run and to avoid soreness or injury. Similar to fuelling the physical body for the distance, we need to feed the spiritual body for the endurance race of earthly living into eternity.

Don't take offence!

In John's Gospel, Jesus says, 'Those who eat my flesh and drink my blood have eternal life, and I will raise them up on the last day.' In essence, what he is suggesting is that we need to 'chew' on his word, meditating on Scripture to increase our awareness and understanding of who he really is – the Son of Man, the Holy One of God. We are not only physical beings, we are spiritual beings and, like physical hunger, spiritual hunger necessitates we nourish the spirit self. From my experience, I find making time to study the Bible and other Christian literature, having a discipline of prayer and regular fellowship with other Christians are part of my dietary requirements to sustain my faith and nourish my spiritual life.

The message of Christ can often be hard-hitting and even 'offend' some people. But in the all-important matter of life and death, Jesus pulls no punches and makes no effort to minimize the reality of the choice we all have to make: to follow God or not. The gospel message of our Lord Jesus Christ cannot and should not be sugar-coated. Jesus was direct in communicating with the disciples, and now us, that he came not to fill our physical bellies but to satiate our spiritual longings, granting us eternal life. The followers of the day expected a saviour who could save them from hunger, but Jesus came to do much more than that. He came to give his life for the sins of the world. They wanted a political Messiah and not one who desired their souls to be saved.

Like those disciples, in a generation where we are caught in the net of a cost-of-living crisis, it is easy to understand how difficult a message it is to grasp. To see beyond the physical and navigate our world with a spiritual lens.

God, on our side

Nonetheless, Jesus' hard saying, while revealing a difficult truth, also offers good news for his hearers. Jesus states emphatically, 'No one can come to me unless it is granted by the Father.' We simply need to trust in Jesus, as Lord and Saviour, the one who came to die on the cross and was resurrected for our sins.

Thankfully, God, the reconciler, is on our side: 'Our help is in the name of the LORD, who made heaven and earth' (Ps. 124.8). No matter where we've been, what we've done, or the circumstances of our lives, God loves us and will never give up on us. The enemy will seek every means to kill, devour and destroy, but God is our 'everlasting light' (Isa. 60.19). We may face significant opposition, hatred and rejection in this world, but God is our Redeemer (Isa. 60.16). If God is for us, who can be against us?

An awesome promise

We are created in God's image and reflect the beauty of God the Father, the Son and the Holy Spirit. We are called to worship God with our whole selves: mind, body and spirit. Many in our society search for the meaning of life, the purpose for their existence. As Christians, we find fulfilment in a world groaning with all manner of distractions and dysfunction because we immerse ourselves in the pursuit of knowing God. We have an enormous appetite for Jesus. It is the desire to grow in Christ which draws us to the communion table week after week, that place where we acknowledge our sinfulness and all that Christ sacrificed for us on the cross. It is as we 'eat the flesh of the Son of Man and drink his blood' that we remember the awesome promise of eternal life.

Catherine Okoronkwo

Hymn suggestions

We have a gospel to proclaim; Guide me, O thou great Redeemer; Breathe on me, breath of God; I know that my Redeemer lives.

Fourteenth Sunday after Trinity (Proper 20)
21 September
(For St Matthew, Apostle and Evanglist, see p. 339.)
Principal Service **God or Wealth?**
(*Continuous*): Jer. 8.18—9.1; Ps. 79.1–9; *or* (*Related*): Amos 8.4–7; Ps. 113; 1 Tim. 2.1–7; **Luke 16.1–13**

What a challenging Gospel today! This portion of Luke has baffled people down the centuries, especially verse 9 where Jesus seems to commend the use of dishonest means to win friends. Commentators agree that this is a difficult passage, and have come up with many possible interpretations to ease confusion. These range from 'Jesus can't possibly have said this, so it must be a mistake', to 'It's all about forgiveness of debts', to 'Jesus is showing he understands the complexity of human nature', and various other clever and complex ways of reading the original. So, if you did a double-take when you heard the Gospel, don't worry! Everyone struggles with this passage.

We could spend a whole sermon going over possible interpretations, but instead let's focus on that last saying of Jesus. It's almost a throwaway line, but let's not lose it: 'You cannot serve God and wealth.'

Values

If you had to write down a list of your values, what would be on your list? What really matters to you? Often when Jesus is telling a parable it encourages us to work out our priorities. It helps us look again at our lives through kingdom spectacles: from a godly perspective. Jesus is asking us what drives us. Is it our faith or is it our things? Because: 'You cannot serve God and wealth.'

Wealth here means more than money. It means possessions, attachments, time, power and influence. It means all the things we think belong to us, but are actually gifts from God, given to us in trust to use wisely. As soon as we begin to think of money, land or people as commodities we own or could exploit, we are in real danger. How we use what we've been given by God demonstrates our faithfulness and commitment. Our money and possessions are not for our private glory but for the glory of God and the welfare of all.

Serving wealth

Of course, we know that! The people of God know that God is more important than money. But look at God's people in the reading from Amos. They were convinced of their holiness. They worshipped faithfully. But God berates them through Amos who indicates that the wealthy in Israel can't wait for worship to be over so that they can return to the marketplace. They are using wealth, power and influence to exploit others. They deceive with faulty scales. They sell the sweepings of the wheat. They trample on the poor. God warns them: 'I never forget any deeds.' The Lord knows when people serve wealth rather than God: 'You cannot serve God and wealth.'

Back to the Gospel. Jesus is indeed showing his understanding of the complexity of human nature. No one is all bad, and everyone is capable of doing good. Though the manager is motivated by trying to save his skin it works out well for others who have their debts reduced. If you can be faithful with a very little, suggests Jesus, then you can be faithful in much. Conversely, if you are dishonest in a little you will be dishonest in much; it's a slippery slope. We all know how a very little lie can soon become a very big deceit.

Serving God

How do we make sure we serve God rather than wealth? How do we remain faithful and learn to use our God-given money, possessions, time and influence appropriately for the kingdom?

Paul writing to Timothy commends the importance of prayer. He suggests that we should pray for everyone, even those we don't agree with or who are our enemies. When we pray for others, we want the best for them and that changes our attitude towards them.

When we are regular and faithful in prayer it reminds us and demonstrates in a tangible way that God comes first in our lives, before anything else. When we pray, we are focused on God and that helps to align our will with the will of God. It helps us to see the world through God's eyes, and expands our hearts to hold more of God's love, for both ourselves and others, leading us naturally to move away from things and focus on God: 'You cannot serve God and wealth.'

Prayer

If you're not used to praying, not sure how to do it, or have fallen out of the habit start by praying the Lord's Prayer, slowly and thoughtfully every day. Pray for your family, your neighbours, work colleagues, friends and those you meet each day, lifting them to God for blessing. Sit quietly and allow the Holy Spirit to bring to mind those for whom you might pray. Listen to what the Spirit wishes to say to you, stirring in your heart the next steps on your journey of faith.

And for all of us, regular in prayer or not yet, let's go home and look at everything we own. Let's remind ourselves that everything we have belongs to God and is to be used for God's good purposes. Let's remember the words of Jesus: 'You cannot serve God and wealth.'

Catherine Williams

Hymn suggestions

As the deer pants for the water; Take my life and let it be; Be thou my vision; My worth is not in what I own (Keith and Kristyn Getty).

Fourteenth Sunday after Trinity (Proper 20)
21 September
Second Service   **Who is Jesus?**
Ps. [128] 129; Ezra 1; **John 7.14–36**

So many questions!

Our reading from John's Gospel today throws us straight into the middle of a dynamic and tumultuous scene, as Jesus comes to teach in the Temple. There are 11 questions in this passage, most of which aren't answered, adding to the sense of tussle and confusion. But the questions at the heart of the encounter, in their different ways, are raising important issues – who is Jesus, what is the source of his authority, and what do we do with the answers to these questions?

Circling in

There are three sets of voices in the passage – Jesus, the crowd, and 'the Jews', which in John's Gospel usually refers to the religious leaders, which is probably the case here as the narrative distinguishes them from the crowd. Each voice or group of voices are coming at the situation from a slightly different direction, and yet they are all circling in to the same place.

Jesus is trying to get the religious leaders to acknowledge who they think he is, to admit that what he is doing and saying is real and true. The last time he was in Jerusalem, he healed a man on the Sabbath. While the Pharisees on the surface seem most affronted by Jesus not observing the Sabbath, the fact that he performed a miracle is clearly in their minds, and now he has shown not only that he heals with authority but he also teaches with authority. Jesus' questions are trying to get them to admit that what is troubling them is not his observance, or otherwise, of the law, but that he may in fact be the Messiah.

The crowd's questions are circling towards the same truth. At first, they can't believe that the authorities could want to kill Jesus, after his teaching and miracles that draw them to him. But then some of the crowd recognize that the authorities do want to kill Jesus and start to suspect the reason they want to kill him – the authorities know he is the Messiah but are refusing to accept it. The crowd recognize Jesus' miracles as signs that he is the Messiah, asking what more could they expect: 'When the Messiah comes, will he do more signs than this man has done?'

The authorities, however, seem to be fully in denial of what is going on. Rather than asking the big questions like the crowd, they are nit-picking. They are surprised by his learning, but instead of engaging with the content of his teaching they question how he can speak like this. Instead of asking about who has sent Jesus, they get exercised about whether they will be able to find Jesus when they want to arrest him. They clearly feel their authority has been challenged, but aren't ready to acknowledge what seems evident to the crowd – Jesus' authority is from God.

What sort of answers are we looking for?

I wonder what questions about Jesus this episode leaves us with. The tumult and questions we hear in this scene from John's Gospel may leave our own minds in a spin of curiosity and uncertainty about what we are seeing and hearing. What do we think that Jesus' teaching and miracles point to? Do we believe they are true? Why do we think Jesus was killed, and what does that tell us about him? What about the people who reject Jesus and his teachings today – what do they tell us about Jesus? Do we believe that Jesus is the Messiah, the Son of God? What sort of answers are we even looking for?

The religious authorities, the Pharisees and chief priests, are looking for facts, for information, zooming in on the details because the big picture is too much for them to handle. That might be where we get stuck too, looking for information to answer our questions about Jesus but not facing who he really is.

A step of faith

Jesus' answer to the very first question in this passage offers us a different approach. He says, 'Anyone who resolves to do the will of God will know whether the teaching is from God or whether I am speaking on my own.' It might be that sometimes we need to start not with information but with commitment. As we commit to do God's will, as we commit to follow Jesus, we learn to know God more closely and to recognize God in the life and person of Jesus. Like the crowds drawn to Jesus by his teaching and his actions, if we allow ourselves to be drawn to him, we will see more clearly the truth of who he is. We can ask all the questions in the world of Jesus, but sometimes what we really need is to take a step of faith.

Kat Campion-Spall

Hymn suggestions

At the name of Jesus; I cannot tell why he whom angels worship; Seek ye first the kingdom of God; Will you come and follow me.

Fifteenth Sunday after Trinity (Proper 21)
28 September
Principal Service   **When the Tables are Turned**
(*Continuous*): Jer. 31.1–3a, 6–15; Ps. 91.1–6, 14–end [*or* 91.11–end]; *or* (*Related*): Amos 6.1a, 4–7; Ps. 146; 1 Tim. 6.6–19; **Luke 16.19–end**

We call it the parable of Dives and Lazarus. But it is only the poor man to whom St Luke gives the dignity of a name. The rich man is nameless, despite the courtesy of a Latin epithet. But this little tale won't have its hard edges smoothed off. Throughout there is a great gulf fixed between the two. The rich man in his castle does not notice the poor man at his gate, not in a way that makes a difference, though he knows who he is when it comes to entreating Abraham. And to Lazarus, the rich man too is far off, living in another country, and they do things differently there.

But the distance between the two is not equal. The rich man would have to travel far to enter Lazarus' world, and no doubt for the wealthy of every age, to cross the threshold of the life and experience of the poor is a long and difficult journey. But not as long and difficult as crossing back in the other direction. The powerful and privileged pass by the poor every day, usually on the other side. The door is always open to them. But Lazarus is for ever excluded from the domain of the rich, on the far side of a gate with no way through. So, when the dining tables are turned, so to speak, and Dives is shut out just as Lazarus had been, we say it is only what he deserved, what they *both* deserve. We say there is justice in things after all.

This morality play is of a piece with the Hebrew prophets as we heard in Amos: God does not trust the rich and powerful to use their privilege wisely or compassionately. On the other hand, those without power or wealth or a voice of their own are called *God's* poor in the Hebrew Bible. They are his special treasure and concern. In St Luke, it is just this prophetic line of justice and compassion that Jesus stands in, the one who announced that he was sent 'to bring good news to the poor' (Luke 4.18).

The parable doesn't tell us that Lazarus was good or wise or devout, only that he was poor. It's the rich man whose career is mercilessly scrutinized, for St Luke has a great deal to say about wealth and its pitfalls. Here, the rich man's failure comes down to one thing: he did not *see* what was required of him on his own doorstep, did not *hear* the sighs and groans at his gate, did not *heed* the voices of the law and his own conscience. In the Bible's language, listening and obeying mean the same thing, to hear the word of God and do it. And, says the parable, our habits of paying attention, or not, have eternal consequences. The rich man in Hades, at last thinking about someone other than himself, asks Abraham to send Lazarus to warn his brothers of the fate that awaits them, for surely a man returning from the dead will awaken even the most dormant of consciences. 'Not so,' replies Abraham, for even someone come back from the tomb will not persuade those who won't listen to Moses and the prophets.

When you are rich, many voices clamour for attention. When you are poor, life is simpler: there are fewer distractions and fewer choices to make. Perhaps the poor are blessed in Luke's Gospel because it is easier for them to hear the word of God and welcome the kingdom: what other hope do they have? In terms of worldly fortune, probably none of us should compare ourselves with Lazarus: we know more about the compromises of prosperity than squatting hungrily outside a locked gate while dogs lick our sores. So how do we *listen* to the word of God and conscience in such a way that our vision begins to be purified and our actions are shaped by self-giving love? What would it mean to kneel to wash Lazarus' scarred and wasted feet?

The Eucharist is a workshop where disciples are crafted; God gathers us to hear his word and feed us not with crumbs that fall from a distant despot's dining table but in the intimacy of divine friendship with his own fractured yet glorified body. Communion in holy things hints at what we shall become. But it also directs us to go and do likewise, to protect and care for those in need just as God cares for us.

For the truth is that in the divine scheme of things, we are all nobodies, even the rich and powerful of this world. But mercy has found us and made us into somebodies whose lives have been given back to us again. So, what matters as we hear this tough, uncomfortable parable is, simply, what we decide to do next.

Michael Sadgrove

Hymn suggestions

O God of earth and altar; Beauty for brokenness; The kingdom of God is justice and joy; When I needed a neighbour.

Fifteenth Sunday after Trinity (Proper 21)
28 September
Second Service   **Summoning Praise**
Ps. 134, 135 [*or* 135.1–14]; Neh. 2; John 8.31–38, 48–end

On the road

There was a reassuring familiarity to trips on the minibus back when I was a member of the 10th Romford Boys' Brigade Company. Part of the routine was the singing of a medley of songs that only seemed to come out when we were on the road. One of our regular trips was to a swimming pool for competitions and galas. The pool was a half-hour drive from the Baptist church where we met. After swimming, we would pile into the fish and chip shop next to the pool and buy portions of what were surely the worst chips known to the human race. We affectionately described these squelchy treats as 'carpet flavoured' and masked their flavour with heaps of salt and bucketloads of vinegar. As the minibus set off home, there would be relative quiet as we scoffed our chips hungrily. However, after around five minutes had passed the singing would begin, nearly always initiated by my friend Sean.

'Everybody dance now'

It is a particular skill to get other people singing. Sean was adept at doing it and was usually aided by his best friend, Robert. The songs we sang on the minibus required you to join in. Sean's playlist was predictable, loaded with songs that contained call and response and others with lots of repetition: 'Everywhere we go', 'Found a peanut' and 'This is the song that doesn't end'. The minibus would often be rocking as we belted out our rowdy, energetic choruses. In the centre of it all was Sean, waiting to unleash the showstopper. This was back in the early 1990s and C+C Music Factory's 'Gonna make you sweat (Everybody dance now)' was a massive cultural phenomenon, particularly Martha Wash's iconic vocals 'Everybody Dance Now'[47] and the catchy beats in the chorus, compelling you to move. Sean's Martha Wash impression was impeccable, his timing was usually perfect. The group would be launched into rapture. Filled with song, dance and greasy carbohydrates, minibus journeys flew by in no time at all.

Summoning praise

Psalm 134 is a short and sweet psalm of praise and blessing associated with being on the move. As a Song of the Ascents, in fact, the last of the 15, it might have been at the end of a playlist used by pilgrims on the way to feast days in Jerusalem or concluding a sequence in some other form of liturgical worship in the Temple.[48] Whatever the specific use of the psalm, it is undeniably addressed not to God but to fellow worshippers. It is a summons to praise loaded with repetition, calling 'all you servants of the LORD' in the 'house of the LORD' to 'Lift up your hands … and bless the LORD'. The exhortation to movement and song is clear. Less clear is the possibility that verse 3 is probably a response by those addressed in the first two verses. It is as if the congregation have encouraged the servants of the Lord, whether they are ministers or some others, to worship the Lord. These 'ministers' respond to assure the people of the Lord's blessing for those who exhort others to worship.[49] Psalm 134 has all the hallmarks of a song ideal for being on the road: call and response, repetition and even dance moves in standing, lifting up hands and the 'bowing the knee' implied by the literal meaning of the Hebrew word translated here as worship.[50]

Keep on moving

As autumn takes hold and the nights draw in, the call to praise might feel slow to be heard and responded to in our lives. This psalm draws us together in unity and solidarity as worshippers of a living God who, despite being the God who made the universe, meets us now in the places where we seek to draw near to him. When the chips are soggy, when the chips are down, Psalm 134 is a summons for each of us as friends and companions to encourage each other to find the spark that will initiate fresh worship of the Lord. Even when the road ahead feels long or the journey tiring, the catchy beats from the rhythm of God's Holy Spirit move us to sing and dance so that we might praise the one worthy of all worship and be filled afresh with the knowledge of the blessing of his presence wherever we find ourselves.

Matt Allen

Hymn suggestions

How great is our God; O praise ye the Lord; Praise to the Lord, the Almighty; The sun comes up, it's a new day dawning.

Sixteenth Sunday after Trinity (Proper 22)
5 October
Principal Service   Divine Dissatisfaction
(*Continuous*): Lam. 1.1–6; *Canticle*: Lam. 3.19–26, *or* Ps. 137 [*or* 137.1–6]; *or* (*Related*): Hab. 1.1–4; 2.1–4; Ps. 37.1–9; 2 Tim. 1.1–14; **Luke 17.5–10**

The birth of a hospice

When I was a curate in Sedgefield, in County Durham, I had the great privilege of getting to know a remarkable woman called Mary Butterwick. I met her because I was supporting a parishioner, who in 30 years of ministry I have never forgotten, who lived with motor neurone disease. The parishioner received care in what became the Butterwick Hospice, and that is where I met Mary.

Being unhappy

Mary was a woman of great energy and determination. Her husband had died in a local hospital, and she was not all that happy about how he died, and after a vision from God and with almost no resources to do so, she founded a hospice, which today is the Butterwick Hospice in Stockton-on-Tees.[51] I saw the hospice grow from a fragile beginning when I first knew it, to a fully fledged purpose-built building, and because faith was so important to Mary, the chapel was built at the heart of it. I have always found Mary's story deeply inspiring – the idea that out of a sense of disgruntlement, something better can come, through God's grace.

Exile

In both Old Testament readings set for today, there is a sense of unhappiness, and of being bereft, particularly in Lamentations, which is then captured so poetically in Psalm 137, a psalm of exile. What is it to be in the wrong place, a place that doesn't feel right, that is not home? Rather like being ill in hospital, or a refugee in another country, as the writer of this psalm seems to be. That longing for something different is all there in these readings. I think that's worth paying attention to. I wonder if a lot of our busyness these days is displacement activity to avoid the uncomfortable emotions of longing, feeling away from safety, of loneliness and feeling disjointed. Yet if God is in all things, he is surely in this too.

Familial life

I visited a parishioner recently who is in her early nineties, and I was really moved as she talked to me about how she prayed each night, starting with the members of her family. I had also recently seen a 13-year-old who was exploring Christianity, who said something similar. I wonder if we have lost a bit of that sense of how significant that can be. I have had a sense for a long time that the power of prayer is deeply interconnected, rather like an underground system of plant roots, or like a spider's web. In today's second letter of St Paul to Timothy, we gain a picture of that as the writer refers to the faith of Lois, the recipient's grandmother and Eunice his mother.

Prayer, I feel, is really counter-cultural, as it is not always obvious where the results of it lie, and yet I believe that we are all the answer to many people's prayers, throughout the centuries. We are containers of prayers answered.

The mustard seed

Compared to the other Scripture passages set for today, the Gospel reading is relatively short. But it comes sandwiched between the parable of the rich man and Lazarus and the healing of some lepers, and you can sense in the apostles' request to Jesus, 'Increase our faith!', some desperation. It is an obvious fact, but one I think worth returning to often, that God is not like us. His ways are different from our ways, and my experience is that he works on a very different scale from human beings. Just as scientists might need microscopes to study much about human existence and the world at large, so we as Christians might need a heightened spiritual sensitivity to what God is doing around us and within us. His ways are often gentle, quiet and in the smallest of things. Hence the mustard seed. But his grace allows extraordinary things to happen, through prayer and faith.

Hope

When Mary Butterwick was sitting with her husband dying, I imagine that she could not have foreseen what good could come of that, just as those in exile in Babylon could not see what God was doing in that painful experience, along with those who have been through genocide and holocaust. Mary is but one example of someone who, through faith, grace and determination, transformed a situation of great sadness into one that has made countless lives better. Can we too trust that God can do this?

Jonathan Lawson

Hymn suggestions

Let us build a house; Amazing grace; Seek ye first the kingdom of God; Firmly I believe and truly.

Sixteenth Sunday after Trinity (Proper 22)
5 October
Second Service   Who Can You See?
Ps. 142; Neh. 5.1–13; **John 9**

From the margins to the centre

John loves his little jokes. He has just had Jesus proclaim, 'I am the light of the world!' And yet right in the next chapter, people struggle to see what he is doing! John problematizes the idea of light and sight. Those who really see, those who have light, are not those you think. A man born blind is a prism for light, he sheds light and truth on the harsh culture of his day. In the course of the story, everything is turned upside down.

The man starts as an object of other people's talk. He is not named – marginalized, with no voice, defined by others. But Jesus heals. The physical condition is not the main focus, however. The man undergoes a complete transformation, as marginalized and dominant characters exchange places: the man gains sight, salvation, a voice and a perspective that exposes the dominant culture; the Pharisees lose their privileged perspective as those who interpret Scripture and define righteousness. The man's speech grows in confidence, as does his spiritual maturity. He goes from being done to, to being the one who voices teaching and wisdom.

Jesus challenges several misconceptions and prejudices. First, he denies that physical suffering is a result of inner sin or problems. Blaming the victim makes life easier for the man's neighbours and family. It gives them a licence not to help, an excuse to walk by and make no effort to change the way they live to make it possible for others to flourish. It also means they don't have to deal with the frightening randomness of life, because if they identify a cause for suffering, then there must be a way to fix it. Accepting that the man's condition was unexplained propels them into a more frightening world, where they could share his fate. Turning him into someone not-like-them was the easy thing to do. Jesus instead calls them to see the man as like-them, another human being, and someone with wisdom to contribute to their shared community.

Light and dark challenged

Jesus challenges his hearers to ask, what is darkness? The kind of hardness of heart that walks by and fails to see another person as made in the image of God is the problem. The imagery of light and darkness, of sight and blindness can strike an uncomfortable note today, but it is central to John's Gospel – in particular because Jesus subverts it, subverts the categories, and tells people that they fail to recognize light, that they struggle to see the world and fellow human beings as they are, and fail to see what needs to be challenged and transformed.

Within this way of thinking, sin involves love of darkness – love of secrets, fear of truth, and the tendency to close oneself and one's community off into small, enclosed spaces that we have control of. It is easier not to recognize our responsibilities towards other human beings, like the neighbours towards the blind man – that is love of untruth because it does not acknowledge common humanity, interdependence and responsibility. It is also easier to shut ourselves off into small groups of people who are like us – but these places are 'dark', because they are small and enclosed, and don't allow the full breadth of perspective, truth and wisdom that is possible when we meet with others who are different. Jesus challenges his hearers to open themselves up, and let the light in. Let other people in.

Light comes gradually

But light comes slowly; wisdom comes gradually, in this story. We see stages of faith and a movement towards increased understanding. The more the man is asked to repeat his story, the more his understanding grows. He goes from talking about Jesus as 'this man called Jesus' to 'a prophet' to 'comes from God' to 'the Son of Man' to 'Lord, I believe' and worshipping Jesus. Revelation happens one step at a time – at the pace this man can cope with. Other encounters in John are faster, like the woman at the well, and others are slower, like Nicodemus. There is no one-size-fits-all. Faith grows, and Jesus encourages it, but there is not one road map to faith.

Faith eventually leads to discipleship, and discipleship to cost. There is healing and faith, but the consequences are ambiguous. It leads to confrontation with the Pharisees, a need to take up a stance which could be deadly. As elsewhere in John, the light has come into the world but the world has not recognized it.

It would be easy to stand in judgement over the crowd and Pharisees. Yet the story asks us to examine ourselves: what might we be unable or unwilling to see? What parts of our lives do we choose to keep hidden, or barricaded from others we fear, or fail to love? What would Jesus' invitation to allow the light of God to shine within and among us look like here, in this place, today?

Isabelle Hamley

Hymn suggestions

Amazing grace; Light of the world, you came down into darkness; Longing for light, we wait in darkness; O for a thousand tongues to sing.

Seventeenth Sunday after Trinity (Proper 23)
12 October
Principal Service **Healing on the Way**
(*Continuous*): Jer. 29.1, 4–7; Ps. 66.1–11; *or* (*Related*):
2 Kings 5.1–3, 7–15c; Ps. 111; 2 Tim. 2.8–15; **Luke 17.11–19**

What I love about the story of the healing of the ten lepers is that it feels almost accidental. We are told that Jesus is 'on the way to Jerusalem'. He is on the way to the capital, to the place where his life will end and ours begins, and this miracle occurs en route. I wonder how often we have waited to get *there*, wherever there is, to be at the destination of our planning, and have missed the signs and wonders of God on the journey itself. There is always the offer of healing on the way because Jesus is always there right by our side.

Jesus does things differently

There is a sense that we are witnessing in this story something rather audacious. The lepers were not meant to speak to Jesus. As outsiders in their society because of their illness, they had to keep their distance. This distance also represents their society's view of their spiritual state, which conflated illness with sin, and ensured that people suffering in body or mind were often permanently excluded. But Jesus, the great interrupter, breaks up this narrative of exclusion. As Chelsey Harmon reminds us:

So here's this man who has multiple reasons to be at a distance. He is a Samaritan, a foreigner. He is a leper who must announce his suffering to others whenever they come close – otherwise, they run the risk of becoming unclean. (Leviticus 13.45) Even after he is healed of his leprosy, he will still be at a distance. Except, that is, when it comes to Christ.[52]

Jesus does things differently. There must have been hope when the man called out to Jesus that something would happen, that something would change. Healing was on the way because Jesus heard the leper's voice. Jesus saw him, saw his physical suffering and the mental anguish of the separation from home, friends and community, and Jesus responded.

Jesus calls us into his presence

Jesus heals ten lepers but only one returns to say thank you. Chelsey Harmon highlights Jesus' question: 'The questions that Jesus asks in verses 17 and 18 are rhetorical (based on the Greek grammar). The middle question in particular is quite powerful: Jesus literally says, "But the nine, where?"'[53] It would seem that the other nine have forgotten the journey and focused on arrival and the destination. They have forgotten where they were, who had seen past their physical and mental isolation, and who had brought them back to life. The gaze is now firmly fixed on what is ahead. It may be easy to judge them, but which one of us would want to go back to that place of entrapment, pain and darkness, when we have been lifted from those surroundings? Whatever made them not turn back can be easily seen in each one of us. The wonderful thing is that we can see that, while we may forget, Jesus does not forget us. Healing on the way is made manifest because Jesus continues to call the lepers into his presence. Jesus is still asking where the others are, not because he needs their expression of thanks but because he wants to see them again in this new stage of their life.

Jesus sets us on a new path

The voice that cries out for help and healing becomes the voice that loudly praises God. With healing on the way, the change is seen and heard by many around us. While the healing we seek may not be the healing we find in life, we see that Jesus is attentive to the needs of the lepers and they are set on a new path. And therein lies the rub. We can follow Jesus and then stop and go in the other direction. We can hear Jesus' words and then pretend that there was no movement in our minds or the depths of our hearts. We can even feel the transformative force of the love of God in our lives and still refuse to acknowledge the source. The fact that what once was can be totally changed by God in the illuminative and disruptive person that is Jesus Christ makes us yield our position. Healing on the way moves us from standing where we were to bowing down to worship our divine Creator, as our cry of despair becomes a cry of joy. To have healing on the way, which is a permanent option with Jesus, allows us to see God and ourselves anew.

Mariama Ifode-Blease

Hymn suggestions

O for a thousand tongues to sing; We cannot measure how you heal; I searched the world (Graves into Gardens, Elevation Worship); Come as you are (Crowder).

Seventeenth Sunday after Trinity (Proper 23)
12 October
Second Service **The Power of Walls**
Ps. 144; **Neh. 6.1–16**; John 15.12–end

Sometimes those of us who preach are told, 'Don't be so political!' I find that such things are most often said to me when I preach something with which my interlocutor disagrees. By contrast, if the same person agrees with the social comment I offer, no accusations of political bias are forthcoming. While I don't ever want to be controversial for the sake of it, I also refuse to accept we can or should avoid politics in our preaching. For politics concerns human interactions; the word itself is derived from the Greek word *polis*, meaning the city. Politics concerns the affairs of the city. As the book of Nehemiah reminds us, the Bible is unafraid of the stuff of politics: it closely attends to political or 'city' affairs and shows how the story of God's people unfolds in the space between holiness and politics.

The politics of walls

Nehemiah, a Jewish Persian official, has been granted permission to rebuild the walls of ruined Jerusalem in the wake of the Babylonian exile. Just as he prepares to complete those walls, he is effectively accused of treachery towards Persia: of preparing to reassert Jerusalem's old position as the centre of the old and destroyed kingdom of Judah. More than that, Nehemiah is accused of preparing to be king himself! Nehemiah, who longs for the holiness of God to be known in Jerusalem, finds himself accused of political shenanigans.

Perhaps it is unsurprising that Nehemiah finds himself embroiled in intrigue and political controversy. After all, he is building a wall. Walls may have many functions, but they are also often political symbols. For example, the wall proposed and partially built by the Trump administration in the United States was as much a political symbol as a physical barrier. It laid down a marker about who was and who wasn't welcome in modern America.

In the ancient world, walls were powerful symbols of effective and functioning cities, enabling them to project prestige and power. Walls afforded security for their inhabitants. They gave them reassurance, a sense of safety and enabled them to sleep easily at night, without fear of ambush. Walls granted protection to those on one side and kept those on the other out. They also provided a defensible barrier. If a kingdom wished to rise high, it needed cities with walls.

The risk of walls

I find the charges of rebellion brought by Sanballat and others against Nehemiah understandable. In the political culture of their day, don't they have grounds for suspecting that Nehemiah might be using the wall building as a pretext for claiming power and position from the great King Artaxerxes? Even in our own day, politicians of all stripes have used 'capital projects' as a way of bolstering their power and position. Of course, Sanballat and his colleagues, including some of the Jewish nobles, misunderstand Nehemiah's motivations. They make their accusations to ensure that the status quo is not disrupted. Sanballat of Samaria would not welcome the political and economic implications of a renewed Judah. He reads Nehemiah's actions through a purely human perspective – a perspective that is merely political. Nehemiah has a richer and deeper motivation which invites us into the ground of holiness and hope.

The holiness of walls

Nehemiah wants nothing more or less than a renewed and invigorated relationship between God and his people. In short, he wishes to ensure that the people can dwell in the covenant with joy and hope. Nehemiah understands that for this to happen the people need a sense of awe and promise shaped around place.

He is not interested in reviving Jerusalem for the sake of his own political ambitions or even to project powers that might threaten the Persian Empire. Rather, Nehemiah wants a symbol of shelter, sanctuary and safety where God can be praised, served and known by a people who have been in exile for so long. He longs for a place where traumatized people can safely sing of the God who is shelter and offers sanctuary to the needy and bewildered.

In Psalm 144, King David sings of God who is 'my rock and my fortress, my stronghold and my deliverer'. He also says that in the days of God's blessing, there will be no breaching of walls, no going into captivity, no cry of distress in the streets. The people will be happy and blessed: 'Happy are the people whose God is the LORD.' For David, a man who knew what it was to be hunted by his enemies in the wilderness, sanctuary is ultimately to be found in the divine. Nehemiah knows, however, that a people returning from exile will need a physical sign that God is a stronghold and deliverer. In rebuilding and completing the wall of ruined Jerusalem, he offers a token of God's blessing.

Rachel Mann

Hymn suggestions

For I'm building a people of power; We would be building, temples still undone; Christ is made the sure foundation; Jerusalem the golden.

Eighteenth Sunday after Trinity (Proper 24)
19 October
Principal Service   **A Human Being Crammed Full of Heaven**
(*Continuous*): Jer. 31.27–34; Ps. 119.97–104; *or* (*Related*): Gen. 32.22–31; Ps. 121; 2 Tim. 3.14—4.5; **Luke 18.1–8**

The need to pray

Prayer is an intricate thing. In Christian culture, it's something we do in private and in public. It's something we do by ourselves and with others. It's something that we need religious professionals to do and something we want everyone to do. It's something we do without really knowing what it's doing. It's something very personal which sits right at the very heart of our corporate life together. It's something as simple as having a single thought in your head and as complicated as centuries of diverse traditions and practices. In the face of intricacy, we humans are hardwired to simplify and do something practical, to start somewhere, to be engrossed in the how. Perhaps that's why we often read this parable as instructions from Jesus about how to pray. It can be read, though, as a story about the why, the reason for prayer, about prayer and our needs as human beings. 'Then Jesus told them a parable about their need to pray …'

Nevertheless, she persisted

The story involves two larger-than-life, stereotyped characters. On the one hand, there is a widow; one of the most exploited, marginalized and vulnerable people in the world of the Bible and, I would suggest, in today's world as well. On the other hand, there is a judge; one of the most powerful, rich and respected people in the world. The widow is described as longing for justice, and the judge as someone who is indifferent to justice and has no respect for anyone, including those the law tells him to look after – the poor and widows. They are trapped in opposing worlds and outlooks and, if we are not careful, we further trap them in a storyline about an extreme binary relationship.

The writer of Luke wanted to give people a full and accurate account of the life of Jesus and emphasizes that, at the beginning of his ministry, Jesus laid out his manifesto and put the poor, the captives, the blind and the oppressed right at the centre (Luke 4.18). Sticking to this focus leads us, as readers, to centre the woman in this story. We see her as a woman in her own right, with her own sense of agency, rather than see her as a means to an end for a powerful man. We see her as a woman with the self-awareness that she is a victim and the wisdom to know and name the perpetrators of that injustice. She is a woman who has the self-efficacy to initiate a campaign for justice. She is a woman who believes in her ability to verbally reason and persuade. She is a woman who radiates the sort of spirit that isn't phased by social niceties and is quite happy to embarrass people to get justice. 'I will grant her justice, so that she may not finally come and slap me in the face' is one way of understanding the biblical text. Less 'nag', more 'nevertheless, she persisted'.

The need to touch and handle the unswerving goodness of God

The central picture of this story, therefore, is that of a human being crammed full of heaven. This is a woman who can envisage a future full of justice and fairness and who is on fire with a sense of the divine within. That picture gives us the why of prayer. We pray because we need to touch and handle the unswerving goodness of God. And this is an insistent and strong need which, if we keep meeting it, builds up our spirit and our soul until we too are crammed full of heaven.

Prayer, then, never mind the technique or the tradition, is a constant, persistent active seeking and pursuit of the God of justice and fairness, of grace and love. It's a tenacious hanging on and a belief in that spark of hope deep down inside. It's a deep-down, pit-deep, quiet confidence in the unswerving goodness of God, even when the world around us at a personal level and in society seems confused, unjust and those in power are corrupt. It's that ability to look up at the hills and say, even if through gritted teeth, our help does come from the Lord. It's the breath, even if it only comes out as a whisper, that sings about God who keeps us in grace and guides us when perplexed.

This is important stuff. The writer of Luke tells one more story about prayer and then has Jesus inverting cultural norms for one last time, blessing children and telling the rich to sell everything, before approaching Jerusalem. It is a picture and a suggestion, perhaps even a new belief for the disciples to carry with them into the tension and trauma which is to come.

Esther Elliott

Hymn suggestions

Prayer is the soul's sincere desire; What a friend we have in Jesus; We sing a love that sets all people free; God will make a way.

Eighteenth Sunday after Trinity (Proper 24)
19 October
Second Service   **Home Rediscovered**
Ps. [146] 149; **Neh. 8.9–end**; John 16.1–11

Exile is a terrible thing. To be taken away from home, whether that means physical removal to another place, the severing of relationships, or the loss of the familiar, is a bewildering and painful experience. No matter what the manifestation of exile, the longing to feel at home with community, context and culture is strong.

By the rivers of Babylon

Nehemiah was an exile in Babylon, with an exalted position (cupbearer to the king). He nonetheless knew that 'home' was Jerusalem, the city of his ancestors. He'd seen Ezra and a group of exiles return to Jerusalem some 20 years previously, and reports of them being somewhat beleaguered had torn his heart. He cried out to God, recognized the unfaithfulness of his people, and was downcast. The king could see that, and sent him to Jerusalem, appointing him governor. Nehemiah rebuilt the city walls and re-established justice in the community. The law of Moses was read, to call the community back to their identity as God's people.

There we wept

Being called 'home' to this identity revealed to the Israelites just how far from 'home' they had strayed. Their initial reaction was to weep in penitence and shame, and also because they had realized just what a half-life they had been living by comparison. However comfortable exile seems to be, it's still exile, and when you are brought face to face with the life you could have been living, the gap between exile and home is a cause of grief. Like the prodigal son in the parable, the people of Israel have come to themselves and realized just how far from their Father they were. They wept at the separation they had created and accepted.

Sing the Lord's song

But Nehemiah's message, like the prodigal father's, was 'Do not weep, but rejoice! What matters is not that you've been away, but that you've found your way home!' And so the people rejoiced, and they revelled in being once more at home with God, and they symbolized that homecoming by once again celebrating Sukkot, the Festival of Booths, as their ancestors had done and as the Lord had commanded. A festival to celebrate the Exodus from Egypt, and now a celebration of their exodus from exile, and their homecoming to God.

And they all lived happily ever after? Not quite.

Carried away to captivity

One of the characteristics of fallen humanity is that we seem to have an inescapable propensity to stray, to wander from home, to be prodigal daughters and prodigal sons, and to send ourselves into exile, captive to our own selfish ends.

It's this propensity to stray from God that leads to the warning Jesus gives to his disciples in our second reading: they need to be kept from stumbling, but there will be people who stray so far from home that they will think they are doing God's will by rejecting and even killing God's people. How on earth can we guard against straying that far, ending up in exile that deep?

The meditations of our hearts

The answer, says Jesus, is that the Advocate is sent to guide us, to infuse and inform our hearts. Like the pillars of cloud and fire that guided the Israelites through the desert, the Holy Spirit provides direction to keep us travelling with God, not away from God – provided we remain open to that guidance and allow ourselves to be led home.

As the prophet Isaiah said, we have all like sheep gone astray and turned to our own way. We do it all the time. It's that pesky propensity for prodigal perambulation. We seem unable to resist it; but God is the prodigal Father, who yearns to have us home, and yearns to throw a party for us that we may rejoice, not grieve.

Remember Zion

I wonder where there is exile in our lives today. We will each answer that in different ways. We may not feel the exile very deeply, just as Nehemiah didn't until he had news of those who'd returned from exile to 'home'. We may not even have realized there is exile, just as those whom Nehemiah found in Judaea had become unable to see their exile until they heard God speak to them once again. We may have become so at home in our exile that, like those of whom Jesus spoke, we believe we are doing God's will when we turn on God's people.

We know we yearn for 'Zion', in the sense that we yearn to be at home in God; but unless we realize that our natural tendency is to wander off, unless we remain open to the guidance of God, the leading of the Advocate, we can stumble further and further into exile without even noticing.

So we need to come to ourselves again and again; to take bearings, to recognize where we have wandered to, to let God remind us where home is and guide us there, rejoicing. Listen for his voice. Look for his love. Lean into his life.

Enough of exile. Time to come home.

Bill Braviner

Hymn suggestions

Let us build a house where love can dwell; Lead us, heavenly Father, lead us; Just as I am; Our Father, we have wandered (Kevin Nichols).

Last Sunday after Trinity (Proper 25) 26 October
(For Bible Sunday, see p. 256.)
Principal Service Do Better, Be Better!
(*Continuous*): Joel 2.23–end; Ps. 65 [*or* 65.1–7]; *or* (*Related*):
Ecclus. 35.12–17, *or* Jer. 14.7–10, 19–end; Ps. 84.1–7;
2 Tim 4.6–8, 16–18; **Luke 18.9–14**

In primary school, I was shy and insecure, often quiet and choosing not to be on show. So, I would need to be nudged by the teacher to answer a question, because I would not be one to put my hand up. My report cards often read, 'Should be more confident in class.' In secondary school, I became more secure in myself and that self-confidence grew. As a young Christian, I must confess I have fallen into the arrogance of thinking myself 'better' than others. God, I thank you that I am not like … (and I proceed to fill in the blank with a self-righteous and opinionated thought). Not so far removed from the attitude of the Pharisee. Thankfully, although flawed and imperfect, God is constantly encouraging us to grow in Christ, to be filled with the gifts of the Holy Spirit. With God we always have an opportunity to do better, to be better.

Comparisons and competition

Jesus' parable causes us to face the truth of who we are in Christ, the reality of our life and relationship as believers. When the Pharisee says, 'God, I thank you that I am not like other people: thieves, rogues, adulterers, or even like this tax-collector. I fast twice a week; I give a tenth of all my income', it is natural to wonder what the Pharisee is hiding beneath this rhetoric of being better than the lowly tax-collector. It is clear the Pharisee has turned his faith and spiritual practice into a competition. But why? Who is the Pharisee trying to convince? God or himself? His prayer is directed not so much to God but to himself.

But isn't this the reality of the human condition? We so often compare ourselves with others and keep score. And I believe this has been exacerbated in our present-day social media culture where we are overwhelmed by celebrities and influencers telling us that, to have enviable lifestyles and sought-after lives, we need to dress a certain way, eat particular foods, drive the latest model of car. To encourage us to purchase the newest, brightest and most fashionable item modelled on Instagram or TikTok, we are reduced to comparing ourselves to others who are achieving dreams. But, more often than not, beneath all the presentations of 'picture-perfect lives' we might find people who are struggling with emptiness, loneliness and addictions of all kinds.

Beauty for brokenness

Looking closely, both the Pharisee and the tax-collector are living in a broken world. They are not so different, because although they are from different socio-economic tracks, there is a lack in both their lives. The difference between the two is that one knows that they need God, while the other does not. There have been times in my life when I have been both Pharisee and tax-collector. Jeremiah 14 asks us, 'Why should you be like a stranger in the land, like a traveller turning aside for the night? Why should you be like someone confused, like a mighty warrior who cannot give help?' (Jer. 14.8–9a).

Rather than looking at, even casting judgement, on others whom we deem 'less than', perhaps this parable invites us to be honest about where we're at in our relationship with Jesus. Jeremiah goes on to remind us, 'O LORD, [you] are in the midst of us, and we are called by your name; do not forsake us!' (Jer. 14.9b). In the regrets of decisions made, in the pain of grief, in the distortion of sickness, in all that disturbs and distracts us from our hearts and flesh singing 'for joy to the living God' (Ps. 84.2), we are encouraged to surrender to the reality that we all need God in our lives. Throughout Scripture, we are offered the strength of God and, as Graham Kendrick's song 'God of the poor',[54] reminds us, there is beauty in brokenness, where God offers us friendship, refuge and rest. As we journey with God this week, let us keep pursuing eternity as we serve God's purposes here on earth: 'I have fought the good fight, I have finished the race, I have kept the faith' (2 Tim. 4.7).

Catherine Okoronkwo

Hymn suggestions

Guide me, O thou great Redeemer; Breathe on me, breath of God; I know that my Redeemer lives; Beauty for brokenness.

Last Sunday after Trinity (Proper 25)   26 October
Second Service   **All is Vanity!**
Ps. 119.1–16; **Eccles. 11 and 12**; 2 Tim. 2.1–7;
Gospel at Holy Communion: Matt. 22.34–end

Vanity of vanities

It's a rare treat today to hear from the book of Ecclesiastes, which features only five times every three years in the Sunday cycle of Bible readings. The most familiar part to many will be the start of chapter 3, 'for everything there is a season', which is often read at funerals, but apart from that Ecclesiastes may be something of a mystery. It's presented as the words of 'the Teacher', a king in Jerusalem, who after much seeking after wisdom is sharing what he has learned. The section we hear today is the final two chapters of the book, the Teacher's conclusions. 'Vanity of vanities, says the Teacher; all is vanity.' Vanity here means ephemeral, intangible, vaporous – whatever we strive for seems to slip through our fingers. Everything in life comes and goes, and however hard we work, in the end we will die and lose the fruits of our labours. We are left with what feels like a bleak picture. This doesn't necessarily feel like an inspiring, hopeful passage of Scripture that can build us up in faith – perhaps that's why we don't hear from Ecclesiastes more often!

Our whole duty

We are all mortal. We are all finite. The world doesn't turn around you, or me, or any one of us. The great cycle of the seasons, of life and death, will continue, whatever you or I do. 'When clouds are full, they empty rain on the earth; whether a tree falls to the south or to the north, in the place where the tree falls, there it will lie.' And there's nothing any of us can do to change that. But rather than allowing that to drag him into a pit of despair at the futility of life, for the Teacher it is a reminder that our simple task in life is to 'Fear God, and keep his commandments; for that is the whole duty of everyone.' And that can feel quite liberating!

Even if we don't have a groaning to-do list for work, most of us have a list of things that need doing around the house and personal admin that needs tackling, before we even get to the piles of books we'd like to read, the list of places we'd like to visit, the friends and family we want to catch up with. And often there are things that feel so important that not being on top of them can cause us a lot of stress and anxiety. Productivity gurus are constantly finding ways to help us squeeze more activity into less time, be more productive, and then, we hope, be happier. But it all just keeps coming, it's never done, something else always is fighting for our attention. And where does 'Fear God, and keep his commandments; for that is the whole duty of everyone' fit into that?

Important business

Sr Joan Chittister is a Benedictine nun. She would talk to the novices at the convent and ask them, 'Why do we pray?' Her answer might surprise you: 'We pray because the bell rings.'[55] That might sound quite dispassionate and functional. But there's some really deep wisdom there. Religious who live their days by the bell have certain set times when, whatever they are doing, the bell rings, they will stop what they are doing, and pray. They lay down the thing that has been absorbing them, bothering them, delighting them, and focus, for a while, on God. Whether or not they want to, whether or not they feel like it, whether or not they are ready. When the bell rings, they pray.

We're so caught up in all sorts of things that feel really important – that are really important. But the most important thing is God. And so, to get into a habit of saying, it's time to stop, to pray, and the important thing will still be there when I've finished, well, that takes the pressure off a bit, doesn't it? 'Just as you do not know how the breath comes to the bones in the mother's womb, so you do not know the work of God, who makes everything,' says the Teacher. It's not our job to be on top of everything, to have everything under control, to get everything done. That's God's business. Do God's work, yes, love our neighbour, yes, but each of us is just a tiny part of God's great creation and it's not all down to you! None of us can control the passage of time – we can't make a day longer so we can fit more in, or slow down the years to avoid ageing and death. To live as if we could – that is vanity. But to live within the boundaries of the seasons and cycles of life, taking as our most important task to 'fear God, and keep his commandments' – that is wisdom.

Kat Campion-Spall

Hymn suggestions

Great is thy faithfulness; Lord of all hopefulness; O God, our help in ages past; Through all the changing scenes of life.

Bible Sunday 26 October
Principal Service **Nobody's Poster Boy**
Isa. 45.22–end; Ps. 119.129–136; Rom. 15.1–6; **Luke 4.16–24**

'Who would you choose to play you in a film of your life?' may be a popular conversation starter, but it's one that always stumps me. I struggle to remember the names of famous film stars, and certainly couldn't claim any resemblance with their faces. It's an enchanting idea, though, that my life story might be considered remarkable enough for the big screen; after all, we all tend to imagine ourselves as the hero in our own stories.

A hero emerges

When Jesus opened up the great story of Scripture in the Nazareth synagogue, the congregation were enthralled. Isaiah's words draw the hearer to the heart of an ongoing epic: the tale of God's gracious calling for his people Israel, and the promise of an anointed one who would fulfil that vocation bringing blessing upon blessing, not just to Israel but to the ends of the earth.

In announcing the fulfilment of Isaiah's words, Jesus set out a messianic manifesto for his ministry. At last, here was the one who would both establish and declare God's good news for all who knew the burdens of material and spiritual poverty; he would be the one to break the chains of oppression in the name of the God of justice. No wonder the congregation were excited to hear that this long-awaited moment of the Lord's favour was to take place not only now, in their lifetime, but here, in their own town.

So the great story of Scripture was to become, for the Nazarenes, their story. A story over which they could claim some ownership, and perhaps within it a special role, since its hero had emerged as one of their own. But Jesus muted their excitement with a warning and a challenge. After the joy would come expectations and demands; the people who at that moment were amazed by him would soon seek to manage and utilize him. They would ask for miracles and signs that put Nazareth on the map and they would entreat him to prioritize their own well-being over others: after all, healing begins at home.

Claimed for a cause

We don't have to look far across the vast spectrum of Christianity to see how tempting it is to claim and utilize Jesus for our own agendas. Of course, it's much easier to spot when groups with whom we disagree hold up Jesus as the poster boy for their programmes. But whether we advocate right- or left-wing politics, whether our aims are altruistic or self-interested, whether we care for local or global concerns, all of us can be prone to co-opt the words and actions of Jesus to advance our preferred causes.

In doing so, we risk relegating Jesus to a sidekick in our own narratives, rather than recognizing him as the protagonist of the one great story of God and humanity. It's Jesus who was there at the beginning, the one for whom and through whom all things were made and the one who sustains all that exists.

The pages of Scripture reveal the story of that creation and humanity's journey within it through the experiences of those God chose, called and used in his service. It's a cumulative testimony, spanning centuries, and Jesus says it all points to him. It's a story of overflowing love, out of which we are made. It's a story of our alienation, into which he comes to find us. It's a story of our search for belonging and his gathering of a family. Our brokenness and his healing, our sin and his redemption, our wandering and his shepherding. From the first light spoken over the formless earth to the eternal light of the Holy City, the whole Bible illuminates Jesus, the true light of the world.

Today's casting call

On this Bible Sunday, we too might catch the excitement of the folks sitting in the synagogue as Jesus read from Isaiah's scroll, expounding the ancient words for their contemporary hearts. I hope we'll share their joy as we glimpse again how the story of Scripture is continually unfolding in our own world, our own lives.

But let's heed the warning too. In this great saga we were never meant to be the heroes and Jesus has not been drafted in to play the supportive friend, the wise mentor or even the love interest! He's not to be claimed for our personal cause any more than he was to promote the renown of Nazareth. Jesus is the start and the summation of the whole of God's story.

It is our privilege, though, to take up the role written for us as one of his beloved people; not a nameless extra making up the backdrop but one of those who are known and called into the adventure alongside him. Now, in our lifetime, and here, in our home town, we can follow Jesus in bringing good news, breaking chains of injustice and proclaiming freedom for all who look to him. As the Scripture is continually fulfilled in Jesus, may it come to life again in us, his people, today.

Claire Jones

Hymn suggestions

O for a thousand tongues to sing; God has spoken by his prophets; What gift of grace is Jesus my redeemer; How firm a foundation.

Fourth Sunday before Advent   2 November
(For All Saints' Day, see p. 348.)
Principal Service   **Would the Real Zacchaeus Please Stand Up?**
Isa. 1.10–18; Ps. 32.1–8; 2 Thess. 1; **Luke 19.1–10**

I imagine most of us are familiar with the story of Zacchaeus. It is a well-trod story of a rich tax-collector who exploits his position to line his pockets at the expense of his neighbours. One day, Jesus comes through town and Zacchaeus climbs a tree to get a better look, only to be spotted by Jesus, who calls him down and invites himself over for tea. Zacchaeus sees the errors of his ways and is ready to turn his life around by repaying the people four times what he has wrongfully taken. This is a classic bad-guy-turns-good-guy morality tale. But what if there is more to the story than this? What if our interpretation is overly simplistic and Zacchaeus was not such a bad man?

Would the real Zacchaeus please stand up?

When Jesus first calls Zacchaeus down from the tree, we read that Zacchaeus 'was happy'. This is a curious response for someone who was purportedly a dishonest man. You would think he would prefer to stay hidden and not draw attention to himself, especially given the animosity of the crowd. Nevertheless, Zacchaeus climbs down, and the crowd grumble that Jesus is going to the house of a sinner.

Zacchaeus responds by standing up and saying to Jesus, 'if I have defrauded anyone of anything, I will pay back four times as much'. At this point, we might be forgiven for thinking that this is the moment where Zacchaeus has a change of heart. We celebrate his newfound generosity that goes way beyond what the law would have demanded.

But this is not what Zacchaeus is saying. Zacchaeus is speaking in hyperbole. He is deliberately exaggerating how much he will pay back anyone he has supposedly defrauded, to highlight the absurdity of the claims made against him by the crowd. The key word here is 'if'. 'If I have defrauded anyone of anything.' Zacchaeus is maintaining his innocence before the Lord. The crowd are mistaken about him and have painted a false picture.

The term 'chief tax-collector' does not exist anywhere else in the Bible. It is a name the crowd has created for Zacchaeus. Zacchaeus has been labelled by a made-up term. His reputation has been tarnished and he has been judged accordingly. Zacchaeus has been 'cancelled'. If you have ever been subject to malicious rumours or gossip, you may know what this is like. Everyone thinks they know Zacchaeus, but nobody really does.

Jesus calls us by name

But Zacchaeus has heard a rumour of his own too. Jesus, 'the friend of tax-collectors', has come to town. The first thing Jesus does is call Zacchaeus down by name. In Hebrew, the name Zacchaeus means 'pure' or 'innocent'. Notice that Jesus does not say come down, 'chief tax-collector', the name that everyone else uses for him. He says to come down, innocent one.

Jesus sees the real Zacchaeus and invites himself around to his home for tea. Perhaps this is the first time that Zacchaeus has had a friend who will sit and eat with him, and not judge him. Jesus sees the real Zacchaeus.

At the beginning of the story, we read that Zacchaeus is prevented by the crowds from seeing Jesus. This emphasis on sight is reminiscent of the story of blind Bartimaeus that proceeds this one. Bartimaeus was at the opposite end of society and very poor. The crowds painted a false picture of him too. And yet in the corresponding account in Mark's Gospel, Bartimaeus becomes the image of the true disciple.

How easy it is for us to be like the crowds judging either the very rich or the very poor, without seeking to understand or know them like Jesus did.

Jesus breaks down the walls that divide us

Jesus' final words are significant. He says, 'Today salvation has come to this house because he too is a son of Abraham. For the Son of Man came to seek out and to save the lost.' Notice that diminutive three-letter word, 'too'. Zacchaeus is a son of Abraham 'too'. By declaring this, Jesus is not only restoring Zacchaeus' identity but also the identity of the crowd. Jesus declares that they are brothers and sisters, that they are all sons and daughters of Abraham and Sarah. Jesus has restored Zacchaeus and the crowd into one people. That is a picture of what salvation looks like.

The passage starts with Jesus entering Jericho. In the Old Testament, Jericho was where God's people walked around the city until the walls came tumbling down. Here, Jesus walks into the city and the dividing walls that people have created also come tumbling down. The good news is that Jesus will stop at nothing to restore us back into a community. And while some of us may be able to identify with Zacchaeus, let this be a lesson for those of us who – if we are being honest with ourselves – probably identify more closely with the crowds.

Mark Nam

Hymn suggestions

Lord Jesus Christ, you have come to us; Make me a channel of your peace; Come down, O love divine; Oh, kneel me down again (Humble King, Brenton Brown).

Fourth Sunday before Advent   2 November
Second Service   **Compassionate and Steadfast**
Ps. 145 [*or* 145.1–9]; **Lam. 3.22–33**; John 11.[1–31] 32–44

Compassion is quite beautiful. It allows itself to be concerned with the well-being of those with whom it sees, hears and touches. It cares. In this passage, compassion is tied to steadfast love. Steadfast love is that which remains and does not waver. Although compassion and steadfastness are distinct character traits, both are in God.

Compassion in this Lament is a response to grief. It sees grief, knows it and feels it in the bones. It allows this feeling to be poured out in solidarity and love. The same God who is compassionate is steadfast and constant. This means that God will not be devoured by compassion to the point of debilitation. What a marvel that God is both compassionate and steadfast.

Compassion and love in God

God's people, whether they were living in exile, being surrounded by enemies, having times of fruitfulness, or experiencing grief, had with them one who was full of compassion and steadfast love. Personality tests might tell us that we are either emotion-led or reason-led. I guess 'reason' relates to steadfastness. It's measured, cautious and stable. Perhaps emotion relates to compassion. It's a passion felt in the heart. Those who conceive the personality tests tell us that both reason and emotion are equally important. It's true. And here, in God, they are intertwined in a unity and flow of love, truth and action. Compassion flows from steadfast love, and God is steadfast even in moving towards us in compassion and solidarity.

But there is a troubling note in our passage. It is implied that God can be the cause of grief. This is a concerning prospect. However, it then states that God does not willingly afflict grief. I don't know if I can make sense of that, even if the writer of our passage feels recourse to say it. Without ignoring this, we can say that the primary focus is not the grief caused but God's response. Our grief calls out to God and meets with compassion. Both compassion and steadfastness speak into pain. Grief, tragedy, trauma and hardship will come our way. We might not be able to explain why God has allowed these things to arrive at our door, but seemingly God's compassion and steadfast love remain.

Compassion and love with us

I imagine that most of us will have known grief. We may also have known God's silence – not just meditative silence, but an empty and dry silence that feels as though it will have no end. God is not absent from these times. Here is where the steadfastness of God's love is. We may not feel the warm breath of God on our backs, we may not feel God reaching out to us in compassion, but God's steadfast love remains.

The mercies of this God are new each morning. We rise from our beds, and they are there. We venture again into the world of work, family and care of others, and they are there. We tire and they are there. We err and they are there. And when the world breaks with the tensions of life, God's compassion continues to stir and flow. Just as Jesus had compassion on a crowd or a leper; just as he reached out his hands to give life; just as he poured out the Holy Spirit, drawing up a community of faith from the absence of his death, so God reaches out to us in compassion now.

Compassion and love from us

The passage also asks some things of us. Because God is compassionate and steadfast in love, we can be patient. We don't need to force people's hands. We don't need to rush people out of their pain and grief. But we can listen to and feel the grief of others. We can sit with them for a while in their silence. We likewise don't need to force God's hand. That doesn't mean that we have to let life pass us by. Likewise, we can learn a simple trust in God which means that we wait and allow for the silences that will come our way.

As we live in God's compassion, the life that comes from God lives through us towards our neighbours, our communities and our circumstances. Likewise, as we live in the steadfast love of God, we will reflect this same love into where we have been placed.

Mark Amos

Hymn suggestions

The Lord is gracious and compassionate; Love divine, all loves excelling; Who can sound the depths of sorrow; Here is love vast as the ocean.

Third Sunday before Advent 9 November
(For Remembrance Sunday, see p. 267.)
(For Remembrance Sunday All-Age, see p. 362.)
Principal Service **Alive to God**
Job 19.23–27a; Ps. 17.1–9 [*or* 17.1–8]; 2 Thess. 2.1–5, 13–end; **Luke 20.27–38**

It seems strange, but often the religious leaders opposed Jesus. While they studied the religious law and gave themselves to worship, they didn't understand his teaching and felt it undermined their authority. So, when Jesus went to Jerusalem and began to teach in the Temple every day, 'The chief priests, the scribes and the leaders of the people kept looking for a way to kill him' (Luke 19.47).

Challenging Jesus

The people were spellbound by Jesus' teaching and it was difficult for the religious leaders to try to catch him out. Ultimately, they resorted to interview techniques that are still often used today. They first asked a direct question and, when that didn't yield the desired response, they tried the 'softly, softly' approach, perhaps hoping to catch Jesus off guard. The direct question put to Jesus was this: 'Tell us, by what authority are you doing these things? Who is it that gave you this authority?' When that didn't work, they tried another tack and asked him if it was lawful to pay taxes to Caesar. Again, they were wrong-footed by Jesus' response. Then, some of the Sadducees decided to engage him in a theological conundrum: citing the law of Moses that required a man to marry his brother's widow and raise children, they presented a case of seven brothers. After the first died, the others married their brother's widow one by one, but she remained childless. Finally, the woman also died. They asked Jesus: 'In the resurrection ... whose wife will the woman be?'

Hearing their question, I can imagine Jesus sighing with weariness and disappointment. Sadducees did not believe in the resurrection of the dead; he knew they were asking these questions in order to accuse him of not respecting the religious law. Those who questioned Jesus were not focusing on relationship with God or caring for the needs of others. Rather they were trying to trap Jesus by speaking of the future of the dead. Patiently, Jesus tried again to explain to them the difference between being bound by the shackles of religious law and being free and alive to God. He drew them back to the present reality of living in relationship with God claiming: 'He is God not of the dead, but of the living; for to him all of them are alive.'

On hearing his response, the Gospel writer says that the religious leaders knew he had 'spoken well' and 'they no longer dared to ask him another question'. However, I wonder if those who heard Jesus' response may have gone away to ponder: What does it mean to be alive – truly alive – to God?

Alive to God

In a series of addresses given in 1986 at Oxford during a week-long mission to the university, John V. Taylor (formerly Bishop of Winchester), claimed that what matters most is being alive to God. He put it this way:

> God is not hugely concerned as to whether we are religious or not. What matters to God, and matters supremely, is whether we are alive or not. If your religion brings you more fully to life, God will be in it; but if your religion inhibits your capacity for life or makes you run away from it, you may be sure that God is against it, just as Jesus was.[56]

Taylor claimed that the test of 'aliveness' for an individual or community is 'responsiveness or the ability to respond', and, conversely, the inability or lack of willingness to respond reflects a 'deadness' of spirit. I well remember the silence that fell over the packed Sheldonian Theatre as Taylor spoke. The question we each needed to ask ourselves was obvious: were we dead or alive?

Signs of being alive to God

Ancient Christian spiritual writers described the deadness of spirit that sometimes causes us to be unresponsive to God and to others as *acedia*. Described as a kind of apathy or lack of care, it was seen as a spiritual malaise which took attention away from daily giving oneself to God and caring for others, too. Those who gave themselves to the religious life were warned that it was possible to be 'lifeless' while still appearing religious.

To be 'alive to God' is surely to be fully open and responsive to God and to others, though this is not an easy task. To be genuinely open demands honesty, humility, vulnerability and great sensitivity to the needs of others. While this way of life brings deep joy, inevitably there are also times of hardship, suffering and pain, and in those moments, the temptation may be to give in to lifelessness even while appearing religious. When that happens, perhaps we should remember: God is 'God not of the dead, but of the living'.

Karen E. Smith

Hymn suggestions

Christ is alive, let Christians sing; Holy Spirit, come confirm us; Breathe on me, breath of God; Fill thou my life, O Lord my God.

Third Sunday before Advent   9 November
Second Service   **'I Am Convinced'**
Ps. 40; 1 Kings 3.1–15, **Rom. 8.31–end**;
Gospel at Holy Communion: Matt. 22.15–22

'Don't put a sock in the toaster'

'Don't put a sock in the toaster, never put jam on a magnet.'[57] According to comedian Eddie Izzard, these are just some of Paul's commandments to the church in Corinth. Of course, we know Paul said no such thing. We might, however, be tempted to agree that Paul often seems full of demands and requirements. As a woman preacher, I am well aware of what some people think Paul says about me! But let's imagine Paul, the writer of this letter to the Roman church.

He is writing from Corinth. Corinth is a wealthy place, a new Roman city, thriving on trade. The most significant characteristic of Corinth was its utter shameless immorality. To live like a Corinthian meant living in self-indulgent luxury. It probably felt very foreign to a Jewish Pharisee bent on reforming Judaism in the name of Jesus. The Jews in Corinth seem to have adapted to the Corinthian lifestyle, too. So, when Paul challenged them about it, they turned against him. This is the moment when Paul becomes an apostle to the Gentiles. Imagine, for a moment, what it took. Rejection by his own people in a place that felt very strange to him. A break from the past, from what he knew, and an uncertain future. 'What can we say about all this?' Paul seems to say. 'If God is for us, who is against us.'

Real hope

You may have guessed that much of what Eddie Izzard ascribes to Paul's letters is simply good advice or ways of earning good luck – 'Don't lean over on a Tuesday' is another instruction. Paul is not naively superstitious, though. Nor is he unrealistically optimistic. 'For your sake, we are being killed all day long; we are accounted as sheep to be slaughtered,' he writes. These verses, I think, show us what Christian hope really is. Not superstitious, not optimistic. Honest and realistic. Grounded in understanding what God has done. I love the idea that hope is the ability to hear the melody of the reign of God.

What is life like? People might be against us, or falsely accuse us, but they can ultimately not harm us. If God is for us, who can be against us? And God is so for us that God's Son came to live among us. Like many of us – I know I do this sometimes – Paul risks focusing on Jesus' death. Often the Christian faith seems to focus on death. Jesus died for us. There's hope for us after we die – that sort of thing. But Paul corrects himself: 'Christ who died, or *rather, was raised*.' Jesus came that we might have the fullness of life.

That is the basis of Paul's hope. Nothing can limit us, nothing can constrict our lives, and nothing can make us live in fear or shame or distress if we recall our hope in the love of Christ, the one who loves us.

'I am convinced'

I love Paul's expression here – I am *convinced*. I love it because it seems to me that being convinced of something involves the whole of our beings. We know with our minds, we understand with our hearts, we experience in every fibre of our beings the love of God that holds us, keeps us and cherishes us. Paul is not superstitious, or optimistic. He does not depend on good wishes or positive feelings. He is convinced by both evidence and experience, thought and feeling, that 'neither death, nor life, nor angels, nor rulers, nor things present, nor things to come, nor powers, nor height, nor depth, nor anything else in all creation will be able to separate us from the love of God in Christ Jesus our Lord.'

Conviction underpins everything else: how we think, what we do, how we treat others, what we do with our money, our time, everything. It seems to me that Paul explains the gospel to the Romans in words so that they might live it out, so that words might become flesh. I think that partly because it seems to me that turning word to flesh is the whole trajectory of the gospel. Ideas and beliefs must always be lived: become flesh. When the love of God becomes our flesh, then nothing can separate us from it, because it is who we are.

So, no – don't put a sock in the toaster or jam on a magnet. But do believe this: 'Neither death, nor life, nor angels, nor rulers, nor things present, nor things to come, nor powers, nor height, nor depth, nor anything else in all creation will be able to separate us from the love of God in Christ Jesus our Lord.'

Liz Shercliff

Hymn suggestions

I know whom I have believed; Nothing shall separate us; The Saviour died but rose again; My hope is built on nothing less.

Remembrance Sunday   9 November
(For Remembrance Sunday All-Age, see p. 362.)
God is the God Who Always Sees
(The readings for the day, or for 'In Time of Trouble', or those for 'The Peace of the World' can be used. The readings for the Third Sunday of Advent (Principal Service) are used here.)
Job 19.23–27a; Ps. 17.1–9 [*or* 17.1–8]; 2 Thess. 2.1–5, 13–end; Luke 20.27–38

Remembrance matters

What are we doing at Remembrance? Maybe some feel anxious about glorifying war. Remembrance is not about that. War is terrible. War is immensely costly for those who fight, for those they leave, and for those they fight against. It has always been so. Remembrance matters. It is about community gathering, story-telling, honouring those who have suffered and died in war, making space for those who grieve the loss of comrades, and who live with scars of mind and body because of what they have seen and experienced. The dead and the living are not forgotten by us *because* we come to remember, and neither has God forgotten. God is the God who always sees.

Meaningless platitudes?

To speak of God being present in suffering could sound like meaningless platitudes unless we take seriously both the magnitude of the suffering of war and the unimaginable depth of God's love. The Old Testament reading for today exemplifies the point I want to make, particularly to any here who bear the visible and invisible scars of war.

Hope from the shell hole

Job is a strange book – a kind of thought experiment. If Job suffers terrible loss, physical pain and abandonment, will he curse God? Chapter after chapter we read of his losses – family deaths, terrible physical suffering, mental pain – and the less-than-helpful advice of his friends who basically tell him it's all his own fault. Some mates! Job lives in a shell hole of a life. He feels everyone and everything, especially God, is against him. He makes his objection to this pretty clear, which I admire. If you can't shout at God, where can you go?

Just when you think Job might as well quit everything and curse God to his face, he has a sudden flash of a different perspective. To be honest, the Hebrew, which was the language this was originally written in, is a bit mangled, but hope in dark places is like that, is not easy to translate, and is difficult to discern clearly, yet is undoubtedly there.

Having raged at everything including God, Job suddenly sees a shaft of light illuminating his darkness. In the low points, on the hard days, in the dark pits, that's what we all need – the light that shines in the darkness. Job says:

> For I know that my Redeemer lives,
>   and that at the last he will stand upon the earth;
> and after my skin has been thus destroyed,
>   then in my flesh I shall see God,
> whom I shall see on my side,
>   and my eyes shall behold, and not another.

Whatever you think personally about such faith, these are powerful words. It is remarkable that at his lowest ebb, a man of many battles should find a bedrock of hope. It's a hope that extends beyond death: that says the final full stop is actually a comma. There is more to come than we can easily see. This is foundational for Job and he wants this written down for ever – inscribed in rock with an iron pen, so we remember.

Ultimate hope

Job's words hint at the Christian hope of resurrection, which is much, much more than life after death. The work of resurrection is about rebalancing all disorder. It points to the shalom of God, the mending of broken limbs, the knitting together of shattered minds, the well-being of all creation. Ultimate peace.

God who always sees

For God, outside of time, all history is now, which means God sees and knows all the stories of horror and all the stories of bravery and courage, all the time. Many of these stories are lost to us, but not to God who always sees. None of this is finished until God gathers all things to Godself. Then all injustice and atrocity will be called to account, all wounds healed and all harms vindicated.

Gathering to re-member

In the meantime, at Remembrance, we gather to 're-member'. We bring together all the fragments, the anecdotes, the history and the human stories. The dead are not forgotten; the suffering are not abandoned; there is hope in the here and now, through comradeship, the help of military charities, chaplains, aid agencies, and advocates, through the disciplined act of Remembrance. There is hope too for that much greater future. The hope in the God found in the scrape holes of life; the God who, as Job discovered, simply will not let us go, promising to meet us beyond the no man's land of death in that other country we sing of in that famous hymn:

> And there's another country, I've heard of long ago,
> Most dear to them that love her, most great to them that know;
> We may not count her armies, we may not see her King;
> Her fortress is a faithful heart, her pride is suffering;
> And soul by soul and silently her shining bounds increase,
> And her ways are ways of gentleness, and all her paths are peace.[58]

Kate Bruce

Hymn suggestions

Hope for the world's despair; Dear Lord and Father of mankind; I vow to thee my country; Abide with me.

Second Sunday before Advent 16 November
Principal Service **Looking for Security and Identity**
Mal. 4.1–2a; Ps. 98; 2 Thess. 3.6–13; **Luke 21.5–19**

Soaring edifices

Durham Cathedral. Wandering in that stunning space I find myself gawping up at the huge, carved pillars, with their eye-catching geometrical patterns – pillars which I am reliably informed are the same size in circumference as they are in height. Then there's that drop in floor level as you meander down into the Chapel of the Nine Altars, creating a sense of vastness. Soaring pillars, echoing the Gothic style, draw my eye up into the massive roof space. Solidity. Permanence. Reliability. In all my changing moods Durham Cathedral has been constant, a mark of permanence, solidity, reliability and longevity.

Our passage begins with the disciples gawping up at the incredible edifice of the Temple. Built by Herod the Great, it was famous throughout the ancient world. Its precincts covered some 35 acres. It was a staggering, stunning, soaring piece of architecture.

Can you picture the disciples pointing and staring? This Temple, the symbol of Jewish nationalism, must have given them a sense of identity and security. A vast, indestructible edifice, a key part of their lives. Can you imagine the disciples' consternation when Jesus says to them, 'not one stone will be left upon another; all will be thrown down'.

Looking for security and identity

Depending on when we date Luke's Gospel, Jesus' prediction is either a prophecy of the fall of Jerusalem and the destruction of the Temple, in AD 70, or Luke's reflection on the theological meaning of this catastrophic event after it had happened. Either way, the question remains the same: when all is in turmoil and confusion, where are we to look for our security and identity?

Jesus' words concerning the fate of the Temple make clear the fact that ultimately it was the wrong source of identity and security. The

Temple was replaced by the ancient world's equivalent of Ground Zero. Perhaps the people asked themselves, 'Now where are we to look for our sense of security and identity?'

Jesus' response to the disciples' questions concerning the timing of the destruction of the Temple gives us an insight into how we can approach the question of our ultimate security and identity. This passage guides us to raise our sights, looking above and beyond the secular and religious 'temples' of our day.

Against a backdrop of national and international conflict, of environmental catastrophe, of betrayal between friends and relatives, violence, persecution, even death, Jesus urges his disciples to stand firm. He promises his presence, the inspiration of his Spirit, enabling his people to speak his wisdom in word and action. And he urges his followers to shift their perspective.

Ah ... but

Against this fearful backdrop, Jesus tells them, 'not a hair of your head will perish'. But I want one of the disciples to interject and say, 'Um, Lord ... sorry to be troublesome ... but martyrdom and the perishing of hair seem to me to be quite closely allied.' Matthew's account of this discourse includes the words, 'See to it that you are not alarmed.' Again, I dearly want a disciple to butt in: 'Sorry, but all this talk of war and disaster, death and generalized mayhem is very alarming.'

Many alarms

I wonder how Christ responds to the uncertainty and insecurity, which I guess most of us can own. The voice that says, 'How am I supposed to avoid alarm and fear?' We live in alarming and fearful times. Countless fears. Countless voices. 'I can't pay my bills.' 'Our city is being bombed.' 'We fled our home country and lost relatives when the boat sank.' 'Our child takes heroin.' 'My partner hits me.' 'I can't feed my kids.' 'I'm ill and afraid and can't get a doctor's appointment.' 'My mental health is broken.' 'The river rose. Our home is flooded.'

Our security and identity

The drive of the passage suggests to me that Christ's response might run a little like this: 'Hold on to me in the chaos and uncertainty, in the pain and fear. By my side, you will find security and identity. I am with you. Preach my gospel of love in action and in word, and stay close to me in prayer, in worship, in the mess and muddle of life. I am your security and identity – not your political alliances – personal, national and international; not the changeable things of fickle humanity, not even your physical life. Your source of security and identity lies in my permanence and steadfastness, in the constancy and reliability of my love which breathes through and transcends time and space. Here is your security and identity. Here I am – with you. Trust me.'

Kate Bruce

Hymn suggestions

You call me out upon the waters (Oceans); In my wrestling and in my doubts (My Lighthouse); The church's one foundation; Faithful One, so unchanging.

Second Sunday before Advent   16 November
Second Service   **Lion's Mouth**
Ps. [93] 97; **Dan. 6**; Matt. 13.1–9, 18–23

The first half of the Passion play of Oberammergau ends on a note of deep solemnity. Jesus has been condemned to death, and after he has been taken down offstage into darkness, the huge choir follow him into silence.

Later in the day the second part begins, and the audience is surprised by a tableau. The curtains draw back to reveal … Daniel in the lions' den!

There are tableaux all through the play, making connections between gospel and Torah, Christian text and Jewish text. Each tableau draws the audience into wondering, into asking questions, into reflecting on what this story is all about.

So why, at this moment, *this* particular story? This story so often told to children, with its narrative of a God who intervenes, a God who stops the mouth of the lions. Why *this* story, before the scene of the crucifixion, where Jesus, nailed to a cross, is *not* delivered, but who cries out in despair that God has forsaken him? How do these two stories speak to each other?

A deeper level

Could it be that if we hear the story of Daniel's deliverance, it enables us to glimpse a deeper level in the story of the Passion of Jesus? For Jesus, it seems as if the lions cannot be stopped. Their devouring greed is complete and devastating. So, has Jesus failed? Has God failed, this God who seems to refuse to intervene?

No, says the tableau, God is still the God of Daniel. God will even go all the way to death to protect the people entrusted to God. The story makes the incredible assertion, that what looks like a triumph of evil is – in the depth and reality of things – a triumph of good. A triumph which finds expression in the new life of resurrection, of a love stronger than death.

Daniel was already aware of a greater reality. One he glimpsed in his heart as he prayed at the window of his upper room. He made the mistake of praying, of speaking his intercession to God rather than the king. An invocation that broke the law. And the story of Daniel is about what we speak, and its effects.

Mouths

Daniel seems to be a story of *mouths*. It hinges on the utterance of power. Here is a king who speaks edicts that cannot be changed: words that have such inhuman weight and violence. A king who speaks with the sword of his mouth. Or the mouth of a den of lions, sealed against rescue, inexorable. An ultimate silence, which the king can only assume is the silence of death. And then the mouths of the lions, miraculously stopped, halted in their power. Is this, then, perhaps a story of the mouth, of the power of the human word, backed up by violence – pitted against the quiet strength of the law, the righteousness, the word of God?

And why is this king so dazzled by this word, so that he issues a decree to the whole world, that they should worship the God of Daniel? Another king, another time, might find the word of God to be something weak, only to be ignored. And in our world there seems to be no special reprieve for those thrown to lions, destroyed in concentration camps or genocide? Which word is real? Which is it to be?

Hope

How can this be a story of hope for those oppressed? It offers a fairy-tale ending for Daniel, if not for the satraps and their families! It only begins to become a story of hope when we allow it to point us to the depth of reality. It speaks of human longing for an invisible kingdom, that moves and works to a different rhythm. This kingdom possesses a different value, an entirely different power from the passing tyrannies of the world. It is a dominion, but it never dominates. It is a kingdom, but it neither fights for nor owns any territory in this world. It is a kingdom that will outlast every other kingdom, empire or dynasty.

And here comes the king of this kingdom. A king, finally, who is thrown to lions and wolves, creatures all the more terrible for being human. A king laid, in death, in a burial cave stoppered with a great stone.

Only in the story of *this* king do we see the reality of God's purpose and some basis for the confidence that underlies the story of Daniel. That there is hope, that we are receiving a kingdom that cannot be shaken, that love is stronger than death.

Andrew Rudd

Hymn suggestions

He who would valiant be; Do not be afraid; Lord of all hopefulness; Longing for light (Christ, be our light).

Christ the King (Sunday next before Advent)
23 November
Principal Service **The King on a Cross**
Jer. 23.1–6; Ps. 46; Col. 1.11–20; **Luke 23.33–43**

Should we even speak of kings?

What do you think of when we talk of kings? Our current one? Kings of old? What kind of thoughts or feelings does it bring up? For some it is pageantry and luxury; for others, duty and service; for others, to speak of kings raises the spectre of imperialism and oppression. Whatever our thoughts, most of us won't meet a king, let alone get to know one. Our primary reaction is shaped by culture, history, our experience of power and its misuse, and, sometimes, preconceived ideas.

And to be fair, human kings have rarely shone with justice and the appropriate exercise of power. Human kings tend to be shrouded in wealth and privilege. Maybe that is why it is trendy in some quarters to refuse the image of Jesus as king because Jesus often represents the very opposite of the misuse of political and worldly power.

And yet ... Jesus was put to death precisely for being king. That is what was written on the board beside the cross. It is Jesus' political claims that upset people the most, so much so that he was condemned by the Roman administration.

The radical call of kingship

To talk of Jesus as king is to say that Jesus has a claim over the whole of our lives, and in particular over how we organize ourselves as human beings, politically, socially and economically. Jesus calls us to live in radically new ways that depart from the economy of competition, injustice and inequality that rules the world around us. Jesus calls us to live as people who love one another, who share what they have, who look after those who are vulnerable – the poor, the widow, the orphan and the stranger – a people who order their lives in ways that reflect the life, and the death, of Jesus himself. To speak of Jesus as king is to say that faith isn't private or personal. Faith is about the kingdom, it is about how we live with one another and wider creation; it recognizes that we are social animals and that the call of the gospel is about society, communities, and the organizations, institutions and systems that undergird them. When we take a step of faith, when we are baptized, we step into an alternative kingdom ruled by justice, love and grace. We choose to enter a community with different rules and a different purpose. To call Jesus 'King' is a pretty tall order.

Kingly justice

One of the central roles of the king in the ancient world was to look after justice. Not just as retribution for wrong, but justice as nurturing the common good. Kings had a special commission to care for the needy, the vulnerable and the stranger, to organize the life of their kingdom in a way that would foster the well-being of all. At least in theory. But in the ancient world, just as today, leaders rarely nurture full equality between all people. There were interest groups, lobbies, and kings sought to maintain their own power.

Jesus, meanwhile, grew up to be a man who cared for everyone, but especially the wrong kind of people. He celebrated with the wrong people, offered peace and hope to the wrong people and warned the wrong people of coming judgement. He did not give more time or care to the rich and powerful, and he did not tell the rich they deserved their blessings. He did not curry favour with the privileged but chose to eat and drink with the despised and outcast, to touch lepers and spend time with the sick. He even talked to women – how shocking for a first-century rabbi! Now, on the cross, he is hailed as king, but in mockery.

Kingly justice on a cross

But on the cross, Jesus also acts as the king he is, by redefining justice. On the cross, Jesus takes upon himself all the twisted, distorted notions of justice and salvation that humans have, and enters their consequences. As king, he changes the system from within, by embracing the grief and pain of the condemnation of human beings, of just deserts for their actions. To bring about justice, salvation and transformation, Jesus does not solely enter the path of a victim but stands in solidarity and understanding with sinners, oppressors, robbers and criminals. The whole of humanity is embraced on the cross, and this embrace challenges us to look to Christ the King to seek justice God's way – by embracing difference, by nurturing all humanity and by bringing together justice with compassion and grace. That's a pretty revolutionary kind of king.

And so the crucifixion, which in many ways is a monument to human foolishness, is turned into a witness to God's grace, and a challenge to rethink how we pursue justice and peace within human communities. This is the message of Christ the King, and the invitation to the call to follow in pursuing justice together with grace and embracing those who may be undeserving to the world but are loved and cherished in the sight of God.

Isabelle Hamley

Hymn suggestions

Crown him with many crowns; The king of love my shepherd is; King of kings, majesty; O sacred king, O holy king.

Christ the King (Sunday next before Advent)
23 November
Second Service **A King Over Us**
Morning Ps. 29, 110; Evening Ps. 72 [*or* 72.1–7]; **1 Sam. 8.4–20**; John 18.33–37

This is the last Sunday of the church's year. We end with a Big Theme, the one that pulls the whole story of our salvation together. The message is one of victory and triumph! Of a new kingdom. Christ is king!

The Old Testament reading is about kings. But the mood was very different. It was a time when national leadership was failing. (Does this all sound rather familiar?) Samuel had dominated that era as prophet and judge, but he was now declining. The elders of the people went to Samuel and demanded a change. 'Look, you're an old man. And your sons aren't following in your footsteps. Here's what we want you to do: Appoint a king to rule us, just like everybody else' (1 Sam. 8.4–5, *The Message*). This is called 'speaking truth to power'.

There is much preoccupation with leadership in our times also. In crisis and uncertainty, we want leaders who make us secure. Our expectations rise with our anxiety. When what we need is saving, we need our leaders to be Messiahs. The novelist John Updike once defined a leader as one who, 'out of madness or goodness, volunteers to take upon [themselves] the woes of a people. There are few ... so foolish, hence the erratic quality of leadership in the world.'[59]

Give us a king

Israel's demand for a king was particularly surprising. They had never had one before. They had always functioned as a loose tribal confederacy administered by circuit judges, like Samuel. There are three things to notice about their demand.

First, it was not a very rational request. It was rather mad, actually. It was common knowledge that the kings of the surrounding nations were brutal despots who exploited their people and treated them as slaves. Why are they attracted to *that* kind of leader at all? Then, and now, as the saying goes, be careful what you wish for.

Second, it was not a theological request. Wasn't *God* Israel's king? This looks like a rejection of their own faith. Throughout this period of Israel's life, the relationship between God, faith and earthly kings was an uneasy one.

Finally, it is not a prayerful or faithful request. There is no record of anyone praying or seeking God in this story. Israel bypasses the God of their salvation. We should not be surprised if the outcome is not very faithful or prayerful either. And so it proves. The story of Israel and its kings is a very mixed one.

Not of this world

So, what does it mean to say Christ is king? Just to be told someone is a king or ultimate ruler is not in itself good news. So much ultimate power and authority in this world ends up being brutally oppressive and self-serving. So, it may not be obviously good news to people to hear of a God who is all-powerful, all-conquering. 'My kingdom is not of this world,' said Jesus to Pilate. This does not mean he rules on another planet in another realm. What use is that to us? It means he rules with a quite different understanding of authority and power.

Time and again in his earthly ministry the people most transformed in meeting Jesus were the bottom of the pile in a world that rewarded the privileged and powerful and exploited the poor and most needy.

> They met a king:
> who gives – does not take
> who makes a gift of himself – does not demand a price
> who liberates – not oppresses
> who forgives – does not condemn.

Above all here is a leader who willingly takes on our woes of the world, who gives his very life for us and welcomes us into the kingdom of his risen life. Throughout the New Testament, the joyful message that Christ is king is proclaimed among the world's persecuted, exiled and marginalized people. They were gripped by another reality and astonished at the welcome of a different kingdom that was their true home.

During the Second World War, Bishop Leonard Wilson of Singapore was imprisoned in appalling conditions, and frequently tortured. He is remembered for his gentle witness to Christ his king, to fellow prisoners and jailers alike. Facing brutality and death he would begin each day singing the same hymn.

> Christ, whose glory fills the skies,
> Christ, the true and only Light,
> Sun of righteousness, arise,
> triumph o'er the shades of night;
> Day-spring from on high, be near;
> Day-star, in my heart appear.[60]

There in the ruling darkness of this world, he proclaimed Christ, the true king, and sang for the coming of his kingdom.

It is our song too.

David Runcorn

Hymn suggestions

Christ, whose glory fills the skies; Meekness and majesty; Lord, reign in me; Jesus shall take the highest honour.

Sermons for Saints' Days and Special Occasions

St Andrew the Apostle 1 December
(transferred from 30 November)
Andrew: The Patron Saint of Community Activists
Isa. 52.7–10; Ps. 19.1–6; Rom. 10.12–18; **Matt. 4.18–22**

The patron saint

It was the end of a long, effective meeting of local community activists. We sat down to have some food together. The local MP turned up to join in. There wouldn't be a better time to ask for ideas for a sermon about St Andrew. I was, after all, in Edinburgh, and the group was made up of Scots from all over the country and some New Scots. I explained my task and asked for ideas about what to say about our patron saint. We collectively ran through a list of places named after St Andrew in Edinburgh; a square, the government headquarters building, a timber yard. Someone suggested that whenever the special day was, the children would do something in school. No one could remember when the special day was because it's not a Bank Holiday and people had only started making a fuss about it relatively recently, well in the last 20 years.

The MP remembered the tale that St Andrew had asked to be crucified on a diagonal cross because he didn't feel worthy to be crucified in the same position as Jesus. Someone else said that was why the saltire is the way it is. We were still struggling. One New Scot had her head in Wikipedia on her phone trying to find an interesting fact to add. Then someone remembered that St Andrew isn't just the patron saint of Scotland, he's also the patron saint of some other places, including Ukraine, and that's why Edinburgh is linked with Kyiv. We had the list of places read out from Wikipedia: Barbados, Romania, Russia, Scotland, Ukraine, Sarzana,

Pienza and Amalfi in Italy, Esgueira in Portugal, Luqa in Malta, Parañaque in the Philippines, and Patras in Greece. Suddenly the energy in the room changed. That was a sufficient answer. St Andrew is a symbol that all of humanity is connected, and we have a responsibility to treat each other, friend and stranger alike, with kindness and justice.

Andrew the activist

In truth, whenever I go back to the biblical texts about Andrew, I think he would be at home with people working in the voluntary sector to build a better world. He has our fire, our spirit, our way of getting on with stuff. Andrew, the fisherman, the manual worker, the activist, who also uses his active nature to look out for others. Andrew who hears Jesus' call to a better world and immediately drops his nets to follow him. Andrew who, in John's Gospel, hears John the Baptist say he has found the Messiah and immediately finds his brother and takes him to Jesus too. Andrew who, when others are standing around wondering how to feed a crowd, finds a possible solution and brings a boy with five loaves and two fish to Jesus. Andrew who hears Jesus talking about the destruction of the Temple and with other disciples immediately asks questions because he's worried about his cultural and community heritage. Andrew who cuts through Philip's indecisiveness and takes people to meet Jesus as they have asked. Andrew who, by tradition, after Jesus' death was a travelling evangelist and was eventually martyred for his faith. Andrew who after his death had a book written about his work – 'The Acts of Andrew', which is a wild thing of legends.

Andrew the revolutionary anti-imperialist

In truth, whenever I go back to this text about Jesus' call to Andrew, I also see a call to that way of life of revolutionary activism against all that divides and controls. The verses just before our reading place Jesus right in the heat of a direct encounter with the Roman Empire. Matthew appropriates Isaiah 9, written from within the Assyrian occupation, to assert that a Messiah would come to save the Jewish people. For Matthew, Jesus is now in this space, bringing light to people who have lived in the darkness of Roman occupation for a long time, bringing an alternative rule, the kingdom of heaven, the good things and ways of God to earth. Immediately, Matthew has Jesus choosing fishermen as the first people he calls.

People most likely, and like many others, contracted to work for the occupying Roman Empire, given permission to fish and probably under obligation to provide a quota of their produce to the state. People whose daily lives were deeply controlled by a state intent on imperialist expansion at all costs. Their act of simply walking away was a disruptive, revolutionary act against the occupying force and against their ideology.

Similarly, their other act of following Jesus' way of 'fishing for people' was a knowing commitment to a direct challenge to the empire's way of 'fishing for people' by violence, coercion and control. Jesus will continue to show them what it means, but Andrew leads the way in committing to the non-coercive techniques of building a community by inspiration, collaboration and acts of kindness and justice.

Inspired by Andrew our conversation turned towards what we could do to change negative responses to asylum seekers and refugees. There's plenty else to do as well. Plenty else to be inspired into living for by the patron saint of community activists the world over.

Esther Elliott

Hymn suggestions

Jesus calls us o'er the tumult; When Jesus saw the fishermen in boats upon the sea; Will you come and follow me; Heaven shall not wait.

St Stephen, Deacon, First Martyr 26 December
Where is God to be Found?

2 Chron. 24.20–22, *or* Acts 7.51–end; Ps. 119.161–168; **Acts 7.51–end** (*if the Acts reading is used instead of the Old Testament reading, the New Testament reading is* Gal. 2.16b–20); Matt. 10.17–22

Yesterday was Christmas Day – a day that on the face of it looks all joyous and familiar, at least to us. Angels, shepherds, Mary and Joseph and a stable with a few animals, plus the star (excuse the pun) of the show, the baby Jesus. The reality of course must have been very different. A tough journey, with nowhere to go, and a birth without medical or familial care. A dirty stable. Then, today, we have martyrdom. Being stoned to death. Stephen. How very odd.

St Stephen

Stephen is named by the church as the first deacon: he was most probably a Hellenistic Jew and was one of the 'seven' appointed by the apostles (Acts 6.5). His feast has been celebrated on this day since the late fourth century, and most people have heard of him from the carol, 'Good King Wenceslas', with its mention of the 'Day of Stephen'. In today's reading, we find Stephen brought before the 'council' (Acts 6.12), where false witnesses bring accusations against him (Acts 6.13–14). Stephen then makes his defence through the whole of Acts 7, giving a sweeping history of the people of Israel's relationship with God, and deriding those present for 'opposing the Holy Spirit, just as your ancestors used to do' (Acts 7.51). All very provocative.

Poking bees' nests

I have a confession to make. I can be quite provocative when the need arises. So much so that in a former ministry, a colleague affectionately asked me (at least I think it was affectionately), 'Did you used to poke bees' nests when you were young?' Stephen is being very provocative today in his speech, which is far more radical than it first appears. For just before the passage that we have been given today, he says this: 'Yet the Most High does not dwell in houses made by human hands' (Acts 7.48). The Greek word for 'human hands' is the same as the word used to describe the making of the golden calf in the Greek version of the Bible (Ex. 32.4). What he is saying is incendiary. He is not just saying to them that God is not in the Temple, he is declaring that the Temple is idolatrous, just like the golden calf.

The small print

Jesus is quite clear with his disciples that following him is no easy matter, and today's Gospel has great clarity about this. Stephen is just the beginning, and in two days' time we shall hear again of innocent children murdered in the wake of the Christ-child's birth. This boy's birth starts a revolution, and to follow him is a costly affair. It is a matter of life and death. The New Testament is littered with warnings and examples about this.

Finding God in this

Stephen's speech today is not just a good example of how to wind up devout religious people: he is also making a key point that connects us to the events of yesterday. The magi search for Jesus, because he is not in the place that they expect him to be. They go to the capital, Jerusalem, to the king, because kings generally are born of kings. But Jesus is not there. He is born in poverty, away from home, and soon he will become a refugee. From the beginning, God, in Jesus, is not where he is expected to be. Through his life and death, it becomes clear that God is not to be found just in religious buildings; rather, God can dwell within humanity. By sharing our nature, God in Jesus reveals that we have become the temple within which he can dwell and be worshipped. Stephen has experienced this, and he is filled with the Holy Spirit, which allows him to act in a Christ-like way, praying for those who are killing him and asking forgiveness of God for them. Stephen, then, is a reminder of the outworking of the meaning of yesterday, Christmas Day. A God who comes to show us that we can be living temples to his glory, if only we would let him abide within us. But watch out for what happens next!

Jonathan Lawson

Hymn suggestions

Stephen, first of Christian martyrs; Let our choirs new anthems raise; Good King Wenceslas; Head of thy church triumphant.

St John, Apostle and Evangelist 27 December
The Scandalous Maths of Grace
Ex. 33.7–11a; Ps. 117; 1 John 1; **John 21.19b–end**

Being the favourite

Bryan Stevenson is a well-known social justice activist and lawyer who spends much of his professional life in prisons and on death row. He is also a law professor and founder of an organization called the Equal Justice Initiative. His 2012 TED talk, 'We need to talk about injustice', is one of the most-watched talks on the internet and has become part of the curriculum in some American colleges.[61] In 2023 President Joe Biden awarded Bryan Stevenson with a National Humanities Medal for his achievements. Bryan Stevenson is a great man, and he puts it down to his grandmother.

One day when Stevenson was about eight years old, his grandmother took him to one side and told him to tell no one else what she was about to say. When he promised, she said, 'I've been watching you. You are special. You can achieve whatever you want to achieve.' He was the favourite. It was empowering and enabling.

The beloved Son of Thunder

One of the questions raised by our reading, or at least by the way our reading has sometimes been interpreted, is what did Jesus see in John? Why was John the favourite, the disciple Jesus loved? We know three things about John. He and his brother James asked Jesus to give them privileged seats in the new kingdom. When Jesus and his followers passed through a village and were not welcomed, John and James wanted to call down fire from heaven and destroy it. When a poor foreign woman approached Jesus to heal her daughter, John and James told Jesus to send her away. John, it seems, did not have much to recommend him! And yet, he was the disciple Jesus loved, and he went on to become a prominent leader in the early church.

Jesus nicknamed John and James the Sons of Thunder. We assume we know what that means. They were short-tempered and rumbled furiously. Well, perhaps. In Palestine, though, thunderstorms were rare and usually indicated not the arrival of a storm but a change of season. Perhaps John and James were indicators of the new season being ushered in by Jesus' ministry. Still, there is nothing to indicate why John was Jesus' favourite.

It is not fair

As Jesus is talking to Peter about Peter's discipleship, Peter notices John, and asks Jesus, 'What about him?' 'It's none of your business,' Jesus tells him. And the story goes around that John will not die. Perhaps implied in Peter's question is some resentment about Jesus' favouritism. Maybe Peter wants to know why Jesus is telling him to follow when he hasn't said the same to John. Perhaps it does not seem fair. John just seems to get things right, because he is the favourite.

Being the favourite was inspiring and enabling for Bryan Stevenson. He achieved much, partly because of what his grandmother told him. It was much later that he discovered that she had had the same conversation with all her grandchildren. She had told all of them they were special. Every one of them was her favourite!

I think Peter understood eventually. I think only someone who knew themselves also to be a favourite of Jesus could write so movingly, as Peter does in his first letter, about what it means to be people of God: 'You are a chosen people, a royal priesthood, a holy nation, God's own people' (1 Peter 2.9). That is who we all are.

The maths of grace

If we live in a world where there can only be one favourite none of this makes sense. If we live in a world where love is a finite resource, where the more there are to love, the less love each one gets, then this does not make sense. If Bryan is the favourite grandchild, the others cannot be. If John is the favourite disciple, Peter cannot be.

But grace does not work like that. God's love is not finite. The inspiration and empowerment available to the favourite is available to us all. It is not really being the favourite that leads to achievements, it is grace. Bryan Stevenson's grandmother spent time watching each of her grandchildren, noticing the kind of person they were, and then affirming them in it. That's grace. Jesus spent time with each of his followers – and not just the Twelve – getting to know them and loving them for who they were. That's grace too. Grace has no limits, grace is infinite.

None of us is loved more than anyone else. We are all Jesus' favourites.

All that remains is to live like it.

Liz Shercliff

Hymn suggestions

The love of God is greater far; All I once held dear; Oh the deep, deep love of Jesus; Love came down at Christmas.

The Holy Innocents 28 December
Principal Service **Searching for Glimpses of Light**
Jer. 31.15–17; Ps. 124; I Cor. 1.26–29; **Matt 2.13–18**

Yesterday and today

Today, there are children crying in refugee camps; today, when many are still celebrating, children and their parents are threatened by bombs, guns and conflict; today, there are children whose lives are blighted by the greed, callousness and self-seeking aggrandisement of powerful world leaders. These are children of Christmas too.

At Christmas, the story we read today, of Herod's persecution of Jewish mothers and babies, forcing Mary, Joseph and their precious baby to flee to Egypt, is particularly precious for the children and parents of our broken world. It is precious because it is the story of God-with-us, Immanuel, a story that tells them, you are not alone, you are not invisible, you are not abandoned; and therefore it is a story of hope. It is a story of life that is deeper than what we can see with our eyes and touch with our hands. It is a story that tells us about the real worth of people, even when everything seems to tell a different story.

A story for the world

And so it is quite a logical story for us to be reading the Sunday after Christmas. Christmas is a story about the real world – the good, the amazing, the magical and beautiful, but also the bad, the sad and the mad. The story of the Bible, of God and God's people, is never a story about an ideal world. But it is the story of a God who chooses to love that world, and redeem it so that nothing is beyond God's reach and presence. It is the story of God not simply coming to be with us but coming into the murkiest and most desperate places of the world.

Christmas is a joyful and beautiful time, but the Christmas story of angels, shepherds and kings is only an interlude, a glimpse of heaven. Today is the day after, picking up the thread of normal life again, the long walk of faith, living in hope and faithfulness, the light of Christmas behind us, the light of the resurrection ahead, but long shadows in the present pressing on us.

The Bible is nothing if not realistic. Every mountain-top experience, every amazing story of God breaking in is soon followed by a return to earth with a bump. The Israelites, afraid of the desert, grumble against Moses, soon after they escape from Egypt. The people look out onto the Promised Land and are frightened by those who occupy it. The birth of Jesus is followed by Herod's slaughter and the flight to Egypt. Jesus hears the voice and affirmation of God at his baptism, only to be led straight into the desert to be tempted. Life with God is not spent on the mountain tops but in the valleys and the plains. The glimpses of glory illuminate our path and sustain us on the way.

Taking Christmas into the everyday

Our call is to take Christmas into every day: to search out the mangers, to see God in the face of those who are forgotten, invisible or disregarded. It is to keep going on the path of discipleship even when God seems distant, or when we are unsure. It is the story of keeping up hope even when everything else speaks of despair.

Hope is not optimism. Hope is not grounded in external reality but in the continuing story of God and his people. This story is full of echoes of the story of Israel, their time fleeing from Egypt, and as prisoners of war, refugees and exiles in Babylon. The God that had been with them is the same God that walks with Joseph and Mary. The story looks forward too: throughout history, displacement, war, crazy rulers, refugees and poverty have been constant features. The question for us is, how do we respond today?

Refugees, displacement and the truth of Christmas

Scripture is hugely interested in refugees, in those fleeing from oppression. It stresses that we meet God in the face of the stranger: in places and people we would never expect; outside of Israel; in younger sons, women and those who are poor. God reveals himself when we take the risk to open ourselves up to be surprised and challenged, to move out of our comfort zones and do what we never thought we might. God also meets us in the face of the other when we would rather shut out the world around us because of our own worries and torments. Hope is something we find when we share together the journey of discipleship.

This is why the truth of Christmas works itself out only in the many days that follow. In the patient work of following in the footsteps of Jesus, valuing those who are invisible, seeking the lost, comforting those who struggle, challenging injustice, feeding the hungry, working for peace and justice in every area of our lives and of our world. This is the work of Christmas, for today, and in hope for tomorrow.

Isabelle Hamley

Hymn suggestions

Unto us a boy is born; O Lord, the clouds are gathering; In the bleak midwinter; O Lord, hear my prayer (Taizé).

Naming and Circumcision of Jesus 1 January
A Face of Love
Num. 6.22–end; Ps. 8; Gal. 4.4–7; Luke 2.15–21

How wonderful to begin your life in this world looking into a face of love! Here is a baby, newborn, held in the arms of a mother, or a father, or another person who loves them. Their faces are just far enough apart for newborn eyes to see. Their eyes meet in an intimacy that is brand new, yet as old as the human race. And so, the mirroring begins, where one person learns what love is from the love of another, from the gaze of life that flows from one to another. The face that shines life, identity and love into the child.

And how tragic it is when a child misses out on that loving gaze.

The miracle of presence

Martin Buber, the great Jewish philosopher and theologian, talked about the *I–Thou* relationship when a person is not just an object to another person but becomes seen as a miracle of presence. It may be the work of a lifetime, to allow those we reduce to 'It' to be seen as 'Thou'. And this is always a search for God, because, in such an encounter, and such a gaze, it is God who is revealed in the face of another.

So, when Moses created a priestly blessing for Aaron and his sons to use when they blessed the people of Israel, this is the language he reached for, the simplest yet most profound language of the human face.

Blessing, keeping

'The LORD, bless you and keep you.'

A blessing face ...

A keeping face ...

Each of the three blessings in this prayer starts by visualizing a movement of God towards us, and this movement is then completed by an action: there is a *blessing*, and then a *keeping*. It is as if a child was first held and then lifted into that gaze of love.

This simple intention, *bless* and *keep*, is then spelled out in the beautiful images of encounter.

Shining

'The LORD make his face to shine upon you.'

A shining face ...

It is part of the experience of every newborn child to know the despair of absence, when for a little while the mother's face is out of sight. But now, lifted in her arms, that presence of joy, that fullness of joy is restored.

And maybe every morning, when the sun comes over the horizon to illuminate the beauty of the world, that joy is recapitulated. The light of dawn itself will be a reminder. It will be an image of that rising, that lifting, the face of God shining.

Gracious

'And be gracious to you.'

A gracious face ...

So, as we receive this blessing, it offers us a first glimpse of grace. Grace is the heart of God. Grace is that unconditional, unrestrained self-giving, which we don't deserve. This grace is not a payment for laws well kept, but a generous shining of the face of God.

Lifted

'The LORD lift up his countenance upon you, and give you peace.'

A lifted face ...

A face of peace ...

When Cain felt rejected by God for bringing an inferior offering, his face fell. And in our bad moods, we still use this language: the downward look, the sulk, displeasure, anger. Our face falls, and we can't look another person in the eye.

But in grace, God is pleased. God seeks our attention, looks for us with love, trying to catch our eye. Every time Jesus appeared to his disciples in resurrection, it seems he always lifted his face to them, and allayed their fear, saying, always, 'Peace be with you.'

And to Christians, the story of the incarnation, indeed the whole story of Jesus, is one in which God takes a human face and lifts up his countenance, and gives us peace. Jesus, the human face of God. Jesus, the Christ, the Anointed One, who blesses us, keeps us, shines into grace and peace.

Pause

In this blessing prayer, we have an amazing resource. It is a prayer that has helped and nourished people for more than 2,000 years. It has illuminated those in dark places and given them hope and strength. Its very utterance has communicated God to people.

It might be good to pause with this over-familiar text and allow ourselves to gaze into the face of God. And to allow the gaze of God to fall upon us, a gaze of unconditional love. And though this may start as an exercise of the imagination, it will very quickly lead us into the reality of the blessing of God.

> The LORD bless you and keep you;
> the LORD make his face to shine upon you,
>   and be gracious to you;
> the LORD lift up his countenance upon you,
>   and give you peace.

Andrew Rudd

Hymn suggestions

Like a candle flame; May God's blessing surround you each day; Lord, the light of your love is shining; Christ, be our light.

Epiphany 6 January
Welcoming the New Things of God
Isa. 60.1–6; Ps. 72.[1–9] 10–15; Eph. 3.1–12; **Matt. 2.1–12**

New Year is traditionally a time when we talk about new beginnings. It is an opportunity to turn over a new leaf and start again. It is a time to embrace new things and welcome change into our lives. The Greek word *neos* describes things that are so new, they didn't exist before – they are unprecedented. The prophet Isaiah uses this word to prophesy the new things of God that he will pour upon his people.

As we approach our Gospel reading today, I encourage you to consider how ready you are to receive the *neos* things of God this year. How prepared are you for change? Our passage offers us three examples of ways in which we might respond to this question.

King Herod

Our first example is King Herod. In our passage, Herod learns of a new birth, the birth of the Messiah. God is doing a brand-new thing. It is a *neos* moment. But instead of embracing the good news, we read that he was 'frightened'. Later on, we learn that he tries to kill the Christ-child, by executing all the male children who are two years old and under in the province of Bethlehem.

At this point in the narrative, Jerusalem represents the institutional centre of God's people. How will our institutions – our churches – respond to the new things of God? Instead of welcoming this *neos* moment, Herod is threatened. He is blinded by his own insecurities. Perhaps it is fear of change, fear of being challenged, or fear of losing authority and control. Either way, this leads him to destroy his community.

These are issues that any one of us can face when confronted with change. We can find ourselves feeling threatened and dig our heels in. We can be guilty of trying to snuff out anything new because of our own insecurities and fear.

People who should know better

The second example is a group who should have known better. These are the priests and scholars of the day. These leaders know the Scriptures well. When Herod calls them together, they are able to put together two obscure passages to ascertain where the Messiah is going to be born. They are learned people.

And yet despite how smart they are, they fail to realize that the Messiah has already come. Unlike the magi, they have not noticed the star. They have not perceived this new thing. In the Gospels, people like this are described as spiritually blind, they can't see past the ends of their noses. When they learn that God's promise has been fulfilled, they do not accompany the magi to worship Jesus. Spiritual pride prevents them from doing so. They do not want to accept that God has revealed himself to these outsiders.

There is that old phrase, 'cutting off your nose to spite your face'. Are there occasions when we might see something new starting up, but, for whatever reason, we are offended by it? Perhaps it is because we were unaware of it at the time or we haven't been consulted, and so we choose not to get involved. We cut off our noses to spite our faces and miss out on the *neos* things of God.

The magi

Our final example is the magi, who have seen the star and recognize that God is doing something new, something unprecedented. Unlike Herod and the religious leaders, we read that they saw 'his star'. This wording is significant. They are not content with just following a light. They are seeking out the source. They are seeking out Jesus himself.

They go on a long journey, across plains and mountains, to get there. Along the way, they encounter people like Herod, the priests and the scholars, but they do not allow these detractors to close their hearts and minds. After visiting the Christ-child, God warns them in a dream not to return to Herod. The Bible says the Holy Spirit will be our counsel and our guide. It can be easy to close ourselves to the new things of God, but the magi didn't. They pressed on, listened to God, and eventually found their way to Jesus, the *neos* gift of God.

The story ends with the magi kneeling down and worshipping Jesus in a 'house'. Joseph was a carpenter, so this would have been a labourer's home. Jesus is found among everyday people, like you and me. God's 'house' – the church – is for everyone to come and receive the *neos* gifts of God's grace.

As 2025 unfolds, how ready are you to receive the *neos* things of God? Will you be like Herod, whose insecurities and fears drove him to snuff them out? Will you resemble the priests and scribes who, despite recognizing the Messiah, are unable to let go of their spiritual pride? Or will you follow the example of the magi, who scan the skies expectantly for the new things of God, and who persevere until they arrive at that place where all people can encounter Jesus in new and vibrant ways?

Mark Nam

Hymn suggestions

We three kings; What child is this; Christ from whom all blessings flow; Be thou my vision.

Week of Prayer for Christian Unity
18–25 January
One Body
Readings for the Unity of the Church:
Jer. 33.6–9a; Ezek. 36.23–28; Zeph. 3.16–end; Ps. 100, 122, 133; **Eph. 4.1–6**; **Col 3.9–17**; 1 John 4.9–15; Matt 18.19–22; John 11.45–52; John 17.11b–23

'Division' cannot be the final word for the church. The unity of the Spirit is the eternal last chapter, flowing to all corners of space and time, to all people, all circumstances and all eventualities. There is 'one body', just as there is one God, one faith and one baptism. This one body, in all its splendid multiplicity, is the truth at the heart of these passages, the truth, perhaps, at the heart of creation. Creation is groaning towards this living body. We acknowledge, however, that such unity can't be taken for granted or imposed. We acknowledge, that is, that we are not there yet.

Difference is not the enemy

When we look around, we can't help but see division. It is real and it affects all aspects of life, whether in the church or wider society. This doesn't mean that the unity of the Spirit is a pipe dream. It is a promise, here already, even while it is still coming; written on our hearts, even while on a distant shore.

These divisions in the world and in our churches are not, and cannot, be final. There are wars and rumours of wars today, but they cannot be final; there is discrimination today that singles out, divides and pulls down, but this cannot be final. There is new language that can be applied to these divisions and what they give birth to: 'othering', 'identity politics', 'culture wars'. However, these cannot become the formative ideals of the body of Christ.

Sadly, in our churches, the dividing lines of the world creep up on us and seek entrance. The body of Christ cannot become finally determined by this dividing pattern.

We might feel our differences intensely when we come together as a diverse community. We realize that we have to rub shoulders with people quite different from ourselves. But we must push against the cultural norm that says if we disagree with the views of others, we just dismiss them or walk away.

The church must not dismiss those who look, think, act or speak differently. To do so would be to follow after a different spirit, a different God, created in our own image according to our own preference. Such a God has nothing to do with the Spirit of unity.

Some of us have the marks of division scarred into us. They are our experiences, our reality, our trauma. Some of us perceive these divisions only from afar. But we can all recognize that unity is not always the lived reality of the church catholic.

We do have very real differences. One to another, we read the book of Scripture with different eyes, different motivations and different desires. And it's OK, I think, to question each other's views if we feel it necessary. Likewise, if we see injustice, we might well speak up. However, we must surely acknowledge the unlikelihood that we will agree upon the interpretation of each of our texts. But such a reality need not be threatening. Difference is not the enemy.

Division is not the final word

There is a cost to unity. It means that we might not get our own way. It might mean that even those things that we think are foundational principles are shaken and remoulded as we seek after relationship.

Unity, of course, is not uniformity. The unity of the Spirit is not sameness. As much as we are called to be one body, we are not called to be replicas of each other, nor are we called to merely replicate that which went before. The unity of the Spirit is dynamic, bringing out diverse gifts, personalities, stories, practices and ideas. The Spirit is not static and does not require a static community in which to be manifest.

We say, therefore, that we believe in this Spirit and therefore venture that division will not have the last word. We say that the categories of slave and free, barbarian and Scythian, are not finally determinative. We say that there is beauty in diversity. We hope for a resurrection life where the word 'division' will no longer have a place and where all will flourish and live and rejoice. Indeed, we have hope that such a life is knocking at the door on earth now, as it is in heaven.

Mark Amos

Hymn suggestions

When I needed a neighbour; Be thou my vision; Jesus, united by thy grace; Make me a channel of your peace.

Conversion of St Paul   25 January
The 'C' word

Jer. 1.4–10, *or* Acts 9.1–22; Ps. 67; **Acts 9.1–22** *(if the Acts reading is used instead of the Old Testament reading, the New Testament reading is* Gal. 1.11–16a); Matt. 19.27–end

'Honour your father and your mother'; words that were deeply important to a young Saul, and that remained so as he grew through rabbinic training in Tarsus, devoted to the faith of his family, immersed in the traditions of his people. He honoured not only his father and mother but the entire people of Israel with his zeal for the law. He was well enough regarded to have ended up in Jerusalem as a young man, a Pharisee among Pharisees.

Order! Order!

No surprise, then, that Saul should be at the forefront of efforts to keep Israel pure, to confront and deal with threats from those who would pervert the teaching of the law to which Saul and his fellow Pharisees were so deeply committed. Keeping God's order was vital, and so Saul was determined to rid Israel of the new, heretical sect that Jesus had started. He was ringleader when they stoned Stephen, he was zealous for hunting out followers of 'the Way', and he was eager to go wherever he may find them – even Damascus.

He knew, you see, that he was right.

Blitzgrace!

Until that is, he knew he wasn't.

Despite all the voices surrounding Saul that reinforced his views, despite their pointing to the unchanging tradition of the faith, despite the clear meaning of Torah which he'd spent his life studying, there came a moment when the same Jesus he was persecuting managed to get through. It took something intense and dramatic to do it, but then Saul was an intense and dramatic man.

Brought up short, Saul was thrown off his carefully cultivated balance just long enough that Jesus was able to reach into his mind, his heart, his soul, and shine his light. On the road to Emmaus, the risen Christ had done this slowly and carefully for two disciples who didn't get it; here he seems to do it suddenly for someone so deeply versed in the law that once seeing how Jesus fulfils the law, everything fell into place in an instant. Saul is no less passionate and intense, but now his passion and intensity are for the truth he's been enabled to see, the gospel he has now received. He hasn't changed his mind; he's had the courage to let Jesus change his mind, and his heart, and his life.

Courage under fire?

This is great for the kingdom of God, for the growth of the church, for the spread of the gospel, and we all know where it will lead for Saul. But how about a word for the existing disciples in Damascus, whom Saul had been on his way to root out and arrest? What of those who'd heard he was coming and were living in deep fear? They didn't know about Saul meeting Jesus, they only knew what they'd heard in the news ...

There's another conversion story in this passage, and one that we can so easily pass over with merely a nod; the conversion of Ananias. Not a conversion in the sense of his becoming a follower of Jesus, but a conversion of courage.

Of all the disciples in Damascus, it's Ananias to whom Jesus reaches out. No blinding lights this time, because Ananias is already open to hearing from the Lord, but a call to go to Saul and pray with him and for him.

Ananias is understandably afraid. Does Jesus know what he's asking? It's a daft question, but we all do it. Ananias doesn't get a reassuring 'Do not be afraid', like so many before him, nor does he get a 'Take heart, it is I', as Peter did on the lake. Ananias just gets 'Go'. And so he goes.

Ananias' conversion isn't from unbelief to belief, nor even from panic to confidence, but from fear to trust. Not that he was no longer afraid as he went to meet Saul, because I'm sure his knees were knocking a bit, but that he knew he could trust God. If Jesus was asking him to do this thing, then it's in his hands and he can be trusted. Ananias was encouraged in his vocation – given the courage to do what needed to be done despite the fear and trepidation, and despite the human logic that said (not unreasonably), 'Stay away!' He was encouraged to know that 'God's got this'.

The 'C' word

The story of Saul's conversion, and the story of Ananias' conversion; both are stories of *change*, that word which can so often be anathema to people in our churches. But change is a sign of life; and openness to change that Jesus wants for us is a sign of discipleship, of being open to his will above our own.

Where, I wonder, do we need to let God into our minds, our thinking, our attitudes, our passions? Where do we need to let God tell us, 'Go', follow this path, take up this challenge, embrace this opportunity, face this issue? How do we need to be converted today?

Bill Braviner

Hymn suggestions

And can it be; Christ, whose glory fills the skies; All to Jesus I surrender; Just as I am.

St Joseph of Nazareth 19 March
Guardians of Jesus
2 Sam. 7.4–16; Ps. 89.26–36; Rom. 4.13–18; **Matt. 1.18–end**

Joseph is a reticent figure in the Gospels. He's an understated character who does what he does 'quietly', the word used in today's Gospel to describe how he was minded to dismiss the pregnant Mary for her presumed immorality or maybe because she had been a rapist's victim. Joseph's dilemma is not any the less because it is God and not another man who has 'violated' the woman he is betrothed to, the uninvited intruder on this quiet, god-fearing couple.

Joseph in the Gospels is a guardian or carer, an honoured

role in any society that upholds the dignity of elderly people, the disabled, children, or the vulnerable – any who for different reasons cannot look after themselves. He takes on the role, not necessarily willingly or easily (for how would we know?) but obediently and conscientiously, certainly.

Awareness

What kind of vocation is this? First, we can see beginning in Joseph's guardianship the quality of *awareness*. Like his namesake in Genesis, he understands dreams, often associated with wisdom in Jewish piety. For that Joseph of old, reading dreams extended into an ability to read not only events and circumstances but also the mysteries of human behaviour and motivation so that he could steer a safe path and deliver the people entrusted to him. Matthew repeats five times how Joseph is asleep and has dreams, as if to say, here is someone who attends to his unconscious, who has emotional and spiritual intelligence. The flight into Egypt, the return to Judaea and the choice of Nazareth as the family home are all determined by his interior awareness, his dreams, his *in*-sight. Good guardians cultivate awareness so as to interpret what the duty of care requires in *these* times and *these* places. In our own roles, it means knowing ourselves, cultivating 'inscape' and having insight into the lives of others.

Responsiveness

Next, we see in Joseph a deep *responsiveness*. It isn't enough that his dreams hold meaning. He must understand what they require of him. 'He did as the angel of the Lord commanded.' Every guardian knows the responsiveness that's needed if caring is to be 'good enough' and life-affirming. Once embarked on, there is no turning back, as the long risky journeys of the holy family in the infancy story make clear. Jesus, who will 'save his people from their sins', must himself be kept safe if God's purpose is to be realized. Joseph's responsiveness is the slender thread on which the salvation of the world hangs, like Mary's 'Yes'. It calls for courage to live out whatever it may mean to care for particular people or the institutions we are part of and are called to serve. It can take us into hard, uncomfortable places. We may wish, Jeremiah-like, that we had never embarked on it. Yet it is unthinkable that we could have done anything else but respond to the times and to the God who invites us to act as guardians on his behalf.

Cherishing

Third, Joseph is an example of true *cherishing*. His care of the infant Jesus is moving, because it is governed not by the biological drive of the parent but by the choice to stay with and care for the one who was thrust upon him. However, Joseph goes far beyond obligation. He must have loved much to sacrifice everything for the sake of Mary and her son. *Affect* means the engagement of our emotional selves so that our full humanity is released into play in our relationships. I see Joseph as the most humane of guardians because of his love for the child that was both not-his and his. I am saying that we must *love* Jesus as Joseph did, and care about his welfare. Which comes down to loving him as he, the good shepherd, will himself embody the most tender and intimate quality of care. This is not only about how we deepen our relationship with Jesus, but also how we 'care' about Jesus in the way we handle the New Testament texts that bear witness to him, and how we cherish him as we take our part in the liturgy and say our prayers. Yes, and how we speak about him and uphold his integrity and reputation; how we recognize and serve him in the least of his brothers and sisters; how we reverence all of life that is *his* life as well as creation's.

Reticent

Perhaps the best guardians are always reticent, not intruding too much lest they crush the very life they are responsible for instead of giving it room to flourish. In the Gospel, Joseph recedes into the background after these opening stories; when all is done that was asked for, we need to be humble enough to withdraw from the stage on which we've made a brief appearance. But with what joy can we imagine him acknowledging that his work is finished, when Jesus the Messiah is safely delivered to the world, longed-for Immanuel at last among us.

Michael Sadgrove

Hymn suggestions

For all the saints who showed your love; The God whom earth and sea and sky; Lord of all hopefulness; Let us build a house where love can dwell.

Annunciation of Our Lord to the Blessed Virgin Mary 25 March
Finding a Voice
Isa. 7.10–14; Ps. 40.5–11; Heb. 10.4–10; **Luke 1.26–38**

In the many encounters between the divine and human beings in the Bible, an abiding mark of God's authentic and definitive work of love and salvation is his call on ordinary people's lives. God calls and his people are invited to respond. Perhaps this is never clearer than in the annunciation, the Blessed Virgin Mary's encounter with the angel Gabriel in Luke's Gospel.

The voice of power

Gabriel comes to Mary as God's messenger. Angel, in Latin, quite literally means 'messenger, envoy or one that announces'. Gabriel is, then, the herald and ambassador of God. He has been despatched into the world as God's representative (if you want to get a glimpse of what this means, think of how a human ambassador represents a head of state). Indeed, in the Hebrew biblical traditions about angels, Gabriel is yet more: he also represents the very presence of God. As such, Gabriel speaks first: 'Greetings, favoured one! The Lord is with you.' Gabriel comes to announce favour and God's very presence and blessing to Mary. This is an awesome and awe-filled moment: the ambassador, herald and presence of God has come to deliver a message that will change the universe.

A voiceless child

To whom has Gabriel come? Not a king or emperor or princeling, but a young woman, the daughter of peasants. It is perhaps unsurprising that Mary is perplexed and bewildered by Gabriel's eloquent, ambassadorial greeting. She is, perhaps, even suspicious of it. What has she done to deserve it? It is clear that, in so far as she is being invited to respond, she is initially unclear how to do so. Perhaps Mary senses risk and danger in God's approach and, however we interpret what comes next, it is clear her instinct is right: for not only is she told that she is favoured by God, but that she is going to have a God-blessed son, the result of being 'overshadowed' by the power of the Holy Spirit. Yet, as she points out, she is a 'virgin' – in Greek, a 'parthenos' or 'maiden'. This means that she is a young girl, perhaps little more than a child who hasn't yet had her first period. What response does this child make? 'Here am I, the servant of the Lord; let it be with me according to your word.'

Feminist analyses of this encounter are well known. These have ranged from concerns about the extent to which Mary is set up as a compliant handmaid through to questions about whether she is old enough to grant her consent to God's plan.[62] It certainly doesn't take much imagination to see how, for some, the images created by this encounter are troubling. A girl meeting the majesty of God is one thing; a girl being told she will conceive a son via the 'overshadowing' power of the Holy Spirit is another. One can readily see how it is possible to read God's call on Mary as massively skewing power towards God.

A voice for the voiceless

Yet Luke makes Mary's response significant; Mary's willingness to unite her will and purposes to those of God is no mere afterthought. There is an extraordinary, quiet and deeply prophetic determination in Mary's words. I am reminded of Isaiah in Isaiah 6.8, saying, 'Here am I.' Isaiah says this in full awareness that he is not really up to the call: he describes himself as a 'man of unclean lips'. Yet still, God calls and equips him for his task. Mary joins a long line of those who will take their place in God's wondrous work of transformation, justice and love. Mary speaks and claims her place. She will not simply be done to but transform God's invitation into service and action.

There is no doubt that Gabriel's encounter with Mary continues to raise questions in the modern era about consent and agency. I do not underestimate these. However, I also find in the first chapter of Luke a young woman seeking dignity in the face of divine majesty. Here is a peasant girl daring to speak to God's ambassador. Mary, a girl with no voice and little agency, has courage and finds her own authority. When she meets Gabriel, she may not realize it, but she has all the authority of a queen. Indeed, we can see why, for some, she is the Queen of Heaven. As she embraces God's invitation to be the bearer of God, the *Theotokos*, she finds her prophetic voice. A short while after her encounter with Gabriel, Mary will proclaim her famous Magnificat. Her words of justice, comfort and challenge echo down the ages, words which shape us still. The young girl who met the presence of God disrupts and transforms our world still.

Rachel Mann

Hymn suggestions

Tell out my soul; My soul proclaims the greatness (Bernadette Farrell); The angel Gabriel (Annunciation Carol); Blest are the pure in heart.

St George, Martyr 28 April (transferred from 23 April)
Battling in the Strength of Christ
1 Mac. 2.59–64, *or* **Rev. 12.7–12**; Ps. 126; 2 Tim. 2.3–13; John 15.18–21

Letters to a persecuted church

Packed tightly in a single room of a family home, the Christians in Laodicea waited with bated breath. That morning, a scroll had arrived; the final copy, sent on from John, banished to the island of Patmos, to the seven churches in Asia Minor. Quickly word had spread and now, in the cooler evening air, they listened.

Life had not always been easy for the Laodiceans. Just 30 years ago, during the reign of Nero, there had been an earthquake so great it had completely destroyed the town. But they were a strong and independent people, not needing any help and rebuilding the city. Maybe that was why John was now dismissing them for being lukewarm and having no need of God. Surely, they bristled, self-sufficiency was a good thing.

But perhaps, John hinted, things were coming where it would be impossible to rely on your own strength. Although they had been largely unaffected, they had already lived through the persecutions of Christians under Nero. Now persecutions came again, the Emperor Domitian declaring that no Christian would be exempt from punishment unless they renounced their faith. As a church, they had tried to remain unnoticed by the authorities, to stay safe. But perhaps it was as John now warned; all was not well with the Roman Empire.

So, they listened intently as John's fantastic prophecy now rolled over them. A tale of a great war in heaven; of a battle between Michael and all the angels, and a great dragon and his angels. A war in which the dragon was hurled down, defeated. Where God was triumphant and, as the kingdom of God rushes in, all rejoice. As the storm clouds of persecution threaten them, it was a tale of hope, that good would overcome.

A persecuted man

Around 200 years later, one man knows exactly what it is like to face persecution. Roman emperors have come and gone, and now the latest one, Diocletian, was raging again against those of Christian faith. It turned into the most systematic persecution Christians would ever face; with manuscripts burnt, buildings demolished and as many as 3,000 Christians executed. One of those was George, a soldier in the Roman army, who died a martyr's death in AD 303, for keeping firm in his Christian faith and refusing to make sacrifices to pagan gods.

Searching for a hero

As centuries pass, battles remain, and people look for heroes. St George was canonized in AD 494, but it was during the Middle Ages his fame spread. As soldiers battle in the Crusades, the legends of his life grow. The story-book tales of battling with dragons gain new impetus, as George becomes the ideal knight of their imagination; the model of Christian chivalry. Visions of the saint on a shimmering white stallion urge the Crusaders on to victory; Richard I calls upon his name for protection and Shakespeare immortalizes him as an ally of the King and country, in his famous Agincourt speech, delivered by Henry V. By the fifteenth century, the feast of St George, which we celebrate today, was ranked as one of the principal feasts of the year.

Fighting the dragons of today

The dragons that both Michael and St George fought are the stuff of myth and legend. But, just as the apocalyptic writing of John had a real message for the persecuted early church, a message of both warning and comfort, we can find both challenge and strength in legends of dragons and epic cosmic battles.

For there are still dragons out there today. Just look at the world around us. There are many situations that seem insurmountable; there are foes we don't know how to beat, and there are evil powers that rise up in the background while we're looking the other way. These dragons of today might be individuals whose desire for power and control threatens and oppresses; but they are also the very real evils of inequality, poverty, injustice, hatred and greed. And while we may not be donning our highly polished battle armour to ride into battle, we are called to see these ills, to name them, and to work to free others from them; to fight with the oppressed and the vulnerable the cords of injustice that bind them, suppress them and scare them.

In this Easter season, we remember the victory that Christ has won; a victory over sin, over death and over the gates of hell. And today, as we celebrate the feast of St George, we remember his example too, as one who had the courage to stand up for what he believed in. With him, we remember all those who came after him, from whom his legend grew; people who found in his story the impetus to be brave, to defend the innocent, and to battle against all the dragons that threaten our lives. But as we listen to those tales of hope, we remember too what John reminded the Laodiceans: whatever dragons we battle, we do so in the strength of Christ and him alone.

Chris Campbell

Hymn suggestions

All for Jesus; Fight the good fight; He who would valiant be; Thine be the Glory.

St Mark the Evangelist 29 April
(transferred from 25 April)
Calling Time
Prov. 15.28–end, *or* Acts 15.35–end; Ps. 119.9–16; Eph. 4.7–16; **Mark 13.5–13**

We humans like to think that we build for ever. And our great cathedrals, palaces, fortifications and heroic statues are meant to convey that impression. Yet it doesn't take much to topple our *grands projects*. Earthquake, wind and fire, indeed, but warfare, terrorism and arson – they can all bring down in a matter of hours what it took years or even centuries to construct. Shelley's famous sonnet pictures the detritus of a once proud royal statue lying forlornly in the desert:

> Nothing beside remains. Round the decay
> Of that colossal wreck, boundless and bare
> The lone and level sands stretch far away.[63]

Ramses II (for it was he) certainly believed that the kingdom of

Egypt would last for ever. How fleeting are even the most permanent monuments of human civilization!

The disciples are admiring the splendour of Herod's Temple: 'Teacher, what large stones and what large buildings!' And Jesus says to them: 'Do you see these great buildings? Not one stone will be left here upon another; all will be thrown down.' This alarming prediction makes them press him further: 'When will this be, and what will be the sign that all these things are about to be accomplished?' The warning of this 'little apocalypse' is clear: be ready, for you do not know the day or the hour. 'Tower and temple fall to dust,' says the hymn,[64] nothing lasts for ever. When you visit Jerusalem and place your hands in the crevices of the Western Wall, which is all that is left of the Temple, you're reminded that humanity's grandest designs are subject to the same law as everything else: earth to earth, ashes to ashes, dust to dust.

Jesus' teaching in the thirteenth chapter of St Mark is held by some to be the core of this tense, edgy Gospel, the earliest of the four. Why would the evangelist and disciple whom we are celebrating today write like this? Mark says that the kingdom Jesus came to proclaim is 'good news', *gospel*. Where's the joy in a message so charged with warning?

The clue is in the last verse of the reading: 'The one who endures to the end will be saved.' And that in turn looks forward to the end of this apocalyptic chapter: 'What I say to you, I say to all: Keep awake' (Mark 13.37). It's of a piece with Jesus' entry on the stage in St Mark, where he says, 'The time is fulfilled, and the kingdom of God has come near; repent and believe in the good news' (Mark 1.15). His calling time is nothing less than a summons to become *disciples*, to turn away from the old life and learn to live in a radically new way because of what God is about to do. For Mark, nothing less than obedience to this call is what it means to follow Jesus. To embrace God's reign over human life is a matter of the utmost urgency and of the utmost seriousness.

Today's Gospel drives home how provisional everything is: our possessions, our relationships, our institutions, our achievements, our very lives. All this, says the apocalyptic Jesus, will be swept away when God winds up history and brings in his kingdom. Mark's message is as stark as that. And even if we step back from the imagery and ascribe it to the end-of-the-world milieu in which first-century Christians believed they were living, we can't escape the vividness of Jesus' teaching, its summons to look afresh at things and consider what we rate as truly important in this life.

So, the announcement of God's kingdom should call us to scrutinize our values, hopes and longings, and decide how we are going to live in the future: that's St Mark's summons to become disciples. 'Repent and believe in the good news.' Mark doesn't make it easy – far from it. But who wants to give their lives to a faith that's no more than a Sunday hobby, that makes no real demands on us and costs us nothing?

We honour St Mark and his Gospel because he points us accurately to where true happiness is found. It's not in anything transient, not even the towers and temples on which we stake our lives. Lasting joy is the gift of the one thing that outlives the changes and chances of time and history: God's kingdom. It's the only hope we have. If we are true to the one Mark bears witness to, who lived among us and taught us the way of truth; who endured godforsakenness at Golgotha but whom the grave could not hold. If we say 'Yes' to his call to follow, and walk as those who are learning to love God with all our heart and our neighbours as ourselves, then we shall have understood St Mark aright. Which is the best possible reason for celebrating him.

Michael Sadgrove

Hymn suggestions

The kingdom is upon you; Disposer supreme, and Judge of the earth; Love's redeeming work is done; Thy kingdom come, O God.

SS Philip and James, Apostles 1 May
Enough
Isa. 30.15–21; Ps. 119.1–8; Eph. 1.3–10; **John 14.1–14**

Making a choice

As a child of the 80s, I grew up amid an odd cultural phenomenon which seemed to last from late childhood through to being a young adult. Everybody seemed to have to make choices between two competing brands or options. It was Sega or Nintendo, Thunder-Cats or He-man, Big Daddy or Giant Haystacks, McDonald's or Burger King. It was *Neighbours* or *Home and Away*, WWF or WCW, Oasis or Blur, *Friends* or *Frasier*, FIFA or Pro Evolution Soccer and, for Sophie, 'Daddy or chips'.[65] For some reason, it was not enough to like something, you had to decide what you ultimately thought to be best.

Being Philip

One of the saints being remembered today is Philip. Although I can honestly say that I am not picking my favourite, I am choosing to focus on Philip over James. Through John's Gospel, Philip wrestles with his own sense of what will be enough. When Jesus first calls Philip in John 1, Philip responds positively to Jesus as the one written about in the Scriptures. Without being prompted, Philip convinces Nathanael to give Jesus a chance too. Philip knows that it would be enough for Nathanael to simply 'come and see' for himself. Among his friends, at the start of the journey, Philip knows that seeing Jesus is enough.

Later, in John 6, we meet Philip again. Confronted with a crowd of thousands of hungry people, Jesus tests Philip by asking him where bread might be bought for the people to eat. Philip's response to Jesus is telling: 'Six months' wages would not buy enough bread for each of them to get a little' (John 6.7). What is striking here is that Philip does not answer Jesus' question. What is on his mind is his assessment that they do not have enough money to buy enough bread. Jesus had asked *where* bread might be bought. Philip gets caught up with how bread might be bought. In his fishing around for an alternative earthly solution, rather than meeting the eye of the one who would reveal himself as the living bread from heaven, Philip does not consider that Jesus might be enough.

No choice

After a brief cameo, where Philip passes on the request of a group of Greek people who wish to see Jesus, he next appears in today's Gospel reading. Philip is among those disciples in the upper room with Jesus. This private encounter between Jesus and his disciples is intense and emotional and Jesus' followers keep misfiring. Peter tells Jesus, 'You will never wash my feet' (John 13.8), then gets his feet washed. Thomas complains: 'How can we know the way?' (John 14.5). Then Jesus declares himself to be the way, the truth and the life. Now, Philip steps up for his big moment: 'Lord, show us the Father, and we will be satisfied' (John 14.8). In response to Philip's request, Jesus seems staggered that Philip does not know him, that Philip has not realized that to see Jesus is to see the Father.

Philip has a deeply held and longstanding concept of the one true God of Israel, the one who is Lord and Father. Pushed to make a choice it would be no contest between the transcendent God of ancient Scripture, the one beyond all time and space, the one beyond all telling, the one beyond human sight, who is the parent of all things living, and the alternative – a man from Nazareth, inspiring, impressive but not immortal or ineffable. When push comes to shove, for Philip, at this moment in the upper room, Jesus is all well and good but only seeing the Father is enough.

Being enough

I think it is too easy to criticize Philip here. In the intensity of the situation, everything is emotionally charged. Jesus himself is 'troubled in spirit' (John 13.21). From the beginning of his following of Jesus, he has known that Jesus is part of God's big story. Now, he is being confronted with the truth of who Jesus is. Today we celebrate Philip and recognize his merits and raw enthusiasm. There is something about Philip which is likeable if not a little frustrating. He is engaged in his circumstances. Yes, he sets about tasks he hasn't been assigned and he answers questions that haven't been asked. He requests things that show that he just wants to make sense of it all.

Philip, along with all who would face the profound challenge of believing in Jesus and, seeing that, alienate them from their community, finds himself confronted with the extraordinary truth that Jesus doesn't just fit into the big story, Jesus is the big story.

Jesus is not a means to an end, but the means and the end. To know Jesus is to know the Father, to see Jesus is to see the Father, and to love Jesus is to love the Father. It is not either/or. Philip names out loud a question that many in every generation would want to ask and hears an unequivocal and stunning answer: Jesus is enough.

Matt Allen

Hymn suggestions

I have decided to follow Jesus; To God be the glory; Jesus, Jesus, holy and anointed one; Jesus is the name we honour.

St Matthias the Apostle 14 May
God's Friends

Isa. 22.15–end, *or* Acts 1.15–end; Ps. 15; **Acts 1.15–end** (*if the Acts reading is used instead of the Old Testament reading, the New Testament reading is* 1 Cor. 4.1–7); **John 15.9–17**

The disciples are in a quandary. They have lost one of their number. Judas has betrayed Jesus, himself and them. There is a need to replace him, a pressing need to restore the number of apostles to 12, to symbolize the 12 tribes of Israel. Had they waited they would have realized that God already had this covered. Soon Paul will be called as an apostle, but the disciples can't possibly imagine such an extraordinary turn of events. Neither can they see that they have the apostle to the apostles in their midst. For us with hindsight, Mary Magdalene might seem the obvious replacement, but such a move is beyond comprehension too!

Two selected

Instead, two men from among the followers of Jesus are chosen as possible replacements. They have both been part of the Lord's company from when Jesus was baptized by John until the ascension. They have both travelled the journey, stayed the course and remained faithful. Selected are Joseph Barsabbas, also known as Justus, and Matthias. Who are they? Neither of them has been mentioned in the Scriptures until now. Why were their names put forward and not others? We know that the Lord called 70 and sent them out in mission (Luke 10.1), so there must be many more followers of Jesus whose names are unknown to us. If from time to time you feel unseen, unnoticed by the church, take heart – not every Christian achieves celebrity status!

Casting lots

The disciples reach their decision by praying and then casting lots. Casting lots as a way of discerning the will of God had good precedence. The high priest's breastplate contained two stones – the Urim and Thummin – which were used to discern God's will on contested matters. King Saul uses this method to reach a conclusion in 1 Samuel 14.40–42. The disciples use this trusted method and the lot falls on Matthias.

What was Matthias thinking while the process was going on? Did he want to be an apostle? He was with the believers throughout the time of Jesus' ministry, but this is the first time we hear about him. He has been faithful and content to serve in the shadows. Now he is thrust into the limelight. We don't know much about what happens to him after this but legend has it that he takes the gospel to Ethiopia. God's calling is sometimes very surprising and requires courage and some growing into.

But there's another person in this story too. What about Joseph called Barsabbas, the other contender on whom the lot does not fall? What happens to him? Was he relieved, do you think? Or did he feel inadequate and disappointed in the outcome? Did he say wistfully in later life, 'I was nearly an apostle, you know,' or generously, 'I'm so glad Matthias was chosen; he made such a good apostle.' The lot falls on Matthias, but that doesn't mean that Joseph Barsabbas isn't chosen. Hopefully, Joseph Barsabbas went on to discover his true calling and knew God's peace.

God's calling

Celebrating St Matthias is a good time to consider whether God is calling us to something new, to step up and take risks, and to develop our gifts and leadership potential. We are members together of the body of Christ, so our calling is never just individual but part of a bigger plan through which God is revealed in our churches and communities. The Gospel set for today is helpful here: 'I am the vine, you are branches,' says Jesus to the disciples, and he asks them 'to abide' (to be at home) in his love. He then goes on to explain that though they are called to serve, they are not servants but friends. And this idea of friendship – with God and with each other – is one that we can all learn to exercise.

Friendship

It's very easy for Christians to fall into the trap of being competitive. We compare our churches, numbers, income, styles of worship, faithfulness and all sorts of other factors to make ourselves feel important. Even when we don't say it, we often think it. This is not Christ-like. Jesus speaks of the great love that sacrifices itself for others. The message that we bear is that through the cross and resurrection of Jesus, everyone can be friends with God. Friendship is about getting along together, wanting the best for each other, sharing problems and solutions, being generous with resources, having empathy, building each other up, serving and celebrating together. Jesus has appointed us to go and bear fruit – 'fruit that will last' – and exercising friendship within our communities will enable that to happen.

So on this day when we remember that the lot fell on Matthias and not on Joseph Barsabbas let's celebrate that we are all chosen and called, whether acknowledged or not. Let's think again about what it is that God is calling each of us to and look for ways to encourage and release the gifts in our church and communities. Let's commit ourselves to Jesus' commandment to love, to the challenge of friendship with God and with each other, which will reach out and transform all we encounter.

Catherine Williams

Hymn suggestions

I, the Lord of sea and sky; Will you come and follow me; Give thanks for Christ's apostles; The highest and the holiest place.

Visit of the Blessed Virgin Mary to Elizabeth
31 May
Pregnancy and Prophecy – the Start of a Revolution
Zeph. 3.14–18; Ps. 113; Rom. 12.9–16; **Luke 1.39–49 [50–56]**

Courage and confidence

Mary has just received two pieces of stunning news in quick succession: first, that she (who is very young) is pregnant; second, her cousin Elizabeth (who is very old) is also pregnant, and at an advanced stage. Having given her consent to the divine plan for her own pregnancy, Mary leaves in a rush to visit Elizabeth. Luke's narrative style seems to suggest she drops everything and goes without a word to anyone that she's leaving. It is a distance of 80–100 miles, taking around four to five days to walk. It is an act of courage (to go seemingly alone) and confidence (that God could be trusted to be telling the truth about these two pregnancies).

Here is a challenge to us. Are we paying attention to God when an unexpected or unlikely call comes our way? Are we willing to go, with haste, and share God's good news with others? Do we have confidence in God that we can trust his message even when it seems impossible?

Pregnancies and prophecies

Mary arrives at the house and announces her arrival. Elizabeth hears her cousin's voice, and her baby leaps for joy! In that instant, they both know who is here with them. They both recognize the baby, barely conceived, within Mary. This knowledge has not come to them via human means – how could it? Elizabeth and her unborn baby are attuned to the divine truth, and Elizabeth speaks words of prophecy: 'You are blessed.' She names Mary as the mother of the Lord, the promised Messiah. Her baby leaps for joy.

In response, Mary speaks words of prophecy over God's people. She voices prophetic promises that this baby she carries will bring in God's kingdom in mighty ways, raising up those on the margins and lowering those in elevated positions within society, bringing justice, mercy and hope.

Two pregnant women, speaking words of prophecy in a household and not a temple, in joy and celebration of God who has surprised them both with an unexpected calling.

This is a challenge to any who feel that prophecy belongs within certain structures, genders and religious spaces. Here, the mother of John the Baptist and the mother of Jesus stand in a domestic setting and are inspired by the Holy Spirit to speak out words of prophecy and revolution (in Mary's words of the Magnificat).

Where might God be gifting people with prophetic words today, in the unexpected places and the unlikely people? Are we paying attention, or are we missing what God is saying and through whom he is saying it?

Revolution and joy

We might be forgiven for characterizing revolutionaries through history as grim-faced men, with furrowed brows and muscular postures, full of angry passion for change. Mary's response is a masterpiece of revolution. This is a joyful, hopeful poem of what is possible: mercy, justice, hungry people full, lowly people raised up, proud people scattered, powerful people brought down, and ancient promises fulfilled, throughout the generations to come. This is a vision of the world and society turned upside down, through the direct involvement of God. Those on the margins, those forgotten and overlooked, are at the very heart of this revolution. And this revolution begins with two pregnant women who speak words of prophecy with joy.

In our discipleship, in our church leadership, in our worship, in our prayer, are we speaking and living words of joyful revolution? Or have we settled into a comfortable, quiet, sedate neutral way of being?

Mary's words of revolution have a sense that these are not just future visions but present realities. God is lifting the lowly, scattering the proud, filling the hungry, and will do so in the future. Have we become complacent, with a message that says we hope God will do these things at some point in the future, but with no imminent expectation that God might just be doing them now?

Mary returns home

After three months with Elizabeth, Mary returns home. She is now three months pregnant, at the point of beginning to show, and will be facing her community with news of her pregnancy and all that will entail. There will be questions, rumours, heartache and decisions to make with Joseph.

Months from now, when other prophetic words are spoken over her and the newborn baby Jesus, Mary will treasure what is said in her heart. Does she treasure these words of prophecy and revolution shared with Elizabeth as she journeys through her pregnancy? Does she return to them over the years, seeing the shoots of revolution throughout Jesus' three-year ministry as an adult? Does she get a hint as Jesus grows up through childhood?

We are now the bearers of her words of prophecy and revolution. May we declare them and live them with joy, bringing hope, mercy and justice to all people.

Kt Tupling

Hymn suggestions

Tell out my soul; Meekness and majesty; Beauty for brokenness; Jesus Christ is waiting.

St Barnabas, Apostle   11 June
He Calls Us Friends

Job 29.11–16, *or* Acts 11.19–end; Ps 112; Acts 11.19–end
(*if the Acts reading is used instead of the Old Testament reading, the New Testament reading is* Gal. 2.1–10); **John 15.12–17**

Raised as a Third Culture Kid in the Middle East, specifically attending primary schools in Jerusalem and Damascus, due to my father's job with the United Nations, I have never made strong and lasting friendships easily. In my present ministry context in Swindon, it never ceases to surprise me that congregation members, now in their seventies and eighties, have known each other since the year dot. How enviable to have such long-lasting friendships! To have friendships is one thing, but to be a good friend to another is another thing. I wonder what you expect from a friendship? For me, the qualities I look for in a friendship are honesty, being available, and trustworthiness – and this goes both ways. For sure, love is at the heart of friendships that grow us and encourage mutual flourishing. So, what does Jesus teach us about friendship?

Sacrificial love

In John's Gospel, we continue with the teachings of Jesus which he gave to his disciples on his last evening with them. From this discourse, we find that Jesus shows his love for us in the following ways:

- He calls us his friends.
- He lays his life down for his friends.
- He chooses us to be his friends.

Interestingly, in this passage we are looking at, Jesus uses the word 'friends' three times. Jesus proves that we are his friends because, he says, 'I have made known to you everything that I have heard from my Father.'

Earlier, in John 14.15, we are reminded that if we love God, we will keep his commandment to love our neighbours. Doing the will of God demands loving God with all our heart, soul, mind and strength. In kingdom terms, love is laying down your life for a brother or sister in Christ. However, in our privileged society, where we can worship God freely, many of us will never be in a position where we are called to make such a sacrifice. But, perhaps, 'laying down one's life' looks different. Might raising our head above the parapet for our UK minority ethnic (UKME) brothers and sisters be an act of laying down our lives for our friends? Might giving up our position of power and privilege for another be an act of laying down our lives for our friends? Might choosing not to look the other way, or be complicit to injustices against groups of people attacked and maligned by society, be an act of laying down our lives for our friends? Jesus reminds us that we were made in God's image, to be his hands and feet offering sacrificial and serving love, moving us towards an act and expression of love to one another.

Friendship builds community

From the Acts and Galatians passages, we observe how a friendship between Paul and Barnabas served in doing God's work of sharing the gospel message of Christ to the Gentiles (Gal. 2.9 and Acts 11.25–26). Thus, the love of friendship and fellowship with other believers has the power to produce fruit for the kingdom of God. In turn, this same love can transform communities where forgiveness, reconciliation and restoration are hallmarks of Jesus' gospel message.

As we commemorate Barnabas today, who was a dependable friend who encouraged, was generous and compassionate in service of God's mission, may we be inspired to be the friend that Jesus, 'friend of sinners', calls us to be as we serve our communities.

Catherine Okoronkwo

Hymn suggestions

What a friend we have in Jesus; Blessed assurance, Jesus is mine; And can it be (Amazing love); How deep the Father's love for us.

Day of Thanksgiving for the Institution of the Holy Communion (Corpus Christi)   19 June
Tokens of Love
Gen. 14.18–20; Ps. 116.10–end; **1 Cor. 11.23–26**; John 6.51–58

Give me sunshine

Sitting one Sunday afternoon recently on a park bench – admittedly in a dog collar – a complete stranger got up from the bench and, as he was leaving, remarked, 'The sun changes everything.' I love that. The idea that sunshine, particularly in Great Britain, can be transformative. It wouldn't be too hard to stretch that to, 'The Son changes everything.'

Grief

Grief is a really tough experience, much hidden in modern society, and yet it is something that we will all go through during the course of our lives. It is not uncommon when grieving to gain a sense of the one who has died through nature or through the senses. A butterfly, bird or plant may be a vivid reminder of the deceased, and equally a scent, a voice or a piece of music can seem to bring that person instantly back and into the present. To start with it can feel quite a shock – over time it can be a comfort too.

The Repair Shop

The Repair Shop is a very popular television series on British television, where members of the public bring items of special significance to them which have aged or gone into disrepair to be repaired or restored. Very commonly, the object in question is of great personal value, not because it is worth lots of money but because it holds a memory or set of memories about a beloved person who has died. The object in question has become a container of something far more than it appears. Its outward appearance does not do justice to its inner meaning for those who possess it. The narrative that goes with the object brings it meaning, and thus the power of the restorer is to bring back to life something of supreme value. It is quite something to witness those who see their sacred object restored, literally brought back to life, after the Repair Shop workers have transformed it.

Sacraments

Today the church celebrates Corpus Christi, the institution of the Eucharist, or Communion, or the Lord's Supper, one of two (or seven) sacraments, depending on your church tradition. When I was at school, one of the school chaplains described sacraments to us as like a kiss: a physical and outward expression of an inward feeling or desire. I have always loved that, the idea that in the sacraments God kisses us. After the ascension, with Jesus no longer physically in the world, the sacraments provide us with something physical to hold on to about God: water, light and oil in baptism; bread and wine in communion. We can touch them, feel them, ingest them. They can become part of us.

Transformation

In today's Epistle, St Paul reminds us of the story of how the Eucharist came to be. The words Jesus spoke over the bread and the wine the night before he died. These words are important because they are connected to the narrative of his life and the sacrifice that he has made. Like the precious things brought to the Repair Shop, they are far more than they seem at first glance, because of the narrative attached to them. Jesus' sacrifice of his life on the cross, the greatest expression of love a human can give to another, is captured in the sharing of bread and wine, where his words have been spoken over them, the words that St Paul repeats for us today. This is my body, given for you. My blood, shed for you. The ordinary is transformed into the extraordinary. They still look like bread and wine, but now they are so much more, connecting us with Jesus intimately, with his death and resurrection, but also with Christians across the world and throughout the ages. Indeed, with the whole company of heaven.

Tokens of love

Today's Gospel reminds us that this meal is real food. It really feeds and sustains us, especially when everything else fails. It is food for the journey, and it brings us wholeness. Each time we receive the Lord's Supper, we physically receive God's love. There, in front of us, within us. These tokens of love are a gift to us, to all people. I wonder what communion means to you? Can we too be containers of his love? Can we witness to his gospel by being that which is transformed: the ordinary to the extraordinary? Tokens of his love.

Jonathan Lawson

Hymn suggestions

Sweet sacrament divine; Soul of my Saviour; This is my body; Broken for me, broken for you.

Birth of John the Baptist   24 June
Learning to Listen
Isa. 40.1–11; Ps 85.7–end; Acts 13.14b–26, *or* Gal. 3.23–end; **Luke 1.57–66, 80**

When the news spread around the village that Elizabeth was pregnant, no one believed it at first – even Zechariah was left speechless. When the child was born, everyone assumed that he would be given his father's name. However, Elizabeth said that he would be called John. When Zechariah confirmed the name, his speech was restored. Everyone was amazed and acknowledged that 'the hand of the Lord' was on John. So, they asked, 'What then will this child become?'

Hearing God's call

As a child, John probably heard the story surrounding the circumstances of his birth many times. Having been told that their child would be 'great in the sight of the Lord' (Luke 1.15), Elizabeth and Zechariah may have impressed upon him that God had important work for him to do, and they would have schooled him in the teaching of the prophets and the law. Yet, while such instruction in the faith was important before John could begin to 'prepare the way of the Lord', he needed to hear for himself a call from God.

There are many stories in the Bible of God's call coming to people: Moses heard a voice speaking to him out of a 'burning bush' (Ex. 3.1–12), while centuries later in the Temple, Isaiah heard a voice saying, 'Whom shall I send?' (Isa. 6.1–8). Today, with these stories in mind, we often associate a 'call' of God with a vocation to Christian ministry or membership in a religious community. Yet,

God speaks to us all in many different ways and places, though we may not always be open or ready to listen to what God is saying to us.

One day, while I was out walking, I saw a group of children who were happily playing together until suddenly there was a disagreement. As they began to argue, one young girl put her fingers to her ears and shouted, 'I can't hear you, I have got bananas in my ears.' The scene has remained etched in my memory, a reminder, I suppose, of how easy it is to close my ears to others and to God too.

Learning to listen

To open our ears to genuinely listen to God and to others takes courage, and may require us to have our own views challenged. It also means that, at times, we listen 'into the silences' within ourselves or others.[66] The thought of listening in this way may seem a fearsome prospect. If we were to hear God speaking, what might we be asked to do? What habits or old ideas would we need to shed? How might life change for us?

Scripture suggests that John the Baptist understood the importance of spending time alone listening to God. Before John began his ministry, the Gospel writer says that 'he was in the wilderness until the day he appeared publicly to Israel'. This reference to the wilderness has been interpreted as a way of highlighting John's prophetic ministry. As foretold, John was a voice crying out, 'Prepare the way of the Lord.' However, while the words of the prophet imply that the desert is a place from which people are to be delivered, for John and for Jesus too, the wilderness was a place of formation; a place where one may be drawn out of one's self and closer to God. Of course, as we seek to listen, we may not always expect an immediate response from God or assume a direct answer.

On one occasion, Mother Teresa was asked by a reporter, 'What do you say to God when you pray?' She replied, 'I listen.' Not satisfied, the reporter asked, 'Then what does God say to you?' She replied, 'He listens.'[67] Perhaps an awareness of God's comforting, consoling presence is God's speech and may constitute God's call.

The challenge of listening

While this may sound strange, I wonder if what is needed in the church today is for Christians to enter into the wilderness. I don't mean going to a deserted landscape! Rather, I wonder if in the midst of our busy, noisy lives, we may discover God speaking as we become aware of the silent depths in ourselves and in others. It might happen in a chance meeting with a stranger, while drinking coffee with a friend, or even sharing in worship.

Even now, what might God be saying? Do you hear words of comfort, challenge, affirmation or rebuke? Perhaps, the word to you is, 'Do not hesitate. Go home and make that phone call today.' Or perhaps it is, 'Let go of the anger that has boiled in you for years, just let it go.' Or the Lord may be saying, 'I know you are disappointed, but rest assured that you have done your best.' Whatever the word for you or me may be today, there is no doubt that God speaks and listens to us all; we will hear if we are prepared to listen.

Karen E. Smith

Hymn suggestions

O Jesus, I have promised; Dear Lord and Father of mankind; Wait for the Lord (Taizé); I, the Lord of sea and sky.

SS Peter and Paul, Apostles 29 June
(or transferred to 30 June)
Belt, Sandals, Cloak, Follow

Zech. 4.1–6a, 10b–end, *or* Acts 12.1–11; Ps. 125; **Acts 12.1–11**, *or* 2 Tim. 4.6–8, 17–18; Matt. 16.13–19

Today we are celebrating the feast of St Peter and St Paul – two of our greatest forebears in the faith. We celebrate both saints today because tradition has it that they were martyred together in Rome during the reign of Nero. Peter was crucified, choosing to be placed on the cross upside down since he did not consider himself worthy to die in the same way as Jesus. Paul, as a Roman citizen, was beheaded. They are an unlikely pairing, so different from each other. Different classes and different levels of education. Peter was married, and Paul was single. Peter was a long-standing disciple who lived alongside Jesus and witnessed his death and resurrection; Paul was a convert after the resurrection who met the ascended Jesus in a vision. But together they spread the gospel, building the church through faithful witness to Christ.

Identifying Jesus

'Who do you say that I am?' asks Jesus of Peter in the reading from Matthew. 'You are the Messiah, the Son of the living God,' Peter replies. While Peter often got it wrong there were times, and this is one of them, when he got it spectacularly right. During Paul's conversion on the road to Damascus in Acts 9 the tables are turned and it is Paul who asks, 'Who are you, Lord?' Jesus responds, 'I am Jesus, whom you are persecuting' (Acts 9.5). Like Peter, like Paul, the questions and answers we have regarding the identity of Jesus shape our future witness to the good news of Jesus Christ, and our roles and responsibilities as disciples.

The onward journey

Peter finds himself called blessed for his response to Jesus, who looks into the impetuous and sometimes flaky disciple and sees what Peter will become. Peter will be rock-solid, faithful and committed to building the church, trustworthy enough to carry the keys of the kingdom. By the time we meet Peter again in the reading from the book of Acts, he has been through the most extraordinary experiences. He's been broken by his denial. He's witnessed the death and resurrection of Jesus, been forgiven and restored. He and the other disciples have been filled with the Holy Spirit who sends them out. Peter is given to the world.

And now we find him in prison, very likely to be executed the next day, like James. Remarkably he is able to sleep, so deeply in fact that the angel who comes to rescue him has to shake him awake. Such trust, such faith! From prison, Peter is rescued by an angel, a messenger of God who makes sure Peter is ready for the journey ahead. 'Fasten your belt and put on your sandals ... wrap your cloak around you and follow me,' are the angel's instructions.

Rescuing angels

When were you last rescued by an angel? When were you called out of a dark and difficult place by God, ministered to, made fit and well, given a new road to walk and reminded to follow? The road of faith can be long, and there will be adventures and challenges. Prisons come in many forms but God is a God of liberation and longs to set us free. Remember to fasten the belt of truth around you, remember your feet are protected by sandals of the gospel;

wrap yourself in your cloak of righteousness and faith and follow where the Spirit leads, even if it seems as if it might be too far, too soon, too dangerous or too foolish. Nothing is impossible with God.

God comes to rescue and restore. Angels come in many guises, and through the power of God a little faith can go a very long way indeed. Peter and Paul's experiences of being called, blessed, broken and sent model for us the Christian journey. There will be adventures, there will be hardships, and we may need to be rescued from time to time. But always there is hope.

Belt, sandals, cloak, follow

Like Peter and Paul, we can only fulfil our calling as disciples of Christ through the power of the Holy Spirit who we look to, to counsel, comfort, energize and embolden us. We are to continually stir up the Spirit throughout our Christian journey, with all its ups and downs, joys and challenges, as we seek to live life fully and sacrificially after the pattern of Jesus.

Jesus takes ordinary people like you and me, makes us precious and blessed in the sight of God, breaks open our safe and contained lives by the power of the Holy Spirit and sends us out into the world so that all may know they are loved beyond measure and saved for eternity. So, heeding the courage and example of Peter and Paul, 'Fasten your belt and put on your sandals ... wrap your cloak around you and follow me.'

Catherine Williams

Hymn suggestions

Will you come and follow me; For all the saints; Dominus Jesus Christus (Taizé); Peter's song (Face to Face, Michael O'Brien).

St Thomas the Apostle 3 July
Jesus of the Scars
Hab. 2.1–4; Ps. 31.1–6; Eph. 2.19–end; **John 20.24–29**

I wonder who you secretly would like to be? Do you have a celebrity, a writer, a person, a film character whom you want to emulate, or would love to be like? Or, maybe a saint or spiritual leader? Does thinking about them ever make you feel as if you don't measure up?

The poison of comparison

Comparison can help us know who we are, and it can help us lose who we are. It can help us discern our way, and lead us astray. Comparison and competition threaten the common life of the disciples in the Gospel that we read. In the passage just before, Jesus appears to the disciples meeting together, wishes them peace, then shows them his hands and his side, at which point they rejoice (John 20.20).

But one of them is missing. Thomas isn't there. We don't know why. They were all meeting together, behind closed doors, afraid of persecution, and he wasn't there. And when he finally arrives, he hears this story. They have seen the Lord! They did better than him in their shared quest to follow Jesus. Thomas is a little grumpy. The disciples had seen his hands and side, well, he, Thomas, wants to outdo them and says, 'Unless I see the mark of the nails in his hands and put my finger in the mark of the nails and my hand in his side, I will not believe.'

Thomas' disappointment at being left behind, comparing himself, almost prevents him from responding to the invitation to follow Jesus. Comparison led him astray. You simply cannot compete when it comes to a relationship with Jesus. That's not how it works. God works in different ways in different places; God will work in our lives in different ways and at a different pace. God speaks to all of us in different ways. Our calling is not to compare these, but to bring them together, learn from one another, support one another, and complement one another as each brings their gifts. Each of us is called in specific ways, to embody the love of God exactly where we are, and as we are, and to nurture our gifts and opportunities responsibly. To see where God is at work around us, not keep looking and comparing how God is working over the fence, or across the road – though hearing stories of God at work elsewhere can be inspiring. It just should not become a point of comparison.

Touching the scars

Embodiment is a big theme in the resurrection appearances. There are lots and lots of references to Jesus' body, his hands, his feet, his side, the nails, the scars. The Jesus that appears really is the same Jesus that had been with them for all those years. Isn't it extraordinary that Jesus is recognized by his scars?

It isn't all the good stuff of being on earth that prompts recognition here, not words he had said before, not gestures, not shared memories. Nor is he recognized through his power, by the fact that he appeared in a locked room, or, indeed, even appeared at all. He is the Jesus of the scars, the Jesus who engages with a broken and difficult world that struggles to believe and even more to follow. The scars are a profound reminder that God meets us in the difficult and painful places and is willing the bear the cost of walking alongside us.

We don't always compare ourselves just because we want to be better than others. Often, we compare ourselves because we lack confidence, because somewhere inside us we are broken, unhealed, afraid, all too aware that we are limited and vulnerable.

I don't think it is a coincidence that this episode majors on the scars. They speak of vulnerability and love, they speak of continuity, of reliability, and of the permanence of God being with us. They speak of a God who shares our struggles, who is big enough to take the worst that we can throw at him, and still come and meet us and gently move us. The scars tell us that the knowledge and brokenness of the world are still carried by Jesus, and taken into the very heart of God.

The scars of Christ hold out the hope of the world. They make a bridge between the perfection of heaven and the brokenness and mixed blessings of earth. They assure us that we, whoever we are, whatever we are facing, are welcome into the heart of God, and that God-with-us, Immanuel, will walk with us on the road. We don't need to be perfect. We don't need to compete. What we are called to is to walk with the God of life.

Isabelle Hamley

Hymn suggestions

Thine be the glory; Everyone needs compassion; Love divine, all loves excelling; Before the throne of God above.

St Mary Magdalene   22 July
All Desires Known
Song of Sol. 3.1–4; Ps. 42.1–10; 2 Cor. 5.14–17;
John 20.1–2, 11–18

Is desire too heady a topic for a sermon? Too risky? Where might talk of desire take us? Buckle up for a sermon on desire. Fundamentally, all humans desire love. Think of the gaze between infant and caregiver; the eye contact between lovers; the countless artistic expressions of the quest for love – poems, songs, artwork, dance. Lack of love causes illness. Images of orphans chained to their cots rocking back and forth in distress come to mind, development arrested through lack of love. Loneliness can increase blood pressure and blood sugar levels, and lead to poor sleep, heart issues and a weakened immune system. Google it. I did!

God reaches the parts no other objects of desire can reach

Of all the forms of love, there is one that is foundational. It's the desire the Psalmist expresses so eloquently. 'As a deer longs for flowing streams, so my soul longs for you, O God' (Ps. 42.1). Augustine wrote in his *Confessions*: 'Our hearts are restless till they find their rest in God.' Ultimately God reaches the parts no other objects of desire can reach.

The words of the Collect for Purity are resonant: 'Almighty God, unto whom all hearts are open, all desires known and from whom no secrets are hid …'[68] Human desire can be messed up and muddled – and God knows this. So, let's be honest with ourselves. Why worship a golden calf, in whatever form, when you can worship the one who brings all life into being and who is the source of all love? Underneath the false starts and mistaken obsessions of desire derailed is the genuine desire for God, for the worth conferred by knowing we are seen by God and loved beyond measure. When we listen to the inner voice of love and really attend, it cries for the one who made us and in whom all desire is fulfilled.

Mary Magdalene knew this love, saw it in Jesus and received it from him. Let's look at her experience. Spoiler alert: it's not all hearts and flowers!

Mary's story

Bleak. Utterly bleak. Surely this is Mary Magdalene's experience as she stands with the others at the foot of the cross. Burning sorrow and biting emptiness. Hope snuffed out by the pall of grief. Mary's reaction demonstrates her deep love and her great longing. Others fled and denied ever knowing Jesus, but Mary Magdalene remained. She was a steady presence. What did Mary do when Jesus bowed his head and gave up his spirit? My guess is she looked on as Joseph of Arimathea took the body from the cross. She must have followed as they carried him to the place of burial. She knew where to go early the next morning.

When the new day dawns, why does she go to the tomb? According to John's Gospel, the spices had already been wrapped in with the body the night before – so she didn't go with that purpose in mind. What desire drove her? In grief there is a longing, to be near the deceased, to connect with them in some way, and the overriding ache for death not to be true. Perhaps near his grave she sought solace.

Her longing finds echoes in the Song of Songs where the woman seeks the one she loves with such intensity. She runs through the city with wild energy, questioning people as to the whereabouts of her love. With similar intensity we see Mary running, telling Simon Peter that she doesn't know where Jesus is, and repeating her searching questions with the angels in white. 'Where is he?' Her longing has a singular focus – laser-like. In a moment of lovely irony, she even questions Jesus as to his whereabouts. Blinded by tears and dismay, she is simply unable to see what she most desires and least expects. Mary only discerns Jesus' presence when he speaks her name in the old familiar way. Then, like the woman in the Song of Songs, she wants to hold him and not let go: desire fulfilled. Like Peter at the transfiguration, she wants to seize the moment for ever. But to cling and cling is to remain static. Mary must let Jesus go to tell her story: 'I have seen the Lord.'

All desire fulfilled?

Fulfilment of the desire for God is dynamic – we never 'arrive' – because there is always more of God to discover, to experience, to know. Perhaps we can get a little too satisfied, a little too cosy with the god we know, content in the safe routines and ways of worship. Perhaps we cling too much to the old familiar ways when God is always inviting us out into deeper water and new discovery. Perhaps when we are too at ease in Zion, God comes and provokes us into restlessness so that we might seek more, find more, grow more and be more. More our truest selves, and our best communities, where loneliness is banished and all desires known and healed.

Kate Bruce

Hymn suggestions

Come, thou fount of every blessing; Longing for light, we wait in darkness; Purify my heart; Jesus be the centre (Vineyard Songs).

St James the Apostle   25 July
Not Sitting but Serving

Jer. 45.1–5, *or* Acts 11.27—12.2; Ps. 126; Acts 11.27—12.2 *(if the Acts reading is used instead of the Old Testament reading, the New Testament reading is* 2 Cor. 4.7–15*)*; **Matt. 20.20–28**

The Gospel writers differ in their accounts of who asked the question in our Gospel reading. In the Gospel according to Mark, two brothers, James and John, posed the question, but in Matthew's narrative it was their mother who asked Jesus to grant her sons a special place – one on his right and one on his left in his kingdom. In the end, it doesn't really matter whether it was the disciples seeking power or status, or a mother wanting the best advantage for her children, because in both accounts it is evident that the disciples do not understand what it means to seek the kingdom of God.

The kingdom and the rule of love

Although Jesus spoke of the kingdom of God – God's rule or reign – many times, the disciples continued to believe that he would establish his kingly rule on earth. Perhaps they thought of it in terms of triumph over the Roman Empire which had dominated their lives for so long. Yet, Jesus was not interested in political power. Instead, he described the kingdom as a new reality discovered by those seeking to love as God loves. The kingdom is not grasped by power, but discovered as it grows through love and harmony in selfless service to others.

The question

As the disciples waited to see how Jesus would respond to their request, he said to them, 'You do not know what you are asking. Are you able to drink the cup that I am about to drink?' They replied, 'We are able.' Of course, they did not know what they were asking. In fact, none of the disciples realized what was required of those who wanted to follow Jesus because when they heard the request of James and John, they were very angry, perhaps wishing that they had asked the question first! On hearing the reply of James and John, and seeing the anger of the other disciples, Jesus said, 'Whoever wishes to be great among you must be your servant, and whoever wishes to be first among you must be your slave.'

Not sitting but serving

What a striking contrast between the way the disciples and Jesus imagined the kingdom. The disciples had a regal setting in mind: sitting in splendour and being served by others. Jesus said that they would not be sitting, but on their knees serving.

The Catholic Worker movement was founded in 1933 by Peter Maurin and Dorothy Day and today is still dedicated to serving and caring for the poor. Committed to living as a servant of Christ, Day often spoke of the need 'to serve' rather than 'to be served'. She wrote:

> The greatest challenge of the day is: how to bring about a revolution of the heart, a revolution which has to start with each one of us? When we begin to take the lowest place, to wash the feet of others, to love our brothers [and sisters] with that burning love, that passion which led to the Cross, then we can truly say, 'Now I have begun.'[69]

The disciples did not envisage themselves as servants, and we may not either. A subservient role does not sit well in a world that prizes dominance, power and control. The voices of culture echo around us: 'Put me first.'

Are we able?

After the death and resurrection of Jesus, I imagine that James and John and the other disciples reflected many times on their conversations with Jesus. Recalling the Lord kneeling at their feet as they shared the Last Supper together, and then witnessing his agonizing death on the cross, I wonder if they remembered, with some embarrassment, their own grand vision of sitting on his right and his left. Did they realize that the cup they were to share was, indeed, a cup of suffering?

According to Scripture, St James, whom we remember today, suffered a martyr's death. Tradition has it that his body was brought to Santiago de Compostela in Spain for burial. Today, many pilgrims journey along what has become known as the Way of St James (The Camino) to that holy site. Wherever our pilgrimage with Christ may be taking us, perhaps we may acknowledge that we are never 'able' – in our own strength – to be servants of Christ. Yet, saying humbly to one another, 'We have begun', we may journey on in faith, trusting that under the Spirit's guidance, step by step, we may discover more and more what it means to follow in the way of Christ who came 'not to be served but to serve, and to give his life a ransom for many'.

Karen E. Smith

Hymn suggestions

You servants of God, your master proclaim; Brother, sister, let me serve you; The kingdom of God is justice and joy; Will you come and follow me (Iona).

Transfiguration of Our Lord 6 August
Mountain-top Experiences
Dan. 7.9–10, 13–14; Ps. 97; 2 Peter 1.16–19; **Luke 9.28–36**

Immediately before our Gospel passage, Jesus informs his disciples that he will undergo great suffering and eventually must go to Jerusalem to die. Not only that but the disciples will too, if not physically, then at least metaphorically. Eight days after making these shocking revelations, Jesus takes Peter, James and John up a mountain with him, which brings us to our Gospel reading.

New perspectives

Scholars are unsure which mountain Jesus took them up, but the important thing to remember is that they went up. When you go up any mountain, you see things differently. That is what is significant about the mountain. Jesus knew that his disciples needed time away from the turmoil and worries of everyday life. And so it is with us. Leonardo da Vinci once said:

> Now and then go away, have a little relaxation, for when you come back to your work, your judgement will be surer. Go some distance away because the work appears smaller, and more of it can be taken in at a glance, and a lack of harmony or proportion is more readily seen.[70]

Jesus took his friends up a high mountain to help them gain perspective on who he was and who they were.

Up the mountain they go and suddenly Jesus' clothes become dazzling white and his face shines. There is much debate about what happened here. Some say that it was Jesus' glory – his divinity – breaking through, which up until now had been hidden by his humanity. But if that were the case, how do we explain Moses and Elijah shining gloriously too? They were not divine. Perhaps, then, it was not the 'God' bit of Jesus shining through, but rather Jesus' humanity shining with divine glory. Humanity glorified in Jesus. This would tie in with Daniel's prophecies that speak of the faithful shining like stars. God has always intended humanity to be glorious, and Jesus is our perfect example. That is the perspective change his disciples needed. We are to shine like stars.

Pitching our tents

The presence of Moses and Elijah is significant. Moses represents the law and Elijah represents the prophets. Jesus is the fulfilment of both the law and the prophets. This revelation has a tremendous impact on Peter. Remember, Peter has been upset by Jesus' talk of his impending suffering and death. It does not match Peter's picture of what the Messiah should be.

But here, Jesus is shining in glory as the fulfilment of the law and the prophets. This vision is much more agreeable to Peter. He must be thinking, 'Now this is more like it. This is what a Messiah should be like!' In his excitement, Peter blurts out, 'Master, it is good for us to be here; let us make three dwellings, one for you, one for Moses, and one for Elijah.'

Peter was likely thinking back to when God's presence dwelt in a tent among the Israelites. It is only natural that Peter suggests they set up three tents – one each for Jesus, Moses and Elijah – to prolong this heavenly experience. Perhaps then Jesus would stop talking about suffering and death.

But notice in verse 34 it says, 'While he was saying this, a cloud came and overshadowed them.' It is as though God had to shut Peter up by interrupting him with a cloud. That is pretty embarrassing! However, I have sympathy for Peter here. Have you ever had such an amazing experience that you wished it could stay like that for ever?

Rather than enjoying something for a season, and then moving on to what God has in store for us next, we keep trying to go back and relive the glory days. Peter is reluctant to move on. He wants to pitch his tent and have everyone stay right there, on the mountain top.

But here is the point. We cannot live in those times for ever. We cannot allow fear to hold us back. What is your equivalent of Peter's tent? What is the thing that tempts you to set up camp and not join Jesus in his walk to Jerusalem and the cross?

Commissioned for more

That is exactly what happens next in the story. A voice comes from the cloud and says, 'This is my Son, my Chosen; listen to him!' In the corresponding account found in Matthew 17, the voice says, 'This is my Son, the Beloved; with him I am well pleased; listen to him!'

You might recognize these words from before. It is what God said to Jesus at his baptism. Jesus has now turned to face Jerusalem, and here we have the words again. At this key moment in Jesus' walk to the cross, he receives his Father's affirmation for the next stage. Perhaps one of the things you need to hear right now is God's affirmation reminding you that you too are God's beloved child and that he is with you wherever you go.

Mark Nam

Hymn suggestions

Christ, whose glory fills the skies; Amazing grace; Darkness like a shroud; Lord, the light of your love is shining.

The Blessed Virgin Mary 15 August
The Power and Potential of God
Isa. 61.10–end, *or* Rev. 11.19—12.6, 10; Ps. 45.10–end; Gal. 4.4–7; **Luke 1.46–55**

Mary's song of praise is both an intimate and public declaration of the power and potential of God to turn the world upside down so that things can be better. Her words are uttered in the house of her cousin Elizabeth, who welcomes her with open arms as in the painting *Mary and Elizabeth* by Danish artist, Carl Heinrich Bloch (1866).[71] In Mary's words, we see something of the mystery of God and a confirmation that God simply does not see the world in the way that we do. The question for us is, what part will we play in this co-creative process of the world being remade?

God can do great things

Mary's position as a marginalized young woman, without wealth, marital status or social importance, and her elevation, is mirrored in the new world order described later in her song. In Mary, we see every woman who has had to endure exclusion, who has found herself alone and frightened, who has had nowhere else to go and who is at the mercy of her community's judgement. In Mary's meeting with Elizabeth, we see the evidence of a double miracle: an impossible birth is the gift given to both women. Elizabeth had been told she could never have children, and Mary had not yet had sexual relations with her husband Joseph. This is a difficult passage to read for those who are unable to have children biologically, and challenges our understanding of science. Read sensitively, the passage is not meant to condemn or isolate those who have had the emotional and difficult challenges of fertility treatment. And the miracle does not make a mockery of this lived reality. Rather, the power and potential of God urges us to believe still that God can do great things, and that these great things are often related to things that we do not believe are possible; these great things can be seen in our own lives.

Say goodbye to the status quo

In this passage, we hear echoes of the Hebrew Scriptures. As Eric Franklin writes:

Mary's song is strongly influenced by that of Hannah in 1 Samuel 2.1–10 which, celebrating the birth of the young Samuel, sees the wonder of God's action in this event as an illustration of the nature of God's whole work for his people.[72]

The work for the people of God means that things cannot stay as they are. There will be some radical shifting of the status quo that will have a direct impact on the proud, the powerful and the rich. Now, if you are in one of these groups, this is a sober read. What can you do? How can you respond? Well, you can join in this work, the work to make the world different and better. And if you don't join in, Mary's song reveals to us that the work will happen anyway. The world will be transformed because the way things are is not a reflection of our potential as children of God. The power and potential of God seek a world in balance and one in which justice is the centre. Social stratification is revised with equity as its framework. God does this as part of a reordering for the amelioration of the whole world, not for a select group or the privileged minority.

The faithful promises

In this Gospel extract we see the power and potential of God to be consistent in God's promises, and to be constant in the expectation of something better from us. God's promises to humankind as presented in the person of Jesus Christ are about freedom, grace and hope. In Mary's words, we see that these promises are ancient. Yet the promises are still valid for us today. We can turn to God and see a constancy that moves us towards a faithful companionship with our divine maker. God made us, and then God did not abandon us. In the same way that God walked with Mary and Elizabeth, against all odds, God walks with us now. The God who calls us is faithful not because we are faithful back but because God has the power and potential to keep waiting for us to let God's promises be fulfilled in and through us. Mary's decision to respond to the request from God reminds us that the choice very much remains ours. Our God is patient and persistent in love. Our lives are made to respond to that love.

Mariama Ifode-Blease

Hymn suggestions

Tell out my soul; God of creation, there at the start (So Will I, Hillsong); Heaven shall not wait; Hildegard von Bingen's Marian antiphon Quia ergo femina.

St Bartholomew the Apostle 24 August
(or transferred to 25 August)
Being Chosen

Isa. 43.8–13, *or* Acts 5.12–16; Ps. 145.1–7; Acts 5.12–16 (*if the Acts reading is used instead of the Old Testament reading, the New Testament reading is* 1 Cor. 4.9–15); **Luke 22.24–30**

Reserved seats

Attending an ordination of a friend of mine many years ago in Ely Cathedral, I asked a person in one of the seats if the seat next to her was taken. She replied that it wasn't, and then went on to say: 'There are no reserved seats in heaven.' I love that. When a seat is reserved, I suppose that we have a sense that somehow that person must be important or significant, at least at major events or services. Monarchs and archbishops don't generally have to search for a seat. Their seating is mostly prominent and set aside.

Self-worth

I am fortunate to have the privilege of deep conversations with people about their faith. What frequently surprises me is that both clergy and laity alike often do not have a sense that God loves them. Really loves them. That they are beautiful in God's eyes. I wonder if you know that, or more importantly if you have ever experienced that? At the heart of the Christian faith is the given that each and every one of us is loved by God with a love beyond our imagining. That he delights in us. After all, we are his creation.

Chosen

I recently officiated at an emotionally very demanding funeral, where the deceased had died at a young age, leaving behind his husband and their adopted son. The son spoke at the funeral and his words were heartbreakingly painful. One of the things he said was, 'And how could I not love you, since you chose me?' I had never thought of adoption like that before. A sense of being the chosen one. Jesus says in John's Gospel (15.16), 'You did not choose me but I chose you.' As we celebrate the life and witness of St Bartholomew today, we recognize that he was called and chosen by God and that each of us too is called and chosen by him. This is recognized in the confirmation liturgy when the bishop says, 'God has called you by name and made you his own.'

Power

Today's Gospel reading follows straight after the story of the Passover meal that Jesus had just shared with his 12 disciples. At that meal, Jesus spoke of the coming of his kingdom and of the one who was to betray him. It is after that, that the passage we have today falls. What follows is a vying for power among the disciples. Is that because they are feeling insecure about who is the betrayer? Or are they simply after the best seats in the kingdom? Or is it a bit of both? In 30 years of ordained ministry, my experience has been that almost every church argument is at the end of the day about power. Nothing changes! But I would also observe that that need for power generally comes out of insecurity: out of a lack of sense of self-worth and of being valued. I would suggest that when we know how much God loves and adores us, simply because we exist (not through what we achieve or do), then the need for reserved seats and status slips away.

Failure

Having said before this Gospel passage that someone would betray him, Jesus goes on, after today's reading, to make clear that Peter too will mess up big time. There is no romanticized version of discipleship. It comes with and through failure written into it. It is deeply counter-cultural, as St Paul so eloquently puts it in today's Epistle. St Bartholomew himself, of whom we know so little, is said to have undergone the most gruesome of deaths, being flayed alive. But his status does not lie in that alone: it lies in him being called and chosen; of being a faithful friend to the one who called, even to death. This raises some interesting questions for us, I would suggest. Do I know (and have I experienced) myself loved by God? If so, am I happy just to be myself, and not to have to strive for a sense of worth through status, work or privilege? Do I know deep down that I am called and chosen? That God knows me by name? If I do, how then can I witness, like St Bartholomew, to that love in my day-to-day life, as a true servant of my Lord and saviour, Jesus Christ?

Jonathan Lawson

Hymn suggestions

Saints of God! Lo, Jesu's people; O Lord, all the world belongs to you; For all thy saints, O Lord; The eternal gifts of Christ the King.

Holy Cross Day   14 September
(or transferred to 15 September)
The Crucified God
Num. 21.4–9; Ps. 22.23–28; **Phil. 2.6–11**; John 3.13–17

'Though he was in the form of God … [he] emptied himself.'

This passage in Philippians is thought to have originated as a very early Christian hymn. The verses tell of a God who willingly, freely, surrendered all, emptied himself and became a slave for this world, even to death on the cross. They sing of his glorious raising up and ascension to the highest place. He is there for us. The one who descended to the depths now reigns as the risen Lord of all.

Making space

Medieval theologians loved a good debate. One question that stretched their understanding more than most was this one. If God is everywhere, filling all things with his presence, how is there any room for this world to exist, let alone you and me? Their solution was wonderfully imaginative. They decided God must make this space for us by doing the equivalent of sucking in his stomach!

But this hymn in Philippians sings of a God who does far more than hold his breath to make a bit of room. He pours out his very being, and utterly empties himself for us. The life we are given is this vast, generous space he creates through his free and utter self-sacrifice. In the Hebrew language the root of the word 'to save' literally means to be brought into a 'broad place'.

In Christ

In the corner of the room where I pray, I have a small wooden cross, made for me by a friend. It is unusual. It is not an empty cross. Nor is it a traditional crucifix with the figure of Jesus stretched across it. Instead, the cross is formed by bringing together two jagged pieces of wood. The space between the meeting of the two pieces reveals the shape of a painfully contorted figure. His arms are thrust wide and deep into the two sides, making them complete and whole. Jesus, the crucified one, is present in the empty space in the midst. I love that image of the cross. There, amid broken and sharply fractured pieces, Christ has emptied himself. He makes a gift of himself as a hospitable space in which our lives may grow and flourish in his love and mercy. This is what it means to be 'in Christ'.

Not clinging

The opening verses of the hymn are a bit puzzling. 'Though he was in the form of God, he did not regard equality with God as something to be exploited' or grasped. But why would he even want to exploit? Would it even cross his mind? He is God. He has no need. He dwells in fullness.

A more helpful translation would be something like this – '*simply because* he was in the form of God', he did not cling to equality with God. It is not in God's nature to be possessive. To be like God is not to grasp, cling or possess. Even to us and our world. That means that on the cross when Jesus empties himself, takes human flesh and gives himself up to death, he is not making some extra special effort, stepping out of character to save the world after all else has failed. On the cross, Jesus is just being himself. This is how God loves. And it always is.

The dance of love

One way the life of God can be imagined is as a circle dance. A circle dance is an endless flow in and out of people, holding and letting go. There is no clinging. The Holy Trinity flow in and out of each other in a divine dance of pure gift. Each freely poured out for the endless joy, love and delight of the other. And like all circle dances, others can be drawn in. Someone grabs your hand. The circle expands. All are welcome.

This is the dance of heaven. Costing not less than everything. One way of imagining the cross is to picture those outstretched arms of Jesus' reaching out to take our hands and draw us into that ever-expanding circle of love. The dance is not complete until we join it. And all are welcome.

Our calling is simply to take others by the hand and invite them into the dance. To teach other voices to sing this hymn of divine love. That every heart will turn from the lifeless clinging and possessing and receive what is simply gift. That every life would be caught up in the endless, joyful dance of the life of God.

David Runcorn

Hymn suggestions

When I survey the wondrous cross; Glory be to Jesus; Jesus shall take the highest honour; Meekness and majesty.

St Matthew, Apostle and Evangelist 21 September
(or transferred to 22 September)
Changing Perspective
Prov. 3.13–18; Ps. 119.65–72; 2 Cor. 4.1–6; **Matt. 9.9–13**

It began as an ordinary working day

Matthew sits in his booth, minding his own business. From his geographical position in Capernaum, he appears to be a customs officer, collecting tolls as people cross the borders. He is viewed as a 'tax-collector' and by association a Roman collaborator, certainly no friend of the Jewish people, by working for the occupying forces. Perhaps he calls out 'next' and looks up to see who is waiting in line.

The man standing in front of him does not look prepared to hand over any amount of money or paperwork. In fact, the man in front of his booth looks nothing like the usual array of businessmen and trade, ready to wrangle over the amount owed. The man standing in front of him simply says two words: 'Follow me.'

Matthew's perspective changes. It moves from money to Messiah – although Matthew would come to name Jesus as such much later in his story. But in this moment, when Matthew could have laughed at Jesus or shrugged him off, and returned to his ledger and his profits, Matthew stands up. He leaves behind the tally and the toll sheet. He follows Jesus, literally.

Perhaps Matthew had been assessing his own life choices and future. Perhaps he had heard rumours of Jesus, his teaching and his ministry, which seemed to throw into question the morals around working for the oppressors. Jesus' apparent preference for the poor and those on the margins seems to resonate with Matthew in a deep way. He gets up, and he follows, without a word or hesitation. He changes his perspective.

From workplace to home

Matthew and Jesus enter a house and eat together, along with others considered on the margins by the religious systems and gatekeepers of the time – tax-collectors and sinners. Whose house is this? It could be the house where Jesus bases himself when he comes to the region, in which case he is willingly host to people who should not be his guests, according to the Jewish food laws. It is said to be Matthew's house (Luke's Gospel), in which case Matthew is going out on a risky limb by inviting Jesus in, and Jesus is taking an equal risk by accepting and eating with him.

The criticisms begin – in a passive-aggressive way – when the critics question the disciples and not Jesus directly. 'Why does *your* teacher …?' (emphasis mine). The critics distance themselves from Jesus. Their perspective is directly at odds with the scene they observe. Jesus, a teacher, should know better than to mix and eat with these people. Why is he doing this?

Challenging the perspective

The critics have categorized the dinner guests as other, as people clearly in need of divine intervention and certainly judgement. Jesus agrees – they are in need of God. They are sinners. They need a physician. Here, in this house, at this meal, they are eating with their physician. Eating and talking with no hint of divine condemnation or judgement. Jesus models to his church the simplicity of sharing himself with the very people the system would dismiss.

Here is our first opportunity to change our perspective. Who are we pushing to the margins, when we should be sitting down and eating with them?

It is interesting to notice what is not being said in the conversation around the table. While acknowledging that the dinner guests are sinners, and being fully aware of Matthew's job, at no point does Jesus tell them they need to repent and be forgiven. He invites Matthew to follow. He doesn't mention corruption and political betrayal. Jesus doesn't insist that the other guests change their sinful lifestyles before eating. They simply sit together, eat together and talk together.

Here is our second opportunity to change our perspective. Are we quick to judge others and preach repentance when what people really need is our presence?

Jesus answers his critics directly, not through the disciples as mediators. He cuts straight through the attempt to sow dissension in the hearts of the disciples by speaking directly to the critics. How often does indirect grumbling about the leadership cause heartache in church communities, and risk causing division and hurt?

Here is our third opportunity to change our perspective. Are we the ones who complain indirectly about our leaders? Are we hearing the 'people are saying' comments and feeling disturbed by complaints? Can we change the perspective and model transparency and honesty in our conversations and criticism?

The story of Matthew's call is an invitation to change our perspective. To stop, stand up and follow.

Kt Tupling

Hymn suggestions

Will you come and follow me; Take my life and let it be; I will offer up my life; In the Lord I'll be ever thankful (Taizé).

St Michael and All Angels 29 September
Fig Trees and Ladders
Gen. 28.10–17, *or* Rev. 12.7–12; Ps. 103.19–end; Rev. 12.7–12, *or* Heb. 1.5–end; **John 1.47–end**

Today's Scripture reading describes Jesus' initial encounter with one of his disciples, Nathanael. Up until this point, other disciples such as Andrew and Peter have come to Jesus eagerly, actively seeking him out. Nathanael on the other hand, is not seeking Jesus at all. Immediately before our passage begins, we hear Nathanael say, referring to Jesus, 'Can anything good come out of Nazareth?' to which a newly recruited disciple called Philip responds, 'Come and see' (John 1.46). This lead-in provides important context for what unfolds next.

Jesus and the sceptics

Jesus sees Nathanael coming towards him and says, 'Here is truly an Israelite in whom there is no deceit!' The first thing to realize is that Jesus is not complimenting Nathanael on his integrity. Jesus is actually being sarcastic. The exclamation mark in the text gives us a clue. Jesus is engaging in a bit of playful banter with Nathanael.

The word 'Israelite' means 'One who can see God'. Jesus is very aware of Nathanael's cynicism, but instead of trying to win him over with a convincing argument, he switches tack and says, 'Here is a man who can see God', and not only that but 'an Israelite in whom there is no deceit'. Through this playful exchange, Jesus places Nathanael higher than their forefather Jacob, who had once been a deceitful man. Jesus is laying the sarcasm on thick.

And you know what? It works. Nathanael is intrigued and says, 'Where did you come to know me?' A dialogue opens up between him and Jesus. Philip dared to say three simple words, 'Come and see', and Jesus does the rest. What an encouragement for those of us praying for family and friends who remain sceptical of our faith.

Jesus speaks to our hearts

Having captured Nathanael's attention, Jesus says, 'I saw you under the fig tree before Philip called you.' There has been much debate as to whether Nathanael was actually sitting under a fig tree. Whether he was or not is not important. What is important is the imagery that a fig tree evokes for Nathanael. It is a fig tree that provided Adam and Eve with the leaves they used to hide from God and one another (Gen. 3.7). It is a fig tree that Jesus later cursed for producing no fruit or signs of life (Matt. 21.18). The image of a fig tree speaks profoundly to Nathaniel because he has been hiding from God all along too. He has been feeling spiritually dead.

Scepticism and cynicism can often become our preferred hiding places, and yet they are not fruitful. They prevent us from engaging with God, ourselves, others and creation fully. This is what had happened to Nathanael, and Jesus calls it out. He sees deeply into his heart.

Jesus informs Nathanael that he saw him before Philip did. In other words, Jesus is saying he has known Nathanael from the very beginning. This is a powerful realization for Nathanael. It is also an encouragement for us to know that Jesus is watching over our loved ones too. Nathanael's eyes are opened, and he declares, 'Rabbi, you are the Son of God! You are the King of Israel!'

Jesus has come for all

Now that Nathanael's eyes have been opened, Jesus says he will see even greater things, and adds, 'Very truly, I tell you, you will see heaven opened and the angels of God ascending and descending upon the Son of Man.'

If you recall, Jesus has already compared Nathanael to Jacob during their opening exchange. Jesus refers to Jacob again, specifically the dream he had in Genesis 28, about a ladder connecting heaven and earth with angels going up and down it.

In the old vision, the ladder connecting heaven and earth was a sign that God would give the land to Jacob's people, Israel. But here, Jesus changes the words slightly and invites Nathanael to see something completely different. In this new vision, there is no ladder. Instead, the angels ascend and descend upon 'the Son of Man'. Jesus is revealing to Nathanael that it is himself, the Son of Man, who is the link between the Father and all of humankind. No longer is God's grace constrained by geographical boundaries or to a particular race or people group. Jesus has come so that all people may have access to the Father. His grace is for everyone.

No one at that time had conceived God like this before. This is the great truth that Jesus revealed to Nathanael that day. Nathanael 'the sceptic' was the first person Jesus revealed this great eternal and global truth to. This is how three small words uttered by Philip, 'Come and see', changed Nathanael's life, and can still change lives today.

Mark Nam

Hymn suggestions

At the name of Jesus; Lord Jesus Christ, you have come to us; Lo! He comes with clouds ascending; Jesus is Lord, creation's voice proclaims it.

St Luke the Evangelist 18 October
The Healing and Wholeness of God
Isa. 35.3–6, *or* Acts 16.6–12a; Ps. 147.1–7; 2 Tim. 4.5–17; **Luke 10.1–9**

What good is the church anyway? For those outside our walls looking in, the answer to this question often shapes their perception of Christian communities. While there's plenty of criticism levelled at churches as national institutions, at a local level it is much easier to find the good news stories.

Traditional projects like soup runs and toddler groups may have run for decades, but in recent years the response of churches to the practical needs of their communities has exploded in myriad directions. Food banks are joined by clothing banks and baby banks. Halls and meeting rooms are open as warm spaces for those struggling to heat their homes. From lunch clubs to night shelters, and community cafes to debt advice services, Christians are doing an awful lot of good in these tough times.

Seeing the need

Today we celebrate St Luke, the doctor and evangelist, and reflect on all the ways that the church is called to offer healing and wholeness to those who need it: physically, socially, emotionally, mentally and spiritually. The imperative to do so is woven through Scripture. Isaiah says, 'Strengthen the weak hands, and make firm the feeble knees.' Jesus instructs his disciples, 'Whenever you enter a town and its people welcome you, eat what is set before you; cure the sick who are there, and say to them, "The kingdom of God has come near to you."'

In Isaiah's day, in Jesus' day and in our own day, there is great need. People are searching and suffering. Physical health and other kinds of well-being don't exist in separate spheres; loneliness, isolation and lack of hope make a big impact on the whole person. So, our aim should be that every time someone comes into contact with our own church, whether for worship or through outreach activity, they are made more 'well' by the time they leave. Human connection, genuine warmth, the building of friendships, offers of prayer, practical support, and the chance to discover faith in Jesus: all of these are ways in which the kingdom of God comes near to those we meet.

Wounded for our healing

But today's readings are not simply a demand that we 'do more'.

I hope that's good news. The work of healing in all its forms can be exhausting, can't it? People are living longer and the numbers in need of pastoral support seem only to grow. Public services are being cut down and the battle for funding intensifies. Volunteers are overstretched and our energy is limited – it's no surprise if you're feeling weary.

The answer is not for us to work ever harder, because healing is not our work. Since the first sin of the first people tore a great gash in the world as it was meant to be, when relationships were ruined, labour became a struggle, life was cut short and death began to reign, from that moment God began the work of healing. God's business has always been restoration. Wholeness. Life. When we trace the salvation story of the Bible, we see how God over and over again ministers to his people, binds up their wounds, steadies their feet and breathes new life into dry bones, until we find the culmination of that work in Jesus. The one who was wounded for our healing, broken for our wholeness and raised to life to bring us with him to eternal life.

Filling up on grace

That redemption and healing is not just for the people we serve in our social action projects. It's for us. It's for us who have messy, chaotic lives, and it's for us who like to think we've got it all together. The people of God are never meant to be the saviours. Rather, we're to say to one another: 'Be strong, do not fear! Here is your God … He will come and save you.' Only then will blindness scatter, and only then will deaf ears be unstopped. Only as God works in us will our healing ministry flourish and have a positive, powerful impact on those we seek to serve.

You can't pour from an empty vessel, as the old saying goes. Before we can be any good to other people, we too need to be filled again and again with the grace that God offers, bringing to him our own aches, our tiredness, our wounds and our pain.

Whether in our bodies, minds or spirit – whether relationships, anxieties, fears or temptations – we're invited to lay them all before God for his work to be done in us, so that our weak hands can be strengthened and our feeble knees made firm.

Take this moment to ask God to strengthen and steady you, and to deepen his healing work in each area of your life day by day. Then you will be ever more ready to see wounds bound up and hope restored, through God's saving power at work and you as his instrument of healing.

Claire Jones

Hymn suggestions

What a friend we have in Jesus; Jesus Christ is waiting; Beauty for brokenness; O for a thousand tongues to sing.

SS Simon and Jude, Apostles 28 October
So that You May Love
Isa. 28.14–16; Ps. 119.89–96; Eph. 2.19–end; **John 15.17–end**

In March 1963 at the Lincoln Memorial in Washington DC, Martin Luther King Jr stood to address a crowd of over 250,000 protest marchers. Some time into the speech, Mahalia Jackson, a gospel singer standing in the wings of the stage, could tell that things were not going well. She whispered to King, 'Tell 'em about the dream, Martin.' He began to speak: 'I have a dream …'[73] Most of us will be familiar with that speech. I wonder, though, how many are familiar with the story behind it. Without Mahalia Jackson, there might have been no speech, no 'I have a dream', one of the most powerful speeches ever given.

Why tell you that story?

Celebrating the little known

Today, we celebrate two other little-known, even unknown, men of the church, St Simon and St Jude. Perhaps you remember St Jude as the patron saint of lost causes. Perhaps you even know St Simon as the patron saint of tanners and woodworkers. When I researched these men, one source simply told me who they were not: Simon, not the well known; Jude, not that Judas. We don't really know about them. And yet the church has decided they merit a feast day between them.

Why celebrate them?

The bones of the story, as far as we can tell, are that St Jude went to Mesopotamia and St Simon went to Egypt as pioneers of the early church in those regions. They met and went together to Persia, where they were martyred. They are not big heroes of the faith. Probably others did similar things who don't even get half a feast day. The question remains, 'Why them?'

Earlier in John's Gospel, Jude asks Jesus a very important question: 'How is it you will reveal yourself to us and not to the world?' Perhaps another way of putting it is, 'How will we know?'

'How will we know?'

In today's Gospel reading, Jesus gives some of the answer. You will know because the world will hate you. You will know because you will be content even when you are treated badly. You will know because you will witness to me. Mainly, though, these are indications of the main thing. 'I am giving you these commands so that you might love one another,' Jesus says. Imagine what that means.

'Tell them about the dream.' You will tell others about the dream of a place where everyone is equal, where structures of political and social power and privilege are resisted. Where nobody expects to be treated better than even their master. Tell them about the dream. Tell them about loving one another.

Perhaps that is what Simon and Jude did. They preached the gospel, and they explained how God loves people and therefore we should love each other. They shared the dream of love.

And they died for it because the 'world' hates a message where the powerful are only equal to the oppressed. The 'world' hates a message where love trumps power and judgement. So why remember St Simon and St Jude?

Dreams are powerful, love is greater

Martin Luther King's speech in 1963 was powerless and unmemorable at first. It is full of reasoned argument and erudite words. That is not the memorable bit. That is not the bit that has inspired generations of people concerned for justice. The speech changed entirely when King spoke those famous words, 'I have a dream …' I think the gospel changes, too, when we remember Jesus' words, 'That you may love.' Perhaps what we need to know about St Simon and

St Jude is not where they were or what they preached, but the very fact that they are little known, yet the churches they helped found in ancient Persia are some of the oldest Christian churches in the world.

Dreams, as we know from the story of Martin Luther King, are powerful. Love is greater still. When Jude asks, 'How will we know?' the answer is love. How will we know, as individuals, that this is what we should do? If it is motivated by love, then it is. How will we know as a church what is the right thing to do? Love will be at the heart of it. Whether it is a local decision or a national decision, surely the right decision shows love.

These two men, defined in at least one commentary as 'not' something, are remembered because they loved enough to give their lives. When you are tempted to think of yourself as not – not as good, not as smart, not as well known – as someone else, remember that all you have to do to be celebrated in God's kin-dom is to love.

Liz Shercliff

Hymn suggestions

A little bit of love goes a long, long way; The people wanted soldiers (Graham Adams); We seek your kingdom; Heal our land.

All Saints' Day   1 November
(or transferred to 2 November)
A Chain of Blessedness

Dan. 7.1–3, 15–18; Ps. 149; Eph. 1.11–end; **Luke 6.20–31**

From there to here

How did we get here? I don't mean, did you get the bus or walk to church today! But, have you ever stopped to think just how extraordinary it is, that over 2,000 years later, and more than 2,000 miles away, we are here, today, gathered in this place, in this building, doing our best to follow Jesus? How did that happen?

Well, one answer is through an unbroken chain of Christians. Each of us will have been taught the faith by others, who were taught by others, who in turn were taught by others – stretching right back to the first followers of Jesus. More of a web, perhaps! In that chain, or web, will be those who built this church, those who translated the Bible into English, those who brought the Christian faith to this country, and those who faithfully prayed, worshipped and lived out the faith as an example to those around them. The saints. And they connect us back to the start, which is where we find ourselves in today's Gospel.

The very beginning

Today's passage from Luke is very early in Jesus' ministry. Jesus has been preaching in the synagogues and gathering disciples, healing people and having a couple of skirmishes with the Pharisees. After a night of prayer on the mountain he has come back and chosen 12 apostles from among his disciples, and we find him on a level place where he has been healing the crowds. And now he speaks, not to the crowds but to the disciples. This is Jesus' very first teaching in Luke that is addressed specifically to the disciples and among them the apostles. And these disciples are the ones at the other end of that chain of saints that stretches across the centuries and the miles.

So where does Jesus start? What does he teach them? He begins by teaching them who the blessed ones are. Unlike Matthew's Gospel with eight beatitudes or blessings, in Luke we have four blessings paired with four woes, each flipped to give its opposite. Those counted among the blessed are the poor, those who hunger now, those who weep, those who are excluded and reviled for Jesus' sake; woe is promised to those who are rich, who are full, who laugh, who are spoken well of. I wonder which group Jesus' first listeners most identified with – poor, hungry, weeping and excluded, or rich, full, laughing and well regarded? I wonder which is a better description of our church today?

Where God is closest

However neat Luke's pairings are, though, it is probably a bit of a false dichotomy to pigeonhole people in one group or the other. After all, those who are hungry have fullness to look forward to, and those who weep are promised laughter. Neither are the woes a suggestion that God will curse or punish those who are full of emptiness, or those who are laughing with weeping. Our lives have many seasons and in our churches will be people in seasons of sorrow and people in seasons of joy; people in times of lack and in times of plenty. But what Jesus tells his disciples is a truth that has played out over the generations, the centuries, the millennia between the time of his first teaching in that level place, and where we are here and now. When we feel satisfied by the things of this life, we tend to rely less on God and are less open to God's transformative power. But when we stare poverty, hunger and weeping in the face, that is often when we feel God is closest, when we somehow understand most deeply how God has blessed us.

God's deepest blessing in the depths

When we think about the saints – the ordinary everyday faithful Christians as well as the ones with a capital S – the stories that inspire us most aren't stories of material riches, fame or worldly success. It's the stories of people who endured hardship, persecution or suffering and who found God's deepest blessings in the depths, and lived the rest of their lives in the light of that learning. This is the first lesson Jesus taught to his disciples and they came face to face with this reality as he was crucified. This is the lesson learned by Christian after Christian in the unbroken chain of witness that stretches from them to us. And this is the lesson we continue to learn in our lives today. Blessedness isn't to be found in riches or reputation. It is in our deepest need for God that we find ourselves most deeply blessed.

Kat Campion-Spall

Hymn suggestions

Blessed are those whose hearts are gentle; Blest are the pure in heart; For all the saints; Ye watchers and ye holy ones.

Commemoration of the Faithful Departed
(All Souls' Day)   2 November
In the Hand of God
Lam. 3.17–26, 31–33, *or* **Wisd. 3.1–9**; Ps. 23, *or* Ps. 27.1–6, 16–end; Rom. 5.5–11, *or* 1 Peter 1.3–9; John 5.19–25, *or* **John 6.37–40**

A vision of love

> Our Lord … showed me a little thing, the size of a hazel-nut, lying in the palm of my hand … I looked at it and thought, 'What can this be?' And the answer came to me, 'It is all that is made.' I wondered how it could last, for it was so small I thought it might suddenly disappear. And the answer in my mind was, 'It lasts and will last forever because God loves it; and in the same way everything exists through the love of God.'[74]

Julian of Norwich had this vision on what she believed at the time to be her deathbed, in 1373, which she later recorded in her book *Revelations of Divine Love*. It's an image that perfectly captures our fragility and even insignificance as humans, and God's perfect love for each of us despite all that.

Facing fragility

When someone close to us dies, we come face to face with human fragility. The fragility of the loved one whose life ends – and while we may have a medical explanation for it, it will often feel inexplicable that someone could so easily pass from life to death.

But we also face our own fragility, both as we have to confront the possibility of our own death in a new way and as we have to come to terms with how our world is shaken by the absence of that person who has been so much part of our life.

The death of someone we love can leave us feeling as if we are in a different world. The things we had taken for granted before suddenly seem much less reliable. Mother Julian's words capture that: 'I wondered how it could last, for it was so small I thought it might suddenly disappear.' It can feel as if the solid ground has disappeared from under our feet and our certainties are no longer certain.

Our reading from Wisdom also talks about the shock of someone dying: 'their departure was thought to be a disaster,' we heard. It is so important to acknowledge these experiences; the struggles of bereavement that often last far longer than people expect. Even if we knew that the person was approaching death, and we had a chance to say goodbye, it can feel like a disaster – the world has changed, and it can be hard to find our way. When someone dies suddenly or at a younger age than we might expect, bereavement can be even more complex and painful.

Held and sustained by God

But both our passage from Wisdom and Mother Julian's image put this into a bigger context. 'The souls of the righteous are in the hand of God,' we are told, '… they are at peace.' And this finds a parallel in Mother Julian's vision of all that is made appearing as small and as fragile as a hazelnut in the palm of her hand, and yet 'it lasts and will last forever because God loves it'.

None of us, living or dead, is too small or too insignificant to be noticed and held and loved and sustained by God. To be in God's hand is to be in a place of peace, of safety, of love. And that sense of being gently and lovingly gathered together shines through in Jesus' words in our New Testament reading as well;

> Everything that the Father gives me will come to me, and anyone who comes to me I will never drive away … And this is the will of him who sent me, that I should lose nothing of all that he has given me, but raise it up on the last day.

Gathered in by Jesus

Jesus carefully welcomes and gathers everyone who comes to him, in life and in death, without losing anyone. There is a real sense of cherishing there, which goes on beyond this life. This day in the church's calendar is a time set aside particularly to remember those who have died. We are remembering them because we love them – present tense – and we are assured that God loves them, as in our reading from Wisdom, 'the faithful will abide with him in love, because grace and mercy are upon his holy ones'. And as we remember them, you might find it helpful to imagine them in God's hand, safe, at peace, and loved. As we remember them, you might also want to imagine yourself in God's hand. Whatever the mix of emotions you might be feeling and memories you might be carrying, all is held and cherished by God, who has made all things and loves all things.

Kat Campion-Spall

Hymn suggestions

Now the green blade riseth; I heard the voice of Jesus say; Be still, my soul; O love that will not let me go.

Harvest Festival
God's Faithful Provision
Deut. 26.1–11; Ps. 100; Phil. 4.4–9, *or* Rev. 14.14–18; **John 6.25–35**

Harvest. It's easy to understand the importance of this festival when you live and worship in a rural community. Where I live in Norfolk, we're surrounded by working farms. We see farmers at work daily. We understand some of the pressures on them and their families. We witness the changing of the seasons and what's happening on the land. We value our local farm shops. We remember to allow extra time when we're driving anywhere – for the 'tractor factor' – on our country lanes.

Some members of our communities imagine Harvest Festival to be a quaint Victorian throw-back embedded in rural England. An opportunity to sing some well-loved traditional hymns and decorate the church with local produce. But harvest is celebrated all over the world. When I worked in Sudan we celebrated in May when the cotton was harvested. Engagement with today's scriptures reminds us that the celebration of Harvest – the first-fruits – goes back millennia.

God has provided

The book of Deuteronomy sets out the command to celebrate the harvest, to bring to the Lord some of the first produce of the land, to ask for God's blessing and to celebrate God's provision for and with everyone. Notice how the command to celebrate the harvest is given before the Israelites are even in the Promised Land. It says,

'*When* you have come into the land that the Lord your God is giving you.' God's people are given instructions about how to give thanksgiving and enjoy the blessings of the land before they have even got there. Before they've ploughed, sowed or reaped.

The promise is that God will provide and they should trust in that promise and make preparations to celebrate. As they bring the offering into God's house so they are to remember what God has done in the past. They recite a creed that rehearses God's saving acts. They tell the story of Abraham, Egypt, of oppression and liberation. They give the best from their land and then gather everyone together for a party. This party is inclusive. Anyone who is in the land, whether from the clan or not, is welcome. God's grace extends to all. Contained within the harvest celebrations is the recognition that God is to be trusted. God has acted in the past, has provided and can be trusted to do so in the future. That provision is for all.

God is providing

Jump forward now to John's Gospel. Jesus is discussing God's continued provision. This comes immediately after the feeding of the 5,000. God has provided for everyone again. The people are intrigued by this man Jesus who can work wonders with food. They've made the connection with Moses giving manna in the wilderness. Jesus reminds them that it's God who provides bread from heaven that gives life to the world. Then he goes on to say the most extraordinary thing: 'I am the bread of life.' 'I am' is the name for God revealed in the Scriptures: 'I AM WHO I AM,' says God to Moses (Ex. 3.14).

Jesus says that whoever comes to him will be fed and satisfied. It's an open invitation. 'Whoever comes' and 'whoever believes' – 'whoever'. There's that grace and generosity again. 'Whoever' is you, whoever is me, whoever is those who've gone before and are yet to come. This is worth celebrating and we do that whenever we share the Eucharist together. Jesus, the bread of life, given for the world. Given for you, that your future with God might be certain and shaped by hope. God has acted in the past. God provided yesterday. God will provide today and tomorrow.

God will provide

And that's what we're doing today. We're remembering back to the roots of our faith. We're recalling that God has provided and will provide. Everything we have comes from God and we give thanks for that by bringing the first fruits here and then letting them go to others more needy than ourselves. We're acting out the belief that all are loved and valued by God. We're longing for a better world, one where there is justice and equality, one where no one is homeless, a refugee or a victim of war. One where no one is hungry, cold, lonely or afraid. We recognize that in Jesus God gives Godself to us. We receive that gift for the strengthening and healing of our bodies and souls, for the healing of the church, the healing of our community, for the healing of the nations, and for the restoration of the cosmos: the harvest of everyone for all time.

God has provided
God is providing.
God will provide.

Catherine Williams

Hymn suggestions

For the fruit of all creation; Great is thy faithfulness; All creatures of our God and king; Morning has broken.

All-Age Services

Palm Sunday 13 April
When the Cheering Stops Will You Stay?
Liturgy of the Palms: **Luke 19.28–40**; Ps. 118.1–2, 19–end [*or* 118.19–end]

Preparation

For this Palm Sunday all-age talk, you need enough 'palms' for everyone, made by cutting large leaf shapes from green paper. In many places, the whole of the Passion narrative might be read, and older children, in particular, might enjoy being part of a dramatic reading. In such cases, a 'talk' might not be necessary. However, this talk would fit well with a shorter service, where only the Liturgy of the Palms is read, but where you want to introduce the congregation to the events that will be remembered during Holy Week.

Script

Today is Palm Sunday and the crowds have gathered. Gathered because they think a new king is coming. A new king, who might just be Jesus. The one whom they've followed. listened to and watched as miracles have been performed. The one about whom word has spread.

The hopeful crowd

As the crowds gather, filled with expectation, suddenly, there is Jesus, riding through them. Reminding the hopeful crowds of the prophecy of Zechariah; that their king will come to them, triumphant and victorious, and yet also humble and riding on a donkey.

As Jesus descends the long road down from the Mount of Olives, cloaks and branches are thrown down in front of him, and the cries go up; the air is filled with cheering and praise: 'Blessed is the king who comes in the name of the Lord!' 'Peace in heaven and glory in the highest heaven!'

In the accounts in Matthew and Mark, the crowd also shouted 'Hosanna!', which means 'Save now!'

I wonder, have you ever been in such a crowd?

A crowd, lining the streets, filled with hope and expectation, almost like a party?

(*Hear any responses to that question; which might include things like a Coronation procession, a Jubilee street party or an Olympic torch relay. Bring out what these different events might have in common.*

Then create such an atmosphere, bring everyone together down the aisle, and use the paper palms to shout and cheer 'Hosanna'.)

The crowd that deserts

But then the singing stops.

Palms are tossed forlorn by the side of the road and cloaks are gathered up hastily. The people wander off in twos and threes, just half a glance over their shoulders as they go.

The crowds fade away.

(*Encourage everyone to throw their palms at random on the floor, and to spread back out around the church.*)

I wonder why they left so quickly?

(*Either solicit answers or share a few examples as follows.*)

Maybe, because they've just arrived in Jerusalem, they need to find somewhere to stay?

Maybe they're hungry and need something to eat, or they want to find and meet up with the family and friends from whom they've become separated on the road?

Or maybe they've seen the menacing glare of the priests, and they are scared, deciding it's better to fade away? The crowds were part of one of the most important moments in history, and then they walk away, and all is quiet.

Perhaps you have also had moments like that. Times when you have been filled with hope and expectation, and then you've needed to walk away, disappointed and unsure.

(*Give some space for people to think about their response, or to talk with their neighbour.*)

Staying with Jesus this Holy Week

This week, we begin Holy Week, probably the most important week of our entire Christian year. It is a week filled with highs and lows; times when the people wave their palms and shout 'Hosanna', and times when they quickly disappear, where the one who rode triumphantly into Jerusalem is left alone as people saunter off, run off or just fall asleep.

It is a week that we walk with Jesus, the son of David, the one who comes in the name of the Lord. A week where we try to stay attentive, not throwing our palms on the ground, but sticking around, using all our senses; to smell the fragrance of costly nard; feel our feet washed with water; taste the bread and wine; hear the cock crow; and know in our hearts the pain of the one we loved being crucified on the cross. It is a week we walk together as a church and in our homes, until we reach the joy of Easter Day.

So go and pick up those palms again.

As you hold your palm, commit yourself to staying with Jesus this week; through all the good bits and the bad bits, the highs and lows of his Passion. Like the disciples, you might not manage it, and it will be hard, but at the start of the week we can at least promise we'll try to stay when the cheering stops.

(*It works well to move straight into a time of prayer, while holding the palm leaf. As well as a prayer for the week ahead, this might include writing prayer intentions onto the leaf. Everyone should then be encouraged to take their leaves home, and to put them somewhere that they will notice them each day of Holy Week.*)

Chris Campbell

Hymn suggestions

All glory, laud and honour; Make way, make way for Christ the King; There's a man riding in on a donkey; We have a King who rides a donkey.

Pentecost 8 June
Empowered by the Holy Spirit

Acts 2.1–21 (*must be used as either the first or second reading*), *or* Gen. 11.1–9; Ps. 104.26–36, 37b [*or* 104.26–end]; Rom. 8.14–17; John 14.8–17 [25–27]

Preparation

For this, you'll need flash paper, which is paper coated in chemicals that burns up totally with a bright flame. It's available via online magic shops. You'll need matches and something safe to burn the paper on (e.g. a cooking tray or Pyrex bowl). As it produces fire, there is always a potential danger in using flash paper, and you should make sure you've practised using it, have an adequate risk assessment in place, and have a fire extinguisher close by. Children and young people should stay well back when it is lit. You should also read storage instructions for flash paper carefully. You'll also need some 'gifts of the Holy Spirit', written on pieces of (preferably red or orange) card.

An optional extra for this talk is a 'dove pan', also available from magic stores. This is a more expensive item, so only suitable if you can borrow one, but can produce an added 'wow' factor. If using this, you do nearly everything the same, but when you burn the flash paper, do so in the bottom section of the pan, before putting on the lid. Have the 'gifts of spirit' ready in the top section, so that when you lift the lid again they are magically revealed!

Script

I wonder if you have ever had to do a very big thing that you thought was totally beyond you?

(*Allow some time for answers.*)

Ten days ago, we celebrated the ascension; and before Jesus was lifted up from his disciples, he commissioned them, to be his 'witnesses in Jerusalem, in all Judea and Samaria, and to the ends of the earth' (Acts 1.8). Imagine that. It feels like a very big thing, and even if we assume the group is larger than the original 12 disciples, it seems like an impossible job for such a small number. No wonder they were left looking at the sky, wondering how they were going to get started! Maybe you've felt like that before too.

(Talk to the congregation more about how the disciples must have felt, and the negative feelings that we sometimes have when faced with a big task; things like fear, inadequacy and worry. You could remind them of the disciples hiding in locked rooms after Jesus' death, and how they kept trying to return to the jobs they knew, like fishing. Then write some of those things on the flash paper. Once you've finished, put the words in a fire-proof bowl or tray, or, if you have one, into the bottom pan of the dove pan.)

The coming of the Holy Spirit

But before Jesus ascended, he had made the disciples a promise. He told them that the Holy Spirit would come and that they would be clothed with power from on high.

Since the ascension, the disciples have been waiting; Peter and Andrew, James and John, Philip and Thomas, Bartholomew and Matthew, James son of Alphaeus, and Simon the Zealot, and Judas son of James, and Mary the mother of Jesus, and Jesus' brothers, and many other women who don't get named. All waiting to see what this power from high would be like, all waiting to see if it would make a difference to how they feel about the task ahead.

And while they waited, they were constantly in prayer.

(Hold a short time of silence ...)

Then came the day of Pentecost, which we heard about in our reading.

Jesus' friends, all the ones we've named, were together in one place. As they sat, suddenly there came a great wind rushing through the room and tongues of fire appeared over the heads of the disciples. With the wind and the tongues of fire, they were filled with the Holy Spirit.

As they were filled with the Holy Spirit, all their worries about not being good enough for the task ahead disappeared.

(At this point, set fire to the negative words. They will burn away quickly with a flash! Then show the congregation that the words they had written have been all burnt up.)

Not only were their worries gone, but the disciples suddenly found they had both the confidence and ability to do what Jesus had asked them to do. As we heard in the reading, they went rushing out, able to speak in all sorts of languages, so that people from across the world could understand the story, the good news that they were sharing.

The gifts of the Spirit

With the coming of the Holy Spirit and the gifts she imparted, the disciples were inspired and able to be Jesus' witnesses in the world. But the story didn't stop with that first Pentecost.

To this day, the Holy Spirit continues to enable and inspire us to be Jesus' witnesses in the world; burning away our own feelings of inadequacy and the things that hold us back, and instead guiding us to follow God's call on our lives. She gives us strength when we feel exhausted; provides us with words of comfort to those in need; offers us patience to deal with people whom we find difficult; and most of all, gives us the confidence to share God's love with those around us.

So I wonder, what do you need to help you share God's love and God's good news better?

(*Take a few suggestions, then bring out the pre-written 'gifts of the Holy Spirit' cards. Hopefully, some of them will match up with what people need, and you can give them to them. But you can also have some blank cards available, to write on suggestions. If using a dove pan, this is where you can lift the lid, to magically reveal the gifts of the Holy Spirit cards. It then works well to move straight into a time of prayer.*)

Chris Campbell

Hymn suggestions

Holy, Holy, Holy; Spirit of God, unseen as the wind; Spirit of the living God; The Spirit lives to set us free.

Remembrance Sunday 9 November
Stories to Remember

(Readings may be those set for 'In Time of Trouble', 'The Peace of the World', or the Third Sunday before Advent. Readings for 'In Time of Trouble' are used here.)
Gen. 9.8–17; Luke 12.1–7

Preparation

For this Remembrance Sunday all-age talk, it is useful to draw from a story either in your own family or one locally (e.g., from one of those whose name you will remember and read out later in the service). An item from their life helps to give a physical connection to them. As an example, I have shared the story of my grandfather.

During the service, it can be moving to have each individual name that will be remembered written onto a poppy, or cross; this is an activity that could be done with young people in advance, or as they arrive.

Script

In our house, we have a suitcase of stories … family stories … And from it, today, I've brought a very special Bible. It's the Bible that was owned by my grandfather, Geoffrey, and was given to him on his confirmation in 1938. He was 13, the same age as some of you here today. (*Ask who has been given a special gift to mark an occasion like a confirmation, going to a new school, a special birthday …*)

Seven years later, aged only 20, Geoffrey married my granny, Barbara. It was wartime and both were engaged in active service; Geoffrey was a young flight sergeant and Barbara served as a sergeant in the MET office, predicting the weather before the planes went up.

Within a few short weeks of their wedding, Geoffrey was seconded to the Glider Pilot Regiment, to be part of Operation Varsity, the crossing of the Rhine. This operation was the largest ever airborne operation on a single day and place. Ultimately, it was successful, but the loss of life was high. The gliders taking part were a particularly easy target and it has been suggested that 20 to 30 per cent of those fighting in Operation Varsity were killed in action.

My grandfather, Geoffrey, was one of them. Within two months after her wedding day, aged only 21, Barbara was a widow. She was also pregnant, with twins, born near the end of 1945: my dad Geoffrey, named after the father he'd never known, and his brother, Antony.

A day for remembering

Geoffrey's story is just one story from the Second World War. Every year on Remembrance Sunday, we remember many others who, like Geoffrey, gave their lives in war and conflict. Across the country, in churches and at war memorials, we remember the names of those who laid down their lives.

(*At this point, take time to go through some of the names of those who have been killed from your area. If some of the names have been written individually onto poppies or crosses, a few young people could stand up to read them out.*)

But Geoffrey and those whose names we have shared are just a few of the many who died in these two wars. It is estimated that the combined military and civilian deaths from the Second World War was an unimaginable 56 million. Though these numbers seem incalculably large, each of those was a real person, with a real story. Behind each name that is read out, up and down the country today, there was a real human life, filled with success and failures, with birthdays, confirmations and wedding days. Lives full of strength and bravery and kindness and love.

I wonder what stories you have heard and told this week? Maybe from friends and family, maybe in your homes, or maybe in your school assemblies? Whose lives have you remembered?

A covenant in the sky

Our reading today comes from the book of Genesis, right at the beginning of the Bible. It is from the end of the story of Noah's ark. This is often one of our favourite stories, as we hear how Noah built a huge boat, an ark, and filled it with animals. But it is also a sad story, because those who weren't on the ark wouldn't have survived the flood.

At the end of the story, as the waters dry up, and the creatures all emerge on to new land, God makes a covenant with Noah. God tells him that the rainbow in the sky would be a promise, that God would never again send a flood to destroy the earth. It is a sign that they would have remembered for a long time, and Noah's children would have told the story of the flood to their children, who would have passed the story on to their children, who would have …

Through the story and the sign of the rainbow, Noah's family and their descendants would remember what had happened, as well as God's promise to them.

The sign of the poppy

Signs and symbols help us to remember stories, and on Remembrance Sunday we have another one. It's an image that many of us have pinned on our chests today, and which reminds us all of individual stories from times of war and conflict. I wonder if you know what that symbol is?

(*Give young people a chance to respond.*)

The poppy has become a symbol of remembrance, and between that and the stories we tell we keep the past alive. Through them, we remember again the sacrifices made by those who served in war and we never forget the huge cost of conflict. As we pass on the stories, we ensure that history never fades from our hearts; we remember how precious peace still is in the world today.

So, whose story will *you* remember this week?

At the going down of the sun and in the morning,
we will remember them.

Chris Campbell

Hymn suggestions

A new commandment; Hope for the world's despair; I've got peace like a river; Make me a channel of your peace.

Notes

1. *Thoughts and Sentiments on the Evil and Wicked Traffic of the Slavery and Commerce of the Human Species, Humbly Submitted to the Inhabitants of Great Britain by Ottobah Cugoano, a Native of Africa 1787* (New York and London: Penguin Group, 1999).
2. *Thoughts and Sentiments*, p. 109.
3. Rowan Williams, *Silence and Honey Cakes: The Wisdom of the Desert* (Oxford: Lion Books, 2003), p. 98.
4. Gillian Rose, *Love's Work* (New York: New York Review of Books, 1995), p. 2.
5. Dietrich Bonhoeffer, *Letters and Papers from Prison* (London: Collins/Fontana Press, 1959), p. 48.
6. W. B. Yeats, 'The Second Coming', first published in *The Dial*, 1920.
7. The Collect for the First Sunday of Advent, The Book of Common Prayer 1662 (Cambridge University Press).
8. Immanuel Kant, *Idea for a Universal History with a Cosmopolitan Purpose* (Cambridge: Cambridge University Press, 2009), Proposition 6, https://s18798.pcdn.co/whatistheworld/wp-content/uploads/sites/13403/2019/01/Kant-Idea-for-a-Universal-History-from-a-Cosmopolitan-Perspective.pdf (accessed 29.11.2023).
9. www.mirror.co.uk/news/uk-news/mum-who-took-incredible-christmas-13764974 (accessed 28.07.2023).
10. Harper Lee, *To Kill a Mockingbird* (London: Heinemann, 1966), p. 230.
11. W. H. Auden, *For the Time Being: A Christmas Oratorio* (London: Random House, 1944), www.thepoetryhour.com/poems/for-the-time-being-a-christmas-oratorio (accessed 21.10.2023).
12. Etty Hillesum, *An Interrupted Life and Letters from Westerbork* (New York: Henry Holt, 1996), p. 44.
13. J. T. Sanders, 'Paul Between Jews and Gentiles in Corinth', *Journal for the Study of the New Testament* (1997), pp. 71–2.
14. W. A. Meeks, *The First Urban Christians* (New Haven, CT: Yale University Press, 1983), pp. 51–73.
15. https://divinehymns.com/lyrics/i-want-to-serve-song-lyrics/ (accessed 13.06.2023).
16. https://www.bbc.co.uk/news/uk-england-derbyshire-52433070 (accessed 13.06.2023).
17. John Polkinghorne speaking at a conference, Lee Abbey, c. 1985.

18 *Common Worship: Times and Seasons* (London: Church House Publishing, 2005).
19 Eric Franklin, 'Luke', in John Barton and John Muddiman (eds), *The Oxford Biblical Commentary* (Oxford: Oxford University Press, 2001), pp. 922–59, p. 946.
20 Lois Malcolm, Commentary on 2 Corinthians 5.1–12, https://www.workingpreacher.org/commentaries/narrative-lectionary/preaching-series-on-2-corinthians-4-of-5/commentary-on-2-corinthians-51-21 (accessed 18.10.2023).
21 George Herbert, 'Easter', in Ronald Blythe (ed.), *A Priest to the Temple* (Norwich: Canterbury Press, 2003), p. 116.
22 *Common Worship: Daily Prayer* (London: Church House Publishing, 2005), p. 634.
23 Henry Vaughan, 'The Revival', in *Collins Albatross Book of Verse* (London: Collins, 1960), p. 233.
24 Olivier Clément, *The Roots of Christian Mysticism* (London: New City, 1995), p. 55.
25 *Common Worship: Services and Prayers for the Church of England* (London: Church House Publishing, 2000), p. 353.
26 Niamh Hughes, *The Confined: A Story of Hidden Children*, BBC Documentary, September 2020.
27 M. Handford, *Where's Wally?* (London: Walker Books, 1987).
28 P. Moran et al., *Where's the Unicorn?* (London: Michael O'Mara Books, 2017).
29 www.telegraph.co.uk/comment/columnists/christopherhowse/6133673/Do-you-believe-in-angels.html (accessed 23.09.2023).
30 www.theguardian.com/uk-news/2019/mar/16/friendship-over-fear-manchester-man-shows-solidarity-with-local-mosque (accessed 09.06.2023).
31 Taken from the Collect for the Second Sunday of Epiphany, www.churchofengland.org/prayer-and-worship/worship-texts-and-resources/common-worship/common-material/collects-and-post-21 (accessed 02.05.2023).
32 https://en.wikipedia.org/wiki/I_Don%27t_Know_How_to_Love_Him (accessed 17.10.2023).
33 https://people.com/parents/angelina-jolie-talks-engagement-to-brad-pitt-motherhood/#:~:text=Angelina%20Jolie%3A%20My%20Kids%20Keep%20Me%20Grounded&text=%E2%80%9CThat's%20who%20you%20are!%E2%80%9D,a%20laugh%20with%20our%20kids.%E2%80%9D (accessed 17.10.2023).
34 www.notable-quotes.com/m/merton_thomas.html (accessed 17.10.2023).
35 J. R. R. Tolkien, *The Fellowship of the Ring* (London: HarperCollins, Kindle edn, 2020), pp. 338–40.
36 Elizabeth Shively, 'Commentary on Mark 7:1–23', www.workingpreacher.org/commentaries/narrative-lectionary/what-defiles-a-person/commentary-on-mark-71-23 (accessed 29.10.2023).

37 www.poetryfoundation.org/poems/45527/lines-composed-a-few-miles-above-tintern-abbey-on-revisiting-the-banks-of-the-wye-during-a-tour-july-13-1798 (accessed 13.10.2023).
38 www.quotescosmos.com/quotes/S%C3%B8ren-Kierkegaard-quote-9.html (accessed 18.10.2023).
39 www.humanists.uk/campaigns/successful-campaigns/atheist-bus-campaign/ (accessed 18.10.2023).
40 Paraphrased from Blaise Pascal, *Pensées*, 3, 233 (1958 edn), p. 66, accessed via Project Gutenberg at https://www.gutenberg.org/files/18269/18269-h/18269-h.htm#SECTION_IIInote (accessed 29.08.2023).
41 Christina Rossetti, 'Lay Up for Yourselves Treasures in Heaven', in Rachel Mann (ed.), *New Selected Poems* (Manchester: Carcanet, 2020), p. 169.
42 George Herbert, 'Prayer (I)', in *The Temple* (London: Penguin Classics, 2017), p. 67.
43 John Bunyan, *The Pilgrim's Progress* (1678), ed. Roger Sharrock (London: Penguin Books, 1981), p. 82.
44 St Augustine, *The Confessions of St Augustine*, trans. John K. Ryan (Garden City, NY: Doubleday, Image Books, 1960), p. 187.
45 R. Atkins, 'Contextual Interpretation of the Letter to Philemon in the United States', in D. F. Tolmie and A. Friedl (eds), *Philemon in Perspective: Interpreting a Pauline Letter* (Berlin: De Gruyter, 2010), p. 205–22.
46 L. J. Kreitzer, *Philemon*, Readings: A New Biblical Commentary (Sheffield: Phoenix Press, 2008), p. 81.
47 www.youtube.com/watch?v=OtkclEB6rmI (accessed 06.11.2023).
48 See, for example, J. Goldingay, *Psalms: Volume 3, Psalms 90–150* (Ada, MI: Baker, 2008), p. 277.
49 Goldingay, *Psalms*, p. 278.
50 Goldingay, *Psalms*, p. 278.
51 www.butterwick.org.uk/ourhospices/thebutterwickstory/ (accessed 09.08.2023).
52 Chelsey Harmon, *Luke 17.11–19 Commentary*, https://cepreaching.org/commentary/2022-10-03/luke-1711-19-3/ (accessed 18.10.2023).
53 Harmon, *Luke 17.11–19 Commentary*.
54 grahamkendrick.co.uk/godofthepoor/ (accessed 21.10.2023).
55 www.theguardian.com/lifeandstyle/2015/may/08/lessons-in-time-management-oliver-burkeman (accessed 27.09.2023).
56 John V. Taylor, *A Matter of Life and Death* (London: SCM Press, 1986), p. 18.
57 www.youtube.com/watch?v=eoBYYElyP4c#:~:text=here%20we%20go%20don't,your%20granny%20in%20the%20bag (accessed 18.10.2023).
58 https://hymnary.org/text/i_vow_to_thee_my_country (accessed 28.05.23).

59 'They Thought They Were Better', *TIME* magazine (21 July 1980), and https://quotepark.com/quotes/1162510-john-updike-a-leader-is-one-who-out-of-madness-or-goodness-v/ (accessed 04.10.2023).

60 Charles Wesley, 'Christ, whose glory fills the skies' (1740), published in 469 hymnals, https://hymnary.org/text/christ_whose_glory_fills_the_skies (accessed 04.10.2023).

61 www.ted.com/talks/bryan_stevenson_we_need_to_talk_about_an_injustice?language=en (accessed 27.06.2023).

62 For a range of views see, for example, Marina Warner, *Alone of All Her Sex: The Myth and Cult of the Virgin Mary* (London: Vintage, 2000); Elizabeth Schüssler-Fiorenza, *In Memory of Her* (London: SCM Press, 1996); Nicola Slee et al., *A Book of Mary* (London: SPCK, 2007).

63 Percy Bysshe Shelley, *Ozymandias*, in *Collins Albatross Book of Verse*, p. 352.

64 Robert Seymour Bridges (1844–1930), 'All my hope on God is founded', https://hymnary.org/hymn/AM2013/584 (accessed 07.10.2023).

65 A television advertisement for McCain chips where a child is asked to decide which she likes best: 'Daddy or chips?' The advert can be watched at: https://www.google.com/search?q=Daddy+or+Chips&oq=Daddy+or+Chips&gs_lcrp=EgZjaHJvbWUyBggAEEUYOTIGCAEQRRg7MgYIAhBFGDsyBggDEEUYO9IBCDI4NDhqMGo3qAIAsAIA&sourceid=chrome&ie=UTF-8#fpstate=ive&vld=cid:1629f360,vid:0fqE5n5W5-I,st:0 (accessed 26.09.2023).

66 Marilyn McEntyre, *Word by Word: A Daily Spiritual Practice* (Grand Rapids, MI: Eerdmans, 2016), p. 6.

67 McEntyre, *Word by Word*, p. 13.

68 Collect for Purity, The Book of Common Prayer 1662.

69 Dorothy Day, *Loaves and Fishes* (Maryknoll, NY: Orbis Books, 1963), p. 215.

70 Matthew Kelly, *The Rhythm of Life: Living Every Day with Passion and Purpose* (London: Touchstone, 2004), pp. 217–18.

71 www.carlbloch.org/Mary-And-Elizabeth.html (accessed 21.10.2023).

72 Franklin, 'Luke', p. 928.

73 www.history.com/this-day-in-history/mahalia-jackson-the-queen-of-gospel-puts-her-stamp-on-the-march-on-washington (accessed 09.08.2023).

74 Julian of Norwich, *Revelations of Divine Love,* trans. Elizabeth Spearing (London: Penguin Books, 1998), p. 7.

www.ingramcontent.com/pod-product-compliance
Ingram Content Group UK Ltd.
Pitfield, Milton Keynes, MK11 3LW, UK
UKHW022050220925
463185UK00008B/161